TWENTIETH
CENTURY
CONTINENTAL
PHILOSOPHY

TWENTIETH CENTURY CONTINENTAL PHILOSOPHY

EDITED, WITH AN INTRODUCTION BY

Todd May

Clemson University

PRENTICE HALL
Upper Saddle River, New Jersey 07458

Library of Congress Cataloging-in-Publication Data
Twentieth century Continental philosophy : a reader / edited with an
  introduction by Todd May.
      p.   cm.
  Includes bibliographical references.
  ISBN 0-13-450826-2
  1. Philosophy.   2. Philosophy, European—20th century—Sources.
  I. May, Todd, [date]
  B804.T8845   1996
  190′.9′04—dc20   96-6794

Acquisitions editor: Angela Stone
Project management: Edie Riker
Buyer: Nick Sklitsis
Editorial assistant: Meg McGuane

This book was set in 10/12 Sabon by Compset, Inc.
and was printed and bound by Courier Companies, Inc.
The cover was printed by Phoenix Color Corp.

© 1997 by Prentice-Hall, Inc.
A Pearson Education Company
Upper Saddle River, NJ 07458

Printed in the United States of America

10   9   8   7   6   5   4   3   2   1

ISBN   0-13-450826-2

Prentice-Hall International (UK) Limited, London
Prentice-Hall of Australia Pty. Limited, Sydney
Prentice-Hall Canada Inc., Toronto
Prentice-Hall Hispanoamericana, S.A., Mexico
Prentice-Hall of India Private Limited, New Delhi
Prentice-Hall of Japan, Inc., Tokyo
Pearson Education Asia Pte. Ltd., Singapore
Editoria Prentice-Hall do Brasil, Ltda., Rio De Janeiro

For Kathleen, David, Rachel, and Joel

CONTENTS

Structuralism

Critical Theory: The Frankfurt School

Hermeneutics

Recent Directions: Poststructuralism

PREFACE

When Prentice Hall first approached me about doing a textbook in twentieth-century continental philosophy, the idea was for me to write a philosophical history. I balked at the proposal, because, among the disputes that characterize recent Continental thought, the meaning of its history is certainly a central one. Instead, I offered to pull together and introduce programmatic writings from the philosophers themselves, in order to allow teachers, students, and other readers the chance to form their own interpretations. Fortunately, continental philosophers have, over the years, issued programmatic or summary writings that allow collections like this one to be constructed.

In pulling this book together, I have opted for longer selections by fewer philosophers—rather than many snippets—in order to give readers the chance to delve into recent continental thought rather than merely glance across it. In philosophy, depth is almost always preferable to breadth. However, I welcome suggestions from readers regarding alternative selections or additional philosophers they would prefer to see in subsequent editions. A book like this is nothing if not a cooperative project encompassing reader and editor.

Finally, I would like to thank the folks at Prentice Hall, at East End Publishing Services, and at the many presses that have generously allowed me permission to reprint their pieces. Without a lot of kindness all around, this book would not have been possible.

Todd May

INTRODUCTION

I want to present you with some scaffolding, rather than presume to be a guide through the building itself. The texts are the building. From Husserl to the contemporary thinkers, the writings are the architecture of twentieth-century Continental philosophy. If you are using this book for a course, then your guide will be the professor with whom you study. And each professor will have a particular take on the architecture. My task in this introduction, then, will *not* be that of giving you a summary of the texts.

Unlike the development of twentieth-century Anglo-American philosophy, the movement of Continental thought—and the writings that compose that movement—are open to many interpretations. Go to any Continentally oriented philosophy conference and you will find as much discussion about what various thinkers have said as you will about whether or not they are right. I leave it then to your own reading and to your professor's wisdom to have the final word on the meaning of the texts included in this volume.

What I want to offer you here in the introduction is some scaffolding. The scaffolding will, of course, be interpretive. But its purpose is not to tell you what the texts say. Rather, what I hope you have gained by the end of these introductory pages is enough of an overview of twentieth-century Continental thought to be able to climb about the outside of the building, peek into the windows, and recognize a bit of what you are seeing. Some of you may want to add to this structure sometime, whether in conversation or more formally through writings or presentations. In that case it helps to have scaffolding, since climbing straight up to the window you want is often difficult and can be treacherous. (More than one philosopher has taken a fall that way.) Others just want to know what is in the building, whether on their own or with a guide. In that case, the scaffolding, by telling you a bit about what's where, may prevent needless confusion.

A moment ago, I said that an important difference between Continental and Anglo-American philosophy is that interpretations of the former are more controversial than interpretations of the latter. That is only one difference between the two traditions. Another is that Continentalists tend to be more historically oriented than Anglo-American philosophers. Continentalists are more self-consciously part of a philosophical tradition and thus are more concerned about articulating their thoughts as responses to and modifications of that tradition. Given the importance of historical responsiveness that characterizes Continental philosophy, the best way to build the scaffolding is to tell a story, a historical story that recounts the unfolding of twentieth-century Continental thought up until a few years back. Rather than approaching this introduction as a map then, as one might do with Anglo-American philosophy (where each part of the map is a thematic area—ethics, epistemology, and so on), I want to approach it by telling the broad story of Continental thought over the past ninety-some years.

Before telling the story, however, let me concede that when I refer to Continental philosophy in these pages, I am referring primarily to philosophical developments in France and Germany. I don't want to shortchange philosophical developments elsewhere on the Continent, although in the end I will. It's just that most of the influential philosophical movements of Continental philosophy have had their seat in France and Germany, so much so that influential thinkers from other countries—for example, Alexandre Kojève, Georg Lukács, and Antonio Negri—have had their impact on the philosophical developments of those two countries. (In many cases, these thinkers have, sooner or later, moved to France or Germany.)

Like everything else in Continental philosophy, the starting point of the story is controversial. Many think the proper starting point is with Karl Marx, since so much of this century's Continental thought is occupied with political concerns. Others, perhaps even the majority, might opt for Friedrich Nietzsche, since his influence has been enormous on many of the thinkers whose work is represented here. Still others might cite Hegel as the point of origin, since much Continental philosophy can be read either as an extension of or reaction to his philosophical system. I prefer instead to begin with Edmund Husserl. Preferring Husserl as the starting point does not reflect any belief that Marx, Nietzsche, or Hegel are unimportant in their influence. The reason for my preference is much more pedestrian. Husserl is the last major philosopher in Continental philosophy to try to develop an absolute, self-grounded first philosophy that would assume the role of queen of the sciences.

The view of philosophy as a first philosophy, as a foundation upon which the rest of our knowledge can be built, is as old as philosophy itself. It assumes its characteristically modern form with Descartes' *Meditations on First Philosophy*, in which Descartes tries to construct an absolute, indubitable philosophical basis for all knowledge. He does so by doubting everything he cannot be certain of and using that which he cannot doubt as the basis for constructing all further philosophical certainties. Husserl's project is essentially the same, although his philosophical approach is different. As he says in *Cartesian Meditations*, "Let the idea guiding our meditations be at first the Cartesian idea of a science that shall be established as radically genuine, ultimately an all-embracing science."[1] If we understand Husserl's project and his approach, then the philosophical approaches of those who take up or (more often the case) take on Husserl's task with varying degrees of sympathy—which includes most of the rest of twentieth-century Continental philosophy—will fall into place more easily.

Husserl called his philosophical approach "transcendental phenomenology." (Transcendental phenomenology is not the approach of his earlier works but was discovered as he began to have doubts about the adequacy of those works.) Like Descartes, Husserl sought to start only with those things of which one could be certain; and in further agreement with Descartes, those things of which one could be certain were to be found in one's consciousness. But unlike Descartes, Husserl's initial move, when he arrived at the realm of subjective certainty, was to describe the phenomena as they presented themselves, rather than reason from them.

Husserl uses the term *epochē* (from the Greek term for *abstention*) to apply to the philosophical journey from everyday thought to the realm of subjective certainty. In our daily lives, we take much for granted. We take for granted that certain behavior is right and other behavior wrong, that the sun will rise tomorrow, that our friends care for us even when they aren't around us, and so on. There are other things we take for granted, however, that are the basis for the taken-for-granteds that I just listed. We take it for granted, for instance, that the chairs upon which we sit exist, they are three-dimensional, and they have sides we don't see. This taking-for-granted comes naturally to us; it does not require any effort or training. Husserl calls it "the natural attitude." To take something for granted, however, is not to justify it or to offer any basis for believing it. If we are to have securely grounded knowledge, then, we must lay aside the natural attitude of taking for granted our fundamental beliefs and find out what, if anything, justifies our believing in what we take for granted. This laying aside of our natural attitude is the epochē.

Husserl often calls the epochē a "bracketing" of the belief-character of the natural attitude. This bracketing must be distinguished, however, from the methodical doubt Descartes engages in. Husserl does not ask us to disbelieve those things we take for granted; rather, he asks us to lay all believing and disbelieving aside. We are to take the phenomena that appear to us, for example perceptual phenomena, exactly as they appear, without either believing in them or doubting them. They are, for Husserl's purposes, pure phenomena. (Thus the "phenomenology" in transcendental phenomenology.)

When we perform the epochē, bracketing the natural attitude, what is left? The appearing-to-oneself of the phenomena that appear. Instead of chair, I have chair-appearances; instead of other people, I have other-people appearances. We are in a realm of pure subjective appearance, and it is from within this realm that our beliefs arise. (For those who have studied Anglo-American philosophy, it is worth noting that these appearances are not sense-data; they are more full-blooded appearances of things as things.) What Husserl wants to know, then, is how those appearances get constituted as the appearances they are.

For Husserl, three things become evident when the epochē is performed. First, the realm of appearances is one that cannot reasonably be doubted. I may doubt that there is a chair in front of me, since perceptual beliefs can be mistaken. (Perhaps I am seeing a shadow.) But I cannot doubt that I am having a chair-appearance. Thus appearances to a subjective consciousness are absolute and indubitable, "apodictic" in Husserl's terms. Second, the constitution of appearances as the specific appearances they are is an operation that is performed by a consciousness, since all phenomena have been reduced to the realm of appearances-to-consciousness. Third, and related to the last point, the understanding of the constitution of appearances is at the same time an understanding of the operation of consciousness. If the phenomena that appear to a consciousness are constituted by that consciousness, then by coming to understand that constitution we are coming to understand how consciousness works. In fact, for Husserl the *only* way we can understand consciousness is through understanding its constitutive character for appearances, because consciousness does not appear to us directly, but only in the mode of constituting appearances. This is why Husserl borrows from his teacher Franz Brentano the formula that all consciousness is consciousness of . . . .

We understand both the constituting character of consciousness and the constituted character of the world as it appears to us, then, by investigating how phenomena appear to a consciousness. Let's take a chair, for example, a specific chair. It presents itself to my consciousness not only as colored, say brown, and of a specific shape. It also presents itself to my consciousness as having sides that are not currently presenting themselves to me; that is, it presents itself as not being exhausted by its current appearance. As Husserl puts it, the chair has "horizons" which are embedded in the presentation but do not directly appear.

All these aspects of presentation must, in Husserl's view, be constituted by my consciousness; by laying aside my belief in the existence of the exterior world through the epochē, I am currently concerned only with phenomena as appearances to a consciousness. This is not to deny that the world may in fact have input into what appears to me. It is to claim that what I can be absolutely sure of lies only in the realm of phenomena inasmuch as they are constituted by my consciousness.

Husserl divides this constitution by consciousness into three parts: noemata, noeses, and transcendental ego. The noemata are the phenomena that appear. The noeses are the constituting acts of consciousness that make the phenomena appear as they do. In the chair example, the noeses are the perception-constituting acts that make the chair appear as brown, of a certain shape, and having the horizons it does. The transcendental ego is the source of the noeses. It is the part of consciousness that cannot be experienced—either directly or indirectly—because it is the source of all experiencing. Noemata can be experienced directly. Noeses can be experienced indirectly, through a reflection on how noemata are constituted; phenomenology engages in exactly that kind of reflection. But the transcendental ego is beyond any experiential grasp. Like Kant's transcendental I, it must be there as the source of experience and the unity that experience has, but it eludes our reflective comprehension.

Transcendental phenomenology, then, is an epistemological enterprise which, through a bracketing of our natural attitude of taking-for-granted that characterizes many of our beliefs, allows us access to a realm of absolute certainty. That realm is the realm of phenomena which is constituted in the immanence of consciousness. (Here it is important to bear in mind that transcendental does not mean transcendent; it means, in the Kantian spirit, both immanent to consciousness and offering the conditions of possibility of experience.) Thus, the Husserlian project, which the rest of twentieth-century Continental philosophy would reject in one or more of its aspects, is to turn philosophy into a science, and indeed the science that would found all other sciences, by rooting it in a realm of indubitable certainty, of apodicticity.

Husserl's most famous student, indeed far more famous than Husserl himself, was Martin Heidegger. Heidegger's work, both his early masterwork *Being and Time* and his latter essays, remains deeply influential in contemporary Continental philosophy; his work is central for philosophical approaches as diverse as the hermeneutics of Hans-Georg Gadamer and the deconstructive project of Derrida and his recent followers Jean-Luc Nancy and Phillipe Lacoue-Labarthe. Recently, Heidegger's fame has been attached to a more political aspect of his life. His association with Nazism, brought back into public light by Victor Farías' *Heidegger and Nazism* and Hugo Ott's more rigorous *Martin Heidegger: A Political Life*, has raised concerns regarding the philosophical intimacy of the relationship between Heidegger's thought and Nazism. I will not pursue this issue further than to note that it has spawned a minor cottage industry, including books by Derrida and Jean-Francois Lyotard.

Throughout his career, Heidegger was interested in what he called the question of Being or the Being-question. What is Being? Not, what is this or that being?, but what is Being? Put another way, the worry to which Heidegger's works are a response is this. There are beings of all sorts in the world, and they have different ways of being—but nevertheless they all are. What is this is-ness, this being or Being, which all beings either are or have or participate in? Now some philosophers in the more analytically oriented wing of Anglo-American philosophy, such as Rudolph Carnap, have dismissed such a question as a misunderstanding of the use of the term "being." But for Heidegger, the question of Being is the driving question of the philosophical tradition.

I should note straight off that Heidegger's concern with this question points him in a different direction from the one pursued by Husserl. Husserl was an epistemologist; he was concerned with our knowledge and the possibility of grounding that knowledge. Heidegger was an ontologist; he was concerned with understanding the Being of what is. Now epistemology and ontology are related. What one can justifiably say depends on what it is to know something; and what one assumes there is will influence what one thinks counts as knowledge. The latter end of that relationship is a particular concern of Heidegger's writings. He often says that the Western philosophical tradition, including Husserl, has made an assumption about Being that has dictated the course of its history, especially its epistemological aspect. That assumption is that Being is somehow like, or on the model of, beings. Rather than asking about Being itself, Western philosophy has asked about Being in terms of beings, and thus has lost or forgotten the most fundamental of all philosophical questions—the question of Being as Being.

In his earlier works, especially *Being and Time*, Heidegger approaches Being through a specific being—the being of the one who asks about Being. Heidegger's view at this time is that in order to approach Being, we need first to understand the being of the asker of the question of Being. We must do so in order to understand the perspective within which the question of Being is asked. The asker of the question of Being is, of course, a human being. However, Heidegger calls the asker *Dasein* (roughly translatable as "being-there") to indicate both that the asker of the question of Being just finds him- or herself there, in the world, alive, and that any being capable of asking the question of Being would be able to be accommodated by his approach.

This focus on *Dasein* has led many, including Jean-Paul Sartre, to interpret Heidegger's early work to be existentialist in character. Heidegger himself disavowed this interpretation (see, for example, p. 56); nevertheless, there is a shift that marks his later thought from the earlier works. In his earlier works, he approaches Being through interrogating the perspective of (more or less) humankind. In his later essays and lectures, he moves away from this "humanist" approach and attempts to broach Being itself. In fact, he claims that the "forgetfulness of Being" that has characterized the Western philosophical tradition—a forgetfulness that comes, as we saw, from reducing Being to beings—is bound to the humanism from which his later works struggle to free themselves.

It is worth pausing a moment over the reason Heidegger thinks that humanism and the forgetfulness of Being are so intimately related, since this relation is a central preoccupation of his post-World War II thought and a key to understanding what he was trying to accomplish with his later essays (which have been dismissed by many as obscure or overly mystical). Why is it that Being has always been thought of in terms of beings? It is because beings are what are present to us, they are what we have direct access to. (The idea of presence will return when we consider the work of Jacques Derrida.) There is a correlation— a correlation that is no accident—between our particular understanding of

Being and our epistemic and perceptual access to the world. (This much, by the way, Husserl might well have agreed to.) Put a bit crudely, Being has been understood as what is accessible to human beings.

This understanding of Being, an understanding that has been in philosophical ascendence since just after the pre-Socratics, gives pride of place to human beings in the ontological order of the world. It is human being, rather than Being itself, that is to be the focus of philosophy (and of our understanding of the world generally), since Being is only that to which human being has access through its access to beings. The upshot of this is that a certain understanding of Being, a view that holds it to be under the sway of human being, has determined our general philosophical perspective and its specific approaches for the past 2,500 years. It is a general perspective that Heidegger, and many he has influenced, like Derrida, call "metaphysics."

This view of Heidegger's explains two aspects of his later philosophy that have often been misunderstood. First, it explains his turn away from the approach of *Being and Time* in his later works. Rather than asking after Being by asking first after human being, he thought the proper philosophical path was to turn directly to Being itself. Second, it explains Heidegger's ontologically oriented interpretation of thinkers who have often been thought to have more epistemological concerns; Kant, for instance. Kant's thought is a good example of how the understanding of Being in terms of beings accessible to human being can shape a philosophical approach. Kant's turn toward consciousness as the proper subject matter of philosophy reflects an assumption that Being—or at least what is worth understanding about it—is reducible to human categories. Now it might be objected here on Kant's behalf that since he was doing epistemology, not ontology, the reduction to human categories was a justifiable philosophical strategy rather than a neglect or forgetfulness of Being. I don't want to address that dispute here. Let met just point out that Heidegger might reply that the very privileging of the epistemological project, particularly as a project of investigating consciousness, reflects an understanding of Being as parastical on human being.

It is not difficult to see, in Heidegger's critique of Kant, his divergence from Husserl. Husserl, like Kant, was an epistemologist who sought the foundations of our knowledge in consciousness. So, while Heidegger agreed with Husserl that there was a correlation between our understanding of Being and our epistemic and perceptual grasp of the world, he saw this as a sign of our forgetfulness of Being rather than as a clue to the proper path for philosophy to pursue.

Heidegger's often cited critique of technology also stems from his critique of "metaphysics." The problem of technology, for Heidegger, has to do not with the technology itself, but with our way of conceiving Being. By situating humankind above Being, as its master rather than its guardian, we have come to think of our world as something to be controlled and manipulated. Our blind march under the banner of technological progress—and our refusal to face the problems of environmental degradation, nuclear proliferation, dehumanization, and so forth—is a reflection of this "humanism"; it is that which needs to be addressed in order to avoid a future technological cataclysm.

How are we to do so? How are we to turn away from "metaphysics" and "humanism" and think in another, less destructive fashion? Heidegger's thoughts here are among his most difficult to fathom. He speaks of "letting be" and of allowing the "advent of Being," and, drawing upon a reference made in *Being and Time*, translates the Greek term *aletheia*, which has been rendered as "truth," instead of as "unconcealment." What is clear from these hints is that Heidegger is suggesting that we replace our view of ourselves as masters of Being with a view that allows Being sway. We must become more receptive to Being rather than manipulative of it. Poetry, in Heidegger's eyes, is one way to do so. In philosophical thought, such a receptivity requires an entirely new philosophical language, one not loaded with the "metaphysics" of the tradition. In many of his later essays, Heidegger struggles to articulate such a language.

I have focused, in this discussion of Heidegger, on his later works rather than his earlier ones. This may seem puzzling to some, since much of his fame rests on *Being and Time*. Moreover, in Anglo-American philosophy, the Heidegger that has been adopted by neo-pragmatists such as Richard Rorty is primarily the early Heidegger. However, in the Continental tradition, it is his later work—and his earlier work as seen through the eyes of the later work—that has been more influential. This is especially true of the most recent wave of French thought, including such thinkers as Derrida and Lyotard. (Among German philosophers, Heidegger's work is most influential in hermeneutics. This influence does stem from the earlier work, and it will be discussed later.) It is possible to read in *Being and Time* and some of the earlier works many of the themes that came to preoccupy Heidegger later, but those in the Continental tradition who draw upon those works often do so from the perspective of Heidegger's later, more fully articulated, anti-humanist and anti-metaphysical view.

At this point, I would like to turn to two successive generations of French thought—existentialism and structuralism—before swinging back to the development of German philosophy, in order to trace a more-or-less coherent unfolding of borrowings and reactions that have characterized it. A look at these two generations of thought will help us see three things: the immediate influence of Heidegger's early thought, the rejection of Husserl's foundationalist project, and the emergence of several themes that are parallel (although not identical) to developments in Germany during this time.

One thinker who drew upon many of Heidegger's early themes, while ignoring the larger framework in which they were embedded, is Jean-Paul Sartre. Sartre is the most famous proponent of the philosophy known as existentialism, which, although rejected in many of its facets, has had its central tenet embraced to this day by most subsequent philosophers. That central tenet is that life has no pre-given meaning, that we exist for no larger cosmic purpose. Sartre put the matter to rest by saying that existence precedes essence; we exist and then create our essence. It would not be wrong, however, to say that the existentialist formula is existence without essence.

Sartre, of course, is not the first thinker to articulate the idea of human life's being without a larger purpose. Think, for instance, of Darwin's evolutionary doctrine, currently in vogue in intellectual circles to explain just about everything. Many have claimed that among the implications of Darwinian thought is that humans are merely a biological happenstance, without purpose in some larger scheme of things. (Darwin himself resisted using the term "evolution" to describe his theory because of its progressivist connotations.) Even from within the parameters of philosophy, Sartre's position had precedents in the thought of Nietzsche and especially the Danish religious philosopher Sören Kierkegaard. For Kierkegaard, the events that happen in this world can be seen as signs of God's will or plan only by someone who is willing to take a "leap of faith" to interpret them that way. Faith is not given objectively but engaged in subjectively without guarantee of that faith's being warranted.

In that light, Sartre can be read as a Kierkegaard without the faith. For Sartre, unlike religious existentialists such as Gabriel Marcel or Martin Buber, the denial of the existence of God is central to existentialism. It is, in fact, from that denial that existentialism sets out. Without God, there is no larger purpose which humans are here to fulfill, no grand scheme within which we have a role. We are a cosmic accident; we just happen to be here.

Sartre interprets Heidegger's concept of *Dasein* in precisely this way and thus gives it an existentialist twist. For Heidegger, *Dasein*, being-there, is characterized by "throwness," by being thrown into the world without its assent and finding itself there with neither purpose nor guidance. Although for Heidegger the analysis of *Dasein* is only part of the larger project of a fundamental ontology of Being, for Sartre the fact of the throwness of humanity is the key piece in the puzzle of understanding ourselves and our world.

Sartre's existentialism is a taking account of what he sees to be the implications of the nonexistence of God, of humanity's just being-there. The first and most central implication is the radical freedom of human being. If there is no God, no essence of humanity, then there is nothing human being is constrained to be. We are radically free in the sense that there are no cosmic bonds on our behavior and no purposes we are constrained to fulfill. Now Sartre reads this radical freedom, particularly in his earlier works, as a pervasive fact about our lives. In his eyes, we are free to do or to be anything—at least within the limits of our physical capabilities. The only thing we cannot do is escape this freedom that we ourselves are: "Man is condemned to be free." (See p. 106 in Sartre's essay.)

For Sartre (as for Heidegger and Kierkegaard), the fact of throwness and the freedom it implies creates in people the experience of existential anguish. This anguish stems from the lack of foundation or justification to which our life choices can appeal. We cannot, ultimately, justify our lives and our decisions because, ultimately, there is no justification to be had. The reasons we give ourselves for our choices may be acceptable to us, and even to others, but that acceptance isn't guaranteed by anything. It rests on nothing, and thus is itself a matter of choice. That we are alone and without support, that we are radically free, cause us anguish (also referred to as "anxiety" or "dread") in the face of our existence. This anguish need not be a consciously experienced emotion. It lies at the center of our being and can be called to consciousness by a reflection on our existential situation.

Sartre views anguish, and the recognition of absolute freedom that gives rise to it, as largely intolerable to us. We spend much of our energy trying to avoid it, acting as though our lives had a pre-given meaning or an ultimate justification. Sartre labels this pretense "bad faith," a term that has, since his coining, often been invoked (and often misunderstood). Bad faith is the attempt of a being without ground or foundation to act as though it actually did have one. Sartre introduces the term in his early grand work *Being and Nothingness* and does so in the context of an ontology that is worth considering for a moment.

In *Being and Nothingness*, Sartre distinguishes two fundamental types of Being: Being-in-itself and Being-for-itself. Being-in-itself is the being of nonconscious beings. It is pure material being. Being-for-itself (a term Sartre borrows from Hegel) is conscious being. Conscious being is nothingness, precisely because it is radical freedom; it isn't anything but is the possibility of being anything. We could say that it is "no thing." Seen in these terms, bad faith is the attempt by a for-itself to become an in-itself. When consciousness, for-itself, attempts to give itself a foundation, it is attempting to abandon the very being of what it is. This is because when it has a foundation it will no longer be the nothingness of pure freedom. Therefore, if it were to succeed (which it cannot), it would become the other kind of Being, being-in-itself. Bad faith is this failed attempt or pretense to escape one's freedom by trying to discover or create a foundation that justifies one's being.

As you can see, freedom is, for Sartre, a pervasive fact of human existence. Many subsequent thinkers have rejected the pervasiveness of this freedom. Heidegger rejected Sartre's existentialism as another form of humanism; given our discussion of Heidegger's own views, it is not difficult to see why. Other Continental thinkers have followed Heidegger's lead and turned away from Sartre's emphasis on human freedom and self-creation. Sartre himself, after becoming Marxist, tempered his views on human freedom. It is important to see, however, that what later thinkers (including Sartre) reject is not the idea of freedom as lack of foundation or essence, but freedom from social constraints that determine us in our daily lives. Lacan, Horkheimer and Adorno, Habermas, Foucault, and others who reject Sartre's privileging of consciousness do not do so because they believe human being really does have an essence, but because they believe that what constrains us is not so much cosmic, ontological, or transcendental as it is material or empirical.

One of the first thinkers to introduce the notion of constraints was Maurice Merleau-Ponty. The constraints to which he points are, at first, more corporeal than social and political. However, by accepting Sartre's broadly existential view while rejecting the ontology of a disembodied consciousness (a for-itself that is in no way an in-itself), Merleau-Ponty paves the way for much of the French thought that follows him.

Merleau-Ponty's writings, perhaps more than those of any other Continental figure, merit the label "existential phenomenology." They are phenomenological in the wealth of description they employ; Merleau-Ponty was loathe to account for the structures of experience without an exhaustive description of the experiences whose structures he sought to understand. He was critical of both the empirical sciences and the rationalist philosophy of his time for moving too quickly to explanation without a full understanding of the phenomenological character of what was to be explained. His writings are existential in their rejection of any transcendental source of the kind to which Husserl appealed. For Merleau-Ponty, an exhaustive description of experience reveals, among other things, that an epoché that leaves one solely within the realm of consciousness is impossible. In his most influential work, *Phenomenology of Perception* (of which the selection included here is a precis), he writes, "The most important lesson which the reduction teaches us is the impossibility of a complete reduction."[2]

The level at which Merleau-Ponty approaches experience—that of perception—is hardly news in the philosophical tradition. As we saw, Husserl starts with perception in order to discover what can be known absolutely. What is news is the way Merleau-Ponty treats perception. He sees it as a corporeal experience, an experience of the body, and not merely a mental experience. Perhaps a better way to put the point would be to say that he approaches it beneath the division of experience into the bodily and the mental. A division between mind and body is assumed in Husserl's thought in order to perform the "complete reduction" that Merleau-Ponty thought impossible. It is also reflected in Sartre's ontological division into the for-itself and the in-itself. For Merleau-Ponty, a division of this kind would be justified only if it emerged in the phenomenological character of experience, rather than being imposed upon that experience. And, as it turns out, no such distinction does emerge. The mind is embodied and the body is already mind.

The phenomena that resist a strict distribution into mind and body are many, but I will let one of Merleau-Ponty's more commonly cited examples suffice: phantom-limb syndrome. Often, people who have had limbs amputated feel pain, but they don't experience that pain in what is left of their limbs. Their experience is of pain in the amputated limb, as though it were still there and capable of pain. Now, if there were a strict separation of body and mind, such an experience would be impossible. If, on the one hand, one said with the empiricists of Merleau-Ponty's day that the mind is a passive receptor of signals coming from the body, then one could not explain how signals could come from a limb that was no longer there. On the other hand, however, if one said with the rationalists of the day that the body is solely an organ used by the mind, then one could not explain how such a signal could be experienced in the mind as coming from the body. One would have to see it as a purely mental hallucination, which would not explain why that hallucination was experienced *there*, where the limb was.

The phantom-limb syndrome resists any division into mind and body, whether primacy is given to the body (empiricism) or the mind (rationalism). The lesson of the phantom-limb syndrome, and of the other phenomena to which Merleau-Ponty calls attention, is that we need to think of a person's primitive orientation toward the world as an embodied orientation. By "embodied" here we mean not merely bodily, as opposed to mental, but, if you'll excuse the expression, mind-in-bodied. Our bodies take up an orientation toward the world, and we live ourselves through that orientation. Merleau-Ponty sometimes calls that orientation our "comportment" to the world, and refers to it, in a borrowing from Heidegger's *Being and Time*, as "being-in-the-world." The first level of orientation through which we encrust ourselves into the world is perception. From there, we move to higher order orientations like reflection and deliberation.

To see how this approach solves the problem of the phantom-limb syndrome, consider someone whose embodied orientation toward the world is suddenly changed by the loss of a limb. The orientation does not immediately change, any more than the death of a loved one stops one from thinking about her as though she were still alive. Instead, the orientation becomes frustrated, as the world does not respond to one in the way one has been used to. The phantom-limb syndrome, then, is a consequence of being oriented a certain way. One's orientation does not leave one immediately upon the loss of a limb, so one feels the pain *there*, where the limb used to be. Gradually, however, the orientation changes, and accompanying that change is a diminishing of pain in the lost limb.

You may have noticed as this account of Merleau-Ponty's thought has proceeded that not only is the mind-body dualism undercut by his thought, but the self-world dualism also begins to be effaced. My orientation to the world, my being-in-the-world, should not be pictured as this "me," separate from the world, that somehow drops in on it. Rather, through my orientation, I am—to use an expression French philosophy is fond of—"always already" part of the world, entwined with it. This entwining happens primarily through perception, which Merleau-Ponty describes not as a distant viewing of the world, but as a way of being in it. In his last writings, Merleau-Ponty uses the term "flesh" to describe this self-world intertwining. The flesh is both my flesh and the flesh of the world; it is the place where there is no distinction to be drawn between me and the world. The flesh is, of course, the site of perception, which Merleau-

Ponty thinks is our most primitive, and thus most foundational, relation to the world.

Merleau-Ponty's thought can be seen as straddling a divide in contemporary French philosophy. On the one hand, he retains two themes that French thought will soon reject: a focus on subjective experience and an assumption of a primitive relation to the world through perception. On the other hand, he introduces new elements that have become benchmarks of the proceeding structuralists and poststructuralists: a devaluing of consciousness in its Husserlian interpretation and an emphasis on the way in which subjective experience is structured and not just structuring. In some of his later writings, he focuses on the idea of subjective experience being structured by appeal to the linguistics of Ferdinand de Saussure, a figure whose work is crucial for all successive French thought.

I have saved Saussure's work for this point in the scaffolding, even though he is chronologically closer to Husserl, because it was not until the rise of structuralism that his thought began to have a noticeable influence on contemporary Continental philosophy. Since the rise of structuralism, however, Saussure's influence has continued to grow, and, although his name is not as widely known philosophically as Husserl's or Heidegger's, his impact on contemporary Continental philosophy is surely as great.

Recall that one of the ways Merleau-Ponty moved away from Husserlian philosophy is by removing the epistemic privilege traditionally enjoyed by consciousness, conceived as a purely mental consciousness. Saussure, in effect, does much the same thing, although his focus is on language rather than on the body. If the lesson of Merleau-Ponty's thought is that conscious experience is mediated by a body that can never be reduced to or mastered by consciousness ("the impossibility of a complete reduction"), then the lesson of Saussure's thought is that conscious experience is mediated by a language that can never be reduced to or mastered by consciousness. Although the full implications of this mediation do not emerge until Derrida, much of it can be seen through an examination of Saussure's views on language.

Saussure was a linguist, but unlike many previous linguists, was interested in language as a synchronic rather than diachronic phenomenon. Synchronic studies are cross-sectional rather than longitudinal; they study a phenomenon as it looks at a given point in time, rather than following its development over time. Many linguists before Saussure saw the study of language as a study of the development of language, or of languages. Emergence, influence, and decline were central themes. For Saussure, on the contrary, understanding language was as much or more understanding it as a whole at a given time. In particular the meaningfulness of linguistic signs and the articulation of phonemes could not be understood without recourse to a synchronic account of language.

When one focuses synchronically, what immediately becomes evident is that a language functions holistically, rather than atomistically. Words (or better, morphemes) do not take their meaning in a purely individual fashion, but by reference to the entire language in which they fit. The same is true of phonemes, which take their phonetic value by contrast to other sounds in the language. To see how this is so, it is easier to start with phonemes. There are many ways to pronounce the "c" sound in the word "cat," for instance. Different people will pronounce it with slightly different inflections. What makes it a "c" sound, then? Its contrast to, for example, the "th" sound in "that" and the "b" sound in "bat." What defines the range of a phoneme, then, is not the specific sound, but its difference from the other sounds recognized in the language spoken by a certain community. If it were the specific sound that defined the range, as a more atomistic account of phonemes would have it, then no two people would ever pronounce the same phoneme.

What holds for phonemes also holds for morphemes, although here the situation is slightly more complicated. (Saussure does not use the term "morpheme" but instead "sound-image." I think, however, that I do his thought no harm by substituting the term "morpheme" for the moment.) The meaningfulness or significance of most morphemes points in two directions. First, and most important, like phonemes, morphemes are defined by their differences from other morphemes. What makes a given morpheme what it is is its place in a system of morphemes. The morpheme "cats," for instance, can refer to a variety of different beings; what makes them all fall under the category of "cat," however, is their differences from dogs, people, whales, and so forth. Second, but parasitic on the first, is that morphemes also refer to mental concepts. (For Saussure, it is the reference to mental concepts and not their reference to the world that is the primary reference relation.) That is to say, morphemes gain their signification or meaningfulness both by taking up a place in a linguistic system of morphemes and by reference to the mental concepts which they signify. To use the terms Saussure invokes—and which come to occupy a central place in structuralist discourse—signifiers (morphemes) signify primarily by playing a role in a system of signifiers, and this role allows them to stand for signifieds (mental concepts).

There are two implications of this view of signification that become central to the focus of structuralist and poststructuralist philosophical approaches. First, the signification or meaningfulness of a signifier depends not primarily upon the relation of that signifier to an idea or to the world; it depends on the system of signifiers of which it is a constituent part. Its signification derives from its differences from all the other signifiers of that language. As Saussure puts it, "in language there are only differences." (See p. 97 in this volume.) Second, signifiers are, in an important sense, arbitrary. There is no natural or essential relationship between a signifier and its signified. Since signification is determined within a system of signifiers, the relation of signifier to signified can happen in any number of ways. That the sound "tree" refers to a particular concept—the concept "tree"—is a nonessential feature of that sound and of the relationship between the sound and the concept.

Before turning to the structuralists themselves, it is worth pausing briefly to see how far Saussure's view of language takes us from Husserlian concerns. Recall that Husserl's goal was to arrive at an absolute foundation for knowledge. This goal required him to privilege consciousness in its (epistemic) relation to the world. If Saussure is right in his view of language, such a privileging of consciousness is impossible. This is because the concepts with which consciousness operates are a product of the current (synchronic) state of a particular language rather than a result of consciousness itself. Consciousness, then, is dependent on language and its signifiers rather than the other way around. This inversion of the priority of language and consciousness is held to by both French and German thought up until the present day (although German thought does not trace this inversion directly to Saussure).

In France, the first wave of thinkers to embrace Saussure's views of language are the structuralists. The structuralists adopt Saussure's view not merely as a view of language, but also apply it generally to the study of human beings. The two thinkers represented in this collection, Claude Lévi-Strauss and Jacques Lacan, applied structuralism to anthropology and psychoanalysis, respectively. Another major structuralist, Roland Barthes, appealed to Saussure's structuralism in developing his literary theory. And yet another structuralist, Louis Althusser, used structuralism to construct a version of Marxism directly opposed to the existential Marxism of Sartre. For Althusser, a scientific Marxism is one that reads off the structural relations of a society without reference to human intentions or goals, and that designs its revolutionary strategy from such a reading. Sartre, by contrast, in his *Critique of Dialectical Reason*, sees the relations of a society as a result of intersecting individual human actions, which is a more atomistic approach than the holistic one taken by Althusser.

The two pieces included in this collection by Lévi-Strauss and Lacan are chosen both because they present good introductions to the approach of these thinkers and because they display the grounding of structuralism in Saussurean linguistics. Turning first to Lévi-Strauss (whose thought helped determine the direction of Lacan's work), we can see the use of structuralist principles for anthropological interpretation. Lévi-Strauss holds that anthropology can reveal the nature of the human mind through an interpretation of the symbols of other cultures. This view is in contrast to many anthropologists, for example Benjamin Whorf, for whom the revelation of anthropology is the diversity rather than the identity of the products of the human mind. But for Lévi-Strauss, that diversity is only a surface phenomenon, one that holds interest only to those who approach anthropology atomistically rather than structurally.

If each symbol of another culture is interpreted individually, then it will certainly seem that humanity is capable of constructing a wide variety of symbols. Further, inasmuch as human life is symbolically driven, it will seem that human life can be practiced in a variety of irreducible ways. However, if we stop reading cultural symbols in isolation from one another and begin to approach them as forming a system, then the similarity of seemingly disparate forms of symbolic behavior becomes evident. Moreover, what goes for cultural symbols also goes for other human practices. Cultural life generally is the realization of a small number of human possibilities for constructing social systems. Although in appearance diverse, seen in the depth of their structure cultural systems are few in number.

Lévi-Strauss' most famous example of nonsymbolic cultural structures is that of the kinship system, articulated fully in his work *The Elementary Structures of Kinship* and noted more briefly in the essay included in this volume. Kinship structures, he argues, are organized around the social issue of how the women of a society are to be circulated. The forms of circulation are limited in number, and moreover, are organized as a form of social exchange. In a nod to Saussure, he notes that the recognition of the nature of kinship structures "can only be achieved by treating marriage and kinship systems as a kind of language." (See p. 133 in this volume.) Thus marriage, like more symbolic forms of communication, should be understood as a social structure rather than as an isolated series of alliances among families.

For Lévi-Strauss, the structures determinative of human societies are enactments of the possibilities for social organization of which the human mind is capable. Thus, by understanding the nature of the structures of human society, we can gain a deep insight into the nature of the human mind. To say that these structures are enactments of the possibilities of which the human mind is capable, however, is not to say that these structures are consciously organized by the participants of a society. In fact, most people have no idea that they are participating in organizing and reproducing the structures Lévi-Strauss describes. They, like the anthropologists whose work Lévi-Strauss rejects, see themselves at a more surface level, as involved in more isolated, individual, and localized events and practices, without a holistic or structural significance. Thus the social structures enacted by the human mind are, for the most part, unconscious structures. As members of a particular human society, we play roles we are unaware of playing, and our actions contribute to structures we are unaware exist.

The idea that the significance of our actions escapes us, and that it can be understood only by distancing ourselves from our conscious intentions, takes us far from Husserl's primacy of consciousness and Sartre's radical freedom. It even removes us from Merleau-Ponty's view of consciousness as an embodied phenomenon. Jacques Lacan's psychoanalytic structuralism shares with Lévi-Strauss this rejection of the primacy of conscious experience. Like Lévi-Strauss, Lacan sees human behavior—and not just social participation, but all behavior—as the product of the unconscious operation of the human mind. Where Lacan diverges from Lévi-Strauss is in seeing unconscious operation less as a matter of innate human structures and more as a matter of individual human history. In other words, for Lacan, what needs to be understood at the structural level are not general human characteristics that can be seen across societies, but more individualized characteristics that attach to particular life histories. This is not to deny that there are general human structures but rather to assert that those structures are interesting less in what they tell us about humanity in general and more in what they allow us to learn about individuals.

As a psychoanalyst, Lacan subscribes to Freud's three central posits: the unconscious, the interpretation of behavior as a result of conflict, and the Oedipal complex. However, Lacan gives each of these posits a Saussurean interpretation. This interpretation introduces the idea of language as a structuring phenomenon in psychoanalysis in a more rigorous way than Freud had done. For Freud, language played an important role in the formation of an individual's unconscious. This can be seen in the method of free association, in which it is the connections among words associated by the analysand that allows the analyst access to the structure of the analysand's unconscious. Although relying on language, however, Freud never offered a systematic theory about the way language operates in the unconscious. Lacan's contribution to—and modification of—psychoanalysis lies in his introduction of structural linguistics into the study of the unconscious.

One of Lacan's oft-repeated slogans is "the unconscious is structured like a language." To see how, we need to recall that for Saussure, the linguistic significance of a signifier is a matter of its difference from other signifiers in the language. For followers of Saussure, for example the linguist Roman Jakobson, this insight can be extended in order to provide an analysis of the tropes of metaphor and metonymy. Metaphor is the substitution of one signifier or set of signifiers for another: Melville's Moby Dick is a metaphor for death, the elusive meaning of life, and perhaps several other signifiers. Metonymy concerns a more contiguous use of signifiers. Referring to a ship in terms of its sails ("the sails set off to sea") is an example of metonomy. The difference between metaphor and metonymy, roughly, is that while metaphor brings disparate terms together by some sort of link, metonymy glides from one register to another among terms that are already linked.

For Jakobson, as for Lacan, metaphor and metonymy are the two methods by which signification is generated. We can leave aside the issue of linguistic generation, however, and turn directly toward psychoanalytic generation. For Lacan, metaphor and metonymy are the ways in which the significance of words for individuals in their own histories is generated. Recall that in Freudian thought, people's desires are often, for one reason or another, unacceptable to them. Those desires are then repressed. But repression does not operate without leaving some trace on a person's behavioral repertoire, often in the form of a symptom or a quirk. The repressed desire is displaced onto another level, where it appears and is (partially) satisfied by a form of behavior seemingly far removed from the original desire. In a classic example, a male child who wishes to sleep with his mother represses this unacceptable desire but may later develop a fetish for women's shoes. This fetish is the displacement of the desire for the mother.

How do these unconscious displacements work? In Lacan's view, they work by metaphor and metonymy, by channeling desire according to the movement of signifiers in relation to one another. That is why the method of free association is the psychoanalytic method par excellence. In following the associations of the analysand, one is tracing back the metaphoric and metonymic tropes through which the analysand's desires have been progressively displaced. What happens if one keeps tracing back? Will one get to an original desire? No. Original desire resists psychoanalytic access because of the way the unconscious itself is formed.

For Freud, the unconscious is formed by primal repression, which occurs mostly during the Oedipal period. Lacan's linguistic interpretation of the Oedipal stage is that it is the stage of the child's real accession to language. In a French play on words, he interprets the castration complex—*le non-du-père* ("the No of the father")—as the accession to language—*le nom-du-père* ("the name of the father"). The accession to language, however, involves the casting of original desire into the abyss of the unconscious. It cannot be signified directly because it does not happen in language; it happens before language. On the other hand, all signifiers, through metaphor and metonymy, signify it indirectly, because it is the lost signified to which all language (futilely) points. As for Freud the identification with the father is, for the boy, the symbolic substitute for the desire to have the mother; for Lacan the access to the symbolic realm of language is the substitute for the original desire (what Lacan sometimes calls the desire to be the phallus of the mother) that cannot itself be caught within the nets of signification.

In giving a structuralist interpretation of psychoanalysis, Lacan makes use of the two central implications of Saussure's thought I called attention to above: Signification is a matter of differences within language rather than reference relationships and signifiers are, in an important sense, arbitrary. In Lacan's thought, the arbitrariness of signifiers allows them to become representatives of an individual's desire. As money is often said to be fungible—it can be transferred from one place to another in order to fulfill a variety of purposes—so signifiers are fungible, coming to represent a variety of desires in a variety of different ways. In addition, their coming-to-represent those desires happens through the intralinguistic means of metaphor and metonymy rather than through word-world relationships. Lacan preserves the Saussurean thought that in language there are only differences but accounts for that thought not only in terms of the system of language itself but also in the relation of people's desire to language. Lacan refers to the "sliding of the signified under the signifier" (see p. 145 in this volume) to indicate that the signified—and ultimately, the primal signified of original desire—is never reached; rather, signification reaches only other signifiers.

Lacan, like Lévi-Strauss, inverts the Husserlian order in which consciousness has primacy over signification. He also helps inaugurate a theme that has dominated French thought to this day: that of the primacy of structure over consciousness. In some ways, and at the same time, there was an analogous theme emerging independently in Germany, and it is perhaps a good time to tack back to that country in order to see the development of thought there.

Recent German thought, particularly since the rise of Nazism, has not followed as neat a developmental sequence as the thought of France. This is not surprising, given Nazism's ravaging of German intellectual culture. Many of Germany's foremost intellectuals were forced into or chose exile during the Nazi period, devastating, among other things, the continuity of Germany's philosophical tradition. This is not to say, and we will see that it is not the case, that Germany has not produced a formidable body of philosophy since the early 1930s. Rather, it is to say that that body of philosophy is not characterized by the kind of evolution we have seen in recent French thought.

Among German trends, three stand out.[3] Two of those trends bear a significant Heideggerian influence. German existentialism, whose primary representative was Karl Jaspers, drew upon and developed many of the Heideggerian themes that we noted in the discussion of Sartre. Hermeneutics, to which we will turn shortly, was influenced by the interpretive orientation in *Being and Time*, which Heidegger himself thought of as hermeneutical. Finally, the Frankfurt school, or, as it has come to be known, critical theory, is not only distant from Heidegger's thought but at moments defines itself in opposition to it.

The Frankfurt school, which first emerged with the formation of the Institute for Social Research in (of course) Frankfurt in 1923, has produced or deeply influenced over the years many of Germany's most influential thinkers, including Theodor Adorno, Walter Benjamin, Erich Fromm, Max Horkheimer, Herbert Marcuse, and Jürgen Habermas. The backbone of the Frankfurt school has always been its Marxism, but this Marxism has been influenced by psychoanalysis and, with Habermas—its foremost contemporary representative—theories of language and communication. The Institute was dismantled by the Nazis in 1933 (although it was reformed briefly in Geneva and then in New York), and many of its members went into exile. In fact, some of its most prominent publications, including *Dialectic of Enlightenment* (from which this volume's selection is drawn), were written in exile. In response to the emergence of Nazism, the development of an understanding of Nazism and its relation to Western culture generally and capitalism specifically has been an abiding theme of critical theorists.

Although there are many different trends within critical theory, what binds them all together is the attempt to understand, from a broadly Marxist perspective, why the capitalist economic system has been so resilient. In other words, why have Marx's predictions about the demise of capitalism and its replacement by communism not only failed to materialize but in fact come to seem more distant now than in the time Marx wrote? In order to seek the answer to this question, the critical theorists have looked almost exclusively at the nature of the capitalist system (instead of looking, for example, at the dynamic of worker resistance). Their conclusion, and this is the specifically critical theoretical contribution to the history of Marxism, is that capitalism is not merely an economic system but a cultural one as well. Earlier, the Italian Marxist Gramsci had utilized the term "hegemony" to refer to the ideological domination of capitalist thought, a domination that resisted incorporation into Marx's concept of superstructure. But it was the critical theorists who, in various ways, discussed the specific cultural aspects of capitalism that allowed it to remain dominant throughout the twentieth century.

For the critical theorists, and more specifically for Horkheimer and Adorno, a cultural system is not merely a set of rituals specific to a certain culture. It is also a way of thinking that characterizes that culture. For medieval culture, for instance, there was a certain religious way of thinking that defined what was proper in the realm of thought and what was improper. The same is true of capitalist cultures. In capitalism, there is a mathematical, calculative way of thinking that defines what earns the status of proper thought and what does not. (In this view of capitalism as dominated by a calculative rationality, the critical theorists converge with Heidegger, who is often otherwise an object of critical theoretical scorn. However, while Heidegger wants to replace capitalist rationality with meditative thinking, the critical theorists want to replace it with Hegelian-Marxist dialectical thinking.)

The problem with this calculative way of thinking, which shows its dominance most clearly in the natural sciences but can be seen as well in economic cost-benefit analyses and in the generally utilitarian ways people approach their lives, is that it precludes critique of the existing order. When one is concerned with how much one might gain and the chances of one's gaining it, one is not concerned with the question of whether the whole game of gain and loss as defined by the current economic system is just or meaningful. Thus, capitalism becomes self-sustaining by its convergence with the scientistic legacy of the Enlightenment. That legacy, which supposedly freed us from the bondage of superstition, has at the same time bound us to a way of thinking that precludes our getting critical distance from the society in which we live. Scientism is capitalism's own mythology.

The view of our domination by calculative rationality is made most explicit in Horkheimer and Adorno's *Dialectic of Enlightenment*. It is, however, present in the writings of many other critical theorists, for example Marcuse and Habermas. The ability of capitalism to sustain itself by precluding the resources for critique is the key reason, according to critical theory, that it has been able to survive Marx's predictions of its demise. This ability is reflected not only at the level of theoretical activity, but also at all levels of culture. In their analyses of the self-sustaining capacity of capitalism through its effects on culture, critical theorists offer different approaches. But they converge on the idea, captured in Marcuse's image of the "one-dimensional man," that culture is monochromatically capitalist, with little offered in the way of alternative perspectives.

In contrast to Horkheimer and Adorno, however, who were pessimistic about the possibility of resisting the domination of capitalist culture, thinkers like Marcuse and Habermas attempt to discover and construct ways of thinking that provide a vision of culture's alternative to the one capitalism provides. Marcuse, for example, used psychoanalytic thought in *Eros and Civilization* to construct an alternative view of who we are that resists capitalist encroachment. We will see Habermas' alternative later in this introduction, but it is worth calling attention at this moment to his critique of the Horkheimer and Adorno's project. Habermas points out that if the situation is exactly as Horkheimer and Adorno describe it, then there is no way out of our present predicament. If we are completely dominated by calculative rationality, then there is no theoretical place to stand from which to offer a critique of the present order. Indeed, their own critique would be impossible were calculative rationality all there is to current modes of thought. Thus, there must be some theoretical place, currently existing, from which critique and a new vision can emerge. The task of critical theory is to articulate and strengthen it.

It is worth pausing a moment to note an important convergence between German critical theory and French structuralism. Both movements turn their attention to structures that are, for the most part, outside the conscious awareness and control of individuals. The explanation of who we are and why does not refer to our self-making, as it does for Sartre and Husserl, but rather to our being made. Although some of these thinkers offer the possibility of some sort of self-making—psychoanalytic intervention for Lacan or participatory discourse for Habermas—they agree in seeing the proper explanatory approach for the human situation as one that in good part (if not wholly) focuses on areas outside of conscious intentions.

This inversion of the Husserlian project characterizes Continental philosophy to this day. Although much can be said about the nontheoretical as well as the theoretical motivations for this inversion, let me suggest in passing the importance of Nazism and the Holocaust. Since the Holocaust, there has been a general distrust in European philosophy of both the powers and the beneficence of human beings. Theoretical justification aside, I believe that this general distrust has helped motivate the turning away from conscious intention toward unconscious or social structures.

In addition to existentialism and critical theory, the other prominent postwar movement arising in Germany is hermeneutics. Actually, hermeneutics is not a recent approach, although in its current practice it differs markedly from earlier hermeneutics. The practice that came to be known as hermeneutics began with the medieval scholastics as biblical interpretation. The bible, of course, is notoriously hard to draw a strict meaning from. Medieval scholars sought to create practices of interpretation that, rather than countenancing a variety of interpretations of scripture, each of which could be seen to have equal plausibility, would offer a more unified biblical interpretation. Although its biblical moorings have been jettisoned, hermeneutics as textual interpretation, and the practice of interpretation generally, has emerged as a central philosophical movement in the twentieth century.

Although resurrected by Schleiermacher and Wilhelm Dilthey in the eighteenth and nineteenth centuries, current-day hermeneutics derives from the hermeneutical approach developed by Heidegger in *Being and Time*. As I noted earlier, in that work Heidegger approaches the question of Being through first trying to understand the being of the asker of the question of Being. This approach involves Heidegger in the question of interpretation at two levels. First, he is interpreting Dasein, the asker of the question of Being. Second, he discovers in this interpretation that Dasein itself is an interpreting being, and that interpreting is central to its being. Thus, the nature of interpretation becomes a key issue in *Being and Time*.

In his interpretation of the nature of interpretation, Heidegger calls attention to the fact that interpretation is always a matter of perspective, in the sense that interpretation always arises from within a particular orientation or horizon. There is no such thing as objective—in the sense of outside all perspectives—interpretation. The implication of this is that whatever is learned by the interpretation is always learned from a certain angle. It may enrich the interpretive perspective, but the learning it offers is always in some way attached to the perspective from which the interpretation is made. Heidegger calls this implication the "hermeneutic circle." He does not see the hermeneutic circle as a vicious one, however, in which we only discover in texts what we put into them. The circle would only be vicious if hermeneutic perspectives could not be widened or altered by what they interpret. Rather, he sees the hermeneutic circle as a condition of all interpretation, without which interpretation would be impossible, since there would be nothing to orient it. As Gadamer says, "the way that we experience one another, the way that we experience historical traditions, the way that we experience the natural givenness of our existence and of our world, constitutes a truly hermeneutic universe, in which we are not imprisoned, as if behind insurmountable barriers, but to which we are opened."[4] (Readers of Ludwig Wittgenstein's writings might see an analogy here between Heidegger's idea that interpretation always happens from within a particular perspective and Wittgenstein's idea that justification always happens from within a particular language game.)

Another way to state this point closer to the terms used in hermeneutics, is that before setting out to interpret an object, one already has an understanding of that object, and interpretation occurs from within the horizon of that understanding. That understanding is a product of the traditions in which one is raised. Gadamer provocatively uses the word "prejudice" to refer to the influence of tradition on one's understanding of objects. He claims that prejudice has received a bad name in our Enlightenment culture, because the dominance of science has opposed itself to prejudice as objectivity to superstition. However, if all interpretation emerges from within a horizon of understanding influenced by traditions, then the epistemic issue is not one of objectivity versus superstition, but of good versus bad prejudices. One of Gadamer's concerns, a concern he inherits from Heidegger, is that the dominance of science in our culture has obscured the hermeneutic necessity of prejudice, and in doing so has moved us to devalue other kinds of experiences—such as art—as having an inferior status to the objectivity of science.

It is important to note here that the hermeneutic necessity to which Heidegger and Gadamer point is not some form of idealism. Their position is not that there is a world on the one hand over and against the interpreter on the other. Heidegger's idea of being-in-the-world is supposed to guard against that mistake. The proper picture for the hermeneutical situation is rather that one's prejudices are part of the way one is in the world, and that interpretive engagement with that world allows for different ways of being in that world. (Also worth noting is that the term "world" as Heidegger and Gadamer use it is not conceived in scientific terms as a collection of meaningless objects; the world already appears to us in our being in it as a meaningful world.)

If all interpretation occurs on the basis of a traditionally given understanding, a pre-understanding or "fore-having" as Heidegger calls it, and if the interpretation itself is also bound to tradition, then what is the mechanism through which tradition informs interpretation? For hermeneutics, it is language. Our traditions are sedimented in our language: in the kinds of words we use, in the meanings those words have, in the justifications we permit ourselves to offer one another. Moreover, interpretative activity, as opposed to our initial understanding of an object, is a linguistic activity. Interpretation is discursive, and as such is subject to the traditions—the prejudices—that are sedimented in language use.

In interpretation, then, what happens is that a horizon of understanding and interpretive resources is brought to bear upon the object of its investigation in order to learn what it is that that object has to teach. When the object of investigation is either human or a human product, however, the situation becomes more complicated. That is because humans have themselves a horizon within which they come to grips with the world, and their products reflect those horizons. If one is to interpret humans or their products fruitfully, then, one has to be able to enter into these more or less foreign horizons within which humans comport themselves with the world and their products are produced. There will, of course, never be a full fusion of horizons—the interpreter with the interpreted—but rather the interpreter has to use the resources of his or her tradition in order to comprehend the horizons, and through them the objects, of interpretation. Gadamer calls this back-and-forth movement of interpretation between the horizon of the interpreter and the horizon of the interpreted "dialectical." As can be seen, dialectical interpretation is far removed from the purported objectivity of science, but closer, in the eyes of Heidegger and Gadamer, to real knowledge.

Aside from Gadamer, the most prominent philosopher to carry forward the hermeneutical approach is the French philosopher Paul Ricoeur. Ricoeur is a bit anomalous in recent French philosophy, in part because hermeneutics has existed outside the mainstream of the development of French thought from structuralism to poststructuralism. Ricoeur's anomaly, however, also has to do with his philosophical method. Ricoeur works less by offering a new philosophical approach and more by investigating various approaches and trying to play them off against one another in order to discover what is right in each. (In this he has some affinity with Merleau-Ponty, although the latter thinker has not been known to be an extraordinarily accurate interpreter of the works of others. Merleau-Ponty's approaches to Husserl and Saussure, for example, often make them sound suspiciously Merleau-Pontian.) As a result, Ricoeur has contributed critically to many of the philosophical debates that have arisen in post-World War II Continental philosophy. He has written on existentialism and phenomenology, psychoanalysis, religion, deconstruction, and narrative theory.

In the end, Ricoeur's approach is hermeneutical, although he sees deep affinities between hermeneutics and phenomenology, to which the selection in this volume attests. In addition, this selection shows Ricoeur's method at work. He attempts to locate the weaknesses of phenomenology in its Husserlian idealist formulation, to show how hermeneutics offers a corrective to those weaknesses, and then to offer a rearticulation of phenomenology that shows how hermeneutics and phenomenology are mutually supportive when one abandons Husserl's idealist approach. His discussion both develops the hermeneutical approach and adds new dimensions to the selections from Husserl, Heidegger, and Gadamer.

Many of the philosophical positions I have discussed up to this point still have forceful adherents in Continental philosophy. And yet I have entitled the final four sections of this book "Recent Directions." I don't want you to think by my use of that heading that the recent directions Continental philosophy has taken have replaced earlier positions. They are, to be sure, developments of those earlier positions. But rather than substituting for them, we should think of the recent directions in Continental philosophy as broadening the field of reflection and research. In addition, the division into poststructuralism, feminism, deconstruction, and critical theory is a bit arbitrary. What I intend by these divisions is less a strict delineation of separate movements and more a broad distinction among several streams that often flow one into another.

One of these streams I have labeled "poststructuralism." My labeling here is a bit idiosyncratic, since poststructuralism can refer not only to the philosophers whose work I place under this head, but also to deconstructionist philosophy. I make the distinction because I believe that the idea of structure—or at least something like structure—still plays an important, if different role, for thinkers like Lyotard and Foucault (as well as Gilles Deleuze) from the role it plays for Derrida and his followers. One, admittedly oversimplified, way to state this role is to say that for poststructuralists there are structures determining human experience, but those structures are smaller, more variegated, and more diffuse than they are for the structuralists.

Jean-François Lyotard merits the dubious distinction of popularizing the term "postmodernism" which has come to be a term more often abused than understood. For Lyotard, the term has a more precise meaning, characterizing a certain aspect of social life. Even for Lyotard, however, there has been an ambiguity in applying the term. Although the aspect of social life he characterizes when speaking of postmodernism is always the same, he wavers between thinking that it is an aspect of social life throughout history and thinking that it is a peculiarly contemporary phenomenon. The selection included in this volume shows him opting for the former.

Lyotard thinks of postmodernism as the situation of breakdown in grand legitimating narratives. We humans tell ourselves stories, narratives, which depict for us who we are and how we got here. The stories told in different cultures are very different, of course. But every culture tells itself stories that situate the identity of the people in it. In each culture, some of these narratives occupy a special place. They are the legitimating narratives of the culture, the narratives that confer legitimacy upon the culture itself. These legitimating narratives tend to be "grand" narratives, because the story they tell places the entire culture in a certain perspective, a perspective from which it can appear to itself to be justified or worthy. In *The Postmodern Condition* (to which the selection in this volume is an appendix), Lyotard points to two grand narratives, that, since the Enlightenment, have been the legitimating narratives of Western culture. The first of these two grand narratives is one of the progressive freeing of people from the bonds of ignorance and slavery; it is a narrative of humanity struggling with superstition and eventually gaining the upper hand. The second one is also progressive, but rather than referring to the progress of humanity it refers to the progress of the spirit; it is a (Hegelian) narrative of the spirit's gradual self-realization in the unfolding of history.

The current condition of Western society—the postmodern condition—is that we in the West do not find these grand legitimating narratives to be compelling any more. The narratives of legitimation have broken down. The reasons for this are many and include both the effect of Nazism on our view of ourselves as progressing and the tendency of much (though by no means all) of current scientific practice to delegitimize any form of narrative. However it came about, the postmodern condition is a condition in which the overarching stories we tell about ourselves in order to give ourselves a place and a meaning are no longer stories to which we can give our assent.

The demise of grand narratives of legitimation has had two effects, one of them negative and another positive. The negative effect has been that capitalism and capitalist discourses such as the efficiency talk have been able to dominate social life. Since capitalism has not had to justify itself by appeal to a grand narrative, it can operate without justification. This operation allows it to expand without being limited by another critical discourse. (One can see here a moment of convergence between Lyotard's poststructuralism and the critical theory of Horkheimer and Adorno.)

The positive effect is that space has been created for a series of smaller narratives and practices. People's practices do not have to confine themselves to the parameters laid out by the grand narratives of legitimation. This is because, with the decline of those narratives, alternative narratives and practices do not face the either/or of justifying themselves by the standards of the grand narratives or being seen as unjustified. They, like capitalism, can operate in a space unconstrained by the justificatory limits imposed by the stories of the progress of humankind away from superstition and of the progressive self-realization of spirit. Unlike capitalism, however, inasmuch as these narratives and practices are small and not overarching, they provide alternative spaces for living rather than new and onerous constraints upon living.

It is through Lyotard's discussion of smaller narratives and practices that the "post" in his poststructuralism emerges. Recall that for the structuralists, people's experience is determined by structures that molded their existence in ways that they are often not conscious of. Lyotard's vision is opposed to the structuralists in a crucial way but retains an important element from structuralism as well. The point of opposition is that, in his commitment to the decline of grand narratives, he is also committed to the decline of explanations of our experience by appeal to a single determining factor, be it the unconscious, the structure of the human mind, the mode of economic production, or whatever. Lyotard sees human experience as much more variegated than single-determining-factor accounts would admit. In fact, it is a virtue of the postmodern condition that it allows for the recognition of this variegation.

The continuity with structuralism is that Lyotard continues to explain our experience by reference to external structures rather than to human consciousness. He does not return to a Husserlian view of consciousness or a Sartrean view of freedom; rather, he sees human experience as a matter of structures and practices that are external to consciousness. These structures are irreducible to a single factor, but this irreducibility does not provide Lyotard with any motive for returning to a pre-structuralist emphasis on human consciousness as the source of experience and the proper object of philosophical reflection.

There is, in Lyotard's thought, a certain ambivalence of which he is often aware. At times, he holds the postmodern condition and its proliferation of smaller narratives and practices to be our condition. At these times, the reason to talk in terms of smaller narratives and practices is that such talk provides an accurate explanation of our current situation. However, at other times, Lyotard sees these narratives and practices not as matters of *explanation* but of *valorization*. From this point of view, the reason to talk in terms of smaller narratives and practices is that such talk allows us to escape the hold capitalism has upon us. In this ambivalence, Lyotard contrasts sharply with Michel Foucault, for whom the appeal to smaller narratives and practices is always a matter of explanation rather than valorization. We must, in Foucault's view, always look locally rather than globally lest we miss the determining factors of who we are and what our experience consists of.

Foucault's thought is often divided into three periods: archaeological, genealogical, and ethical. In the first period his work resembles that of the structuralists more closely, since he sees certain areas of experience (the experience of madness, of medicine, of knowledge) as dominated by a single underlying theme for a period of time before changing to domination by another single, underlying theme. The idea of a single underlying theme for each period of time presents the image of layers of themes lying one atop the next throughout history; thus the idea of Foucault's histories as archaeologies. Those themes are, like Lacan's unconscious and Lévi-Strauss' structures of the human mind, not within the conscious grasp of those who act under their sway. Foucault adamantly rejected the label "structuralist," however, and not without some justification. Unlike the structuralists, he does not make a methodological appeal to Saussure's approach to language, and thus can be distinguished from the structuralists on that important score.

Foucault's second period of genealogical writings contains the work for which he is best known. In his genealogical period, he retains two key themes from his earlier writings. First, he tries to understand how our experience is structured by factors that are not generally within our conscious awareness. Second, he sees that the way our knowledge—or at least what we think we know—operates is crucial in structuring that experience. What kinds of claims count as knowledge, how those claims arise, whose claims get to count as knowledge and under what conditions—these are themes that preoccupy both Foucault's archaeological and genealogical periods.

In addition to the themes he retains, however, Foucault also adds two new themes that give his work another dimension: the locality of determinants and the pervasiveness of power. In sharp contrast to his earlier works, Foucault's genealogical writings do not locate the emergence of certain kinds of knowledge and their effects upon experience in a single underlying theme. Rather, the emergence of a kind of knowledge is the product of a variety of practices that come together in often unexpected ways and which give rise to a product that could not have been predicted by historians (or by anybody else, for that matter) previous to the emergence. Foucault calls the tracing of the practices that lead to an emergence of a kind of knowledge, following Nietzsche's term in the latter's *Genealogy of Morals*, a "genealogy." With this focus upon local practices as determinants of knowledge, and thus of our experience, Foucault moves decisively away from the structuralist camp.

Foucault has claimed that the other new theme, that of power, exists often in a nascent form in his earlier works. It comes to the fore, however, in his genealogical works. The idea is this. The structuring of our identities and our experience by knowledge is not a politically neutral affair. The kinds of things we think we know, the social recognition granted to certain people as experts in their areas, and the behavioral allowances granting expertise confers, all have effects of power on people in a society. By power, Foucault means "a way in which certain actions may structure the field of other possible actions."[5] Thus, what we can do and become is structured by relations of power that inhere in the local practices that both constitute knowledge and give rise to other types of knowledge. Foucault introduces the term "power/knowledge" to indicate this nexus in which both power and knowledge operate inseparably.

To see how power/knowledge works, let me offer a brief (i.e., oversimplified) summary of some themes from Foucault's most influential work, *Discipline and Punish*, a history of the emergence of both the prison and the domination of psychological knowledge in France. The idea of imprisoning criminals as the central means of punishment is a relatively recent idea. Before the turn to imprisonment, torture was the preferred mode of punishment. Torture, however, did not always achieve its desired results, since among its consequences was a general sympathy for the object of torture. Prison reformers arose who demanded a form of punishment that was gentler but also more nearly inevitable than torture, since torture was only selectively applied. The goal of these reformers was to promote a general respect for obeying laws by making the law seem just but also inescapable.

At around the same time, certain techniques of discipline that had once characterized monasteries were gaining acceptance in schools, factories, and armies. These techniques consisted of instilling routine patterns of motion in people's bodies, breaking down activities into their smallest behavioral components, and then arranging those components into their most efficient order. (Think here of the construction of an assembly line.) In order to instill discipline, however, one needs to have constant vigilance over the people in whom one is instilling discipline. Thus, observation, efficiency testing, and psychological evaluation are incorporated into the disciplinary project.

According to Foucault, the beginning of psychological practice, particularly psychotherapeutic practice, can be traced to the disciplinary project that spreads itself across the social field. This spreading is not smooth; it is taken up in different but related ways in different areas—schools, factories, the military—and often one area borrows from another. Discipline finds particular application in the area of punishment. Imprisonment and disciplinary rehabilitation replace retribution as the dominant practice and goal in dealing with criminal behavior. Rather than being punished for acts committed, people are now rehabilitated from their criminal personalities. "Behind the offender, to whom the investigation of the facts may attribute responsibility for an offence, stands the delinquent whose slow formation is shown in a biographical investigation."[6] With the emergence of the figure of the delinquent, and concomitantly with the idea of normality as the optimal functioning state of an individual, society becomes ruled in part by a new form of knowledge—psychological knowledge. Not just for the delinquent, but for all of us inasmuch as we are subject to the authority of schools, work, and so forth. We are subject to the disciplinary project and the psychological knowledge that is inseparable from it.

In this summary, we can recognize the four themes I noted earlier—the formation of our experience by factors that often elude our conscious awareness, the importance of knowledge in that formation, the emergence of that knowledge through the intersection of local practices, and the effects of power caused by that knowledge. Like Lyotard, Foucault focuses on smaller rather than grand structures or practices; in addition, Foucault is interested in the political effects of those smaller structures or practices. Both Foucault and Lyotard are "micropolitical" thinkers. However, Foucault does not valorize the smaller as opposed to the larger; instead, he tries to trace the effects of the interactions of smaller practices in the constitution of our lives and our experience.

If we turn to French feminism, we see a very different picture from the one presented by the poststructuralists. The French feminists are every bit as political as Foucault and Lyotard, but they hold to the structuralist program of appealing to a single dominant factor that determines identity and experience. Specifically, French feminists, particularly Luce Irigaray, Julia Kristeva, and Hélène Cixous, have articulated their views within (and often against) the psychoanalytic framework defined by the thought of Jacques Lacan. In order to see their work clearly, let me first highlight an aspect of Lacan's thought I passed over briefly earlier.

For Lacan, as for Freud, the single most important defining moment in the formation of a person's identity comes during the Oedipal stage. For Freud, the Oedipal stage is when the boy comes, through fear of castration, to identify with the father. In contrast, for Lacan the Oedipal stage is when the accession to language occurs, and with it the emergence of chains of signifiers which are invested by desire. Despite this difference, Freud and Lacan are in agreement about two other aspects of the Oedipal stage that are crucial for the French feminists. One is that the stage is articulated in masculine terms. In Freud's case, it is the father (through the castration threat) that motivates the Oedipal movement and it is the boy upon whom the father's threat falls. (Freud does discuss an Electra complex for girls, but it is a bit of an afterthought.) In Lacan's case, it is the *non (nom)-du-père*, the "no (name) of the father" which is the motivator, and presumably, although not as straightforwardly, the boy who gets motivated. The second point of agreement is that it is at the Oedipal stage that the unconscious is formed, through primal repression. The repression at the Oedipal stage is the repression that creates the unconscious and its desires that will remain forever inaccessible to the subject whose unconscious it is.

In the Oedipal stage—the central stage for human development—there is very little psychoanalytic room for the role of women. The mother appears only as a shadowy figure, and surely not as a protagonist; and the daughter's development is parasitic upon what is essentially a drama played out between the son and the father. Irigaray and Kristeva (and also Cixous) enter the psychoanalytic discussion at this point where the woman is missing. They enter the discussion in very different ways, but their work is framed within—and often against—Lacan's psychoanalytic perspective.

Luce Irigaray articulates her feminist themes in point-by-point contrast to the masculinist framework of the linguistic order established by the Oedipal stage. Recall that for Lacan the symbolic order—the order of language—is formed at the Oedipal stage, while the more inchoate unconscious is primally repressed. Inasmuch as the symbolic order is Oedipal then, it is also a residue of male practice. But that is not all. The symbolic order is the order of identity, of reducing things to sameness. This is because one of the key functions of language is to bring the disparateness of experience under the constraining sway of linguistic categories. In Kantian terms, the manifold is synthesized when it is submitted to language.

This "identitarian" (my term, with apologies) character of language leads in turn both to a solidification of experience and an emphasis on the visual at the expense of the tactile. The solidification comes from the resistance of the symbolic order of language to fluid, changeable, uncategorizable phenomena. In logic, for instance, the principle of identity states that anything is either A or not-A. The principle of identity tries to solidify the disparate into categories, disallowing as incoherent what does not congeal into a particular category. The emphasis on the visual derives from the specular mode of categorization. It is as though the linguistic categorizer were stepping back from experience, holding it at a distance, and taking its measure. The sense most suited to such holding at a distance is the visual. The visual stands back and compares, while the other senses are closer to, more immersed in, the phenomena they sense.

For Irigaray, then, the masculinity defined by the Oedipal stage is symbolic, identitarian, solidified, and specular. Irigaray does not dispute any of this but instead proceeds to articulate the feminine in contrasting terms. Where the masculine is symbolic, the feminine is corporeal; where the masculine is identitarian, the feminine is differential; where the masculine is solidified and visual, the feminine is fluid and tactile. And, in addition to these, where the masculine is oriented to consciousness, the feminine resides mostly in the unconscious.

By articulating the feminine in terms of corporeality, difference, fluidity, and tactility, what image is Irigaray constructing of the feminine? In some ways, a very traditional one, although the use to which she puts this image differs markedly from its use in the traditional articulation. Irigaray agrees, for instance, that the corporeal rather than the symbolic is the realm of the feminine. But this does not mean that women are not thinking creatures. To see why not, recall that for Lacan the unconscious is created by a primal repression, and thus that one's identity is formed as much—if not more—by what one represses as by what is conscious to one. It is as though the masculine project of solidification and identity were trying to repress the fluid and the different that are also part of who one is, of one's "identity," if we can still use this term. Thus feminism, rather than being an (inferior) alternative to masculinism, is rather a haunting of masculinism, its repressable but never eliminable other. And, in this reading, the difference between men and women lies less in the parasitical nature of the formation of women's identity upon that of men, but in the access women—who are never straightforwardly "oedipalized"—have to the unconscious, feminist side of human being.

The articulation of the feminine in the terms Irigaray has given it puts a strain on theoretical articulation. This is because philosophical writing is traditionally masculinist in the very way Irigaray wants to subvert. Thus, her writings are often constructed in such a way as to resist solidification into a single interpretation. Take for instance the title of the piece in this volume: "This Sex Which Is Not One." It has at least two meanings, each of which resonates against the other in a way that is hard to pin down (i.e., to solidify). Irigaray often uses tropes, double-entendres, poetic language, and questions rather than claims in her writing. In one sense, this is in keeping with the psychoanalytic project, since she is revealing unconscious sedimentations of language. But in another sense, she is subverting psychoanalytic thought, since the unconscious she reveals is fluid and shifting, resisting rather than conforming to the symbolic order of interpretation. That resistance, she believes, is characteristic of the repressed feminine of psychoanalysis.

Julia Kristeva, like Irigaray, works within the broad framework of psychoanalysis while trying to discover the feminine that has been repressed in it. Unlike Irigaray, however, she is not as suspicious of the symbolic order, the order of language. For Kristeva, a rejection of the symbolic order is also a rejection of a woman's ability to articulate her own experience. Thus, to reject the symbolic just because it is masculine is to reduce women to silence, a position that women have already known all too well. As she puts it, "A woman has nothing to laugh about when the paternal order falls."[7] But if women must articulate themselves from within the resources of the paternal order, then they seem to face a dilemma: either silence or reduction to the masculine. For Kristeva, the way out of this dilemma is to recognize the feminine as a constituent of the masculine, to recognize the maternal order within the paternal order.

The difference between Irigaray and Kristeva could, at a first approach, be put this way: For Irigaray the feminine is an alternative to the masculine while for Kristeva the feminine is an alternative within it. This is a bit oversimplified, since we have already seen that for Irigaray the feminine does indeed haunt the masculine symbolic order. However, it does capture the contrasting emphases of these two thinkers. Irigaray's work is always struggling against the solidifying and identitarian elements of the symbolic order that she nevertheless turns to. Kristeva, on the other hand, seems less to be engaged in such a struggle and to be more concerned about letting the symbolic order reveal that which is non-symbolic in it. The nonsymbolic that can be revealed within the symbolic she calls the "semiotic."

The semiotic is pre-linguistic. It is bound to the drives that the child has in relation to the mother (hence the feminine component) before the father's intervention, the intervention of the symbolic order. For Lacan, those drives are repressed, but not lost, during the Oedipal stage. Moreover, they become bound to the symbolic order by means of metaphor and metonymy. Kristeva accepts this Lacanian view but calls attention to two generally ignored implications.

First, the drives that are bound to the symbolic order have their source in the maternal relationship; it is before the father's appearance on the scene that they are formed. Second, although bound to the symbolic order, those drives are not reducible to it. They are encrusted in the symbolic but are not themselves symbolic. In that sense, they are a disruption of the symbolic order from within its own parameters.

For Kristeva, then, the task of articulating the feminine is the task of using the symbolic order to reveal what inhabits it but is not reducible to it. It is the task of discovering the semiotic within the symbolic. The difficulty of this task is that it requires one both to engage in and to resist the (identitarian, solidifying) tendencies of the symbolic order, and to do both at the same time. To refuse the symbolic order is to lapse into silence, but to be lured by its ruses into an identification with it is to further the project of repressing the semiotic. In this sense, feminism must engage in a double reading and a double writing if it is to create a space for women in the symbolic order.

In the requirement of a double reading and a double writing, Kristeva's work closely resembles that of Jacques Derrida, for whom language is also haunted by an inarticulable other that is both constitutive of it and repressed by it. Derrida, however, does not work out of a Lacanian framework and has in fact raised questions about that framework from within his own perspective. In Derrida's view, the problem lies not so much within human psychological development as within the development of the Western philosophical tradition. Thus, his work addresses itself to various texts in that tradition in order to show how this other manifests itself. (Although the idea of this other's manifesting itself is a bit misleading, it is not quite as misleading as talking about this other's appearing.)

For Derrida, as for Irigaray and Kristeva, language tends toward identitarianism—toward the privileging of identity at the expense of difference. The place where Derrida takes on this identitarianism, however, is in the philosophical tradition. The reason for this is that it is the philosophical tradition, as much as any discursive project, that has tried to solidify language. And the reason it has done that is, in Derrida's view, that the philosophical project is characterized by the goal—exemplified by Husserl—of giving an absolute and unsurpassable foundation to our experience. Philosophy tries to capture what is to be captured of our experience such that it can be known as exactly what it is and not another way.

If the object of a philosophy is to provide an absolute foundation for experience, then it must somehow be able to control the meaning of the language in which it states its philosophical position. This is because, if the language in which it states its claims is ambiguous, vague, or polyvalent, then it cannot capture the object it needs to capture exactly in words. And if it cannot capture its object exactly, then it cannot claim to provide a foundation for knowledge of that object. What Derrida questions is the possibility of a language that captures its object exactly. Deconstruction is the approach he develops in raising that question.

Actually, deconstruction is concerned not solely with language, but its larger concern relates importantly to language. I would like to outline the larger concern and then show how language fits in. Let's return to the project of giving an absolute foundation to our knowledge. If we are to give our knowledge an absolute foundation, then we must have some sort of immediate access to the object of knowledge, as opposed to merely mediated access to it. As Derrida, picking up on a Heideggerian motif, puts it, there must be a relation of full presence between the knower and the knower's object. This is because, once the relation is mediated, once one's access to it is not direct but by means of some third thing, then one risks picking up any distortion this third thing—the medium—has introduced into one's relation with the object. Thus, Western philosophy has been characterized by a series of positions that try to discover immediate (unmediated) relations between knower and known, while discarding all mediation. The key medium to be discarded is, of course, language, since it seems to affect at least how we relate to the world and certainly how we state our relation to the world.

The problem, in Derrida's view, is that potentially distorting media cannot be eliminated. Or, putting the point another way, one cannot achieve full presence; presence is haunted by, and indeed partially constituted by, absence. Deconstruction is the approach Derrida has developed to show, in individual cases, how that which a philosophical approach discards or marginalizes in order to capture its object exactly and immediately is an uneliminable part of either that object or that capturing.

To see how deconstruction works, let me offer once again a brief (again, oversimplified) summary, this time of Derrida's deconstruction, in *Speech and Phenomena*, of Husserl's work. If Husserl is to offer the philosophical foundation he seeks, then at least two conditions have to be met. First, he must be able to discover an unmediated relationship to the phenomena of experience. The reduction, the epochē, must assure him of the full presence of the presented phenomena to a reflective consciousness. Second, he must, in conformity with what I said above, offer an analysis of language that allows the possibility that his philosophical claims will faithfully reflect the truths to which he has access in the reduction. Putting these two requirements a bit schematically, reflective consciousness must be a perfect reflection of the phenomena under the epochē, and language must be capable of a perfect reflection of that first perfect reflection of the phenomena.

Derrida argues that neither condition can be met. The first condition cannot be met, for one thing, even on Husserl's own analysis of time. Husserl notes that the immediate present, that instant of full presence, is only an idealization, a temporal point that narrows down to nonexistence. Any full temporal present must also contain some retention of the past, even if only an infinitesimal one.

But this means that presence is constituted in part by what is absent, what is no longer—that is, the past. There is no presence without absence, and thus, no immediate presence. One cannot have an experience, even under the reduction, of what is present to one without that experience incorporating a nonpresence—a bit of the absent past.

The second condition cannot be met because language cannot be a mere reflection of conscious experience. Linguistic signs are not empty vessels into which one can pour thoughts; they are defined as much by what is outside consciousness as by what is internal to it. In this, Derrida returns to Saussure's structural analysis of language which, as we have already seen, diminishes the importance of consciousness in the constitution of experience.

Derrida's term *differance*, discussed in the selection in this volume, brings together both the idea of temporal deferral of presence (the denial of Husserl's first condition) and spatial difference (the denial of Husserl's second condition by appeal to Saussure's conception of language as a system of differences). Derrida claims that differance is constitutive of all language, and indeed of all experience. The first implication of this is that foundationalist philosophy, which has been the dominant philosophical project since at least Plato, is futile. It cannot succeed. But a second, related but broader, implication is even more important. It is that our experience and our language are always about more than we can know. Our lives are always and inevitably beyond our cognition, and any attempt to bring them within our cognition (as always, in language) is a betrayal of our experience. Because our language presents itself as identitarian, we are always tempted by that betrayal. But one of the lessons of deconstruction (and here Derrida rejoins Kristeva, but from a different direction) is that in using language we must at once work with it and against it. We cannot escape the use of language and the identitarian illusion it presents: The illusion that it can, rightly employed, capture its object. But, if the deconstructive approach is right, we must use that language in a way that undercuts the illusion even as it engages in it. Many of Derrida's later writings are concerned with this double task of engagement and subversion, a task which makes sense only if the philosophical motivation for it is understood.

While Derrida questions the possibility of giving a philosophical ground to discourse, Habermas is employed in trying to find or to construct one. Like Derrida, he believes that the project of discovering an ultimate foundation is futile; but for him, this does not mean that we cannot find more contingent or historically situated ground for discourse. His selection in this volume defends "discourse ethics," which is an attempt to offer some sort of ground for defending normative positions. In order to understand discourse ethics, however, we need to trace Habermas' philosophical itinerary. Discourse ethics, as it turns out, is an answer to a question Habermas has been pursuing over the course of his philosophical career.

Habermas' concerns are closely aligned with those of the Frankfurt school, and in fact he is considered to be the heir of the legacy of critical theory. Like the critical theorists that precede him, he works in the shadow of failed Marxist predictions and seeks to understand both the failure and a possible way out of failure. And, also in keeping with critical theoretical tradition, he sees much of this failure in capitalism's ability to co-opt social and cultural practices. However, as mentioned above, Habermas also believes that the Frankfurt school painted itself into a corner by claiming that all of reason has become a tool of capitalist production and reproduction. The question he faces, then, is how to conceive of reason, or at least some part of it, that can offer the resources necessary to build both a critique of existing political relationships and the vision of alternative and more just relationships.

For Derrida, this question would be a repetition of the traditional philosophical project of offering foundations and of denying that which is both excluded from (but at the same time constitutive of) those foundations. But Habermas worries that if we follow what he sees as the Derridean path of refusing to give grounds for our commitments, then the political choices we make will be wholly arbitrary. Arbitrariness in political choice is a particular concern for a thinker whose country authored the Holocaust because if all choices are equally unjustified, then there is no theoretical space from which one could offer a critique of an unjust social order. (In contrast, Derrida's take on the Holocaust is that it is not so much a failure of reason but the success of a certain kind of reason—a reason that marginalizes what it sees as different from it.)

In his earliest major work *Knowledge and Human Interests*, Habermas identifies what he calls different cognitive "interests" to which different types of inquiry respond. The three interests to which he calls attention are technical, practical, and emancipatory. The technical interest is most fully realized by the natural sciences, which, by disclosing the nature of the world, can allow us to act more effectively in it. The practical interest is addressed more by hermeneutical sciences, sciences of interpretation like history and the human sciences. These sciences allow us to understand ourselves and our products more fully in order to help us build a community of mutual understanding and interest. The emancipatory interest requires sciences of a more self-reflective sort, of which psychoanalysis might provide an example. The problem the emancipatory interest addresses is that of a distorted understanding of who one is that derives from the capitalist mechanisms to which critical theorists have called our attention. But there is a problem that the emancipatory interest faces that separates it from the other two interests. Since the emancipatory interest is more critical, it is always in danger of co-optation by capitalism, and its history is of one of being reduced either to technical or practical interests. In addition, the positivist self-understanding of philosophy (and of epistemic practice generally) has led to a divorce of the idea of knowledge from that of interest, so that interests are seen as opposed to, rather than bound to, the process of inquiry. The task of a critical theory, then, is to point out and develop the emancipatory interest.

In later writings, Habermas moves away from the three-interest model and recasts the concept of an emancipatory interest. He turns instead to the idea that there are different types of discourse, each with its own proper norms and constraints. Each of these different discourses is bound to different types of actions in which people may be engaged. (The concept of action in Habermas' later writings plays much the same role that the concept of interest does in his earlier ones.) For instance, instrumental or goal-directed action corresponds to technical and strategic discourse with its norms of efficiency, while dramaturgical action corresponds to self-expressive discourse with its norms of truthfulness or sincerity. In this view, the problem that capitalism presents is that it fosters the domination of instrumental or strategic discourse and its incursion into other forms of discourse, which in turn distorts those discourses, preventing them from realizing the type of action that is proper to them. Everything becomes a matter of strategy. Here the link with the critique of the Frankfurt school is very close.

But Habermas still faces the problem of articulating an alternative to the strategic domination of various aspects of discourse. How is it that the norms of a type of discourse ought to be set, if not by the actions of whomever can, by whatever strategy, succeed in setting them? His answer—an answer that leans heavily on the work of his colleague Karl Otto-Apel—is that those norms should be set through a process of unforced and participatory agreement among all those who will be subject to them. Everyone who is going to be a participant in a certain type of discourse, bound by its constraints, should have a say in setting the norms of that discourse. Moreover, that say should not be given under threat of any kind of coercion. What determines which norms will be adopted by the discourse is not force, but the weight of reasons. Only norms that are freely ratified by all the participants in the discussion after all the reasons for and against one or another norm are in should be accepted.

The idea of setting norms of discourse through uncoerced discussion by all participants in that discourse is the heart of Habermas' discourse ethics. It answers the question of how to conceive an alternative to capitalist-dominated discourse. But it does so procedurally; Habermas does not offer an alternative discourse, but a procedure for constructing discourses that will allow people to institute their own alternatives. In that sense, he is interested less in prescribing for others where their good lies and more in creating a space, undistorted and uncoerced by capitalist strategic relations, for them to develop the discourses whose rules they will live by.

NOTES

1. *Cartesian Meditations: An Introduction to Phenomenology,* tr. Dorion Cairns. The Hague: Nijhoff, 1977, p. 7.
2. *Phenomenology of Perception,* tr. Colin Smith. London: Routledge and Kegan Paul, 1962, p. xiv.

3. In calling attention to the three following trends, I do not mean to slight the work that has been done philosophically in Germany in other areas, for instance in philosophy of science. My intention in both this introductory essay and in the selection of readings is to address traditional Continental, as opposed to traditional Anglo-American, themes and trends. It would be a mistake, however, to assume either that there is an abyss that lies between the two traditions or that there are no philosophers working in Germany and France who focus upon the themes and approaches associated with Anglo-American philosophy. Regarding the first mistake, the German philosopher Ernst Tugenhadt has articulated Anglo-American philosophy of language alongside both Heideggerian and Hegelian approaches; regarding the second mistake, Jacques Bouveresse, although writing in France, is concerned more with Anglo-American philosophical themes and approaches than with those I have called "Continental."

4. *Truth and Method*, New York: Crossroad Publishing Co., 1975 (orig. pub. 1960), p. xiv.

5. "The Subject and Power," tr. Leslie Sawyer. Afterword to *Michel Foucault: Beyond Structuralism and Hermeneutics*, by Hubert L. Dreyfus and Paul Robinow. Chicago: University of Chicago Press, 1982, p. 222.

6. *Discipline and Punish: The Birth of the Prison*, tr. Alan Sheridan. New York: Random House, 1977 (orig. pub. 1975), p. 252.

7. *About Chinese Women*, tr. Anita Barrows. New York: Unizen Books, 1977 (orig. pub. 1974), p. 30.

EDMUND HUSSERL

INTRODUCTION TO THE IDEA OF PHENOMENOLOGY

THE TRAIN OF THOUGHTS IN THE LECTURES

Natural thinking in science and everyday life is untroubled by the difficulties concerning the possibility of cognition. *Philosophical thinking* is circumscribed by one's position toward the problems concerning the possibility of cognition. The perplexities in which reflection about the possibility of a cognition that "gets at" the things themselves becomes entangled: How can we be sure that cognition accords with things as they exist in themselves, that it "gets at them"? What do things in themselves care about our ways of thinking and the logical rules governing them? These are laws of how we think; they are psychological laws—Biologism, psychological laws as laws of adaptation.

Absurdity: to begin with, when we think naturally about cognition and fit it and its achievements into the natural ways of thinking which pertains to the sciences we arrive at theories that are appealing at first. But they end in contradiction or absurdity—Inclination to open scepticism.

Even this attempt to look at these problems scientifically we can call "theory of knowledge." At any rate what emerges is the idea of a theory of knowledge as a science which solves the above-mentioned difficulties, gives us an ultimate, clear, therefore inherently consistent insight into the essence of cognition and the possibility of its achievements. The critique of cognition in this sense is the condition of the possibility of a metaphysics.

Reprinted from *The Idea of Phenomenology*, tr. William P. Alston and George Nakhnikian. Introduction by George Nakhnikian. The Hague: Martinus Nijhoff, 1964, pp. 1–12. Reprinted with permission of Kluwer Academic Publishers.

The *method* of the critique of cognition is the phenomenological method, phenomenology as the general doctrine of essences, within which the science of the essence of cognition finds its place.

What sort of method is this? How can a science of cognition be established if cognition in general, what cognizing means and can accomplish, is questioned? What method can here reach the goal?

A. The First Step in the Phenomenological Orientation

1) Right away we become dubious whether such a science is at all possible. If it questions all cognition, every cognition chosen as a starting point is questioned. How then can it ever begin?

This, however, is only a specious difficulty. In "being called into question," cognition is neither *disavowed* nor regarded as in *every* sense doubtful. The question is about some accomplishments imputed to cognition, whereas in fact it is even an open question whether the difficulties pertain to all possible types of cognition. At any rate, if the theory of knowledge is to concern itself with the possibility of cognition it must have cognitions of the possibilities of cognition which, as such, are beyond question; indeed, cognitions in the fullest sense, cognitions about which absolutely no doubt of their having reached their objects is possible. If we are uncertain or unclear as to how it is possible for cognition to reach its object, and if we are inclined to doubt that such a thing is possible, we must, first of all, have before us indubitable examples of cognitions or possible cognitions which really reach, or would reach, their respective objects. At the outset we must not take anything as a cognition just because it seems to be one; otherwise we would have no possible, or what comes to the same thing, no sensible objective.

Here the *Cartesian method of doubt* provides a starting point. Without doubt there is *cogitatio,* there is, namely, the mental process during the [subject's] undergoing it and in a simple reflection upon it. The seeing, direct grasping and having of the *cogitatio* is already a cognition. The *cogitationes* are the first absolute data.

2) What follows naturally is our *first question in the theory of knowledge:* What distinguishes the certainty in these examples from the uncertainty in other instances of alleged cognition? Why is there in certain cases a tendency toward scepticism and toward asking the sceptical question: How can cognition reach a being, and why is there not this doubt and this difficulty in connection with the *cogitationes*?

People answer at first—that is indeed the answer ready at hand—in terms of the pair of concepts or words *immanence* and *transcendence.* The "seeing" cognition of the *cogitatio* is immanent. The cognition belonging to the objective sciences, the natural sciences and the sciences of culture (*Geisteswissenschaften*) and on closer inspection also the mathematical sciences, is transcendent. Involved in the objective sciences is the *doubtfulness of transcendence,* the question: How can cognition reach beyond itself? How can it reach a being that is not to be found within the confines of consciousness? There is not this difficulty with the "seeing" cognition of the *cogitatio.*[1]

3) Next, one is inclined to interpret, as if this were obvious, immanence as genuine immanence (*reelle Immanenz*)[2] and even perhaps to interpret it psychologically, as *immanence in something real (reale Immanenz):* the object of cognition too, is within the cognitive process as a real actuality, or in the [stream of] ego-consciousness of which the mental process is a part. That the cognitive act can hit upon and find its object in the same [stream of] consciousness and within the same real here and now, that is what is taken for granted. The neophyte will say, at this point, that the immanent is in me, the transcendent outside of me.

On a closer view, however, *genuine immanence (reelle Immanenz)* differs from *immanence in the sense of self-givenness as constituted in evidence (Evidenz).* The genuinely immanent (*reell Immanente*) is taken as the indubitable just on account of the fact that it presents nothing else, "points" to nothing "outside" itself, for what is here intended is fully and adequately given in itself. Any self-givenness other than that of the genuinely immanent (*reell Immanente*) is not yet in view.

4) So for the moment no distinction is made. The first step toward clarity now is this: the genuinely immanent (*reell Immanentes*), or what would here mean the same, the adequately self-given, is beyond question. I may make use of it. That which is transcendent (not genuinely immanent) I may not use. Therefore, I must accomplish a *phenomenological reduction: I must exclude all that is transcendently posited.*

Why? [Because] if I am in the dark as to how cognition can reach that which is transcendent, not given in itself but "intended as being outside," no cognition or science of the transcendent can help to dispel the darkness. What I want is *clarity.* I want to understand *the possibility* of that reaching. But this, if we examine its sense, signifies: I want to come face to face with the essence of the possibility of that reaching. I want to make it given to me in an act of "seeing." A "seeing" cannot be demonstrated. The blind man who wishes to see cannot be made to see by means of scientific proofs. Physical and physiological theories about colors give no "seeing" (*schauende*) clarity about the meaning of color as those with eyesight have it. If, therefore, the critique of cognition is a science, as it doubtless is in the light of these considerations, a science which is to clarify all species and forms of cognition, *it can make no use of any science of the natural sort.* It cannot tie itself to the conclusions that any natural science has reached about what is. For it they remain in question. As far as the critique of cognition is concerned, all the sciences are only *phenomena of science.* Every tie of that sort signifies a defective μετάβασις (foundation). This comes about only by way of a mistaken but often seductive *shifting between problems:* between explaining cognition as a fact of nature in psychological and scientific terms and elucidating cognition in terms of its essential capabilities to accomplish its task. Accordingly, if we are to avoid this confusion and remain constantly mindful of the meaning of the question concerning these capabilities, we need *phenomenological reduction*.

This means: everything transcendent (that which is not given to me immanently) is to be assigned the index zero, i.e., its existence, its validity is not to be assumed as such, except at most as *the phenomenon of a claim to validity*. I am to treat all sciences only as phenomena, hence not as systems of valid truths, not as premises, not even as hypotheses for me to reach truth with. This applies to the whole of psychology and the whole of natural science. Meanwhile, the proper *meaning of our principle* is in the constant challenge to stay with the objects as they are in question *here* in the critique of cognition and not to confuse the problems *here* with quite different ones. The elucidation of the ways in which cognition is possible does not depend upon the ways of objective science. To bring knowledge to evident self-givenness and to seek to view the nature of its accomplishment does not mean to deduce, to make inductions, to calculate, etc. It is not the same as eliciting, with reasons, novel things from things already given or purportedly given.

B. The Second Level of the Phenomenological Orientation

We now need a *new stratum of considerations* in order to achieve a higher level of clarity about the nature of phenomenological research and its problems.

1) First, the Cartesian *cogitatio* already requires the phenomenological reduction. The psychological phenomenon in psychological apperception and objectification is not a truly absolute datum. The truly absolute datum is the *pure phenomenon*, that which is reduced. The mentally active ego, the object, man in time, the thing among things, etc., are not absolute data; hence man's mental activity as his activity is not absolute datum either. *We abandon finally the standpoint of psychology, even of descriptive psychology.* And so what is also *reduced* is the question which initially drove us: no longer how can I, this man, contact in my mental processes something existing in itself, perhaps out there, beyond me; but we now replace this hitherto ambiguous question, unstable and complex, because of its transcendent burden, with the *pure basic question:* How can the pure phenomenon of cognition reach something which is not immanent to it? How can the absolute self-givenness of cognition reach something not self-given and how is this reaching to be understood?

At the same time the concept of *genuine immanence (reellen Immanenz)* is reduced. It no longer signifies immanence in something *real (reale Immanenz)*, the immanence in human consciousness and in the real (*realen*) psychic phenomenon.

2) Once we have the "seen" phenomena, it seems that we already have a phenomenology, a science of these phenomena.

But as soon as we begin there, we notice a certain constriction. The field of absolute phenomena—taken one at a time—does not seem to be enough to fulfill our intentions. What good are single "seeings" to us, no matter how securely they bring our *cogitationes* to self-givenness? At first it seems beyond question that on the basis of these "seeings" we can undertake logical operations, can compare, contrast, subsume under concepts, predicate, although, as appears later, behind these operations stand new objectivities. But even if what here seems beyond question were taken for granted and considered no further, we could not understand how we could here arrive at universally valid findings of the sort we need.

But one thing seems to help us along: *eidetic abstraction.* It yields inspectable universals, species, essences, and so it seems to provide the redeeming idea: for do we not seek "seeing" clarity about the essence of cognition? Cognition belongs to the sphere of *cogitationes.* Accordingly, we must through "seeing" bring its universal objects into the consciousness of the universal. Thus it becomes possible to have a doctrine about the essence of cognition.

We take this step in agreement with a tenet of Descartes's concerning *clear and distinct perceptions.* The "existence" of the *cogitatio* is guaranteed by its absolute *self-givenness,* by its givenness in *pure evidence (Evidenz).* Whenever we have pure evidence (*Evidenz*), the pure viewing and grasping of something objective directly and in itself, we have the same guarantees, the same certainties.

This step gave us a new objectivity as absolutely given, i.e., the *objectivity of essences;* and as to begin with the logical acts which find expression in assertions based upon what is intuited remain unnoticed, so now we get the field of *assertions about essences,* viz., of what is generally the case as given in pure "seeing." That is to say at first undifferentiated from the individually given universal objects.

3) Yet do we now have everything; do we have the fully delineated phenomenology and the clear self-evidence to put us in the position of having what we need for the critique of cognition? And are we clear about the issues to be resolved?

No, the step we took leads us further. It makes clear to us in the first place that *genuine (reell) immanence* (and the same is true of transcendence) is but a special case of the *broader concept of immanence as such.* No longer is it a commonplace and taken on face value that the *absolutely given and the genuinely immanent* are one and the same. For that which is universal is absolutely given but is not genuinely immanent. *The act of cognizing* the universal is something singular. At any given time, it is a moment in the stream of consciousness. *The universal itself,* which is given in evidence (*Evidenz*) within the stream of consciousness is nothing singular but just a universal, and in the genuine (*reellen*) sense it is transcendent.

Consequently, the idea of *phenomenological reduction* acquires a more immediate and more profound determination and a clearer meaning. It means not the exclusion of the genuinely transcendent (perhaps even in some psychologico-empirical sense), but the exclusion of the transcendent as such as something to be accepted as existent, i.e., everything that is not evident givenness in its true sense, that is not absolutely given to pure "seeing." But, of course, everything of what we said remains. Inductive or deductive scientific conclusions or facets, etc., from hypotheses, facts, axioms, remain excluded and are allowed only as "phenomena"; and the same with all reference to any "knowing" and "cognition": inquiry must concern itself always with *pure "seeing"* and, therefore, not with the genuinely immanent. It is inquiry within the sphere of pure evidence, inquiry into essences. We also said that its field is the *a priori within absolute self-givenness.*

Thus the field is now characterized. It is a field of absolute cognitions, within which the ego and the world and God and the mathematical manifolds and whatever else may be a scientifically objective matter are held in abeyance, cognitions which are, therefore, also not dependent on these matters, which are valid in their own right, whether we are sceptics with regard to the others or not. All that remains as it is. The root of the matter, however, is *to grasp the meaning of the absolutely given, the absolute clarity of the given,* which excludes every meaningful doubt, in a word, *to grasp the absolutely "seeing" evidence which gets hold of itself.* To a certain extent in the discovery of all this lies the historical significance of the Cartesian method of doubt. But for Descartes to discover and to abandon were the same. We do nothing but clearly formulate and develop consistently what was always implicit in this age-old project. We part company in this connection with psychologistic interpretations of evidence in terms of feelings.

C. The Third Level of the Phenomenological Orientation

Once more we need a new level of considerations, to give us greater clarity about the meaning of phenomenology and to develop further its problems.

How far does self-givenness reach? Is it contained in the givenness of the *cogitatio* and in the ideations which grasp it in its generality? Our phenomenological sphere, the sphere of absolute clarity, of immanence in the true sense, reaches no farther than self-givenness reaches.

We are once again led somewhat deeper, and in depths lie the obscurities and in the obscurities lie the problems.

Everything seemed at first simple and hardly requiring hard work. The prejudice about immanence as genuine immanence, as if the latter were what mattered, one may cast off, and yet one remains at first wedded to genuine immanence, at least in a certain sense. It seems, at first, that in "seeing" essences we have only to grasp in its generality the genuinely immanent in the *cogitationes* and to establish the connections rooted in essences. This, too, seems an easy matter. We reflect; we look back at our own acts; we appraise their genuine contents, as they are, only under phenomenological reduction. This appears to be the sole difficulty. And now, of course, there is nothing further than to lift that which is "seen" into consciousness of universality.

The matter, however, becomes less cozy when we take a closer look at the data. First, the *cogitationes,* which we regard as simple data and in no way mysterious, hide all sorts of transcendencies.

If we look closer and notice how in the mental process, say of [perceiving] a sound, even after phenomenological reduction, *appearance and that which appears stand in contrast,* and this *in the midst of pure givenness,* hence in the midst of true immanence, then we are taken aback. Perhaps the sound lasts. We have there the patently given unity of the sound and its duration with its temporal phases, the present and the past. On the other hand, when we reflect, the phenomenon of enduring sound, itself a temporal phenomenon, has its own now-phase and past phases. And if one picks out a now-phase of the phenomenon there is not only the objective now of the sound itself, but the now of the sound is but a point in the duration of a sound.

Detailed analyses will be given in the course of our special tasks. The above suggestion is enough to call attention to a new point: that the phenomenon of sound perception, even as evident and reduced, demands within the immanent a distinction between *appearance* and *that which appears.* We thus have two absolute data, the givenness of the appearing and the givenness of the object; and the object within this immanence is not immanent in the sense of genuine immanence; it is not a concrete part (*Stück*) of the appearance, i.e., the past phases of the enduring sound are now still objective and yet they are not genuinely contained in the present moment of the appearance. Therefore, we also find in the case of the phenomenon of perception what we found in the case of consciousness of universals, namely, that it is a consciousness which constitutes something self-given which is not contained within what is occurring [in the world] and is not at all found as *cogitatio.*

At the lowest level of reflection, the naive level, at first it seems as if evidence were a matter of simple "seeing," a mental inspection without a character of its own, always one and the same and in itself undifferentiated: the "seeing" just "sees" the things (*Sachen*), the things are simply there and in the truly evident "seeing" they are there in consciousness, and "seeing" is simply to "see" them. Or, to use our previous simile: a direct grasping or taking or pointing to something that simply is and is there. All difference is thus in the things that exist in themselves and have their differences through themselves.

And now how different the "seeing" of things shows itself to be on closer analysis. Even if we retain under the heading of attention the notion of an undifferentiated and in itself no further describable "seeing," it is, nevertheless, apparent that it really makes no sense at all to talk about things which are "simply there" and just need to be "seen." On the contrary, this "simply being there" consists of certain mental processes of specific and changing structure, such as perception, imagination, memory, predication, etc., and in them the things are not contained as in a hull or vessel. Instead, the things come to be *constituted* in these mental processes, although in reality they are not at all to be found in them. For "things to be given" is for them to be *exhibited* (represented) as so and so in such phenomena. And this is not to say that the things once more exist in themselves and "send their representatives into consciousness." This sort of thing cannot occur to us within the sphere of phenomenological reduction. Instead, the things are and are given in appearance and in virtue of the appearance itself; though they are, or are taken as, individually separable from the appearance, they are essentially inseparable from it insofar as the single appearance (the consciousness of the given) is not in question.

Thus this marvelous correlation between the *phenomenon of cognition* and the *object of cognition* reveals itself everywhere. Now let us notice that the task of phenomenology, or rather the area of its tasks and inquiries, is no such trivial things as merely looking, merely opening one's eyes. Already in the first and simplest cases, in the lowest forms of cognition, the greatest difficulties confront pure analysis and the inspection of essences. It is easy to talk of correlation in general but it is very difficult to clarify the way in which an object of cognition *constitutes* itself in cognition. And the task is just this: within the framework of pure evidence (*Evidenz*) or self-givenness *to trace all forms of givenness and all correlations* and to conduct an elucidatory analysis. Of course, to do this we need to take account not only of single acts but also of their complexities, of the consistency or inconsistency of their connections and of the intentions (*Teleologien*) apparent in them. These connections are not conglomerations but distinctively connected and as it were congruent unities, and unities of cognition, which, as unities of cognition have also their unitary objective correlates. Thus they belong themselves to the *cognitive acts,* their types are cognitive types, their native forms are forms of thought and forms of intuition (the word not here to be taken in its Kantian sense).

It now remains to trace step by step the data in all their modifications, those that are, properly speaking, data and those that are not, the simple and the compounded ones, those that so to say are constituted at once and those that essentially are built up stepwise, those that are absolutely valid and those that in the process of cognition acquire givenness and validity in an unlimited progression.

We finally arrive in this way at an understanding of how the transcendent real object can be met (can be known in its nature) in the cognitive act as that which one primarily means by it, and how the sense of this meaning is filled out step by step in a developing cognitive context (if only it has the proper forms which belong to the constitution of the object of experience). We then understand how the object of experience is progressively constituted, and how this manner of being constituted is prescribed. We understand that such a stepwise constitution is required by the very essence of the experienced object.

Along this path one approaches the methodological forms which determine all the sciences and are constitutive of all scientifically given objects, and so also the elucidation of the theory of science and with it implicitly the elucidation of all the sciences; however, only implicitly, i.e., it is only once this enormous work of elucidation has been accomplished that the critique of cognition will be fit to become a critique of the specialized sciences and thereby to evaluate them meta-physically.

These then are the problems of givenness, the problems of the *constitution of objects of all sorts within cognition.* The phenomenology of cognition is the science of cognitive phenomena in two senses. On the one hand it has to do with cognitions as appearances, presentations, acts of consciousness in which this or that object is presented, is an object of consciousness, passively or actively. On the other hand, the phenomenology of cognition has to do with these objects as presenting themselves in this manner. The word "phenomenon" is ambiguous in virtue of the essential correlation between *appearance and that which appears.* Φαινόμενον (phenomenon) in its proper sense means that which appears, and yet it is by preference used for the appearing itself, for the subjective phenomenon (if one may use this expression which is apt to be misunderstood in the vulgar psychological sense).

In reflection, the *cogitatio,* the appearing itself, becomes an object, and this encourages the rise of ambiguity. Finally, we need not repeat once more that in speaking about investigating the objects and modes of cognition, we always mean investigation into essences, which, in the sphere of the absolutely given, exhibits in a general way the ultimate meaning, the possibility, the essence of the objectivity of cognition and of the cognition of objects.

It goes without saying that the *general phenomenology of reason* has to solve also the parallel problems of the correlation between *valuing* and the *things valued,* etc. If the word "phenomenology" were used so broadly as to cover the analysis of everything self-given, the incoherent data would become coherent: analyzing sense-given entities according to their various kinds, etc.— the common element is then in the methodology of the analysis of essences within the sphere of immediate evidence.

NOTES

1. Tr. note: we have rendered Husserl's word *schauen* as "see," the point of the double quotes being that this use of "see" is broader than simply seeing with one's eyes.
2. Tr. note: *reelle Immanenz* has no straightforward translation. The distinction Husserl has in mind is the immanence of universals (essences) vs. the (*reelle*) immanence of mental occurrences and their *contents, e.g., cogitationes,* their contents; also, psychological occurrences such as toothaches. Everything (*reell*) immanent is existentially mind-dependent. Essences, on the other hand, are neither mental *occurrences* nor *contents.* They are intentionally inexistent *objects* of cognitive acts, specifically of "seeings," but they are not ingredients of such acts. Their immanence is simply their *givenness* to "seeing."

MARTIN HEIDEGGER

"LETTER on HUMANISM"

We are still far from pondering the essence of action decisively enough. We view action only as causing an effect. The actuality of the effect is valued according to its utility. But the essence of action is accomplishment. To accomplish means to unfold something into the fullness of its essence, to lead it forth into this full-ness—*producere*. Therefore only what already is can really be accomplished. But what "is" above all is Being. Thinking accomplishes the relation of Being to the essence of man. It does not make or cause the relation. Thinking brings this relation to Being solely as something handed over to it from Being. Such offer-ing consists in the fact that in thinking Being comes to language. Language is the house of Being. In its home man dwells. Those who think and those who create with words are the guardians of this home. Their guardianship accom-plishes the manifestation of Being insofar as they bring the manifestation to lan-guage and maintain it in language through their speech. Thinking does not

This new translation of *Brief über den Humanismus* by Frank A. Capuzzi in collaboration with J. Glenn Gray appears here in its entirety. I [David Farrell Krell] have edited it with reference to the helpful French bilingual edition, Martin Heidegger, *Lettre sur l'humanisme*, translated by Roger Munier, revised edition (Paris: Aubier Montaigne, 1964). The German text was first published in 1947 by A. Francke Verlag, Bern; the present translation is based on the text in Martin Heidegger, *Wegmarken* (Frankfurt am Main: Vittorio Klostermann Verlag, 1967), pp. 145–194. Reprinted from "Letter on Humanism," pp. 190–242, *Basic Writings* by Martin Heidegger. English translation copyright © 1977 by Harper & Row, Publishers, Inc. General Introduction and Introductions to Each Selection copyright © 1977 by David Farrell Krell. Reprinted by permission of HarperCollins Publishers, Inc.

become action only because some effect issues from it or because it is applied. Thinking acts insofar as it thinks. Such action is presumably the simplest and at the same time the highest, because it concerns the relation of Being to man. But all working or effecting lies in Being and is directed toward beings. Thinking, in contrast, lets itself be claimed by Being so that it can say the truth of Being. Thinking accomplishes this letting. Thinking is *l'engagement par l'Être pour l'Être* [engagement by Being for Being]. I do not know whether it is linguistically possible to say both of these ("*par*" and "*pour*") at once, in this way: *penser, c'est l'engagement de l'Être* [thinking is the engagement of Being]. Here the possessive form "*de l'* . . ." is supposed to express both subjective and objective genitive. In this regard "subject" and "object" are inappropriate terms of metaphysics, which very early on in the form of Occidental "logic" and "grammar" seized control of the interpretation of language. We today can only begin to descry what is concealed in that occurrence. The liberation of language from grammar into a more original essential framework is reserved for thought and poetic creation. Thinking is not merely *l'engagement dans l'action* for and by beings, in the sense of the actuality of the present situation. Thinking is *l'engagement* by and for the truth of Being. The history of Being is never past but stands ever before; it sustains and defines every *condition et situation humaine*. In order to learn how to experience the aforementioned essence of thinking purely, and that means at the same time to carry it through, we must free ourselves from the technical interpretation of thinking. The beginnings of that interpretation reach back to Plato and Aristotle. They take thinking itself to be a *technē*, a process of reflection in service to doing and making. But here reflection is already seen from the perspective of *praxis* and *poiēsis*. For this reason thinking, when taken for itself, is not "practical." The characterization of thinking as *thēoria* and the determination of knowing as "theoretical" behavior occur already within the "technical" interpretation of thinking. Such characterization is a reactive attempt to rescue thinking and preserve its autonomy over against acting and doing. Since then "philosophy" has been in the constant predicament of having to justify its existence before the "sciences." It believes it can do that most effectively by elevating itself to the rank of a science. But such an effort is the abandonment of the essence of thinking. Philosophy is hounded by the fear that it loses prestige and validity if it is not a science. Not to be a science is taken as a failing which is equivalent to being unscientific. Being, as the element of thinking, is abandoned by the technical interpretation of thinking. "Logic," beginning with the Sophists and Plato, sanctions this explanation. Thinking is judged by a standard that does not measure up to it. Such judgment may be compared to the procedure of trying to evaluate the nature and powers of a fish by seeing how long it can live on dry land. For a long time now, all too long, thinking has been stranded on dry land. Can then the effort to return thinking to its element be called "irrationalism"?

Surely the questions raised in your letter would have been better answered in direct conversation. In written form thinking easily loses its flexibility. But in writing it is difficult above all to retain the multidimensionality of the realm peculiar to thinking. The rigor of thinking, in contrast to that of the sciences, does not consist merely in an artificial, that is, technical theoretical exactness of concepts. It lies in the fact that speaking remains purely in the element of Being and lets the simplicity of its manifold dimensions rule. On the other hand, written composition exerts a wholesome pressure toward deliberate linguistic formulation. Today I would like to grapple with only one of your questions. Perhaps its discussion will also shed some light on the others.

You ask: *Comment redonner un sens au mot 'Humanisme'?* [How can we restore meaning to the word "humanism"?] This question proceeds from your intention to retain the word "humanism." I wonder whether that is necessary. Or is the damage caused by all such terms still not sufficiently obvious? True, "-isms" have for a long time now been suspect. But the market of public opinion continually demands new ones. We are always prepared to supply the demand. Even such names as "logic," "ethics," and "physics" begin to flourish only when original thinking comes to an end. During the time of their greatness the Greeks thought without such headings. They did not even call thinking "philosophy." Thinking comes to an end when it slips out of its element. The element is what enables thinking to be a thinking. The element is what properly enables: the enabling [*das Vermögen*]. It embraces thinking and so brings it into its essence. Said plainly, thinking is the thinking of Being. The genitive says something twofold. Thinking is of Being inasmuch as thinking, coming to pass from Being, belongs to Being. At the same time thinking is of Being insofar as thinking, belonging to Being, listens to Being. As the belonging to Being that listens, thinking is what it is according to its essential origin. Thinking *is*—this says: Being has fatefully embraced its essence. To embrace a "thing" or a "person" in its essence means to love it, to favor it. Thought in a more original way such favoring [*Mögen*] means to bestow essence as a gift. Such favoring is the proper essence of enabling, which not only can achieve this or that but also can let something essentially unfold in its provenance, that is, let it be. It is on the "strength" of such enabling by favoring that something is properly able to be. This enabling is what is properly "possible" [*das "Mögliche"*], that whose essence resides in favoring. From this favoring Being enables thinking. The former makes the latter possible. Being is the enabling-favoring, the "may be" [*das "Mög-liche"*]. As the element, Being is the "quiet power" of the favoring-enabling, that is, of the possible. Of course, our words *möglich* [possible] and *Möglichkeit* [possibility], under the dominance of "logic" and "metaphysics," are thought solely in contrast to "actuality"; that is, they are thought on the basis of a definite—the metaphysical—interpretation of Being as *actus* and *potentia*, a distinction identified with the one between *existentia* and *essentia*. When I speak of the "quiet power of the possible" I do not mean the *possible* of a merely represented *possibilitas*, nor *potentia* as the *essentia* of an *actus* of *existentia*; rather, I mean Being itself, which in its favoring presides over thinking and hence over the essence of humanity, and that means over its relation to

Being. To enable something here means to preserve it in its essence, to maintain it in its element.

When thinking comes to an end by slipping out of its element it replaces this loss by procuring a validity for itself as *technē*, as an instrument of education and therefore as a classroom matter and later a cultural concern. By and by philosophy becomes a technique for explaining from highest causes. One no longer thinks; one occupies himself with "philosophy." In competition with one another, such occupations publicly offer themselves as "-isms" and try to offer more than the others. The dominance of such terms is not accidental. It rests above all in the modern age upon the peculiar dictatorship of the public realm. However, so-called "private existence" is not really essential, that is to say free, human being. It simply insists on negating the public realm. It remains an off-shoot that depends upon the public and nourishes itself by a mere withdrawal from it. Hence it testifies, against its own will, to its subservience to the public realm. But because it stems from the dominance of subjectivity the public realm itself is the metaphysically conditioned establishment and authorization of the openness of individual beings in their unconditional objectification. Language thereby falls into the service of expediting communication along routes where objectification—the uniform accessibility of everything to everyone—branches out and disregards all limits. In this way language comes under the dictatorship of the public realm which decides in advance what is intelligible and what must be rejected as unintelligible. What is said in *Being and Time* (1927), sections 27 and 35, about the "they" in no way means to furnish an incidental contribution to sociology.[1] Just as little does the "they" mean merely the opposite, understood in an ethical-existentiell way, of the selfhood of persons. Rather, what is said there contains a reference, thought in terms of the question of the truth of Being, to the word's primordial belongingness to Being. This relation remains concealed beneath the dominance of subjectivity that presents itself as the public realm. But if the truth of Being has become thought-provoking for thinking, then reflection on the essence of language must also attain a different rank. It can no longer be a mere philosophy of language. That is the only reason *Being and Time* (section 34) contains a reference to the essential dimension of language and touches upon the simple question as to what mode of Being language as language in any given case has.[2] The widely and rapidly spreading devastation of language not only undermines aesthetic and moral responsibility in every use of language; it arises from a threat to the essence of humanity. A merely cultivated use of language is still no proof that we have as yet escaped the danger to our essence. These days, in fact, such usage might sooner testify that we have not yet seen and cannot see the danger because we have never yet placed ourselves in view of it. Much bemoaned of late, and much too lately, the downfall of language is, however, not the grounds for, but already a consequence of, the state of affairs in which language under the dominance of the modern metaphysics of subjectivity almost irremediably falls out of its element. Language still denies us its essence: that it is the house of the truth of Being. In-

stead, language surrenders itself to our mere willing and trafficking as an instrument of domination over beings. Beings themselves appear as actualities in the
interaction of cause and effect. We encounter beings as actualities in a calculative business-like way, but also scientifically and by way of philosophy, with explanations and proofs. Even the assurance that something is inexplicable
belongs to these explanations and proofs. With such statements we believe that
we confront the mystery. As if it were already decided that the truth of Being
lets itself at all be established in causes and explanatory grounds or, what comes
to the same, in their incomprehensibility.

But if man is to find his way once again into the nearness of Being he must
first learn to exist in the nameless. In the same way he must recognize the seductions of the public realm as well as the impotence of the private. Before he
speaks man must first let himself be claimed again by Being, taking the risk that
under this claim he will seldom have much to say. Only thus will the precious-
ness of its essence be once more bestowed upon the word, and upon man a
home for dwelling in the truth of Being.

But in the claim upon man, in the attempt to make man ready for this claim,
is there not implied a concern about man? Where else does "care" tend but in
the direction of bringing man back to his essence.[3] What else does that in turn
betoken but that man (homo) become human (humanus)? Thus humanitas
really does remain the concern of such thinking. For this is humanism: meditating and caring, that man be human and not inhumane, "inhuman," that is, outside his essence. But in what does the humanity of man consist? It lies in his
essence.

But whence and how is the essence of man determined? Marx demands that
"man's humanity" be recognized and acknowledged.[4] He finds it in "society."
"Social" man is for him "natural" man. In "society" the "nature" of man, that
is, the totality of "natural needs" (food, clothing, reproduction, economic suffi-
ciency) is equably secured. The Christian sees the humanity of man, the humanitas of homo, in contradistinction to Deitas. He is the man of the history of
redemption who as a "child of God" hears and accepts the call of the Father in
Christ. Man is not of this world, since the "world," thought in terms of Platonic
theory, is only a temporary passage to the beyond.

Humanitas, explicitly so called, was first considered and striven for in the
age of the Roman Republic. Homo humanus was opposed to homo barbarus.
Homo humanus here means the Romans, who exalted and honored Roman vir-
tus through the "embodiment" of the paideia [education] taken over from the
Greeks. These were the Greeks of the Hellenistic age, whose culture was acquired in the schools of philosophy. It was concerned with eruditio et institutio
in bonas artes [scholarship and training in good conduct]. Paideia thus understood was translated as humanitas. The genuine romanitas of homo romanus
consisted in such humanitas. We encounter the first humanism in Rome: it
therefore remains in essence a specifically Roman phenomenon which emerges
from the encounter of Roman civilization with the culture of late Greek civiliza-

tion. The so-called Renaissance of the fourteenth and fifteenth centuries in Italy is a *renascentia romanitatis*. Because *romanitas* is what matters, it is concerned with *humanitas* and therefore with Greek *paideia*. But Greek civilization is always seen in its later form and this itself is seen from a Roman point of view. The *homo romanus* of the Renaissance also stands in opposition to *homo barbarus*. But now the in-humane is the supposed barbarism of gothic Scholasticism in the Middle Ages. Therefore a *studium humanitatis,* which in a certain way reaches back to the ancients and thus also becomes a revival of Greek civilization, always adheres to historically understood humanism. For Germans this is apparent in the humanism of the eighteenth century supported by Winckelmann, Goethe, and Schiller. On the other hand, Hölderlin does not belong to "humanism" precisely because he thought the destiny of man's essence in a more original way than "humanism" could.

But if one understands humanism in general as a concern that man become free for his humanity and find his worth in it, then humanism differs according to one's conception of the "freedom" and "nature" of man. So too are there various paths toward the realization of such conceptions. The humanism of Marx does not need to return to antiquity any more than the humanism which Sartre conceives existentialism to be. In this broad sense Christianity too is a humanism, in that according to its teaching everything depends on man's salvation (*salus aeterna*); the history of man appears in the context of the history of redemption. However different these forms of humanism may be in purpose and in principle, in the mode and means of their respective realizations, and in the form of their teaching, they nonetheless all agree in this, that the *humanitas of homo humanus* is determined with regard to an already established interpretation of nature, history, world, and the ground of the world, that is, of beings as a whole.

Every humanism is either grounded in a metaphysics or is itself made to be the ground of one. Every determination of the essence of man that already presupposes an interpretation of being without asking about the truth of Being, whether knowingly or not, is metaphysical. The result is that what is peculiar to all metaphysics, specifically with respect to the way the essence of man is determined, is that it is "humanistic." Accordingly, every humanism remains metaphysical. In defining the humanity of man humanism not only does not ask about the relation of Being to the essence of man; because of its metaphysical origin humanism even impedes the question by neither recognizing nor understanding it. On the contrary, the necessity and proper form of the question concerning the truth of Being, forgotten in and through metaphysics, can come to light only if the question "What is metaphysics?" is posed in the midst of metaphysics' domination. Indeed every inquiry into Being, even the one into the truth of Being, must at first introduce its inquiry as a "metaphysical" one.

The first humanism, Roman humanism, and every kind that has emerged from that time to the present, has presupposed the most universal "essence" of man to be obvious. Man is considered to be an *animal rationale.* This definition is not simply the Latin translation of the Greek *zōon logon echon* but rather a

metaphysical interpretation of it. This essential definition of man is not false.
But it is conditioned by metaphysics. The essential provenance of metaphysics,
and not just its limits, became questionable in *Being and Time*. What is questionable is above all commended to thinking as what is to be thought, but not at
all left to the gnawing doubts of an empty skepticism.

Metaphysics does indeed represent beings in their Being, and so it thinks
the Being of beings. But it does not think the difference of both.[5] Metaphysics
does not ask the truth of Being itself. Nor does it therefore ask in what way the
essence of man belongs to the truth of Being. Metaphysics has not only failed up
to now to ask this question, the question is inaccessible to metaphysics as such.
Being is still waiting for the time when it will become thought-provoking to
man. With regard to the definition of man's essence, however one may determine the *ratio* of the *animal* and the reason of the living being, whether as a
"faculty of principles," or a "faculty of categories," or in some other way, the
essence of reason is always and in each case grounded in this: for every apprehending of beings in their Being, Being itself is already illumined and comes to
pass in its truth. So too with *animal, zōon,* an interpretation of "life" is already
posited which necessarily lies in an interpretation of beings as *zōē* and *physis,*
within which what is living appears. Above and beyond everything else, however, it finally remains to ask whether the essence of man primordially and most
decisively lies in the dimension of *animalitas* at all. Are we really on the right
track toward the essence of man as long as we set him off as one living creature
among others in contrast to plants, beasts, and God? We can proceed in that
way; we can in such fashion locate man within being as one being among others. We will thereby always be able to state something correct about man. But
we must be clear on this point, that when we do this we abandon man to the essential realm of *animalitas* even if we do not equate him with beasts but attribute a specific difference to him. In principle we are still thinking of *homo
animalis*—even when *anima* [soul] is posited as *animus sive mens* [spirit or
mind], and this in turn is later posited as subject, person, or spirit [*Geist*]. Such
positing is the manner of metaphysics. But then the essence of man is too little
heeded and not thought in its origin, the essential provenance that is always the
essential future for historical mankind. Metaphysics thinks of man on the basis
of *animalitas* and does not think in the direction of his *humanitas.*

Metaphysics closes itself to the simple essential fact that man essentially occurs only in his essence, where he is claimed by Being. Only from that claim
"has" he found that wherein his essence dwells. Only from this dwelling "has"
he "language" as the home that preserves the ecstatic for his essence.[6] Such
standing in the lighting of Being I call the ek-sistence of man. This way of Being
is proper only to man. Ek-sistence so understood is not only the ground of the
possibility of reason, *ratio,* but is also that in which the essence of man preserves the source that determines him.

Ek-sistence can be said only of the essence of man, that is, only of the human way "to be." For as far as our experience shows, only man is admitted to

the destiny of ek-sistence. Therefore ek-sistence can also never be thought of as a specific kind of living creature among others—granted that man is destined to think the essence of his Being and not merely to give accounts of the nature and history of his constitution and activities. Thus even what we attribute to man as *animalitas* on the basis of the comparison with "beast" is itself grounded in the essence of ek-sistence. The human body is something essentially other than an animal organism. Nor is the error of biologism overcome by adjoining a soul to the human body, a mind to the soul, and the existentiell to the mind, and then louder than before singing the praises of the mind—only to let everything relapse into "life-experience," with a warning that thinking by its inflexible concepts disrupts the flow of life and that thought of Being distorts existence. The fact that physiology and physiological chemistry can scientifically investigate man as an organism is no proof that in this "organic" thing, that is, in the body scientifically explained, the essence of man consists. That has as little validity as the notion that the essence of nature has been discovered in atomic energy. It could even be that nature, in the face she turns toward man's technical mastery, is simply concealing her essence. Just as little as the essence of man consists in being an animal organism can this insufficient definition of man's essence be overcome or offset by outfitting man with an immortal soul, the power of reason, or the character of a person. In each instance essence is passed over, and passed over on the basis of the same metaphysical projection.

What man is—or, as it is called in the traditional language of metaphysics, the "essence" of man—lies in his ek-sistence. But ek-sistence thought in this way is not identical with the traditional concept of *existentia*, which means actuality in contrast to the meaning of *essentia* as possibility. In *Being and Time* (p. 42) this sentence is italicized: "The 'essence' of Dasein lies in its existence." However, here the opposition between *existentia* and *essentia* is not under consideration, because neither of these metaphysical determinations of Being, let alone their relationship, is yet in question. Still less does the sentence contain a universal statement about *Dasein*, since the word came into fashion in the eighteenth century as a name for "object," intending to express the metaphysical concept of the actuality of the actual. On the contrary, the sentence says: man occurs essentially in such a way that he is the "there" [*das "Da"*], that is, the lighting of Being. The "Being" of the *Da*, and only it, has the fundamental character of ek-sistence, that is, of an ecstatic inherence in the truth of Being. The ecstatic essence of man consists in ek-sistence, which is different from the metaphysically conceived *existentia*. Medieval philosophy conceives the latter as *actualitas*. Kant represents *existentia* as actuality in the sense of the objectivity of experience. Hegel defines *existentia* as the self-knowing Idea of absolute subjectivity. Nietzsche grasps *existentia* as the eternal recurrence of the same. Here it remains an open question whether through *existentia*—in these explanations of it as actuality, which at first seem quite different—the Being of a stone or even life as the Being of plants and animals is adequately thought. In any case living creatures are as they are without standing outside their Being as such and within the truth of Being, preserving in such standing the essential nature of their Being. Of all the beings that are, presumably the most difficult to think about are living creatures, because on the one hand they are in a certain way most closely related to us, and on the other are at the same time separated from our ek-sistent essence by an abyss. However, it might also seem as though the essence of divinity is closer to us than what is foreign in other living creatures, closer, namely, in an essential distance which however distant is nonetheless more familiar to our ek-sistent essence than is our appalling and scarcely conceivable bodily kinship with the beast. Such reflections cast a strange light upon the current and therefore always still premature designation of man as *animal rationale*. Because plants and animals are lodged in their respective environments but are never placed freely in the lighting of Being which alone is "world," they lack language. But in being denied language they are not thereby suspended wordlessly in their environment. Still, in this word "environment" converges all that is puzzling about living creatures. In its essence language is not the utterance of an organism; nor is it the expression of a living thing. Nor can it ever be thought in an essentially correct way in terms of its symbolic character, perhaps not even in terms of the character of signification. Language is the lighting-concealing advent of Being itself.

Ek-sistence, thought in terms of *ecstasis,* does not coincide with *existentia* in either form or content. In terms of content ek-sistence means standing out into the truth of Being. *Existentia* (*existence*) means in contrast *actualitas*, actuality as opposed to mere possibility as Idea. Ek-sistence identifies the determination of what man is in the destiny of truth. *Existentia* is the name for the realization of something that is as it appears in its Idea. The sentence "Man ek-sists" is not an answer to the question of whether man actually is or not; rather, it responds to the question concerning man's "essence." We are accustomed to posing this question with equal impropriety whether we ask what man is or who he is. For in the *Who?* or the *What?* we are already on the lookout for something like a person or an object. But the personal no less than the objective misses and misconstrues the essential unfolding of ek-sistence in the history of Being. That is why the sentence cited from *Being and Time* (p. 42) is careful to enclose the word "essence" in quotation marks. This indicates that "essence" is now being defined from neither *esse essentiae* nor *esse existentiae* but rather from the ek-static character of Dasein. As ek-sisting, man sustains Da-sein in that he takes the *Da*, the lighting of Being, into "care." But Da sein itself occurs essentially as "thrown." It un-folds essentially in the throw of Being as the fateful sending.

But it would be the ultimate error if one wished to explain the sentence about man's ek-sistent essence as if it were the secularized transference to human beings of a thought that Christian theology expresses about God (*Deus est suum esse* [God is His Being]); for ek-sistence is not the realization of an essence, nor does ek-sistence itself even effect and posit what is essential. If we understand what *Being and Time* calls "projection" as a representational positing, we take it to be an achievement of subjectivity and do not think it in the only way the "understanding of Being" in the context of the "existential analysis" of "being-in-the-world" can be thought—namely as the ecstatic relation to the lighting of Being. The adequate execution and completion of this other thinking that abandons subjectivity is surely made more difficult by the fact that in the publication of *Being and Time* the third division of the first part, "Time and Being," was held back (cf. *Being and Time*, p. 88, above). Here everything is reversed. The section in question was held back because thinking failed in the adequate saying of this turning [*Kehre*] and did not succeed with the help of the language of metaphysics. The lecture "On the Essence of Truth," thought out and delivered in 1930 but not printed until 1943, provides a certain insight into the thinking of the turning from "Being and Time" to "Time and Being." This turning is not a change of standpoint from *Being and Time,* but in it the thinking that was sought first arrives at the location of that dimension out of which, *Being and Time* is experienced, that is to say, experienced from the fundamental experience of the oblivion of Being.

By way of contrast, Sartre expresses the basic tenet of existentialism in this way: Existence precedes essence.[7] In this statement he is taking *existentia* and *essentia* according to their metaphysical meaning, which from Plato's time on has said that *essentia* precedes *existentia*. Sartre reverses this statement. But the reversal of a metaphysical statement remains a metaphysical statement. With it he stays with metaphysics in oblivion of the truth of Being. For even if philosophy wishes to determine the relation of *essentia* and *existentia* in the sense it had in medieval controversies, in Leibniz's sense, or in some other way, it still remains to ask first of all from what destiny of Being this differentiation in Being as *esse essentiae* and *esse existentiae* comes to appear to thinking. We have yet to consider why the question about the destiny of Being was never asked and why it could never be thought. Or is the fact that this is how it is with the differentiation of *essentia* and *existentia* not at all a sign of forgetfulness of Being? We must presume that this destiny does not rest upon a mere failure of human thinking, let alone upon a lesser capacity of early Western thinking. Concealed in its essential provenance, the differentiation of *essentia* (essentiality) and *existentia* (actuality) completely dominates the destiny of Western history and of all history determined by Europe.

Sartre's key proposition about the priority of *existentia* over *essentia* does, however, justify using the name "existentialism" as an appropriate title for a philosophy of this sort. But the basic tenet of "existentialism" has nothing at all in common with the statement from *Being and Time*—apart from the fact that in *Being and Time* no statement about the relation of *essentia* and *existentia* can yet be expressed since there it is still a question of preparing something precursory. As is obvious from what we have just said, that happens clumsily enough. What still today remains to be said could perhaps become an impetus for guiding the essence of man to the point where it thoughtfully attends to that dimension of the truth of Being which thoroughly governs it. But even this could take place only to the honor of Being and for the benefit of Dasein which man eksistingly sustains; not, however, for the sake of man so that civilization and culture through man's doings might be vindicated.

But in order that we today may attain to the dimension of the truth of Being in order to ponder it, we should first of all make clear how Being concerns man and how it claims him. Such an essential experience happens to us when it dawns on us that man is in that he eksists. Were we now to say this in the language of the tradition, it would run: the ek-sistence of man is his substance. That is why in *Being and Time* the sentence often recurs, "The 'substance' of man is existence (pp. 117, 212, 314)." But "substance," thought in terms of the history of Being, is already a blanket translation of *ousia,* a word that designates the presence of what is present and at the same time, with puzzling ambiguity, usually means what is present itself. If we think the metaphysical term "substance" in the sense already suggested in accordance with the "phenomenological destruction" carried out in *Being and Time* (cf. p. 64, above), then the statement "The 'substance' of man is ek-sistence" says nothing else but that the way that man in his proper essence becomes present to Being is ecstatic inherence in the truth of Being. Through this determination of the essence of man the humanistic interpretations of man as *animal rationale,* as "person," as spiritual-ensouled-bodily being, are not declared false and thrust aside. Rather, the sole implication is that the highest determinations of the essence of man in humanism still do not realize the proper dignity of man. To that extent the thinking in *Being and Time* is against humanism. But this opposition does not mean that such thinking aligns itself against the humane and advocates the inhuman, that it promotes the inhumane and deprecates the dignity of man. Humanism is opposed because it does not set the *humanitas* of man high enough. Of course the essential worth of man does not consist in his being the substance of beings, as the "Subject" among them, so that as the tyrant of Being he may deign to release the beingness of beings into an all too loudly bruited "objectivity."

Man is rather "thrown" from Being itself into the truth of Being, so that ek-sisting in this fashion he might guard the truth of Being, in order that beings might appear in the light of Being as the beings they are. Man does not decide whether and how beings appear, whether and how God and the gods or history and nature come forward into the lighting of Being, come to presence and depart. The advent of beings lies in the destiny of Being. But for man it is ever a question of finding what is fitting in his essence which corresponds to such destiny; for in accord with this destiny man as ek-sisting has to guard the truth of Being. Man is the shepherd of Being. It is in this direction alone that *Being and Time* is thinking when ecstatic existence is experienced as "care" (cf. section 44 C, pp. 226 ff.).

Yet Being—what is Being? It is It itself. The thinking that is to come must learn to experience that and to say it. "Being"—that is not God and not a cosmic ground. Being is farther than all beings and is yet nearer to man than every being, be it a rock, a beast, a work of art, a machine, be it an angel or God. Being is the nearest. Yet the near remains farthest from man. Man at first clings always and only to beings. But when thinking represents beings as beings it no doubt relates itself to Being. In truth, however, it always thinks only of beings as such; precisely not, and never, Being as such. The "question of Being" always remains a question about beings. It is still not at all what its elusive name indicates: the question in the direction of Being. Philosophy, even when it becomes "critical" through Descartes and Kant, always follows the course of metaphysical representation. It thinks from beings back to beings with a glance in passing toward Being. For every departure from beings and every return to them stands already in the light of Being.

But metaphysics recognizes the lighting of Being either solely as the view of what is present in "outward appearance" (*idea*) or critically as what is seen as a result of categorical representation on the part of subjectivity. This means that the truth of Being as the lighting itself remains concealed for metaphysics. However, this concealment is not a defect of metaphysics but a treasure withheld from it yet held before it, the treasure of its own proper wealth. But the lighting itself is Being. Within the destiny of Being in metaphysics the lighting first affords, a view by which what is present comes into touch with man, who is present to it, so that man himself can in apprehending (*noein*) first touch upon Being (*thigein*, Aristotle, *Met.* IX, 10). This view first gathers the aspect to itself. It yields to such aspects when apprehending has become a setting-forth-before-itself in the *perceptio* of the *res cogitans* taken as the *subiectum* or *certitudo*.

But how—provided we really ought to ask such a question at all—how does Being relate to ek-sistence? Being itself is the relation to the extent that It, as the location of the truth of Being amid beings, gathers to itself and embraces ek-sistence in its existential, that is, ecstatic, essence. Because man as the one who ek-sists comes to stand in this relation that Being destines for itself, in that he ecstatically sustains it, that is, in care takes it upon himself, he at first fails to recognize the nearest and attaches himself to the next nearest. He even thinks that this is the nearest. But nearer than the nearest and at the same time for ordinary thinking farther than the farthest is nearness itself: the truth of Being.

Forgetting the truth of Being in favor of the pressing throng of beings unthought in their essence is what ensnarement [*Ver-fallen*] means in *Being and Time*.[8] This word does not signify the Fall of Man understood in a "moral-philosophical" and at the same time secularized way; rather, it designates an essential relationship of man to Being within Being's relation to the essence of man. Accordingly, the terms "authenticity" and "inauthenticity," which are used in a provisional fashion, do not imply a moral-existentiell or an "anthropological" distinction but rather a relation which, because it has been hitherto concealed from philosophy, has yet to be thought for the first time, an "ecstatic" relation of the essence of man to the truth of Being. But this relation is as it is not by reason of ek-sistence; on the contrary, the essence of ek-sistence derives existentially ecstatically from the essence of the truth of Being.

The one thing thinking would like to attain and for the first time tries to articulate in *Being and Time* is something simple. As such, Being remains mysterious, the simple nearness of an unobtrusive governance. The nearness occurs essentially as language itself. But language is not mere speech, insofar as we represent the latter at best as the unity of phoneme (or written character), melody, rhythm, and meaning (or sense). We think of the phoneme and written character as a verbal body for language, of melody and rhythm as its soul, and whatever has to do with meaning as its mind. We usually think of language as corresponding to the essence of man represented as *animal rationale,* that is, as the unity of body-soul-mind. But just as ek-sistence—and through it the relation of the truth of Being to man—remains veiled in the humanitas of *homo animalis,* so does the metaphysical-animal explanation of language cover up the essence of language in the history of Being. According to this essence language is the house of Being which comes to pass from Being and is pervaded by Being. And so it is proper to think the essence of language from its correspondence to Being and indeed as this correspondence, that is, as the home of man's essence.

But man is not only a living creature who possesses language along with other capacities. Rather, language is the house of Being in which man ek-sists by dwelling, in that he belongs to the truth of Being, guarding it.

So the point is that in the determination of the humanity of man as ek-sistence what is essential is not man but Being—as the dimension of the *ecstasis* of ek-sistence. However, the dimension is not something spatial in the familiar sense. Rather, everything spatial and all space-time occur essentially in the dimensionality which Being itself is.

Thinking attends to these simple relationships. It tries to find the right word for them within the long traditional language and grammar of metaphysics. But does such thinking—granted that there is something in a name—still allow itself to be described as humanism? Certainly not so far as humanism thinks metaphysically. Certainly not if humanism is existentialism and is represented by what Sartre expresses: *précisément nous sommes sur un plan où il y a seulement des hommes* [We are precisely in a situation where there are only human beings].[9] Thought from *Being and Time,* this should say instead: *précisément nous sommes sur un plan où il y a principalement l'Être* [We are precisely in a situation where principally there is Being]. But where does *le plan* come from and what is it? *L'Être et le plan* are the same. In *Being and Time* (p. 212) we purposely and cautiously say, *il y a l'Être:* "there is / it gives" ["*es gibt*"] Being. *Il y a* translates "it gives" imprecisely. For the "it" that here "gives" is Being itself. The "gives" names the essence of Being that is giving, granting its truth. The self-giving into the open, along with the open region itself, is Being itself.

At the same time "it gives" is used preliminarily to avoid the locution "Being is"; for "is" is commonly said of some thing which is. We call such a thing a being. But Being "is" precisely not "a being." If "is" is spoken without a closer interpretation of Being, then Being is all too easily represented as a "being" after the fashion of the familiar sort of beings which act as causes and are actualized as effects. And yet Parmenides, in the early age of thinking, says, *esti gar einai*, "for there is Being." The primal mystery for all thinking is concealed in this phrase. Perhaps "is" can be said only of Being in an appropriate way, so that no individual being ever properly "is." But because thinking should be directed only toward saying Being in its truth instead of explaining it as a particular being in terms of beings, whether and how Being is must remain an open question for the careful attention of thinking.

The *esti gar einai* of Parmenides is still unthought today. That allows us to gauge how things stand with the progress of philosophy. When philosophy attends to its essence it does not make forward strides at all. It remains where it is in order constantly to think the Same. Progression, that is, progression forward from this place, is a mistake that follows thinking as the shadow which thinking itself casts. Because Being is still unthought, *Being and Time* too says of it, "there is / it gives." Yet one cannot speculate about this *il y a* precipitously and without a foothold. This "there is / it gives" rules as the destiny of Being. Its history comes to language in the words of essential thinkers. Therefore the thinking that thinks into the truth of Being is, as thinking, historical. There is not a "systematic" thinking and next to it an illustrative history of past opinions. Nor is there, as Hegel thought, only a systematics which can fashion the law of its thinking into the law of history and simultaneously subsume history into the system. Thought in a more primordial way, there is the history of Being to which thinking belongs as recollection of this history that unfolds of itself. Such recollective thought differs essentially from the subsequent presentation of history in the sense of an evanescent past. History does not take place primarily as a happening. And its happening is not evenescence. The happening of history occurs essentially as the destiny of the truth of Being and from it.[10] Being comes to destiny in that It, Being, gives itself. But thought in terms of such destiny this says: it gives itself and refuses itself simultaneously. Nonetheless, Hegel's definition of history as the development of "Spirit" is not untrue. Neither is it partly correct and partly false. It is as true as metaphysics, which through Hegel first brings to language its essence—thought in terms of the absolute—in the system. Absolute metaphysics, with its Marxian and Nietzschean inversions, belongs to the history of the truth of Being. Whatever stems from it cannot be countered or even cast aside by refutations. It can only be taken up in such a way that its truth is more primordially sheltered in Being itself and removed from the domain of mere human opinion. All refutation in the field of essential thinking is foolish. Strife among thinkers is the "lovers' quarrel" concerning the matter itself. It assists them mutually toward a simple belonging to the Same, from which they find what is fitting for them in the destiny of Being.

Assuming that in the future man will be able to think the truth of Being, he will think from ek-sistence. Man stands ek-sistingly in the destiny of Being. The ek-sistence of man is historical as such, but not only or primarily because so much happens to man and to things human in the course of time. Because it must think the ek-sistence of Da-sein, the thinking of *Being and Time* is essentially concerned that the historicity of Dasein be experienced.

But does not *Being and Time* say on p. 212, where the "there is / it gives" comes to language, "Only so long as Dasein is, is there [*gibt es*] Being"? To be sure. It means that only so long as the lighting of Being comes to pass does Being convey itself to man. But the fact that the *Da*, the lighting as the truth of Being itself, comes to pass is the dispensation of Being itself. This is the destiny of the lighting. But the sentence does not mean that the Dasein of man in the traditional sense of *existentia*, and thought in modern philosophy as the actuality of the *ego cogito*, is that being through which Being is first fashioned. The sentence does not say that Being is the product of man. The "Introduction" to *Being and Time* (p. 86, above) says simply and clearly, even in italics, "Being is the *transcendens* pure and simple." Just as the openness of spatial nearness seen from the perspective of a particular thing exceeds all things near and far, so is Being essentially broader than all beings, because it is the lighting itself. For all that, Being is thought on the basis of beings, a consequence of the approach—at first unavoidable—within a metaphysics that is still dominant. Only from such a perspective does Being show itself in and as a transcending.

The introductory definition, "Being is the *transcendens* pure and simple," articulates in one simple sentence the way the essence of Being hitherto has illumined man. This retrospective definition of the essence of Being from the lighting of beings as such remains indispensable for the prospective approach of thinking toward the question concerning the truth of Being. In this way thinking attests to its essential unfolding as destiny. It is far from the arrogant presumption that wishes to begin anew and declares all past philosophy false. But whether the definition of Being as the *transcendens* pure and simple really does express the simple essence of the truth of Being—this and this alone is the primary question for a thinking that attempts to think the truth of Being. That is why we also say (p. 230) that how Being *is* is to be understood chiefly from its "meaning" ["*Sinn*"], that is, from the truth of Being. Being is illumined for man in the ecstatic projection [*Entwurf*]. But this projection does not create Being.

Moreover, the projection is essentially a thrown projection. What throws in projection is not man but Being itself, which sends man into the ek-sistence of Da-sein that is his essence. This destiny comes to pass as the lighting of Being, as which it is. The lighting grants nearness to Being. In this nearness, in the lighting of the *Da*, man dwells as the ek-sisting one without yet being able properly to experience and take over this dwelling. In the lecture on Hölderlin's elegy "Homecoming" (1943) this nearness "of" Being, which the *Da* of Dasein is, is thought on the basis of *Being and Time*; it is perceived as spoken from the minstrel's poem; from the experience of the oblivion of Being it is called the "homeland." The word is thought here in an essential sense, not patriotically or nationalistically but in terms of the history of Being. The essence of the homeland, however, is also mentioned with the intention of thinking the homelessness of contemporary man from the essence of Being's history. Nietzsche was the last to experience this homelessness. From within metaphysics he was unable to find any other way out than a reversal of metaphysics. But that is the height of futility. On the other hand, when Hölderlin composes "Homecoming" he is concerned that his "countrymen" find their essence. He does not at all seek that essence in an egoism of his nation. He sees it rather in the context of a belongingness to the destiny of the West. But even the West is not thought regionally as the Occident in contrast to the Orient, nor merely as Europe, but rather world-historically out of nearness to the source. We have still scarcely begun to think of the mysterious relations to the East which found expression in Hölderlin's poetry.[11] "German" is not spoken to the world so that the world might be reformed through the German essence; rather, it is spoken to the Germans so that from a fateful belongingness to the nations they might become world-historical along with them.[12] The homeland of this historical dwelling is nearness to Being.

In such nearness, if at all, a decision may be made as to whether and how God and the gods withhold their presence and the night remains, whether and how the day of the holy dawns, whether and how in the upsurgence of the holy an epiphany of God and the gods can begin anew. But the holy, which alone is the essential sphere of divinity, which in turn alone affords a dimension for the gods and for God, comes to radiate only when Being itself beforehand and after extensive preparation has been illuminated and is experienced in its truth. Only thus does the overcoming of homelessness begin from Being, a homelessness in which not only man but the essence of man stumbles aimlessly about.

Homelessness so understood consists in the abandonment of Being by beings. Homelessness is the symptom of oblivion of Being. Because of it the truth of Being remains unthought. The oblivion of Being makes itself known indirectly through the fact that man always observes and handles only beings. Even so, because man cannot avoid having some notion of Being, it is explained merely as what is "most general" and therefore as something that encompasses beings, or as a creation of the infinite being, or as the product of a finite subject. At the same time "Being" has long stood for "beings" and, inversely, the latter for the former, the two of them caught in a curious and still unraveled confusion.

As the destiny that sends truth, Being remains concealed. But the world's destiny is heralded in poetry, without yet becoming manifest as the history of Being. The world-historical thinking of Hölderlin that speaks out in the poem "Remembrance" is therefore essentially more primordial and thus more significant for the future than the mere cosmopolitanism of Goethe. For the same reason Hölderlin's relation to Greek civilization is something essentially other than humanism. When confronted with death, therefore, those young Germans who knew about Hölderlin lived and thought something other than what the public held to be the typical German attitude.

Homelessness is coming to be the destiny of the world. Hence it is necessary to think that destiny in terms of the history of Being. What Marx recognized in an essential and significant sense, though derived from Hegel, as the estrangement of man has its roots in the homelessness of modern man.[13] This homelessness is specifically evoked from the destiny of Being in the form of metaphysics and through metaphysics is simultaneously entrenched and covered up as such. Because Marx by experiencing estrangement attains an essential dimension of history, the Marxist view of history is superior to that of other historical accounts. But since neither Husserl nor—so far as I have seen till now—Sartre recognizes the essential importance of the historical in Being, neither phenomenology nor existentialism enters that dimension within which a productive dialogue with Marxism first becomes possible.

For such dialogue it is certainly also necessary to free oneself from naïve notions about materialism, as well as from the cheap refutations that are supposed to counter it. The essence of materialism does not consist in the assertion that everything is simply matter but rather in a metaphysical determination according to which every being appears as the material of labor. The modern metaphysical essence of labor is anticipated in Hegel's *Phenomenology of Spirit* as the self-establishing process of unconditioned production, which is the objectification of the actual through man experienced as subjectivity. The essence of materialism is concealed in the essence of technology, about which much has been written but little has been thought. Technology is in its essence a destiny within the history of Being and of the truth of Being, a truth that lies in oblivion. For technology does not go back to the *technē* of the Greeks in name only but derives historically and essentially from *technē* as a mode of *alētheuein*, a mode, that is, of rendering beings manifest [*Offenbarmachen*]. As a form of truth technology is grounded in the history of metaphysics, which is itself a distinctive and up to now the only perceptible phase of the history of Being. No matter which of the various positions one chooses to adopt toward the doctrines of communism and to their foundation, from the point of view of the history of Being it is certain that an elemental experience of what is world-historical speaks out in it. Whoever takes "communism" only as a "party" or a "Weltanschauung" is thinking too shallowly, just as those who by the term "Americanism" mean, and mean derogatorily, nothing more than a particular lifestyle. The danger into which Europe as it has hitherto existed is ever more clearly forced consists presumably in the fact above all that its thinking—once its glory—is falling behind in the essential course of a dawning world destiny which nevertheless in the basic traits of its essential provenance remains European by definition. No metaphysics, whether idealistic, materialistic, or Christian, can in accord with its essence, and surely not in its own attempts to explicate itself, "get a hold on" this destiny yet, and that means thoughtfully to reach and gather together what in the fullest sense of Being now is.

In the face of the essential homelessness of man, man's approaching destiny reveals itself to thought on the history of Being in this, that man find his way into the truth of Being and set out on this find. Every nationalism is metaphysically an anthropologism, and as such subjectivism. Nationalism is not overcome through mere internationalism; it is rather expanded and elevated thereby into a system. Nationalism is as little brought and raised to *humanitas* by internationalism as individualism is by an ahistorical collectivism. The latter is the subjectivity of man in totality. It completes subjectivity's unconditioned self-assertion, which refuses to yield. Nor can it be even adequately experienced by a thinking that mediates in a one sided fashion. Expelled from the truth of Being, man everywhere circles round himself as the *animal rationale.*

But the essence of man consists in his being more than merely human, if this is represented as "being a rational creature." "More" must not be understood here additively as if the traditional definition of man were indeed to remain basic, only elaborated by means of an existentiell postscript. The "more" means: more originally and therefore more essentially in terms of his essence. But here something enigmatic manifests itself: man is in thrownness. This means that man, as the ek-sisting counter-throw [*Gegenwurf*] of Being, is more than *animal rationale* precisely to the extent that he is less bound up with man conceived from subjectivity. Man is not the lord of beings. Man is the shepherd of Being. Man loses nothing in this "less"; rather, he gains in that he attains the truth of Being. He gains the essential poverty of the shepherd, whose dignity consists in being called by Being itself into the preservation of Being's truth. The call comes as the throw from which the thrownness of Da-sein derives. In his essential unfolding within the history of Being, man is the being whose Being as ek-sistence consists in his dwelling in the nearness of Being. Man is the neighbor of Being.

But—as you no doubt have been wanting to rejoin for quite a while now— does not such thinking think precisely the *humanitas* of homo humanus? Does it not think *humanitas* in a decisive sense, as no metaphysics has thought it or can think it? Is this not "humanism" in the extreme sense? Certainly. It is a humanism that thinks the humanity of man from nearness to Being. But at the same time it is a humanism in which not man but man's historical essence is at stake in its provenance from the truth of Being. But then doesn't the ex-sistence of man also stand or fall in this game of stakes? So it does.

In *Being and Time* (p. 87, above) it is said that every question of philosophy "recoils upon existence." But existence here is not the actuality of the *ego cogito.* Neither is it the actuality of subjects who act with and for each other and so become who they are. "Ek-sistence," in fundamental contrast to every *existentia* and *"existence,"* is ecstatic dwelling in the nearness of Being. It is the guardianship, that is, the care for Being. Because there is something simple to be thought in this thinking it seems quite difficult to the representational thought that has been transmitted as philosophy. But the difficulty is not a matter of indulging in a special sort of profundity and of building complicated concepts; rather, it is concealed in the step back that lets thinking enter into a questioning that experiences—and lets the habitual opining of philosophy fall away.

It is everywhere supposed that the attempt in *Being and Time* ended in a blind alley. Let us not comment any further upon that opinion. The thinking that hazards a few steps in *Being and Time* has even today not advanced beyond that publication. But perhaps in the meantime it has in one respect come farther into its own matter. However, as long as philosophy merely busies itself with continually obstructing the possibility of admittance into the matter for thinking, i.e., into the truth of Being, it stands safely beyond any danger of shattering against the hardness of that matter. Thus to "philosophize" about being shattered is separated by a chasm from a thinking that is shattered. If such thinking were to go fortunately for a man no misfortune would befall him. He would receive the only gift that can come to thinking from Being.

But it is also the case that the matter of thinking is not achieved in the fact that talk about the "truth of Being" and the "history of Being" is set in motion. Everything depends upon this alone, that the truth of Being come to language and that thinking attain to this language. Perhaps, then, language requires much less precipitous expression than proper silence. But who of us today would want to imagine that his attempts to think are at home on the path of silence? At best, thinking could perhaps point toward the truth of Being, and indeed toward it as what is to be thought. It would thus be more easily weaned from mere supposing and opining and directed to the now rare handicraft of writing. Things that really matter, although they are not defined for all eternity, even when they come very late still come at the right time.

Whether the realm of the truth of Being is a blind alley or whether it is the free space in which freedom conserves its essence is something each one may judge after he himself has tried to go the designated way, or even better, after he has gone a better way, that is, a way befitting the question. On the penultimate page of *Being and Time* (p. 437) stand the sentences: "The *conflict* with respect to the interpretation of Being (that is, therefore, not the interpretation of beings or of the Being of man) cannot be settled, *because it has not yet been kindled.* And in the end it is not a question of 'picking a quarrel,' since the kindling of the conflict does demand some preparation. To this end alone the foregoing investigation is under way." Today after two decades these sentences still hold. Let us also in the days ahead remain as wanderers on the way into the neighborhood of Being. The question you pose helps to clarify the way.

You ask, *Comment redonner un sens au mot 'Humanisme'?* "How can some sense be restored to the word 'humanism'?" Your question not only presupposes a desire to retain the word "humanism" but also contains an admission that this word has lost its meaning.

It has lost it through the insight that the essence of humanism is metaphysical, which now means that metaphysics not only does not pose the question concerning the truth of Being but also obstructs the question, insofar as metaphysics persists in the oblivion of Being. But the same thinking that has led us to this insight into the questionable essence of humanism has likewise compelled us to think the essence of man more primordially. With regard to this more essential *humanitas* of *homo humanus* there arises the possibility of restoring to the word "humanism" a historical sense that is older than its oldest meaning chronologically reckoned. The restoration is not to be understood as though the word "humanism" were wholly without meaning and a mere *flatus vocis* [empty sound]. The "*humanum*" in the word points to *humanitas*, the essence of man; the "-ism" indicates that the essence of man is meant to be taken essentially. This is the sense that the word "humanism" has as such. To restore a sense to it can only mean to redefine the meaning of the word. That requires that we first experience the essence of man more primordially; but it also demands that we show to what extent this essence in its own way becomes fateful. The essence of man lies in ek-sistence. That is what is essentially—that is, from Being itself—at issue here, insofar as Being appropriates man as ek-sisting for guardianship over the truth of Being into this truth itself. "Humanism" now means, in case we decide to retain the word, that the essence of man is essential for the truth of Being, specifically in such a way that the word does not pertain to man simply as such. So we are thinking a curious kind of "humanism." The word results in a name that is a *lucus a non lucendo* [literally, a grove where no light penetrates].

Should we still keep the name "humanism" for a "humanism" that contradicts all previous humanism—although it in no way advocates the inhuman? And keep it just so that by sharing in the use of the name we might perhaps swim in the predominant currents, stifled in metaphysical subjectivism and submerged in oblivion of Being? Or should thinking, by means of open resistance to "humanism," risk a shock that could for the first time cause perplexity concerning the *humanitas* of *homo humanus* and its basis? In this way it could awaken a reflection—if the world-historical moment did not itself already compel such a reflection—that thinks not only about man but also about the "nature" of man, not only about his nature but even more primordially about the dimension in which the essence of man, determined by Being itself, is at home. Should we not rather suffer a little while longer those inevitable misinterpretations to which the path of thinking in the element of Being and Time has hitherto been exposed and let them slowly dissipate? These misinterpretations are natural reinterpretations of what was read, or simply mirrorings of what one believes he knows already before he reads. They all betray the same structure and the same foundation.

Because we are speaking against "humanism" people fear a defense of the inhuman and a glorification of barbaric brutality. For what is more "logical" than that for somebody who negates humanism nothing remains but the affirmation of inhumanity?

Because we are speaking against "logic" people believe we are demanding that the rigor of thinking be renounced and in its place the arbitrariness of drives and feelings be installed and thus that "irrationalism" be proclaimed as true. For what is more "logical" than that whoever speaks against the logical is defending the alogical?

Because we are speaking against "values" people are horrified at a philosophy that ostensibly dares to despise humanity's best qualities. For what is more "logical" than that a thinking that denies values must necessarily pronounce everything valueless?

Because we say that the Being of man consists in "being-in-the-world" people find that man is downgraded to a merely terrestrial being, whereupon philosophy sinks into positivism. For what is more "logical" than that whoever asserts the worldliness of human being holds only this life as valid, denies the beyond, and renounces all "Transcendence"?

Because we refer to the word of Nietzsche on the "death of God" people regard such a gesture as atheism. For what is more "logical" than that whoever has experienced the death of God is godless?

Because in all the respects mentioned we everywhere speak against all that humanity deems high and holy our philosophy teaches an irresponsible and destructive "nihilism." For what is more "logical" than that whoever roundly denies what is truly in being puts himself on the side of nonbeing and thus professes the pure nothing as the meaning of reality?

What is going on here? People hear talk about "humanism," "logic," "values," "world," and "God." They hear something about opposition to these. They recognize and accept these things as positive. But with hearsay—in a way that is not strictly deliberate—they immediately assume that what speaks against something is automatically its negation and that this is "negative" in the sense of destructive. And somewhere in *Being and Time* there is explicit talk of "the phenomenological destruction." With the assistance of logic and *ratio*—so often invoked—people come to believe that whatever is not positive is negative and thus that it seeks to degrade reason—and therefore deserves to be branded as depravity. We are so filled with "logic" that anything that disturbs the habitual somnolence of prevailing opinion is automatically registered as a despicable contradiction. We pitch everything that does not stay close to the familiar and beloved positive into the previously excavated pit of pure negation which negates everything, ends in nothing, and so consummates nihilism. Following this logical course we let everything expire in a nihilism we invented for ourselves with the aid of logic.

But does the "against" which a thinking advances against ordinary opinion necessarily point toward pure negation and the negative? This happens—and then, to be sure, happens inevitably and conclusively, that is, without a clear prospect of anything else—only when one posits in advance what is meant by the "positive" and on this basis makes an absolute and absolutely negative decision about the range of possible opposition to it. Concealed in such a procedure is the refusal to subject to reflection this presupposed "positive" in which one believes himself saved, together with its position and opposition. By continually appealing to the logical one conjures up the illusion that he is entering straight-forwardly into thinking when in fact he has disavowed it.

It ought to be somewhat clearer now that opposition to "humanism" in no way implies a defense of the inhuman but rather opens other vistas.

"Logic" understands thinking to be the representation of beings in their Be-ing, which representation proposes to itself in the generality of the concept. But how is it with meditation on Being itself, that is, with the thinking that thinks the truth of Being? This thinking alone reaches the primordial essence of *logos* which was already obfuscated and lost in Plato and in Aristotle, the founder of "logic." To think against "logic" does not mean to break a lance for the illogi-cal but simply to trace in thought the *logos* and its essence which appeared in the dawn of thinking, that is, to exert ourselves for the first time in preparing for such reflection. Of what value are even far-reaching systems of logic to us if, without really knowing what they are doing, they recoil before the task of sim-ply inquiring into the essence of *logos*? If we wished to bandy about objections, which is of course fruitless, we could say with more right: "irrationalism, as a denial of *ratio*, rules unnoticed and uncontested in the defense of "logic," which believes it can eschew meditation on *logos* and on the essence of *ratio* which has its ground in *logos*.

To think against "values" is not to maintain that everything interpreted as "a value"—"culture," "art," "science," "human dignity," "world," and "God"—is valueless. Rather, it is important finally to realize that precisely through the char-acterization of something as "a value" what is so valued is robbed of its worth. That is to say, by the assessment of something as a value what is valued is admit-ted only as an object for man's estimation. But what a thing is in its Being is not exhausted by its being an object, particularly when objectivity takes the form of value. Every valuing, even where it values positively, is a subjectivizing. It does not let beings: be. Rather, valuing lets beings: be valid—solely as the objects of its doing. The bizarre effort to prove the objectivity of values does not know what it is doing. When one proclaims "God" the altogether "highest value," this is a degradation of God's essence. Here as elsewhere thinking in values is the greatest blasphemy imaginable against Being. To think against values therefore does not mean to beat the drum for the valuelessness and nullity of beings. It means rather to bring the lighting of the truth of Being before thinking, as against subjectiviz-ing beings into mere objects.

The reference to "being-in-the-world" as the basic trait of the *humanitas* of *homo humanus* does not assert that man is merely a "worldly" creature under-stood in a Christian sense, thus a creature turned away from God and so cut loose from "Transcendence." What is really meant by this word could be more clearly called "the transcendent." The transcendent is supersensible being. This is consid-ered the highest being in the sense of the first cause of all beings. God is thought as this first cause. However, in the name "being-in-the-world," "world" does not in any way imply earthly as opposed to heavenly being, nor the "worldly" as op-posed to the "spiritual." For us "world" does not at all signify beings or any realm of beings but the openness of Being. Man is, and is man, insofar as he is the ek-sisting one. He stands out into the openness of Being. Being itself, which as the throw has projected the essence of man into "care," is as this openness. Thrown in such fashion, man stands "in" the openness of Being. "World" is the lighting of Being into which man stands out on the basis of his thrown essence. "Being-in-the-world" designates the essence of ek-sistence with regard to the lighted dimension out of which the "ek-" of ek-sistence essentially unfolds. Thought in terms of ek-sistence, "world" is in a certain sense precisely "the beyond" within existence and for it. Man is never first and foremost man on the hither side of the world, as a "subject," whether this is taken as "I" or "We." Nor is he ever simply a mere subject which always simultaneously is related to objects, so that his essence lies in the subject-object relation. Rather, before all this, man in his essence is ek-sistent into the openness of Being, into the open region that lights the "between" within which a "relation" of subject to object can "be."

The statement that the essence of man consists in being-in-the-world likewise contains no decision about whether man in a theologico-metaphysical sense is merely a this-worldly or an other-worldly creature.

With the existential determination of the essence of man, therefore, nothing is decided about the "existence of God" or his "non-being," no more than about the possibility or impossibility of gods. Thus it is not only rash but also an error in procedure to maintain that the interpretation of the essence of man from the relation of his essence to the truth of Being is atheism. And what is more, this arbitrary classification betrays a lack of careful reading. No one bothers to notice that in the article *Vom Wesen des Grundes* the following appears: "Through the ontological interpretation of Dasein as being-in-the-world no decision, whether positive or negative, is made concerning a possible being toward God. It is, however, the case that through an illumination of transcendence we first achieve an *adequate concept of Dasein,* with respect to which it can now be asked how the relationship of Dasein to God is ontologically ordered."[14] If we think about this remark too quickly, as is usually the case, we will declare that such a philosophy does not decide either for or against the existence of God. It remains stalled in indifference. Thus it is unconcerned with the religious question. Such indifferentism ultimately falls prey to nihilism.

But does the foregoing observation teach indifferentism? Why then are particular words in the note italicized—and not just random ones? For no other reason than to indicate that the thinking that thinks from the question concerning the truth of Being questions more primordially than metaphysics can. Only from the truth of Being can the essence of the holy be thought. Only from the essence of the holy is the essence of divinity to be thought. Only in the light of the essence of divinity can it be thought or said that the word "God" is to signify. Or should we not first be able to hear and understand all these words carefully if we are to be permitted as men, that is, as eksistent creatures, to experience a relation of God to man? How can man at the present stage of world history ask at all seriously and rigorously whether the god nears or withdraws, when he has above all neglected to think into the dimension in which alone that question can be asked? But this is the dimension of the holy, which indeed remains closed as a dimension if the open region of Being is not lighted and in it lighting is near man. Perhaps what is distinctive about this world-epoch consists in the closure of the dimension of the hale [*des Heilen*]. Perhaps that is the sole malignancy [*Unheil*].

But with this reference the thinking that points toward the truth of Being as what is to be thought has in no way decided in favor of theism. It can be theistic as little as atheistic. Not, however, because of an indifferent attitude, but out of respect for the boundaries that have been set for thinking as such, indeed set by what gives itself to thinking as what is to be thought, by the truth of Being. Insofar as thinking limits itself to its task it directs man at the present moment of the world's destiny into the primordial dimension of his historical abode. When thinking of this kind speaks the truth of Being it has entrusted itself to what is more essential than all values and all types of beings. Thinking does not overcome metaphysics by climbing still higher, surmounting it, transcending it somehow or other; thinking overcomes metaphysics by climbing back down into the nearness of the nearest. The descent, particularly where man has strayed into subjectivity, is more arduous and more dangerous than the ascent. The descent leads to the poverty of the ek-sistence of *homo humanus*. In ek-sistence the region of *homo animalis,* of metaphysics, is abandoned. The dominance of that region is the mediate and deeply rooted basis for the blindness and arbitrariness of what is called "biologism," but also of what is known under the heading "pragmatism." To think the truth of Being at the same time means to think the humanity of *homo humanus*. What counts is *humanitas* in the service of the truth of Being, but without humanism in the metaphysical sense.

But if *humanitas* must be viewed as so essential to the thinking of Being, must not "ontology" therefore be supplemented by "ethics"? Is not that effort entirely essential which you express in the sentence "*Ce que je cherche à faire, depuis longtemps déjà, c'est préciser le rapport de l'ontologie avec une éthique possible*" ["What I have been trying to do for a long time now is to determine precisely the relation of ontology to a possible ethics"]?

Soon after *Being and Time* appeared a young friend asked me, "When are you going to write an ethics?" Where the essence of man is thought so essentially, i.e., solely from the question concerning the truth of Being, but still without elevating man to the center of beings, a longing necessarily awakens for a peremptory directive and for rules that say how man, experienced from ek-sistence toward Being, ought to live in a fitting manner. The desire for an ethics presses ever more ardently for fulfillment as the obvious no less than the hidden perplexity of man soars to immeasurable heights. The greatest care must be fostered upon the ethical bond at a time when technological man, delivered over to mass society, can be kept reliably on call only by gathering and ordering all his plans and activities in a way that corresponds to technology.

Who can disregard our predicament? Should we not safeguard and secure the existing bonds even if they hold human beings together ever so tenuously and merely for the present? Certainly. But does this need ever release thought from the task of thinking what still remains principally to be thought and, as Being prior to all beings, is their guarantor and their truth? Even further, can thinking refuse to think Being after the latter has lain hidden so long in oblivion but at the same time has made itself known in the present moment of world history by the uprooting of all beings?

Before we attempt to determine more precisely the relationship between "ontology" and "ethics" we must ask what "ontology" and "ethics" themselves are. It becomes necessary to ponder whether what can be designated by both terms still remains near and proper to what is assigned to thinking, which as such has to think above all the truth of Being.

Of course if both "ontology" and "ethics," along with all thinking in terms of disciplines, become untenable, and if our thinking therewith becomes more disciplined, how then do matters stand with the question about the relation between these two philosophical disciplines?

Along with "logic" and "physics," "ethics" appeared for the first time in the school of Plato. These disciplines arose at a time when thinking was becoming "philosophy," philosophy, *epistēmē* (science), and science itself a matter for schools and academic pursuits. In the course of a philosophy so understood, science waxed and thinking waned. Thinkers prior to this period knew neither a "logic" nor an "ethics" nor "physics." Yet their thinking was neither illogical nor immoral. But they did think *physis* in a depth and breadth that no subsequent "physics" was ever again able to attain. The tragedies of Sophocles—provided such a comparison is at all permissible—preserve the *ēthos* in their sagas more primordially than Aristotle's lectures on "ethics." A saying of Heraclitus which consists of only three words says something so simply that from it the essence of the *ēthos* immediately comes to light.

The saying of Heraclitus (Frag. 119) goes: *ēthos anthrōpōidaimōn*. This is usually translated, "A man's character is his daimon." This translation thinks in a modern way, not a Greek one. *Ēthos* means abode, dwelling place. The word names the open region in which man dwells. The open region of his abode allows what pertains to man's essence, and what in thus arriving resides in nearness to him, to appear. The abode of man contains and preserves the advent of what belongs to man in his essence. According to Heraclitus' phrase this is *daimōn*, the god. The fragment says: Man dwells, insofar as he is man, in the nearness of god. A story that Aristotle reports (*De parte animalium*, I, 5, 645a 17) agrees with this fragment of Heraclitus.

The story is told of something Heraclitus said to some strangers who wanted to come visit him. Having arrived, they saw him warming himself at a stove. Surprised, they stood there in consternation—above all because he encouraged them, the astounded ones, and called for them to come in with the words, "For here too the gods are present."

The story certainly speaks for itself, but we may stress a few aspects.

The group of foreign visitors, in their importunate curiosity about the thinker, are disappointed and perplexed by their first glimpse of his abode. They believe they should meet the thinker in circumstances which, contrary to the ordinary round of human life, everywhere bear traces of the exceptional and rare and so of the exciting. The group hopes that in their visit to the thinker they will find things that will provide material for entertaining conversation—at least for a while. The foreigners who wish to visit the thinker expect to catch sight of him perchance at that very moment when, sunk in profound meditation, he is thinking. The visitors want this "experience" not in order to be overwhelmed by thinking but simply so they can say they saw and heard someone everybody says is a thinker.

Instead of this the sightseers find Heraclitus by a stove. That is surely a common and insignificant place. True enough, bread is baked here. But Heraclitus is not even busy baking at the stove. He stands there merely to warm himself. In this altogether everyday place he betrays the whole poverty of his life. The vision of a shivering thinker offers little of interest. At this disappointing spectacle even the curious lose their desire to come any closer. What are they supposed to do here? Such an everyday and unexciting occurrence—somebody who is chilled warming himself at a stove—anyone can find any time at home. So why look up a thinker? The visitors are on the verge of going away again. Heraclitus reads the frustrated curiosity in their faces. He knows that for the crowd the failure of an expected sensation to materialize is enough to make those who have just arrived leave. He therefore encourages them. He invites them explicitly to come in with the words *Einai gar kai entautha theous,* "Here too the gods are present."

This phrase places the abode (*ēthos*) of the thinker and his deed in another light. Whether the visitors understood this phrase at once—or at all—and then saw everything differently in this other light the story doesn't say. But the story was told and has come down to us today because what it reports derives from and characterizes the atmosphere surrounding this thinker. *Kai entautha,* "even here," at the stove, in that ordinary place where every thing and every condition, each deed and thought is intimate and commonplace, that is, familiar [geheuer], "even there" in the sphere of the familiar, *einai theous,* it is the case that "the gods are present."

Heraclitus himself says, *ēthos anthrōpōi daimōn,* "The (familiar) abode is for man the open region for the presencing of god (the unfamiliar one)."

If the name "ethics," in keeping with the basic meaning of the word *ēthos,* should now say that "ethics" ponders the abode of man, then that thinking which thinks the truth of Being as the primordial element of man, as one who eksists, is in itself the original ethics. However, this thinking is not ethics in the first instance, because it is ontology. For ontology always thinks solely the being (*on*) in its Being. But as long as the truth of Being is not thought all ontology remains without its foundation. Therefore the thinking which in *Being and Time* tries to advance thought in a preliminary way into the truth of Being characterizes itself as "fundamental ontology." [Cf. *Being and Time*, sections 3 and 4, above.] It strives to reach back into the essential ground from which thought concerning the truth of Being emerges. By initiating another inquiry this thinking is already removed from the "ontology" of metaphysics (even that of Kant). "Ontology" itself, however, whether transcendental or precritical, is subject to criticism, not because it thinks the Being of beings and thereby reduces Being to a concept, but because it does not think the truth of Being and so fails to recognize that there is a thinking more rigorous than the conceptual. In the poverty of its first breakthrough, the thinking that tries to advance thought into the truth of Being brings only a small part of that wholly other dimension to language. This language is still faulty insofar as it does not yet succeed in retaining the essential help of phenomenological seeing and in dispensing with the inappropriate concern with "science" and "research." But in order to make the attempt at thinking recognizable and at the same time understandable for existing philosophy, it could at first be expressed only within the horizon of that existing philosophy and its use of current terms.

In the meantime I have learned to see that these very terms were bound to lead immediately and inevitably into error. For the terms and the conceptual language corresponding to them were not rethought by readers from the matter particularly to be thought; rather, the matter was conceived according to the established terminology in its customary meaning. The thinking that inquires into the truth of Being and so defines man's essential abode from Being and toward Being is neither ethics nor ontology. Thus the question about the relation of each to the other no longer has any basis in this sphere. Nonetheless, your question, thought in a more original way, retains a meaning and an essential importance.

For it must be asked: If the thinking that ponders the truth of Being defines the essence of *humanitas* as ek-sistence from the latter's belongingness to Being, then does thinking remain only a theoretical representation of Being and of man, or can we obtain from such knowledge directives that can be readily applied to our active lives?

The answer is that such thinking is neither theoretical nor practical. It comes to pass before this distinction. Such thinking is, insofar as it is, recollection of Being and nothing else. Belonging to Being, because thrown by Being into the preservation of its truth and claimed for such preservation, it thinks Being. Such thinking has no result. It has no effect. It satisfies its essence in that it is. But it is by saying its matter. Historically, only one Saying [*Sage*] belongs to the matter of thinking, the one that is in each case appropriate to its matter. Its material relevance is essentially higher than the validity of the sciences, because it is freer. For it lets Being—be.

Thinking builds upon the house of Being, the house in which the jointure of Being fatefully enjoins the essence of man to dwell in the truth of Being. This dwelling is the essence of "being-in-the-world." The reference in *Being and Time* (p. 54) to "being-in" as "dwelling" is no etymological game.[15] The same reference in the 1936 essay on Hölderlin's verse, "Full of merit, yet poetically, man dwells on this earth," is no adornment of a thinking that rescues itself from science by means of poetry. The talk about the house of Being is no transfer of the image "house" to Being. But one day we will, by thinking the essence of Being in a way appropriate to its matter, more readily be able to think what "house" and "to dwell" are.

And yet thinking never creates the house of Being. Thinking conducts historical eksistence, that is, the *humanitas* of *homo humanus*, into the realm of the upsurgence of the healing [*des Heilens*].

With healing, evil appears all the more in the lighting of Being. The essence of evil does not consist in the mere baseness of human action but rather in the malice of rage. Both of these, however, healing and the raging, can essentially occur only in Being, insofar as Being itself is what is contested. In it is concealed the essential provenance of nihilation. What nihilates illuminates itself as the negative. This can be addressed in the "no." The "not" in no way arises from the no-saying of negation. Every "no" that does not mistake itself as willful assertion of the positing power of subjectivity, but rather remains a letting-be of ek-sistence, answers to the claim of the nihilation illumined. Every "no" is simply the affirmation of the "not." Every affirmation consists in acknowledgment. Acknowledgment lets that toward which it goes come toward it. It is believed that nihilation is nowhere to be found in beings themselves. This is correct as long as one seeks nihilation as some kind of being, as an existing quality in beings. But in so seeking, one is not seeking nihilation. Neither is Being any existing quality which allows itself to be fixed among beings. And yet Being is more in being than any being. Because nihilation occurs essentially in Being itself we can never discern it as a being among beings. Reference to this impossiblity never in any way proves that the origin of the not is no-saying. This proof appears to carry only if one posits beings as what is objective for subjectivity. From this alternative it follows that every "not," because it never appears as something objective, must inevitably be the product of a subjective act. But whether no-saying first posits the "not" as something merely thought, or whether nihilation first requires the "no" as what is to be said in the letting-be of beings—this can never be decided at all by a subjective reflection of a thinking already posited as subjectivity. In such a reflection we have not yet reached the dimension where the question can be appropriately formulated. It remains to ask, granting that thinking belongs to ek-sistence, whether every "yes" and "no" are not themselves already dependent upon Being. As these dependents, they can never first posit the very thing to which they themselves belong.

Nihilation unfolds essentially in Being itself, and not at all in the existence of man—so far as this is thought as the subjectivity of the *ego cogito*. Dasein in no way nihilates as a human subject who carries out nihilation in the sense of denial; rather, Da-sein nihilates inasmuch as it belongs to the essence of Being as that essence in which man ek-sists. Being nihilates—as Being. Therefore the "not" appears in the absolute Idealism of Hegel and Schelling as the negativity of negation in the essence of Being. But there Being is thought in the sense of absolute actuality as unconditioned will that wills itself and does so as the will of knowledge and of love. In this willing Being as will to power is still concealed. But just why the negativity of absolute subjectivity is "dialectical," and why nihilation comes to the fore through this dialectic but at the same time is veiled in its essence, cannot be discussed here.

The nihilating in Being is the essence of what I call the nothing. Hence because it thinks Being, thinking thinks the nothing.

To healing Being first grants ascent into grace; to raging its compulsion to malignancy.

Only so far as man, ek-sisting into the truth of Being, belongs to Being can there come from Being itself the assignment of those directions that must become law and rule for man. In Greek to assign is *nemein*. *Nomos* is not only law but more originally the assignment contained in the dispensation of Being. Only the assignment is capable of dispatching man into Being. Only such dispatching is capable of supporting and obligating. Otherwise all law remains merely something fabricated by human reason. More essential than instituting rules is that man find the way to his abode in the truth of Being. This abode first yields the experience of something we can hold on to. The truth of Being offers a hold for all conduct. "Hold" in our language means protective heed. Being is the protective heed that holds man in his ek-sistent essence to the truth of such protective heed—in such a way that it houses ek-sistence in language. Thus language is at once the house of Being and the home of human beings. Only because language is the home of the essence of man can historical mankind and human beings not be at home in their language, so that for them language becomes a mere container for their sundry preoccupations.

But now in what relation does the thinking of Being stand to theoretical and practical behavior? It exceeds all contemplation because it cares for the light in which a seeing, as *theoria*, can first live and move. Thinking attends to the lighting of Being in that it puts its saying of Being into language as the home of eksistence. Thus thinking is a deed. But a deed that also surpasses all *praxis*. Thinking towers above action and production, not through the grandeur of its achievement and not as a consequence of its effect, but through the humbleness of its inconsequential accomplishment.

For thinking in its saying merely brings the unspoken word of Being to language.

The usage "bring to language" employed here is now to be taken quite literally. Being comes, lighting itself, to language. It is perpetually under way to language. Such arriving in its turn brings ek-sisting thought to language in a saying. Thus language itself is raised into the lighting of Being. Language *is* only in this mysterious and yet for us always pervasive way. To the extent that language which has thus been brought fully into its essence is historical, Being is entrusted to recollection. Ex-sistence thoughtfully dwells in the house of Being. In all this it is as if nothing at all happens through thoughtful saying.

But just now an example of the inconspicuous deed of thinking manifested itself. For to the extent that we expressly think the usage "bring to language," which was granted to language, think only that and nothing further, to the extent that we retain this thought in the heedfulness of saying as what in the future continually has to be thought, we have brought something of the essential unfolding of Being itself to language.

What is strange in the thinking of Being is its simplicity. Precisely this keeps us from it. For we look for thinking—which has its world-historical prestige under the name "philosophy"—in the form of the unusual, which is accessible only to initiates. At the same time we conceive of thinking on the model of scientific knowledge and its research projects. We measure deeds by the impressive and successful achievements of *praxis*. But the deed of thinking is neither theoretical nor practical, nor is it the conjunction of these two forms of behavior.

Through its simple essence the thinking of Being makes itself unrecognizable to us. But if we become acquainted with the unusual character of the simple, then another plight immediately befalls us. The suspicion arises that such thinking of Being falls prey to arbitrariness; for it cannot cling to beings. Whence does thinking take its measure? What law governs its deed?

Here the third question of your letter must be entertained: *Comment sauver l'élément d'aventure que comporte toute recherche sans faire de la philosophie une simple aventurière?* [How can we preserve the element of adventure that all research contains without simply turning philosophy into an adventuress?] I shall mention poetry now only in passing. It is confronted by the same question, and in the same manner, as thinking. But Aristotle's words in the *Poetics*, although they have scarcely been pondered, are still valid—that poetic composition is truer than exploration of beings.

But thinking is an *aventure* not only as a search and an inquiry into the unthought. Thinking, in its essence as thinking of Being, is claimed by Being. Thinking is related to Being as what arrives (*l'avenant*[16]). Thinking as such is bound to the advent of Being, to Being as advent. Being has already been dispatched to thinking. Being *is* as the destiny of thinking. But destiny is in itself historical. Its history has already come to language in the saying of thinkers.

To bring to language ever and again this advent of Being which remains, and in its remaining waits for man, is the sole matter of thinking. For this reason essential thinkers always say the Same. But that does not mean the identical. Of course they say it only to him who undertakes to think back on them. Whenever thinking, in historical recollection, attends to the destiny of Being, it has already bound itself to what is fitting for it, in accord with its destiny. To flee into the identical is not dangerous. To risk discord in order to say the Same is the danger. Ambiguity threatens, and mere quarreling.

The fittingness of the saying of Being, as of the destiny of truth, is the first law of thinking, not the rules of logic which can become rules only on the basis of the law of Being. To attend to the fittingness of thoughtful saying does not only imply, however, that we contemplate at every turn *what* is to be said of Being and *how* it is to be said. It is equally essential to ponder *whether* what is to be thought is to be said—to what extent, at what moment of the history of Being, in what sort of dialogue with this history, and on the basis of what claim, it ought to be said. The threefold thing mentioned in an earlier letter is determined in its cohesion by the law of the fittingness of thought on the history of Being: rigor of meditation, carefulness in saying, frugality with words.

It is time to break the habit of overestimating philosophy and of thereby asking too much of it. What is needed in the present world crisis is less philosophy, but more attentiveness in thinking; less literature, but more cultivation of the letter.

The thinking that is to come is no longer philosophy, because it thinks more originally than metaphysics—a name identical to philosophy. However, the thinking that is to come can no longer, as Hegel demanded, set aside the name "love of wisdom" and become wisdom itself in the form of absolute knowledge. Thinking is on the descent to the poverty of its provisional essence. Thinking gathers language into simple saying. In this way language is the language of Being, as clouds are the clouds of the sky. With its saying, thinking lays inconspicuous furrows in language. They are still more inconspicuous than the furrows that the farmer, slow of step, draws through the field.

NOTES

1. The preparatory fundamental analysis of Dasein tries to define concrete structures of human being in its predominant state, "average everydayness." For the most part Dasein is absorbed in the public realm (*die Öffentlichkeit*) which dictates the range of possibilities that shall obtain for it in all dimensions of its life: "We enjoy ourselves and take our pleasures as *they* do; we read, see, and judge works of literature and art *as they* do; but we also shrink back in revulsion from the 'masses' of men just as *they* do; and are 'scandalized' by what *they* find shocking" (*Sein und Zeit*, pp. 126–27). Heidegger argues that the public realm—the neutral, impersonal "they"—tends to level off genuine possibilities and force individuals to keep their distance from one another and from themselves. It holds Dasein in subservience and hinders knowledge of the self and the world. It allows the life-and-death issues of existence proper to dissolve in "chatter," which is "the possibility of understanding everything without prior dedication to, and appropriation of, the matter at stake" (*Sein und Zeit*, p. 169). (All references to *Being and Time* in this essay and throughout the book cite the pagination of the German edition.)—ED.

2. In section 34 of *Being and Time* Heidegger defines the existential-ontological foundation of language as speech or talk (*die Rede*). It is as original a structure of being-in-the-world as mood or understanding, of which it is the meaningful articulation. To it

belong not only speaking out and asserting but also hearing and listening, heeding and being silent and attentive. As the Greeks experienced it, Dasein is living being that speaks, not so much in producing vocal sounds as in discovering the world, and this by letting beings come to appear as they are. Cf. the analysis of *logos* in section 7 B.—ED.

3. In the final chapter of division one of *Being and Time* Heidegger defines "care" as the Being of Dasein. It is a name for the structural whole of existence in all its modes and for the broadest and most basic possibilities of discovery and disclosure of self and world. Most poignantly experienced in the phenomenon of anxiety—which is not fear of anything at hand but awareness of my being-in-the-world as such—"care" describes the sundry ways I get involved in the issue of my birth, life, and death, whether by my projects, inclinations, insights, or illusions. "Care" is the all-inclusive name for my concern for other people, preoccupations with things, and awareness of my proper Being. It expresses the movement of my life out of a past, into a future, through the present. In section 65 the ontological meaning of the Being of care proves to be *temporality*.—ED.

4. The phrase *der menschliche Mensch* appears in Karl Marx, *Economic-philosophic Manuscripts of 1844*, the so-called "Paris Manuscripts," third MS, p. IV. Cf. *Marx-Engels-Werke* (Berlin, 1973), Ergänzungsband 1, 536. This third manuscript is perhaps the best source for Marx's synceretic "humanism," based on man's natural, social, practical, and conscious species-existence.—ED.

5. Cf. Martin Heidegger, *Vom Wesen des Grundes* (1929), p. 8; *Kant and the Problem of Metaphysics*, trans. J. Churchill (Bloomington, Ind.: Indiana University Press, 1962), p. 243; and *Being and Time*, section 44, p. 230.

6. In *Being and Time* "ecstatic" (from the Greek *ekstasis*) means the way Dasein "stands out" in the various moments of the temporality of care, being "thrown" out of a past and "projecting" itself toward a future by way of the present. The word is closely related to another Heidegger introduces now to capture the unique sense of man's Being—*ek-sistence*. This too means the way man "stands out" into the truth of Being and so is exceptional among beings that are on hand only as things of nature or human production. Cf. Heidegger's definition of "existence" in *Being and Time* and his use of ek-sistence in Reading III, above.—ED.

7. Cf. Jean-Paul Sartre, *L'Existentialisme est un humanisme* (Paris: Nagel, 1946), pp. 17, 21, and elsewhere.—ED.

8. In *Being and Time* (cf. esp. sections 25–27, 38, and 68 C) *Verfallen*, literally a "falling" or "lapsing," serves as a third constitutive moment of being-in-the-world. Dasein is potentiality for Being, directed toward a future in which it can realize its possibilities: this is its "existentiality." But existence is always "thrown" out of a past that determines its trajectory: this is its "facticity." Meanwhile, Dasein usually busies itself in quotidien affairs, losing itself in the present, forgetting what is most its own: this is its *Verfallensein*. (The last-named is not simply a matter of "everyday" dealings, however, since the tendency to let theoretical problems slip into the readymade solutions of a tradition affects interpretation itself.) To forget what is most its own is what Heidegger means by *Uneigentlichkeit*, usually rendered as "inauthenticity."—ED.

9. Heidegger cites Sartre's *L'Existentialisme est un humanisme*, p. 36. The context of Sartre's remark is as follows. He is arguing (pp. 33 ff.) "that God does not exist, and that it is necessary to draw the consequences to the end." To those who assert that the death of God leaves traditional values and norms untouched—and humanism is one

such value—Sartre rejoins "that it is very distressing that God does not exist because with him vanishes every possibility of finding values in some intelligible heaven; we can no longer locate an *a priori* Good since there is no infinite and perfect conscious- ness to think it; it is nowhere written that the Good exists, that we must be honest, that we mustn't lie, precisely because we are in a situation where there are only hu- man beings."—ED.

10. See the lecture on Hölderlin's hymn, "Wie wenn am Feiertage . . ." in Martin Heidegger, *Erläuterungen zu Hölderlins Dichtung*, fourth, expanded ed. (Frankfurt am Main: V. Klostermann, 1971), p. 76.

11. Cf. "The Ister" and "The Journey" [*Die Wanderung*], third stanza and ff. [In the transla- tions by Michael Hamburger (Ann Arbor: University of Michigan Press, 1966), pp. 492 ff. and 392 ff.]

12. Cf. Hölderlin's poem "Remembrance" [*Andenken*] in the *Tübingen Memorial* (1943), p. 322. [Hamburger, pp. 488 ff.]

13. On the notion of *Entfremdung*, estrangement or alienation, see Marx's *first* Paris MS, pp. XXII ff., *Werke*, Ergänzungsband I, 510–22. The relation of estrangement to "world-historical" developments which Heidegger here stresses is perhaps more clearly stated in Marx-Engels, *The German Ideology*, *Werke*, III, 34–36.—ED.

14. Martin Heidegger, *Vom Wesen des Grundes*, p. 28 n. 1.

15. Citing an analysis of the word "in" by Jacob Grimm, Heidegger relates "being in" to *innan, wohnen*, inhabit, reside, or dwell. To be *in* the world means to dwell and be at home there, i.e., to be familiar with meaningful structures that articulate people and things. On the meaning of *dwelling*, see Reading VIII, below.—ED.

16. *L'avenant* (cf. the English *advenient*) is most often used as an adverbial phrase, *à l'avenant*, to be in accord, conformity, or relation to something. It is related to *l'aven- ture*, the arrival of some unforeseen challenge, and *l'avenir*, the future, literally, what is to come. Thinking is in relation to Being insofar as Being advenes or arrives. Being as arrival or presence is the "adventure" toward which Heidegger's thought is on the way.—ED.

FERDINAND DE SAUSSURE

SELECTIONS FROM COURSE IN GENERAL LINGUISTICS

CHAPTER I: NATURE OF THE LINGUISTIC SIGN

1. SIGN, SIGNIFIED, SIGNIFIER

Some people regard language, when reduced to its elements, as a naming-process only—a list of words, each corresponding to the thing that it names. For example:

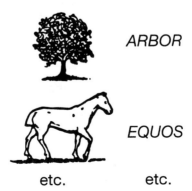

ARBOR

EQUOS

etc.   etc.

Reprinted with permission from *Course in General Linguistics*, tr. Wade Baskin. New York: Philosophical Library, 1959, pp. 66–78 and 111–122.

This conception is open to criticism at several points. It assumes that ready-made ideas exist before words (on this point, . . .); it does not tell us whether a name is vocal or psychological in nature (*arbor,* for instance, can be considered from either viewpoint); finally, it lets us assume that the linking of a name and a thing is a very simple operation—an assumption that is anything but true. But this rather naive approach can bring us near the truth by showing us that the linguistic unit is a double entity, one formed by the association of two terms.

We have seen in considering the speaking-circuit that both terms involved in the linguistic sign are psychological and are united in the brain by an associative bond. This point must be emphasized.

The linguistic sign unites, not a thing and a name, but a concept and a sound-image.[1] The latter is not the material sound, a purely physical thing, but the psychological imprint of the sound, the impression that it makes on our senses. The sound-image is sensory, and if I happen to call it "material," it is only in that sense, and by way of opposing it to the other term of the association, the concept, which is generally more abstract.

The psychological character of our sound-images becomes apparent when we observe our own speech. Without moving our lips or tongue, we can talk to ourselves or recite mentally a selection of verse. Because we regard the words of our language as sound-images, we must avoid speaking of the "phonemes" that make up the words. This term, which suggests vocal activity, is applicable to the spoken word only, to the realization of the inner image in discourse. We can avoid that misunderstanding by speaking of the *sounds* and *syllables* of a word provided we remember that the names refer to the sound-image.

The linguistic sign is then a two-sided psychological entity that can be represented by the drawing:

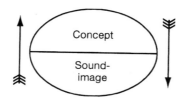

The two elements are intimately united, and each recalls the other. Whether we try to find the meaning of the Latin word *arbor* or the word that Latin uses to designate the concept "tree," it is clear that only the associations sanctioned by that language appear to us to conform to reality, and we disregard whatever others might be imagined.

Our definition of the linguistic sign poses an important question of terminology. I call the combination of a concept and a sound-image a *sign,* but in current usage the term generally designates only a sound-image, a word, for example (*arbor,* etc.). One tends to forget that *arbor* is called a sign only because it carries the concept "tree," with the result that the idea of the sensory part implies the idea of the whole.

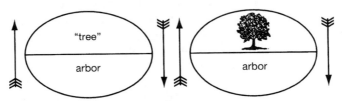

Ambiguity would disappear if the three notions involved here were designated by three names, each suggesting and opposing the others. I propose to retain the word *sign* [*signe*] to designate the whole and to replace *concept* and *sound-image* respectively by *signified* [*signifié*] and *signifier* [*signifiant*]; the last two terms have the advantage of indicating the opposition that separates them from each other and from the whole of which they are parts. As regards *sign,* if I am satisfied with it, this is simply because I do not know of any word to replace it, the ordinary language suggesting no other.

The linguistic sign, as defined, has two primordial characteristics. In enunciating them I am also positing the basic principles of any study of this type.

2. PRINCIPLE I: THE ARBITRARY NATURE OF THE SIGN

The bond between the signifier and the signified is arbitrary. Since I mean by sign the whole that results from the associating of the signifier with the signified, I can simply say: *the linguistic sign is arbitrary.*

The idea of "sister" is not linked by any inner relationship to the succession of sounds *s-ö-r* which serves as its signifier in French; that it could be represented equally by just any other sequence is proved by differences among languages and by the very existence of different languages: the signified "ox" has as its signifier *b-ö-f* on one side of the border and *o-k-s* (*Ochs*) on the other.

No one disputes the principle of the arbitrary nature of the sign, but it is often easier to discover a truth than to assign to it its proper place. Principle I dominates all the linguistics of language; its consequences are numberless. It is true that not all of them are equally obvious at first glance; only after many detours does one discover them, and with them the primordial importance of the principle.

One remark in passing: when semiology becomes organized as a science, the question will arise whether or not it properly includes modes of expression based on completely natural signs, such as pantomime. Supposing that the new science welcomes them, its main concern will still be the whole group of systems grounded on the arbitrariness of the sign. In fact, every means of expression used in society is based, in principle, on collective behavior or—what amounts to the same thing—on convention. Polite formulas, for instance, though often imbued with a certain natural expressiveness (as in the case of a Chinese who greets his emperor by bowing down to the ground nine times), are nonetheless fixed by rule; it is this rule and not the intrinsic value of the gestures that obliges one to use them. Signs that are wholly arbitrary realize better than the others the ideal of the semiological process; that is why language, the most complex and universal of all systems of expression, is also the most characteristic; in this sense linguistics can become the master-pattern for all branches of semiology although language is only one particular semiological system.

The word *symbol* has been used to designate the linguistic sign, or more specifically, what is here called the signifier. Principle I in particular weighs against the use of this term. One characteristic of the symbol is that it is never wholly arbitrary; it is not empty, for there is the rudiment of a natural bond between the signifier and the signified. The symbol of justice, a pair of scales, could not be replaced by just any other symbol, such as a chariot.

The word *arbitrary* also calls for comment. The term should not imply that the choice of the signifier is left entirely to the speaker (we shall see below that the individual does not have the power to change a sign in any way once it has become established in the linguistic community); I mean that it is unmotivated, i.e. arbitrary in that it actually has no natural connection with the signified.

In concluding let us consider two objections that might be raised to the establishment of Principle I:

1) *Onomatopoeia* might be used to prove that the choice of the signifier is not always arbitrary. But onomatopoeic formations are never organic elements of a linguistic system. Besides, their number is much smaller than is generally supposed. Words like French *fouet* 'whip' or *glas* 'knell' may strike certain ears with suggestive sonority, but to see that they have not always had this property we need only examine their Latin forms (*fouet* is derived from *fāgus* 'beech-tree,' *glas* from *classicum* 'sound of a trumpet'). The quality of their present sounds, or rather the quality that is attributed to them, is a fortuitous result of phonetic evolution.

As for authentic onomatopoeic words (e.g. *glug-glug, tick-tock*, etc.), not only are they limited in number, but also they are chosen somewhat arbitrarily, for they are only approximate and more or less conventional imitations of certain sounds (cf. English *bow-bow* and French *ouaoua*). In addition, once these words have been introduced into the language, they are to a certain extent subjected to the same evolution—phonetic, morphological, etc.—that other words undergo (cf. *pigeon*, ultimately from Vulgar Latin *pīpiō*, derived in turn from an onomatopoeic formation): obvious proof that they lose something of their original character in order to assume that of the linguistic sign in general, which is unmotivated.

2) *Interjections*, closely related to onomatopoeia, can be attacked on the same grounds and come no closer to refuting our thesis. One is tempted to see in them spontaneous expressions of reality dictated, so to speak, by natural

forces. But for most interjections we can show that there is no fixed bond between their signified and their signifier. We need only compare two languages on this point to see how much such expressions differ from one language to the next (e.g. the English equivalent of French *aïe!* is *ouch!*). We know, moreover, that many interjections were once words with specific meanings (cf. French *diable!* 'darn!' *mordieu!* 'golly!' from *mort Dieu* 'God's death,' etc.).[2]

Onomatopoeic formations and interjections are of secondary importance, and their symbolic origin is in part open to dispute.

3. PRINCIPLE II: THE LINEAR NATURE OF THE SIGNIFIER

The signifier, being auditory, is unfolded solely in time from which it gets the following characteristics: (a) it represents a span, and (b) the span is measurable in a single dimension; it is a line.

While Principle II is obvious, apparently linguists have always neglected to state it, doubtless because they found it too simple; nevertheless, it is fundamental, and its consequences are incalculable. Its importance equals that of Principle I; the whole mechanism of language depends upon it. In contrast to visual signifiers (nautical signals, etc.) which can offer simultaneous groupings in several dimensions, auditory signifiers have at their command only the dimension of time. Their elements are presented in succession; they form a chain. This feature becomes readily apparent when they are represented in writing and the spatial line of graphic marks is substituted for succession in time.

Sometimes the linear nature of the signifier is not obvious. When I accent a syllable, for instance, it seems that I am concentrating more than one significant element on the same point. But this is an illusion; the syllable and its accent constitute only one phonational act. There is no duality within the act but only different oppositions to what precedes and what follows.

CHAPTER II: IMMUTABILITY AND MUTABILITY OF THE SIGN

1. IMMUTABILITY

The signifier, though to all appearances freely chosen with respect to the idea that it represents, is fixed, not free, with respect to the linguistic community that uses it. The masses have no voice in the matter, and the signifier chosen by language could be replaced by no other. This fact, which seems to embody a contradiction, might be called colloquially "the stacked deck." We say to language: "Choose!" but we add: "It must be this sign and no other." No individual, even if he willed it, could modify in any way at all the choice that has been made; and what is more, the community itself cannot control so much as a single word; it is bound to the existing language.

No longer can language be identified with a contract pure and simple, and it is precisely from this viewpoint that the linguistic sign is a particularly interesting object of study; for language furnishes the best proof that a law accepted by a community is a thing that is tolerated and not a rule to which all freely consent.

Let us first see why we cannot control the linguistic sign and then draw together the important consequences that issue from the phenomenon.

No matter what period we choose or how far back we go, language always appears as a heritage of the preceding period. We might conceive of an act by which, at a given moment, names were assigned to things and a contract was formed between concepts and sound-images; but such an act has never been recorded. The notion that things might have happened like that was prompted by our acute awareness of the arbitrary nature of the sign.

No society, in fact, knows or has ever known language other than as a product inherited from preceding generations, and one to be accepted as such. That is why the question of the origin of speech is not so important as it is generally assumed to be. The question is not even worth asking; the only real object of linguistics is the normal, regular life of an existing idiom. A particular language-state is always the product of historical forces, and these forces explain why the sign is unchangeable, i.e. why it resists any arbitrary substitution.

Nothing is explained by saying that language is something inherited and leaving it at that. Can not existing and inherited laws be modified from one moment to the next?

To meet that objection, we must put language into its social setting and frame the question just as we would for any other social institution. How are other social institutions transmitted? This more general question includes the question of immutability. We must first determine the greater or lesser amounts of freedom that the other institutions enjoy; in each instance it will be seen that a different proportion exists between fixed tradition and the free action of society. The next step is to discover why in a given category, the forces of the first type carry more weight or less weight than those of the second. Finally, coming back to language, we must ask why the historical factor of transmission dominates it entirely and prohibits any sudden widespread change.

There are many possible answers to the question. For example, one might point to the fact that succeeding generations are not superimposed on one another like the drawers of a piece of furniture, but fuse and interpenetrate, each generation embracing individuals of all ages—with the result that modifications of language are not tied to the succession of generations. One might also recall the sum of the efforts required for learning the mother language and conclude that a general change would be impossible. Again, it might be added that reflection does not enter into the active use of an idiom—speakers are largely unconscious of the laws of language; and if they are unaware of them, how could they modify them? Even if they were aware of these laws, we may be sure that their awareness would seldom lead to criticism, for people are generally satisfied with the language they have received.

The foregoing considerations are important but not topical. The following are more basic and direct, and all the others depend on them.

1) *The arbitrary nature of the sign.* Above, we had to accept the theoretical possibility of change; further reflection suggests that the arbitrary nature of the sign is really what protects language from any attempt to modify it. Even if people were more conscious of language than they are, they would still not know how to discuss it. The reason is simply that any subject in order to be discussed must have a reasonable basis. It is possible, for instance, to discuss whether the monogamous form of marriage is more reasonable than the polygamous form and to advance arguments to support either side. One could also argue about a system of symbols, for the symbol has a rational relationship with the thing signified (see p. 83); but language is a system of arbitrary signs and lacks the necessary basis, the solid ground for discussion. There is no reason for preferring *soeur* to *sister, Ochs* to *boeuf*, etc.

2) *The multiplicity of signs necessary to form any language.* Another important deterrent to linguistic change is the great number of signs that must go into the making of any language. A system of writing comprising twenty to forty letters can in case of need be replaced by another system. The same would be true of language if it contained a limited number of elements; but linguistic signs are numberless.

3) *The over-complexity of the system.* A language constitutes a system. In this one respect (as we shall see later) language is not completely arbitrary but is ruled to some extent by logic; it is here also, however, that the inability of the masses to transform it becomes apparent. The system is a complex mechanism that can be grasped only through reflection; the very ones who use it daily are ignorant of it. We can conceive of a change only through the intervention of specialists, grammarians, logicians, etc.; but experience shows us that all such meddlings have failed.

4) *Collective inertia toward innovation.* Language—and this consideration surpasses all the others—is at every moment everybody's concern; spread throughout society and manipulated by it, language is something used daily by all. Here we are unable to set up any comparison between it and other institutions. The prescriptions of codes, religious rites, nautical signals, etc., involve only a certain number of individuals simultaneously and then only during a limited period of time; in language, on the contrary, everyone participates at all times, and that is why it is constantly being influenced by all. This capital fact suffices to show the impossibility of revolution. Of all social institutions, language is least amenable to initiative. It blends with the life of society, and the latter, inert by nature, is a prime conservative force.

But to say that language is a product of social forces does not suffice to show clearly that it is unfree; remembering that it is always the heritage of the preceding period, we must add that these social forces are linked with time. Language is checked not only by the weight of the collectivity but also by time. These two are inseparable. At every moment solidarity with the past checks freedom of choice. We say *man* and *dog*. This does not prevent the existence in the total phenomenon of a bond between the two antithetical forces—arbitrary convention by virtue of which choice is free and time which causes choice to be fixed. Because the sign is arbitrary, it follows no law other than that of tradition, and because it is based on tradition, it is arbitrary.

2. MUTABILITY

Time, which insures the continuity of language, wields another influence apparently contradictory to the first: the more or less rapid change of linguistic signs. In a certain sense, therefore, we can speak of both the immutability and the mutability of the sign.[3]

In the last analysis, the two facts are interdependent: the sign is exposed to alteration because it perpetuates itself. What predominates in all change is the persistence of the old substance; disregard for the past is only relative. That is why the principle of change is based on the principle of continuity.

Change in time takes many forms, on any one of which an important chapter in linguistics might be written. Without entering into detail, let us see what things need to be delineated.

First, let there be no mistake about the meaning that we attach to the word change. One might think that it deals especially with phonetic changes undergone by the signifier, or perhaps changes in meaning which affect the signified concept. That view would be inadequate. Regardless of what the forces of change are, whether in isolation or in combination, they always result in a *shift in the relationship between the signified and the signifier.*

Here are some examples. Latin *necāre* 'kill' became *noyer* 'drown' in French. Both the sound-image and the concept changed; but it is useless to separate the two parts of the phenomenon; it is sufficient to state with respect to the whole that the bond between the idea and the sign was loosened, and that there was a shift in their relationship. If instead of comparing Classical Latin *necāre* with French *noyer*, we contrast the former term with *necare* of Vulgar Latin of the fourth or fifth century meaning 'drown' the case is a little different; but here again; although there is no appreciable change in the signifier, there is a shift in the relationship between the idea and the sign.[4]

Old German *dritteil* 'one-third' became *Drittel* in Modern German. Here, although the concept remained the same, the relationship was changed in two ways: the signifier was changed not only in its material aspect but also in its grammatical form; the idea of *Teil* 'part' is no longer implied; *Drittel* is a simple word. In one way or another there is always a shift in the relationship.

In Anglo-Saxon the preliterary form *fot* 'foot' remained while its plural *fōti* became *fēt* (Modern English *feet*). Regardless of the other changes that are implied, one thing is certain: there was a shift in their relationship; other correspondences between the phonetic substance and the idea emerged.

Language is radically powerless to defend itself against the forces which from one moment to the next are shifting the relationship between the signified and the signifier. This is one of the consequences of the arbitrary nature of the sign.

Unlike language, other human institutions—customs, laws, etc.—are all based in varying degrees on the natural relations of things; all have of necessity adapted the means employed to the ends pursued. Even fashion in dress is not entirely arbitrary; we can deviate only slightly from the conditions dictated by the human body. Language is limited by nothing in the choice of means, for apparently nothing would prevent the associating of any idea whatsoever with just any sequence of sounds.

To emphasize the fact that language is a genuine institution, Whitney quite justly insisted upon the arbitrary nature of signs; and by so doing, he placed linguistics on its true axis. But he did not follow through and see that the arbitrariness of language radically separates it from all other institutions. This is apparent from the way in which language evolves. Nothing could be more complex. As it is a product of both the social force and time, no one can change anything in it, and on the other hand, the arbitrariness of its signs theoretically entails the freedom of establishing just any relationship between phonetic substance and ideas. The result is that each of the two elements united in the sign maintains its own life to a degree unknown elsewhere, and that language changes, or rather evolves, under the influence of all the forces which can affect either sounds or meanings. The evolution is inevitable; there is no example of a single language that resists it. After a certain period of time, some obvious shifts can always be recorded.

Mutability is so inescapable that it even holds true for artificial languages. Whoever creates a language controls it only so long as it is not in circulation; from the moment when it fulfills its mission and becomes the property of everyone, control is lost. Take Esperanto as an example; if it succeeds, will it escape the inexorable law? Once launched, it is quite likely that Esperanto will enter upon a fully semiological life; it will be transmitted according to laws which have nothing in common with those of its logical creation, and there will be no turning backwards. A man proposing a fixed language that posterity would have to accept for what it is would be like a hen hatching a duck's egg: the language created by him would be borne along, willy-nilly, by the current that engulfs all languages.

Signs are governed by a principle of general semiology: continuity in time is coupled to change in time; this is confirmed by orthographic systems, the speech of deaf-mutes, etc.

But what supports the necessity for change? I might be reproached for not having been as explicit on this point as on the principle of immutability. This is because I failed to distinguish between the different forces of change. We must consider their great variety in order to understand the extent to which they are necessary.

The causes of continuity are *a priori* within the scope of the observer, but the causes of change in time are not. It is better not to attempt giving an exact account at this point, but to restrict discussion to the shifting of relationships in general. Time changes all things; there is no reason why language should escape this universal law.

Let us review the main points of our discussion and relate them to the principles set up in the Introduction.

1) Avoiding sterile word definitions, within the total phenomenon represented by speech we first singled out two parts: language and speaking. Language is speech less speaking. It is the whole set of linguistic habits which allow an individual to understand and to be understood.

2) But this definition still leaves language outside its social context; it makes language something artificial since it includes only the individual part of reality; for the realization of language, a community of speakers [*masse parlante*] is necessary. Contrary to all appearances, language never exists apart from the social fact, for it is a semiological phenomenon. Its social nature is one of its inner characteristics. Its complete definition confronts us with two inseparable entities, as shown in this drawing:

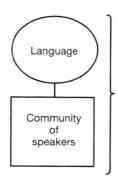

But under the conditions described language is not living—it has only potential life; we have considered only the social, not the historical, fact.

3) The linguistic sign is arbitrary; language, as defined, would therefore seem to be a system which, because it depends solely on a rational principle, is free and can be organized at will. Its social nature, considered independently, does not definitely rule out this viewpoint. Doubtless it is not on a purely logical basis that group psychology operates; one must consider everything that deflects reason in actual contacts between individuals. But the thing which keeps

language from being a simple convention that can be modified at the whim of interested parties is not its social nature; it is rather the action of time combined with the social force. If time is left out, the linguistic facts are incomplete and no conclusion is possible.

If we considered language in time, without the community of speakers—imagine an isolated individual living for several centuries—we probably would notice no change; time would not influence language. Conversely, if we considered the community of speakers without considering time, we would not see the effect of the social forces that influence language. To represent the actual facts, we must then add to our first drawing a sign to indicate passage of time:

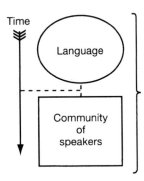

Language is no longer free, for time will allow the social forces at work on it to carry out their effects. This brings us back to the principle of continuity, which cancels freedom. But continuity necessarily implies change, varying degrees of shifts in the relationship between the signified and the signifier.

CHAPTER IV: LINGUISTIC VALUE

1. LANGUAGE AS ORGANIZED THOUGHT COUPLED WITH SOUND

To prove that language is only a system of pure values, it is enough to consider the two elements involved in its functioning: ideas and sounds.

Psychologically our thought—apart from its expression in words—is only a shapeless and indistinct mass. Philosophers and linguists have always agreed in recognizing that without the help of signs we would be unable to make a clear-cut, consistent distinction between two ideas. Without language, thought is a vague, uncharted nebula. There are no pre-existing ideas, and nothing is distinct before the appearance of language.

Against the floating realm of thought, would sounds by themselves yield predelimited entities? No more so than ideas. Phonic substance is nether more fixed nor more rigid that thought; it is not a mold into which thought must of necessity fit but a plastic substance divided in turn into distinct parts to furnish the signifiers needed by thought. The linguistic fact can therefore be pictured in its totality—i.e. language—as a series of contiguous subdivisions marked off on both the indefinite plane of jumbled ideas (A) and the equally vague plane of sounds (B). The following diagram gives a rough idea of it:

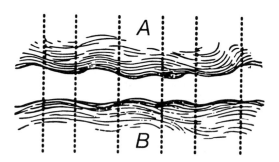

The characteristic role of language with respect to thought is not to create a material phonic means for expressing ideas but to serve as a link between thought and sound, under conditions, that of necessity bring about the reciprocal delimitations of units. Thought, chaotic by nature, has to become ordered in the process of its decomposition. Neither are thoughts given material form nor are sounds transformed into mental entities; the somewhat mysterious fact is rather that "thought-sound" implies division, and that language works out its units while taking shape between two shapeless masses. Visualize the air in contact with a sheet of water; if the atmospheric pressure changes, the surface of the water will be broken up into a series of divisions, waves; the waves resemble the union or coupling of thought with phonic substance.

Language might be called the domain of articulations, using the word as it was defined earlier. Each linguistic term is a member, an *articulus* in which an idea is fixed in a sound and a sound becomes the sign of an idea.

Language can also be compared with a sheet of paper: thought is the front and the sound the back; one cannot cut the front without cutting the back at the same time; likewise in language, one can neither divide sound from thought nor thought from sound; the division could be accomplished only abstractedly, and the result would be either pure psychology or pure phonology.

Linguistics then works in the borderland where the elements of sound and thought combine; *their combination produces a form, not a substance.*

These views give a better understanding of what was said before about the arbitrariness of signs. Not only are the two domains that are linked by the linguistic fact shapeless and confused, but the choice of a given slice of sound to name a given idea is completely arbitrary. If this were not true, the notion of value would be compromised, for it would include an externally imposed element. But actually values remain entirely relative, and that is why the bond between the sound and the idea is radically arbitrary.

The arbitrary nature of the sign explains in turn why the social fact alone can create a linguistic system. The community is necessary if values that owe their existence solely to usage and general acceptance are to be set up; by himself the individual is incapable of fixing a single value.

In addition, the idea of value, as defined, shows that to consider a term as simply the union of a certain sound with a certain concept is grossly misleading. To define it in this way would isolate the term from its system; it would mean assuming that one can start from the terms and construct the system by adding them together when, on the contrary, it is from the interdependent whole that one must start and through analysis obtain its elements.

To develop this thesis, we shall study value successively from the viewpoint of the signified or concept (Section 2), the signifier (Section 3), and the complete sign (Section 4).

Being unable to seize the concrete entities or units of language directly, we shall work with words. While the word does not conform exactly to the definition of the linguistic unit, it at least bears a rough resemblance to the unit and has the advantage of being concrete; consequently, we shall use words as specimens equivalent to real terms in a synchronic system, and the principles that we evolve with respect to words will be valid for entities in general.

2. LINGUISTIC VALUE FROM A CONCEPTUAL VIEWPOINT

When we speak of the value of a word, we generally think first of its property of standing for an idea, and this is in fact one side of linguistic value. But if this is true, how does *value* differ from *signification?* Might the two words be synonyms? I think not, although it is easy to confuse them, since the confusion results not so much from their similarity as from the subtlety of the distinction that they mark.

From a conceptual viewpoint, value is doubtless one element in signification, and it is difficult to see how signification can be dependent upon value and still be distinct from it. But we must clear up the issue or risk reducing language to a simple naming-process (see p. 80).

Let us first take signification as it is generally understood and as it was pictured on page 82. As the arrows in the drawing show, it is only the counterpart of the sound-image. Everything that occurs concerns only the sound-image and the concept when we look upon the word as independent and self-contained.

But here is the paradox: on the one hand the concept seems to be the counterpart of the sound-image, and on the other hand the sign itself is in turn the counterpart of the other signs of language.

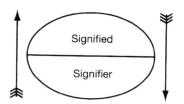

Language is a system of interdependent terms in which the value of each term results solely from the simultaneous presence of the others, as in the diagram:

How, then, can value be confused with signification, i.e. the counterpart of the sound-image? It seems impossible to liken the relations represented here by horizontal arrows to those represented above by vertical arrows. Putting it another way—and again taking up the example of the sheet of paper that is cut in two—it is clear that the observable relation between the different pieces A, B, C, D, etc. is distinct from the relation between the front and back of the same piece as in A/A', B/B', etc.

To resolve the issue, let us observe from the outset that even outside language all values are apparently governed by the same paradoxical principle. They are always composed:

(1) of a *dissimilar* thing that can be *exchanged* for the thing of which the value is to be determined; and

(2) of *similar* things that can be *compared* with the thing of which the value is to be determined.

Both factors are necessary for the existence of a value. To determine what a five-franc piece is worth one must therefore know: (1) that it can be exchanged for a fixed quantity of a different thing, e.g. bread; and (2) that it can be compared with a similar value of the same system, e.g. a one-franc piece, or with coins of another system (a dollar, etc.). In the same way a word can be exchanged for something dissimilar, an idea; besides, it can be compared with something of the same nature, another word. Its value is therefore not fixed so long as one simply states that it can be "exchanged" for a given concept, i.e. that it has this or that signification: one must also compare it with similar values, with other words that stand in opposition to it. Its content is really fixed only by the concurrence of everything that exists outside it. Being part of a system, it is endowed not only with a signification but also and especially with a value, and this is something quite different.

A few examples will show clearly that this is true. Modern French *mouton* can have the same signification as English *sheep* but not the same value, and this for several reasons, particularly because in speaking of a piece of meat ready to be served on the table, English uses *mutton* and not *sheep*. The difference in value between *sheep* and *mouton* is due to the fact that *sheep* has beside it a second term while the French word does not.

Within the same language, all words used to express related ideas limit each other reciprocally; synonyms like French *redouter* 'dread,' *craindre* 'fear,' and *avoir peur* 'be afraid' have value only through their opposition: if *redouter* did not exist, all its content would go to its competitors. Conversely, some words are enriched through contact with others: e.g. the new element introduced in *décrépit* (un vieillard *décrépit*) results from the coexistence of *décrépi* (un mur *décrépi*). The value of just any term is accordingly determined by its environment; it is impossible to fix even the value of the word signifying "sun" without first considering its surroundings: in some languages it is not possible to say "sit in the *sun*."

Everything said about words applies to any term of language, e.g. to grammatical entities. The value of a French plural does not coincide with that of a Sanskrit plural even though their signification is usually identical; Sanskrit has three numbers instead of two (*my eyes, my ears, my arms, my legs,* etc. are dual);[5] it would be wrong to attribute the same value to the plural in Sanskrit and in French; its value clearly depends on what is outside and around it.

If words stood for pre-existing concepts, they would all have exact equivalents in meaning from one language to the next; but this is not true. French uses *louer* (*une maison*) 'let (a house)' indifferently to mean both "pay for" and "receive payment for," whereas German uses two words, *mieten* and *vermieten;* there is obviously no exact correspondence of values. The German verbs *schätzen* and *urteilen* share a number of significations, but that correspondence does not hold at several points.

Inflection offers some particularly striking examples. Distinctions of time, which are so familiar to us, are unknown in certain languages. Hebrew does not recognize even the fundamental distinctions between the past, present, and future. Proto-Germanic has no special form for the future; to say that the future is expressed by the present is wrong, for the value of the present is not the same in Germanic as in languages that have a future along with the present. The Slavic languages regularly single out two aspects of the verb: the perfective represents action as a point, complete in its totality; the imperfective represents it as taking place, and on the line of time. The categories are difficult for a Frenchman to understand, for they are unknown in French; if they were predetermined, this would not be true. Instead of pre-existing ideas then, we find in all the foregoing examples *values* emanating from the system. When they are said to correspond to concepts, it is understood that the concepts are purely differential and defined not by their positive content but negatively by their relations with the other terms of the system. Their most precise characteristic is in being what the others are not.

Now the real interpretation of the diagram of the signal becomes apparent. Thus

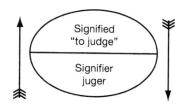

means that in French the concept "to judge" is linked to the sound-image *juger;* in short, it symbolizes signification. But it is quite clear that initially the concept is nothing, that is only a value determined by its relations with other similar values, and that without them the signification would not exist. If I state simply that a word signifies something when I have in mind the associating of a sound-image with a concept, I am making a statement that may suggest what actually happens, but by no means am I expressing the linguistic fact in its essence and fullness.

3. LINGUISTIC VALUE FROM A MATERIAL VIEWPOINT

The conceptual side of value is made up solely of relations and differences with respect to the other terms of language, and the same can be said of its material side. The important thing in the word is not the sound alone but the phonic differences that make it possible to distinguish this word from all others, for differences carry signification.

This may seem surprising, but how indeed could the reverse be possible? Since one vocal image is no better suited than the next for what it is commissioned to express, it is evident, even *a priori,* that a segment of language can never in the final analysis be based on anything except its noncoincidence with the rest. *Arbitrary* and *differential* are two correlative qualities.

The alteration of linguistic signs clearly illustrates this. It is precisely because the terms *a* and *b* as such are radically incapable of reaching the level of consciousness—one is always conscious of only the *a/b* difference—that each term is free to change according to laws that are unrelated to its signifying function. No positive sign characterizes the genitive plural in Czech *žen,* still the two forms *žena: žen;* function as well as the earlier forms *žena: ženb; žen* has value only because it is different.

Here is another example that shows even more clearly the systematic role of phonic differences: in Greek, *éphēn* is an imperfect and *éstēn* an aorist although both words are formed in the same way; the first belongs to the system of the present indicative of *phēmí* 'I say,' whereas there is no present **stēmi*; now it is precisely the relation *phēmí éphēn* that corresponds to the relation between the present and the imperfect (cf. *déiknūmi: edéiknūn*, etc.). Signs function, then, not through their intrinsic value but through their relative position.

In addition, it is impossible for sound alone, a material element, to belong to language. It is only a secondary thing, substance to be put to use. All our conventional values have the characteristic of not being confused with the tangible element which supports them. For instance, it is not the metal in a piece of money that fixes its value. A coin nominally worth five francs may contain less than half its worth of silver. Its value will vary according to the amount stamped upon it and according to its use inside or outside a political boundary. This is even more true of the linguistic signifier, which is not phonic but incorporeal—constituted not by its material substance but by the differences that separate its sound-image from all others.

The foregoing principle is so basic that it applies to all the material elements of language, including phonemes. Every language forms its words on the basis of a system of sonorous elements, each element being a clearly delimited unit and one of a fixed number of units. Phonemes are characterized not, as one might think, by their own positive quality but simply by the fact that they are distinct. Phonemes are above all else opposing, relative, and negative entities.

Proof of this is the latitude that speakers have between points of convergence in the pronunciation of distinct sounds. In French, for instance, general use of a dorsal *r* does not prevent many speakers from using a tongue-tip trill; language is not in the least disturbed by it; language requires only that the sound be different and not, as one might imagine, that it have an invariable quality. I can even pronounce the French *r* like German *ch* in *Bach, doch*, etc., but in German I could not use *r* instead of *ch*, for German gives recognition to both elements and must keep them apart. Similarly, in Russian there is no latitude for *t* in the direction of *t'* (palatalized *t*), for the result would be the confusing of two sounds differentiated by the language (cf. *govorit'* 'speak' and *goverit* 'he speaks'), but more freedom may be taken with respect to *th* (aspirated *t*) since this sound does not figure in the Russian system of phonemes.

Since an identical state of affairs is observable in writing, another system of signs, we shall use writing to draw some comparisons that will clarify the whole issue. In fact:

1) The signs used in writing are arbitrary; there is no connection, for example, between the letter *t* and the sound that it designates.

2) The value of letters is purely negative and differential. The same person can write *t*, for instance, in different ways. The only requirement is that the sign for *t* not to be confused in his script with the signs used for *l, d*, etc.

3) Values in writing function only through reciprocal opposition within a fixed system that consists of a set number of letters. This third characteristic, though not identical to the second, is closely related to it, for both depend on

the first. Since the graphic sign is arbitrary, its form matters little or rather matters only within the limitations imposed by the system.

4) The means by which the sign is produced is completely unimportant, for it does not affect the system (this also follows from characteristic 1). Whether I make the letters in white or black, raised or engraved, with pen or chisel—all this is of no importance with respect to their signification.

4. THE SIGN CONSIDERED IN ITS TOTALITY

Everything that has been said up to this point boils down to this: in language there are only differences. Even more important: a difference generally implies positive terms between which the difference is set up; but in language there are only differences *without positive terms*. Whether we take the signified or the signifier, language has neither ideas nor sounds that existed before the linguistic system, but only conceptual and phonic differences that have issued from the system. The idea or phonic substance that a sign contains is of less importance than the other signs that surround it. Proof of this is that the value of a term may be modified without either its meaning or its sound being affected, solely because a neighboring term has been modified (see p. 93).

But the statement that everything in language is negative is true only if the signified and the signifier are considered separately; when we consider the sign in its totality, we have something that is positive in its own class. A linguistic system is a series of differences of sound combined with a series of differences of ideas; but the pairing of a certain number of acoustical signs with as many cuts made from the mass of thought engenders a system of values; and this system serves as the effective link between the phonic and psychological elements within each sign. Although both the signified and the signifier are purely differential and negative when considered separately, their combination is a positive fact; it is even the sole type of facts that language has, for maintaining the parallelism between the two classes of differences is the distinctive function of the linguistic institution.

Certain diachronic facts are typical in this respect. Take the countless instances where alteration of the signifier occasions a conceptual change and where it is obvious that the sum of the ideas distinguished corresponds in principle to the sum of the distinctive signs. When two words are confused through phonetic alteration (e.g. French *décrépit* from *dēcrepitus* and *décrépi* from *crispus*), the ideas that they express will also tend to become confused if only they have something in common. Or a word may have different forms (cf. *chaise* 'chair' and *chaire* 'desk'). Any nascent difference will tend invariably to become significant but without always succeeding or being successful on the first trial. Conversely, any conceptual difference perceived by the mind seeks to find expression through a distinct signifier, and two ideas that are no longer distinct in the mind tend to merge into the same signifier.

When we compare signs—positive terms—with each other, we can no longer speak of difference; the expression would not be fitting, for it applies only to the comparing of two sound-images, e.g. *father* and *mother*, or two ideas, e.g. the idea "father" and the idea "mother"; two signs, each having a signified and signifier, are not different but only distinct. Between them there is only *opposition*. The entire mechanism of language, with which we shall be concerned later, is based on oppositions of this kind and on the phonic and conceptual differences that they imply.

What is true of value is true also of the unit. A unit is a segment of the spoken chain that corresponds to a certain concept; both are by nature purely differential.

Applied to units, the principle of differentiation can be stated in this way: *the characteristics of the unit blend with the unit itself.* In language, as in any semiological system, whatever distinguishes one sign from the others constitutes it. Difference makes character just as it makes value and the unit.

Another rather paradoxical consequence of the same principle is this: in the last analysis what is commonly referred to as a "grammatical fact" fits the definition of the unit, for it always expresses an opposition of terms; it differs only in that the opposition is particularly significant (e.g. the formation of German plurals of the type *Nacht: Nächte*). Each term present in the grammatical fact (the singular without umlaut or final *e* in opposition to the plural with umlaut and −*e*) consists of the interplay of a number of oppositions within the system. When isolated, neither *Nacht* nor *Nächte* is anything: thus everything is opposition. Putting it another way, the *Nacht: Nächte* relation can be expressed by an algebraic formula *a/b* in which *a* and *b* are not simple terms but result from a set of relations. Language, in a manner of speaking, is a type of algebra consisting solely of complex terms. Some of its oppositions are more significant than others; but units and grammatical facts are only different names for designating diverse aspects of the same general fact: the functioning of linguistic oppositions. This statement is so true that we might very well approach the problem of units by starting from grammatical facts. Taking an opposition like *Nacht: Nächte*, we might ask what are the units involved in it. Are they only the two words, the whole series of similar words, *a* and *ä*, or all singulars and plurals, etc.?

Units and grammatical facts would not be confused if linguistic signs were made up of something besides differences. But language being what it is, we shall find nothing simple in it regardless of our approach; everywhere and always there is the same complex equilibrium of terms that mutually condition each other. Putting it another way, *language is a form and not a substance.* This truth could not be overstressed, for all the mistakes in our terminology, all our incorrect ways of naming things that pertain to language, stem from the involuntary supposition that the linguistic phenomenon must have substance.

NOTES

1. The term sound-image may seem to be too restricted inasmuch as beside the representation of the sounds of a word there is also that of its articulation, the muscular image of the phonational act. But for F. de Saussure language is essentially a depository, a thing received from without. The sound-image is par excellence the natural representation of the word as a fact of potential language, outside any actual use of it in speaking. The motor side is thus implied or, in any event, occupies only a subordinate role with respect to the sound-image. [Ed.]
2. Cf. English *goodness!* and *zounds!* (from *God's wounds*). [Tr.]
3. It would be wrong to reproach F. de Saussure for being illogical or paradoxical in attributing two contradictory qualities to language. By opposing two striking terms, he wanted only to emphasize the fact that language changes in spite of the inability of speakers to change it. One can also say that it is intangible but not unchangeable. [Ed.]
4. From May to July of 1911, De Saussure used interchangeably the old terminology (*idea* and *sign*) and the new (*signified* and *signifier*). [Tr.]
5. The use of the comparative form for two and the superlative for more than two in English (e.g. *may the* better *boxer win: the* best *boxer in the world*) is probably a remnant of the old distinction between the dual and the plural number. [Tr.]

JEAN-PAUL SARTRE

SELECTION FROM "EXISTENTIALISM"

I should like on this occasion to defend existentialism against some charges which have been brought against it.

First, it has been charged with inviting people to remain in a kind of desperate quietism because, since no solutions are possible, we should have to consider action in this world as quite impossible. We should then end up in a philosophy of contemplation; and since contemplation is a luxury, we come in the end to a bourgeois philosophy. The communists in particular have made these charges.

On the other hand, we have been charged with dwelling on human degradation, with pointing up everywhere the sordid, shady, and slimy, and neglecting the gracious and beautiful, the bright side of human nature; for example, according to Mlle. Mercier, a Catholic critic, with forgetting the smile of the child. Both sides charge us with having ignored human solidarity, with considering man as an isolated being. The communists say that the main reason for this is that we take pure subjectivity, the *Cartesian I think,* as our starting point; in other words, the moment in which man becomes fully aware of what it means to him to be an isolated being; as a result, we are unable to return to a state of solidarity with the men who are not ourselves, a state which we can never reach in the *cogito.*

Reprinted with permission from "Existentialism," in *Existentialism and Human Emotions,* tr. Bernard Frechtman. New York: Philosophical Library, 1957, pp. 9–40.

From the Christian standpoint, we are charged with denying the reality and seriousness of human undertakings, since, if we reject God's commandments and the eternal verities, there no longer remains anything but pure caprice, with everyone permitted to do as he pleases and incapable, from his own point of view, of condemning the points of view and acts of others.

I shall try today to answer these different charges. Many people are going to be surprised at what is said here about humanism. We shall try to see in what sense it is to be understood. In any case, what can be said from the very beginning is that by existentialism we mean a doctrine which makes human life possible and, in addition, declares that every truth and every action implies a human setting and a human subjectivity.

As is generally known, the basic charge against us is that we put the emphasis on the dark side of human life. Someone recently told me of a lady who, when she let slip a vulgar word in a moment of irritation, excused herself by saying, "I guess I'm becoming an existentialist." Consequently, existentialism is regarded as something ugly; that is why we are said to be naturalists; and if we are, it is rather surprising that in this day and age we cause so much more alarm and scandal than does naturalism, properly so called. The kind of person who can take in his stride such a novel as Zola's *The Earth* is disgusted as soon as he starts reading an existentialist novel; the kind of person who is resigned to the wisdom of the ages—which is pretty sad—finds us even sadder. Yet, what can be more disillusioning than saying "true charity begins at home" or "a scoundrel will always return evil for good"?

We know the commonplace remarks made when this subject comes up, remarks which always add up to the same thing: we shouldn't struggle against the powers-that-be; we shouldn't resist authority; we shouldn't try to rise above our station; any action which doesn't conform to authority is romantic; any effort not based on past experience is doomed to failure; experience shows that man's bent is always toward trouble, that there must be a strong hand to hold him in check, if not, there will be anarchy. There are still people who go on mumbling these melancholy old saws, the people who say, "It's only human!" whenever a more or less repugnant act is pointed out to them, the people who glut themselves on *chansons réalistes*; these are the people who accuse existentialism of being too gloomy, and to such an extent that I wonder whether they are complaining about it, not for its pessimism, but much rather its optimism. Can it be that what really scares them in the doctrine I shall try to present here is that it leaves to man a possibility of choice? To answer this question, we must re-examine it on a strictly philosophical plane. What is meant by the term *existentialism?*

Most people who use the word would be rather embarrassed if they had to explain it, since, now that the word is all the rage, even the work of a musician or painter is being called existentialist. A gossip columnist in *Clartés* signs himself *The Existentialist,* so that by this time the word has been so stretched and has taken on so broad a meaning, that it no longer means anything at all. It seems that for want of an advance-guard doctrine analogous to surrealism, the kind of people who are eager for scandal and flurry turn to this philosophy which in other respects does not at all serve their purposes in this sphere.

Actually, it is the least scandalous, the most austere of doctrines. It is intended strictly for specialists and philosophers. Yet it can be defined easily. What complicates matters is that there are two kinds of existentialist: first, those who are Christian, among whom I would include Jaspers and Gabriel Marcel, both Catholic; and on the other hand the atheistic existentialists, among whom I class Heidegger, and then the French existentialists and myself. What they have in common is that they think that existence precedes essence, or, if you prefer, that subjectivity must be the starting point.

Just what does that mean? Let us consider some object that is manufactured, for example, a book or a paper-cutter: here is an object which has been made by an artisan whose inspiration came from a concept. He referred to the concept of what a paper-cutter is and likewise to a known method of production, which is part of the concept, something which is, by and large, a routine. Thus, the paper-cutter is at once an object produced in a certain way and, on the other hand, one having a specific use; and one can not postulate a man who produces a paper-cutter but does not know what it is used for. Therefore, let us say that, for the paper-cutter, essence—that is, the ensemble of both the production routines and the properties which enable it to be both produced and defined—precedes existence. Thus, the presence of the paper-cutter or book in front of me is determined. Therefore, we have here a technical view of the world whereby it can be said that production precedes existence.

When we conceive God as the Creator, He is generally thought of as a superior sort of artisan. Whatever doctrine we may be considering, whether one like that of Descartes or that of Leibnitz, we always grant that will more or less follows understanding or, at the very least, accompanies it, and that when God creates He knows exactly what He is creating. Thus, the concept of man in the mind of God is comparable to the concept of paper-cutter in the mind of the manufacturer, and, following certain techniques and a conception, God produces man, just as the artisan, following a definition and a technique, makes a paper-cutter. Thus, the individual man is the realization of a certain concept in the divine intelligence.

In the eighteenth century, the atheism of the *philosophes* discarded the idea of God, but not so much for the notion that essence precedes existence. To a certain extent, this idea is found everywhere; we find it in Diderot, in Voltaire, and even in Kant. Man has a human nature; this human nature, which is the concept of the human, is found in all men, which means that each man is a particular example of a universal concept, man. In Kant, the result of this universality is that the wild-man, the natural man, as well as the bourgeois, are circumscribed by the same definition and have the same basic qualities. Thus, here too the essence of man precedes the historical existence that we find in nature.

Atheistic existentialism, which I represent, is more coherent. It states that if God does not exist, there is at least one being in whom existence precedes essence, a being who exists before he can be defined by any concept, and that this being is man, or, as Heidegger says, human reality. What is meant here by saying that existence precedes essence? It means that, first of all, man exists, turns up, appears on the scene, and, only afterwards, defines himself. If man, as the existentialist conceives him, is indefinable, it is because at first he is nothing. Only afterward will he be something, and he himself will have made what he will be. Thus, there is no human nature, since there is no God to conceive it. Not only is man what he conceives himself to be, but he is also only what he wills himself to be after this thrust toward existence.

Man is nothing else but what he makes of himself. Such is the first principle of existentialism. It is also what is called subjectivity, the name we are labeled with when charges are brought against us. But what do we mean by this, if not that man has a greater dignity than a stone or table? For we mean that man first exists, that is, that man first of all is the being who hurls himself toward a future and who is conscious of imagining himself as being in the future. Man is at the start a plan which is aware of itself, rather than a patch of moss, a piece of garbage, or a cauliflower; nothing exists prior to this plan; there is nothing in heaven; man will be what he will have planned to be. Not what he will want to be. Because by the word "will" we generally mean a conscious decision, which is subsequent to what we have already made of ourselves. I may want to belong to a political party, write a book, get married; but all that is only a manifestation of an earlier, more spontaneous choice that is called "will." But if existence really does precede essence, man is responsible for what he is. Thus, existentialism's first move is to make every man aware of what he is and to make the full responsibility of his existence rest on him. And when we say that a man is responsible for himself, we do not only mean that he is responsible for his own individuality, but that he is responsible for all men.

The word subjectivism has two meanings, and our opponents play on the two. Subjectivism means, on the one hand, that an individual chooses and makes himself; and, on the other, that it is impossible for man to transcend human subjectivity. The second of these is the essential meaning of existentialism. When we say that man chooses his own self, we mean that every one of us does likewise; but we also mean by that that in making this choice he also chooses all men. In fact, in creating the man that we want to be, there is not a single one of our acts which does not at the same time create an image of man as we think he ought to be. To choose to be this or that is to affirm at the same time the value of what we choose, because we can never choose evil. We always choose the good, and nothing can be good for us without being good for all.

If, on the other hand, existence precedes essence, and if we grant that we exist and fashion our image at one and the same time, the image is valid for everybody and for our whole age. Thus, our responsibility is much greater than we might have supposed, because it involves all mankind. If I am a workingman and choose to join a Christian trade-union rather than be a communist, and if by being a member I want to show that the best thing for man is resignation, that the kingdom of man is not of this world, I am not only involving my own case—I want to be resigned for everyone. As a result, my action has involved all humanity. To take a more individual matter, if I want to marry, to have children; even if this marriage depends solely on my own circumstances or passion or wish, I am involving all humanity in monogamy and not merely myself. Therefore, I am responsible for myself and for everyone else. I am creating a certain image of man of my own choosing. In choosing myself, I choose man.

This helps us understand what the actual content is of such rather grandiloquent words as anguish, forlornness, despair. As you will see, it's all quite simple.

First, what is meant by anguish? The existentialists say at once that man is anguish. What that means is this: the man who involves himself and who realizes that he is not only the person he chooses to be, but also a lawmaker who is, at the same time, choosing all mankind as well as himself, can not help escape the feeling of his total and deep responsibility. Of course, there are many people who are not anxious; but we claim that they are hiding their anxiety, that they are fleeing from it. Certainly, many people believe that when they do something, they themselves are the only ones involved, and when someone says to them, "What if everyone acted that way?" they shrug their shoulders and answer, "Everyone doesn't act that way." But really, one should always ask himself, "What would happen if everybody looked at things that way?" There is no escaping this disturbing thought except by a kind of double-dealing. A man who lies and makes excuses for himself by saying "not everybody does that," is someone with an uneasy conscience, because the act of lying implies that a universal value is conferred upon the lie.

Anguish is evident even when it conceals itself. This is the anguish that Kierkegaard called the anguish of Abraham. You know the story: an angel has ordered Abraham to sacrifice his son; if it really were an angel who has come and said, "You are Abraham, you shall sacrifice your son," everything would be all right. But everyone might first wonder, "Is it really an angel, and am I really Abraham? What proof do I have?"

There was a madwoman who had hallucinations; someone used to speak to her on the telephone and give her orders. Her doctor asked her, "Who is it who talks to you?" She answered, "He says it's God." What proof did she really have that it was God? If an angel comes to me, what proof is there that it's an angel? And if I hear voices, what proof is there that they come from heaven and not from hell, or from the subconscious, or a pathological condition? What proves that they are addressed to me? What proof is there that I have been appointed to impose my choice and my conception of man on humanity? I'll never find any proof or sign to convince me of that. If a voice addresses me, it is always for me to decide that this is the angel's voice; if I consider that such an act is a good one, it is I who will choose to say that it is good rather than bad.

Now, I'm not being singled out as an Abraham, and yet at every moment I'm obliged to perform exemplary acts. For every man, everything happens as if all mankind had its eyes fixed on him and were guiding itself by what he does. And every man ought to say to himself, "Am I really the kind of man who has the right to act in such a way that humanity might guide itself by my actions?" And if he does not say that to himself, he is masking his anguish.

There is no question here of the kind of anguish which would lead to quietism, to inaction. It is a matter of a simple sort of anguish that anybody who has had responsibilities is familiar with. For example, when a military officer takes the responsibility for an attack and sends a certain number of men to death, he chooses to do so, and in the main he alone makes the choice. Doubtless, orders come from above, but they are too broad; he interprets them, and on this interpretation depend the lives of ten or fourteen or twenty men. In making a decision he can not help having a certain anguish. All leaders know this anguish. That doesn't keep them from acting; on the contrary, it is the very condition of their action. For it implies that they envisage a number of possibilities, and when they choose one, they realize that it has value only because it is chosen. We shall see that this kind of anguish, which is the kind that existentialism describes, is explained, in addition, by a direct responsibility to the other men whom it involves. It is not a curtain separating us from action, but is part of action itself.

When we speak of forlornness, a term Heidegger was fond of, we mean only that God does not exist and that we have to face all the consequences of this. The existentialist is strongly opposed to a certain kind of secular ethics which would like to abolish God with the least possible expense. About 1880, some French teachers tried to set up a secular ethics which went something like this: God is a useless and costly hypothesis; we are discarding it; but, meanwhile, in order for there to be an ethics, a society, a civilization, it is essential that certain values be taken seriously and that they be considered as having an *a priori* existence. It must be obligatory, *a priori,* to be honest, not to lie, not to beat your wife, to have children, etc., etc. So we're going to try a little device which will make it possible to show that values exist all the same, inscribed in a heaven of ideas, though otherwise God does not exist. In other words—and this, I believe, is the tendency of everything called reformism in France—nothing will be changed if God does not exist. We shall find ourselves with the same norms of honesty, progress, and humanism, and we shall have made of God an outdated hypothesis which will peacefully die off by itself.

The existentialist, on the contrary, thinks it very distressing that God does not exist, because all possibility of finding values in a heaven of ideas disappears along with Him; there can no longer be an *a priori* Good, since there is no infinite and perfect consciousness to think it. Nowhere is it written that the Good exists, that we must be honest, that we must not lie; because the fact is we are on a plane where there are only men. Dostoievsky said, "If God didn't exist, everything would be possible." That is the very starting point of existentialism.

Indeed, everything is permissible if God does not exist, and as a result man is forlorn, because neither within him nor without does he find anything to cling to. He can't start making excuses for himself.

If existence really does precede essence, there is no explaining things away by reference to a fixed and given human nature. In other words, there is no determinism, man is free, man is freedom. On the other hand, if God does not exist, we find no values or commands to turn to which legitimize our conduct. So, in the bright realm of values, we have no excuse behind us, nor justification before us. We are alone, with no excuses.

That is the idea I shall try to convey when I say that man is condemned to be free. Condemned, because he did not create himself, yet, in other respects is free: because, once thrown into the world, he is responsible for everything he does. The existentialist does not believe in the power of passion. He will never agree that a sweeping passion is a ravaging torrent which fatally leads a man to certain acts and is therefore an excuse. He thinks that man is responsible for his passion.

The existentialist does not think that man is going to help himself by finding in the world some omen by which to orient himself. Because he thinks that man will interpret the omen to suit himself. Therefore, he thinks that man, with no support and no aid, is condemned every moment to invent man. Ponge, in a very fine article, has said, "Man is the future of man." That's exactly it. But if it is taken to mean that this future is recorded in heaven, that God sees it, then it is false, because it would really no longer be a future. If it is taken to mean that, whatever a man may be, there is a future to be forged, a virgin future before him, then this remark is sound. But then we are forlorn.

To give you an example which will enable you to understand forlornness better, I shall cite the case of one of my students who came to see me under the following circumstances: his father was on bad terms with his mother, and, moreover, was inclined to be a collaborationist; his older brother had been killed in the German offensive of 1940, and the young man, with somewhat immature but generous feelings, wanted to avenge him. His mother lived alone with him, very much upset by the half-treason of her husband and the death of her older son; the boy was her only consolation.

The boy was faced with the choice of leaving for England and joining the Free French Forces—that is, leaving his mother behind—or remaining with his mother and helping her to carry on. He was fully aware that the woman lived only for him and that his going-off—and perhaps his death—would plunge her into despair. He was also aware that every act that he did for his mother's sake was a sure thing, in the sense that it was helping her to carry on, whereas every effort he made toward going off and fighting was an uncertain move which might run aground and prove completely useless; for example, on his way to England he might, while passing through Spain, be detained indefinitely in a Spanish camp; he might reach England or Algiers and be stuck in an office at a desk job. As a result, he was faced with two very different kinds of action: one, concrete, immediate, but concerning only one individual; the other concerned an incomparably vaster group, a national collectivity, but for that very reason was dubious, and might be interrupted en route. And, at the same time, he was wavering between two kinds of ethics. On the one hand, an ethics of sympathy, of personal devotion; on the other, a broader ethics, but one whose efficacy was more dubious. He had to choose between the two.

Who could help him choose? Christian doctrine? No. Christian doctrine says, "Be charitable, love your neighbor, take the more rugged path, etc., etc." But which is the more rugged path? Whom should he love as a brother? The fighting man or his mother? Which does the greater good, the vague act of fighting in a group, or the concrete one of helping a particular human being to go on living? Who can decide *a priori*? Nobody. No book of ethics can tell him. The Kantian ethics says, "Never treat any person as a means, but as an end." Very well, if I stay with my mother, I'll treat her as an end and not as a means; but by virtue of this very fact, I'm running the risk of treating the people around me who are fighting, as means; and conversely, if I go to join those who are fighting, I'll be treating them as an end, and, by doing that, I run the risk of treating my mother as a means.

If values are vague, and if they are always too broad for the concrete and specific case that we are considering, the only thing left for us is to trust our instincts. That's what this young man tried to do; and when I saw him, he said, "In the end, feeling is what counts. I ought to choose whichever pushes me in one direction. If I feel that I love my mother enough to sacrifice everything else for her—my desire for vengeance, for action, for adventure—then I'll stay with her. If, on the contrary, I feel that my love for my mother isn't enough, I'll leave."

But how is the value of a feeling determined? What gives his feeling for his mother value? Precisely the fact that he remained with her. I may say that I like so-and-so well enough to sacrifice a certain amount of money for him, but I may say so only if I've done it. I may say "I love my mother well enough to remain with her" if I have remained with her. The only way to determine the value of this affection is, precisely, to perform an act which confirms and defines it. But, since I require this affection to justify my act, I find myself caught in a vicious circle.

On the other hand, Gide has well said that a mock feeling and a true feeling are almost indistinguishable; to decide that I love my mother and will remain with her, or to remain with her by putting on an act, amount somewhat to the same thing. In other words, the feeling is formed by the acts one performs; so, I can not refer to it in order to act upon it. Which means that I can neither seek within myself the true condition which will impel me to act, nor apply to a system of ethics for concepts which will permit me to act. You will say, "At least, he did go to a teacher for advice." But if you seek advice from a priest, for example, you have chosen this priest; you already knew, more or less, just about what advice he was going to give you. In other words, choosing your adviser is involving yourself. The proof of this is that if you are a Christian, you will say, "Consult a priest." But some priests are collaborating, some are just marking time, some are resisting. Which to choose? If the young man chooses a priest who is resisting or collaborating, he has already decided on the kind of advice he's going to get. Therefore, in coming to see me he knew the answer I was going to give him, and I had only one answer to give: "You're free, choose, that is, invent." No general ethics can show you what is to be done; there are no omens in the world. The Catholics will reply, "But there are." Granted—but, in any case, I myself choose the meaning they have.

When I was a prisoner, I knew a remarkable young man who was a Jesuit. He had entered the Jesuit order in the following way: he had had a number of very bad breaks; in childhood, his father died, leaving him in poverty, and he was a scholarship student at a religious institution where he was constantly made to feel that he was being kept out of charity; then, he failed to get any of the honors and distinctions that children like; later on, at about eighteen, he bungled a love affair; finally, at twenty-two, he failed in military training, a childish enough matter, but it was the last straw.

This young fellow might well have felt that he had botched everything. It was a sign of something, but of what? He might have taken refuge in bitterness or despair. But he very wisely looked upon all this as a sign that he was not made for secular triumphs, and that only the triumphs of religion, holiness, and faith were open to him. He saw the hand of God in all this, and so he entered the order. Who can help seeing that he alone decided what the sign meant?

Some other interpretation might have been drawn from this series of setbacks; for example, that he might have done better to turn carpenter or revolutionist. Therefore, he is fully responsible for the interpretation. Forlornness implies that we ourselves choose our being. Forlornness and anguish go together.

As for despair, the term has a very simple meaning. It means that we shall confine ourselves to reckoning only with what depends upon our will, or on the ensemble of probabilities which make our action possible. When we want something, we always have to reckon with probabilities. I may be counting on the arrival of a friend. The friend is coming by rail or street-car; this supposes that the train will arrive on schedule, or that the street-car will not jump the track. I am left in the realm of possibility; but possibilities are to be reckoned with only to the point where my action comports with the ensemble of these possibilities, and no further. The moment the possibilities I am considering are not rigorously involved by my action, I ought to disengage myself from them, because no God, no scheme, can adapt the world and its possibilities to my will. When Descartes said, "Conquer yourself rather than the world," he meant essentially the same thing.

The Marxists to whom I have spoken reply, "You can rely on the support of others in your action, which obviously has certain limits because you're not going to live forever. That means: rely on both what others are doing elsewhere to help you, in China, in Russia, and what they will do later on, after your death, to carry on the action and lead it to its fulfillment, which will be the revolution. You even *have* to rely upon that, otherwise you're immoral." I reply at once that I will always rely on fellow-fighters insofar as these comrades are involved with me in a common struggle, in the unity of a party or a group in which I can more or less make my weight felt; that is, one whose ranks I am in as a fighter and whose movements I am aware of at every moment. In such a situation, relying on the unity and will of the party is exactly like counting on the fact that the train will arrive on time or that the car won't jump the track. But, given that man is free and that there is no human nature for me to depend on, I can not count on men whom I do not know by relying on human goodness or man's concern for the good of society. I don't know what will become of the Russian revolution; I may make an example of it to the extent that at the present time it is apparent that the proletariat plays a part in Russia that it plays in no other nation. But I can't swear that this will inevitably lead to a triumph of the proletariat. I've got to limit myself to what I see.

Given that men are free and that tomorrow they will freely decide what man will be, I can not be sure that, after my death, fellow-fighters will carry on my work to bring it to its maximum perfection. Tomorrow, after my death, some men may decide to set up Fascism, and the others may be cowardly and muddled enough to let them do it. Fascism will then be the human reality, so much the worse for us.

Actually, things will be as man will have decided they are to be. Does that mean that I should abandon myself to quietism? No. First, I should involve myself; then, act on the old saw, "Nothing ventured, nothing gained." Nor does it mean that I shouldn't belong to a party, but rather that I shall have no illusions and shall do what I can. For example, suppose I ask myself, "Will socialization, as such, ever come about?" I know nothing about it. All I know is that I'm going to do everything in my power to bring it about. Beyond that, I can't count on anything. Quietism is the attitude of people who say, "Let others do what I can't do." The doctrine I am presenting is the very opposite of quietism, since it declares, "There is no reality except in action." Moreover, it goes further, since it adds, "Man is nothing else than his plan; he exists only to the extent that he fulfills himself; he is therefore nothing else than the ensemble of his acts, nothing else than his life."

According to this, we can understand why our doctrine horrifies certain people. Because often the only way they can bear their wretchedness is to think, "Circumstances have been against me. What I've been and done doesn't show my true worth. To be sure, I've had no great love, no great friendship, but that's because I haven't met a man or woman who was worthy. The books I've written haven't been very good because I haven't had the proper leisure. I haven't had children to devote myself to because I didn't find a man with whom I could have spent my life. So there remains within me, unused and quite viable, a host of propensities, inclinations, possibilities, that one wouldn't guess from the mere series of things I've done."

Now, for the existentialist there is really no love other than one which manifests itself in a person's being in love. There is no genius other than one which is expressed in works of art; the genius of Proust is the sum of Proust's works; the genius of Racine is his series of tragedies. Outside of that, there is nothing. Why say that Racine could have written another tragedy, when he didn't write it? A man is involved in life, leaves his impress on it, and outside of that there is nothing. To be sure, this may seem a harsh thought to someone whose life hasn't been a success. But, on the other hand, it prompts people to understand that reality alone is what counts, that dreams, expectations, and hopes warrant no more than to define a man as a disappointed dream, as miscarried hopes, as vain expectations. In other words, to define him negatively and not positively. However, when we say, "You are nothing else than your life," that does not imply that the artist will be judged solely on the basis of his works of art; a thousand other things will contribute toward summing him up. What we mean is that a man is nothing else than a series of undertakings, that he is the sum, the organization, the ensemble of the relationships which make up these undertakings.

When all is said and done, what we are accused of, at bottom, is not our pessimism, but an optimistic toughness. If people throw up to us our works of fiction in which we write about people who are soft, weak, cowardly, and sometimes even downright bad, it's not because these people are soft, weak, cowardly, or bad; because if we were to say, as Zola did, that they are that way because of heredity, the workings of environment, society, because of biological or psychological determinism, people would be reassured. They would say, "Well, that's what we're like, no one can do anything about it." But when the existentialist writes about a coward, he says that this coward is responsible for his cowardice. He's not like that because he has a cowardly heart or lung or brain; he's not like that on account of his physiological make-up; but he's like that because he has made himself a coward by his acts. There's no such thing as a cowardly constitution; there are nervous constitutions; there is poor blood, as the common people say, or strong constitutions. But the man whose blood is poor is not a coward on that account, for what makes cowardice is the act of renouncing or yielding. A constitution is not an act; the coward is defined on the basis of the acts he performs. People feel, in a vague sort of way, that this coward we're talking about is guilty of being a coward, and the thought frightens them. What people would like is that a coward or a hero be born that way.

One of the complaints most frequently made about *The Ways of Freedom**
can be summed up as follows: "After all, these people are so spineless, how are you going to make heroes out of them?" This objection almost makes me laugh, for it assumes that people are born heroes. That's what people really want to think. If you're born cowardly, you may set your mind perfectly at rest; there's

---

Les Chemins de la Liberté, M. Sartre's projected trilogy of novels, two of which, *L'Age de Raison* (*The Age of Reason*) and *Le Sursis* (*The Reprieve*) have already appeared.—Translator's note.

nothing you can do about it; you'll be cowardly all your life, whatever you may do. If you're born a hero, you may set your mind just as much at rest; you'll be a hero all your life; you'll drink like a hero and eat like a hero. What the existentialist says is that the coward makes himself cowardly, that the hero makes himself heroic. There's always a possibility for the coward not to be cowardly any more and for the hero to stop being heroic. What counts is total involvement; some one particular action or set of circumstances is not total involvement.

Thus, I think we have answered a number of the charges concerning existentialism. You see that it can not be taken for a philosophy of quietism, since it defines man in terms of action; nor for a pessimistic description of man—there is no doctrine more optimistic, since man's destiny is within himself; nor for an attempt to discourage man from acting, since it tells him that the only hope is in his acting and that action is the only thing that enables a man to live. Consequently, we are dealing here with an ethics of action and involvement.

Nevertheless, on the basis of a few notions like these, we are still charged with immuring man in his private subjectivity. There again we're very much misunderstood. Subjectivity of the individual is indeed our point of departure, and this for strictly philosophic reasons. Not because we are bourgeois, but because we want a doctrine based on truth and not a lot of fine theories, full of hope but with no real basis. There can be no other truth to take off from than this: *I think; therefore, I exist.* There we have the absolute truth of consciousness becoming aware of itself. Every theory which takes man out of the moment in which he becomes aware of himself is, at its very beginning, a theory which confounds truth, for outside the Cartesian *cogito,* all views are only probable, and a doctrine of probability which is not bound to a truth dissolves into thin air. In order to describe the probable, you must have a firm hold on the true. Therefore, before there can be any truth whatsoever, there must be an absolute truth; and this one is simple and easily arrived at; it's on everyone's doorstep; it's a matter of grasping it directly.

Secondly, this theory is the only one which gives man dignity, the only one which does not reduce him to an object. The effect of all materialism is to treat all men, including the one philosophizing, as objects, that is, as an ensemble of determined reactions in no way distinguished from the ensemble of qualities and phenomena which constitute a table or a chair or a stone. We definitely wish to establish the human realm as an ensemble of values distinct from the material realm. But the subjectivity that we have thus arrived at, and which we have claimed to be truth, is not a strictly individual subjectivity, for we have demonstrated that one discovers in the *cogito* not only himself, but others as well.

The philosophies of Descartes and Kant to the contrary, through the *I think* we reach our own self in the presence of others, and the others are just as real to us as our own self. Thus, the man who becomes aware of himself through the *cogito* also perceives all others, and he perceives them as the condition of his own existence. He realizes that he can not be anything (in the sense that we say that someone is witty or nasty or jealous) unless others recognize it as such. In order to get any truth about myself, I must have contact with another person. The other is indispensable to my own existence, as well as to my knowledge about myself. This being so, in discovering my inner being I discover the other person at the same time, like a freedom placed in front of me which thinks and wills only for or against me. Hence, let us at once announce the discovery of a world which we shall call intersubjectivity; this is the world in which man decides what he is and what others are.

Besides, if it is impossible to find in every man some universal essence which would be human nature, yet there does exist a universal human condition. It's not by chance that today's thinkers speak more readily of man's condition than of his nature. By condition they mean, more or less definitely, the *a priori* limits which outline man's fundamental situation in the universe. Historical situations vary; a man may be born a slave in a pagan society or a feudal lord or a proletarian. What does not vary is the necessity for him to exist in the world, to be at work there, to be there in the midst of other people, and to be mortal there. The limits are neither subjective nor objective, or, rather, they have an objective and a subjective side. Objective because they are to be found everywhere and are recognizable everywhere; subjective because they are *lived* and are nothing if man does not live them, that is, freely determine his existence with reference to them. And though the configurations may differ, at least none of them are completely strange to me, because they all appear as attempts either to pass beyond these limits or recede from them or deny them or adapt to them. Consequently, every configuration, however individual it may be, has a universal value.

Every configuration, even the Chinese, the Indian, or the Negro, can be understood by a Westerner. "Can be understood" means that by virtue of a situation that he can imagine, a European of 1945 can, in like manner, push himself to his limits and reconstitute within himself the configuration of the Chinese, the Indian, or the African. Every configuration has universality in the sense that every configuration can be understood by every man. This does not at all mean that this configuration defines man forever, but that it can be met with again. There is always a way to understand the idiot, the child, the savage, the foreigner, provided one has the necessary information.

In this sense we may say that there is a universality of man; but it is not given, it is perpetually being made. I build the universal in choosing myself; I build it in understanding the configuration of every other man, whatever age he might have lived in. This absoluteness of choice does not do away with the relativeness of each epoch. At heart, what existentialism shows is the connection between the absolute character of free involvement, by virtue of which every man realizes himself in realizing a type of mankind, an involvement always comprehensible in any age whatsoever and by any person whosoever, and the relativeness of the cultural ensemble which may result from such a choice; it must be stressed that the relativity of Cartesianism and the absolute character of Cartesian involvement go together. In this sense, you may, if you like, say that each of us performs an absolute act in breathing, eating, sleeping, or behaving in any way whatever. There is no difference between being free, like a configuration, like an existence which chooses its essence, and being absolute. There is no difference between being an absolute temporarily localized, that is, localized in history, and being universally comprehensible.

MAURICE MERLEAU-PONTY

"THE PRIMACY OF PERCEPTION AND ITS PHILOSOPHICAL CONSEQUENCES"

PRELIMINARY SUMMARY OF THE ARGUMENT

I. Perception as an Original Modality of Consciousness

The unprejudiced study of perception by psychologists has finally revealed that the perceived world is not a sum of objects (in the sense in which the sciences use this word), that our relation to the world is not that of a thinker to an object of thought, and finally that the unity of the perceived thing, as perceived by several consciousnesses, is not comparable to the unity of a proposition [*théorème*], as understood by several thinkers, any more than perceived existence is comparable to ideal existence.

As a result we cannot apply the classical distinction of form and matter to perception, nor can we conceive the perceiving subject as a consciousness which "interprets," "deciphers," or "orders" a sensible matter according to an ideal

This address to the Société française de philosophie was given shortly after the publication of Merleau-Ponty's major work, the *Phenomenology of Perception*, and it represents his attempt to summarize and defend the central thesis of that work. The following translation gives the complete text of Merleau-Ponty's address and the discussion which followed it, with the exception of a few incidental remarks unrelated to the substance of the discussion. These minimal omissions are indicated by the insertion of suspension points in the text. The discussion took place on November 23, 1946, and was published in the *Bulletin de la société française de philosophie*, vol. 49 (December, 1947), pp. 119–53.—*Translated by James M. Edie.* Reprinted by permission of Northwestern University Press.

law which it possesses. Matter is "pregnant" with its form, which is to say that in the final analysis every perception takes place within a certain horizon and ultimately in the "world." We experience a perception and its horizon "in action" [*pratiquement*] rather than by "posing" them or explicitly "knowing" them. Finally the quasi-organic relation of the perceiving subject and the world involves, in principle, the contradiction of immanence and transcendence.

2. The Generalization of These Results

Do these results have any value beyond that of psychological description? They would not if we could superimpose on the perceived world a world of ideas. But in reality the ideas to which we recur are valid only for a period of our lives or for a period in the history of our culture. Evidence is never apodictic, nor is thought timeless, though there is some progress in objectification and thought is always valid for more than an instant. The certainty of ideas is not the foundation of the certainty of perception but is, rather, based on it—in that it is perceptual experience which gives us the passage from one moment to the next and thus realizes the unity of time. In this sense all consciousness is perceptual, even the consciousness of ourselves.

3. Conclusions

The perceived world is the always presupposed foundation of all rationality, all value and all existence. This thesis does not destroy either rationality or the absolute. It only tries to bring them down to earth.

REPORT OF THE SESSION

. . .

M. Merleau-Ponty. The point of departure for these remarks is that the perceived world comprises relations and, in a general way, a type of organization which has not been recognized by classical psychology and philosophy.

If we consider an object which we perceive but one of whose sides we do not see, or if we consider objects which are not within our visual field at this moment—i.e., what is happening behind our back or what is happening in America or at the South Pole—how should we describe the existence of these absent objects or the nonvisible parts of present objects?

Should we say, as psychologists have often done, that I *represent* to myself the sides of this lamp which are not seen? If I say these sides are representations, I imply that they are not grasped as actually existing; because what is represented is not here before us, I do not actually perceive it. It is only a possible. But since the unseen sides of this lamp are not imaginary, but only hidden from view (to see them it suffices to move the lamp a little bit), I cannot say that they are representations.

Should I say that the unseen sides are somehow anticipated by me, as perceptions which would be produced necessarily if I moved, given the structure of the object? If, for example, I look at a cube, knowing the structure of the cube as it is defined in geometry, I can anticipate the perceptions which this cube will give me while I move around it. Under this hypothesis I would know the unseen side as the necessary consequence of a certain law of the development of my perception. But if I turn to perception itself, I cannot interpret it in this way because this analysis can be formulated as follows: It is *true* that the lamp has a back, that the cube has another side. But this formula, "It is true," does not correspond to what is given to me in perception. Perception does not give me truths like geometry but presences.

I grasp the unseen side as present, and I do not affirm that the back of the lamp exists in the same sense that I say the solution of a problem exists. The hidden side is present in its own way. It is in my vicinity.

Thus I should not say that the unseen sides of objects are simply possible perceptions, nor that they are the necessary conclusions of a kind of analysis or geometrical reasoning. It is not through an intellectual synthesis which would freely posit the total object that I am led from what is given to what is not actually given; that I am given, together with the visible sides of the object, the non-visible sides as well. It is, rather, a kind of practical synthesis: I can touch the lamp, and not only the side turned toward me but also the other side; I have only to extend my hand to hold it.

The classical analysis of perception reduces all our experience to the single level of what, for good reasons, is judged to be true. But when, on the contrary, I consider the whole setting [*l'entourage*] of my perception, it reveals another modality which is neither the ideal and necessary being of geometry nor the simple sensory event, the "*percipi*," and this is precisely what remains to be studied now.

But these remarks on the setting [*entourage*] of what is perceived enable us better to see the perceived itself. I perceive before me a road or a house, and I perceive them as having a certain dimension: the road may be a country road or a national highway; the house may be a shanty or a manor. These identifications presuppose that I recognize the true size of the object, quite different from that which appears to me from the point at which I am standing. It is frequently said that I restore the true size on the basis of the apparent size by analysis and conjecture. This is inexact for the very convincing reason that the apparent size of which we are speaking is not perceived by me. It is a remarkable fact that the uninstructed have no awareness of perspective and that it took a long time and much reflection for men to become aware of a perspectival deformation of objects. Thus there is no deciphering, no mediate inference from the sign to what is signified, because the alleged signs are not given to me separately from what they signify.

In the same way it is not true that I deduce the true color of an object on the basis of the color of the setting or of the lighting, which most of the time is not perceived. At this hour, since daylight is still coming through the windows, we perceive the yellowness of the artificial light, and it alters the color of objects. But when daylight disappears this yellowish color will no longer be perceived, and we will see the objects more or less in their true colors. The true color thus is not deduced, taking account of the lighting, because it appears precisely when daylight disappears.

If these remarks are true, what is the result? And how should we understand this "I perceive" which we are attempting to grasp?

We observe at once that it is impossible, as has often been said, to decompose a perception, to make it into a collection of sensations, because in it the whole is prior to the parts—and this whole is not an ideal whole. The meaning which I ultimately discover is not of the conceptual order. If it were a concept, the question would be how I can recognize it in the sense data, and it would be necessary for me to interpose between the concept and the sense data certain intermediaries, and then other intermediaries between these intermediaries, and so on. It is necessary that meaning and signs, the form and matter of perception, be related from the beginning and that, as we say, the matter of perception be "pregnant with its form."

In other words, the synthesis which constitutes the unity of the perceived objects and which gives meaning to the perceptual data is not an intellectual synthesis. Let us say with Husserl that it is a "synthesis of transition" [synthèse de transition][1]—I anticipate the unseen side of the lamp because I can touch it—or a "horizonal synthesis" [synthèse d'horizon]—the unseen side is given to me as "visible from another standpoint," at once given but only immanently. What prohibits me from treating my perception as an intellectual act is that an intellectual act would grasp the object either as possible or as necessary. But in perception it is "real"; it is given as the infinite sum of an indefinite series of perspectival views in each of which the object is given but in none of which is it given exhaustively. It is not accidental for the object to be given to me in a "deformed" way, from the point of view [place] which I occupy. That is the price of its being "real." The perceptual synthesis thus must be accomplished by the subject, which can both delimit certain perspectival aspects in the object, the only ones actually given, and at the same time go beyond them. This subject, which takes a point of view, is my body as the field of perception and action [pratique]—in so far as my gestures have a certain reach and circumscribe as my domain the whole group of objects familiar to me. Perception is here understood as a reference to a whole which can be grasped, in principle, only through certain of its parts or aspects. The perceived thing is not an ideal unity in the possession of the intellect, like a geometrical notion, for example; it is rather a totality open to a horizon of an indefinite number of perspectival views which blend with one another according to a given style, which defines the object in question.

Perception is thus paradoxical. The perceived thing itself is paradoxical; it exists only in so far as someone can perceive it. I cannot even for an instant imagine an object in itself. As Berkeley said, if I attempt to imagine some place in the world which has never been seen, the very fact that I imagine it makes me present at that place. I thus cannot conceive a perceptible place in which I am not myself present. But even the places in which I find myself are never completely given to me; the things which I see are things for me only under the condition that they always recede beyond their immediately given aspects. Thus there is a paradox of immanence and transcendence in perception. Immanence, because the perceived object cannot be foreign to him who perceives; transcendence, because it always contains something more than what is actually given. And these two elements of perception are not, properly speaking, contradictory. For if we reflect on this notion of perspective, if we reproduce the perceptual experience in our thought, we see that the kind of evidence proper to the perceived, the appearance of "something," requires both this presence and this absence.

Finally, the world itself, which (to give a first, rough definition) is the totality of perceptible things and the thing of all things, must be understood not as an object in the sense the mathematician or the physicist give to this word—that is, a kind of unified law which would cover all the partial phenomena or as a fundamental relation verifiable in all—but as the universal style of all possible perceptions. We must make this notion of the world, which guides the whole transcendental deduction of Kant, though Kant does not tell us its provenance, more explicit. "If a world is to be possible," he says sometimes, as if he were thinking before the origin of the world, as if he were assisting at its genesis and could pose its *a priori* conditions. In fact, as Kant himself said profoundly, we can only think the world because we have already experienced it; it is through this experience that we have the idea of being, and it is through this experience that the words "rational" and "real" receive a meaning simultaneously.

If I now consider not the problem of knowing how it is that there are things for me or how it is that I have a unified, unique, and developing perceptual experience of them, but rather the problem of knowing how my experience is related to the experience which others have of the same objects, perception will again appear as the paradoxical phenomenon which renders being accessible to us.

If I consider my perceptions as simple sensations, they are private; they are mine alone. If I treat them as acts of the intellect, if perception is an inspection of the mind, and the perceived object an idea, then you and I are talking about the same world, and we have *the right* to communicate among ourselves because the world has become an ideal existence and is the same for all of us—just like the Pythagorean theorem. But neither of these two formulas accounts for our experience. If a friend and I are standing before a landscape, and if I attempt to show my friend something which I see and which he does not yet see, we cannot account for the situation by saying that I see something in my own world and that I attempt, by sending verbal messages, to give rise to an analogous perception in the world of my friend. There are not two numerically distinct worlds plus a mediating language which alone would bring us together. There is—and I know it very well if I become impatient with him—a kind of demand that what I see be seen by him also. And at the same time this communication is required by the very thing which I am looking at, by the reflections of sunlight upon it, by its color, by its sensible evidence. The thing imposes itself not as true for every intellect, but as real for every subject who is standing where I am.

I will never know how you see red, and you will never know how I see it; but this separation of consciousnesses is recognized only after a failure of communication, and our first movement is to believe in an undivided being between us. There is no reason to treat this primordial communication as an illusion, as the sensationalists do, because even then it would become inexplicable. And there is no reason to base it on our common participation in the same intellectual consciousness because this would suppress the undeniable plurality of consciousnesses. It is thus necessary that, in the perception of another, I find myself in relation with another "myself," who is, in principle, open to the same truths as I am, in relation to the same being that I am. And this perception is realized. From the depths of my subjectivity I see another subjectivity invested with equal rights appear, because the behavior of the other takes place within my perceptual field. I understand this behavior, the words of another; I espouse his thought because this other, born in the midst of my phenomena, appropriates them and treats them in accord with typical behaviors which I myself have experienced. Just as my body, as the system of all my holds on the world, founds the unity of the objects which I perceive, in the same way the body of the other—as the bearer of symbolic behaviors and of the behavior of true reality—tears itself away from being one of my phenomena, offers me the task of a true communication, and confers on my objects the new dimension of intersubjective being or, in other words, of objectivity. Such are, in a quick résumé, the elements of a description of the perceived world.

Some of our colleagues who were so kind as to send me their observations in writing grant me that all this is valid as a psychological inventory. But, they add, there remains the world of which we say "It is true"—that is to say, the world of knowledge, the verified world, the world of science. Psychological description concerns only a small section of our experience, and there is no reason, according to them, to give such descriptions any universal value. They do not touch being itself but only the psychological peculiarities of perception. These descriptions, they add, are all the less admissible as being in any way definitive because they are contradicted by the perceived world. How can we admit ultimate contradictions? Perceptual experience is contradictory because it is confused. It is necessary to think it. When we think it, its contradictions disappear under the light of the intellect. Finally, one correspondent tells me that we are invited to return to the perceived world as we experience it. That is to say that there is no need to reflect or to think and that perception knows better than we what it is doing. How can this disavowal of reflection be philosophy?

It is true that we arrive at contradictions when we describe the perceived world. And it is also true that if there were such a thing as a non-contradictory thought, it would exclude the world of perception as a simple appearance. But the question is precisely to know whether there is such a thing as logically coherent thought or thought in the pure state. This is the question Kant asked himself and the objection which I have just sketched is a pre-Kantian objection. One of Kant's discoveries, whose consequences we have not yet fully grasped, is that all our experience of the world is throughout a tissue of concepts which lead to irreducible contradictions if we attempt to take them in an absolute sense or transfer them into pure being, and that they nevertheless found the structure of all our phenomena, of everything which *is* for us. It would take too long to show (and besides it is well known) that Kantian philosophy itself failed to utilize this principle fully and that both its investigation of experience and its critique of dogmatism remained incomplete. I wish only to point out that the accusation of contradiction is not decisive, *if the acknowledged contradiction appears as the very condition of consciousness*. It is in this sense that Plato and Kant, to mention only them, accepted the contradiction of which Zeno and Hume wanted no part. There is a vain form of contradiction which consists in affirming two theses which exclude one another at the same time and under the same aspect. And there are philosophies which show contradictions present at the very heart of time and of all relationships. There is the sterile non-contradiction of formal logic and the justified contradictions of transcendental logic. The objection with which we are concerned would be admissible only if we could put a system of eternal truths in the place of the perceived world, freed from its contradictions.

We willingly admit that we cannot rest satisfied with the description of the perceived world as we have sketched it up to now and that it appears as a psychological curiosity if we leave aside the idea of the true world, the world as thought by the understanding. This leads us, therefore, to the second point which I propose to examine: what is the relation between intellectual consciousness and perceptual consciousness?

Before taking this up, let us say a word about the other objection which was addressed to us: you go back to the unreflected [*irréfléchi*]; therefore you renounce reflection. It is true that we discover the unreflected. But the unreflected we go back to is not that which is prior to philosophy or prior to reflection. It is the unreflected which is understood and conquered by reflection. Left to itself, perception forgets itself and is ignorant of its own accomplishments. Far from thinking that philosophy is a useless repetition of life I think, on the contrary, that without reflection life would probably dissipate itself in ignorance of itself or in chaos. But this does not mean that reflection should be carried away with itself or pretend to be ignorant of its origins. By fleeing difficulties it would only fail in its task.

Should we now generalize and say that what is true of perception is also true in the order of the intellect and that in a general way all our experience, all our knowledge, has the same fundamental structures, the same synthesis of transition, the same kind of horizons which we have found in perceptual experience?

No doubt the absolute truth or evidence of scientific knowledge would be opposed to this idea. But it seems to me that the acquisitions of the philosophy of the sciences confirm the primacy of perception. Does not the work of the French school at the beginning of this century, and the work of Brunschvicg, show that scientific knowledge cannot be closed in on itself, that it is always an approximate knowledge, and that it consists in clarifying a pre-scientific world the analysis of which will never be finished? Physico-mathematical relations take on a physical sense only to the extent that we at the same time represent to ourselves the sensible things to which these relations ultimately apply. Brunschvicg reproached positivism for its dogmatic illusion that the law is truer than the fact. The law, he adds, is conceived exclusively to make the fact intelligible. The perceived happening can never be reabsorbed in the complex of transparent relations which the intellect constructs because of the happening. But if this is the case, philosophy is not only consciousness of these relations; it is also consciousness of the obscure element and of the "non-relational foundation" on which these relations are based. Otherwise it would shirk its task of universal clarification. When I think the Pythagorean theorem and recognize it as true, it is clear that this truth is not for this moment only. Nevertheless later progress in knowledge will show that it is not yet a final, unconditioned evidence and that, if the Pythagorean theorem and the Euclidean system once appeared as final, unconditioned evidences, that is itself the mark of a certain cultural epoch. Later developments would not annul the Pythagorean theorem but would put it back in its place as a partial, and also an abstract, truth. Thus here also we do not have a timeless truth but rather the recovery of one time by another time, just as, on the level of perception, our certainty about perceiving a given thing does not guarantee that our experience will not be contradicted, or dispense us from a fuller experience of that thing. Naturally it is necessary to establish here a difference between ideal truth and perceived truth. I do not propose to undertake this immense task just now. I am only trying to show the organic tie, so to speak, between perception and intellection. Now it is incontestable that I dominate the stream of my conscious states and even that I am unaware of their temporal succession. At the moment when I am thinking or considering an idea, I am not divided into the instants of my life. But it is also incontestable that this domination of time, which is the work of thought, is always somewhat deceiving. Can I seriously say that I will always hold the ideas I do at present—and mean it? Do I not know that in six months, in a year, even if I use more or less the same formulas to express my thoughts, they will have changed their meaning slightly? Do I not know that there is a life of ideas, as there is a meaning of everything I experience, and that every one of my most convincing thoughts will need additions and then will be, not destroyed, but at least integrated into a new unity? This is the only conception of knowledge that is scientific and not mythological.

Thus perception and thought have this much in common—that both of them have a future horizon and a past horizon and that they appear to themselves as temporal, even though they do not move at the same speed nor in the same time. We must say that at each moment our ideas express not only the truth but also our capacity to attain it at that given moment. Skepticism begins if we conclude from this that our ideas are always false. But this can only happen with reference to some idol of absolute knowledge. We must say, on the contrary, that our ideas, however limited they may be at a given moment—since they always express our contact with being and with culture—are capable of being true provided we keep them open to the field of nature and culture which they must express. And this possibility is always open to us, just because we are temporal. The idea of going straight to the essence of things is an inconsistent idea if one thinks about it. What is given is a route, an experience which gradually clarifies itself, which gradually rectifies itself and proceeds by dialogue with itself and with others. Thus what we tear away from the dispersion of instants is not an already-made reason; it is, as has always been said, a natural light, our openness to *something*. What saves us is the possibility of a new development, and our power of making even what is false, true—by thinking through our errors and replacing them within the domain of truth.

But finally, it will be objected that I grasp myself in pure reflexion, completely outside perception, and that I grasp myself not now as a perceiving subject, tied by its body to a system of things, but as a thinking subject, radically free with respect to things and with respect to the body. How is such an experience of self, of the *cogito,* possible in our perspective, and what meaning does it have?

There is a first way of understanding the *cogito:* it consists in saying that when I grasp myself I am limited to noting, so to speak, a psychic fact, "I think." This is an instantaneous constatation, and under the condition that the experience has no duration I adhere immediately to what I think and consequently cannot doubt it. This is the *cogito* of the psychologists. It is of this instantaneous *cogito* that Descartes was thinking when he said that I am certain that I exist during the whole time that I am thinking of it. Such certitude is limited to my existence and to my pure and completely naked thought. As soon as I make it specific with any particular thought, I fail, because, as Descartes explains, every particular thought uses premises not actually given. Thus the first truth, understood in this way, is the only truth. Or rather it cannot even be formulated as truth; it is experienced in the instant and in silence. The *cogito* understood in this way—in the skeptical way—does not account for our idea of truth.

There is a second way of understanding the *cogito:* as the grasping not only of the fact that I think but also of the objects which this thought intends, and as evidence not only of a private existence but also of the things which it thinks, at least as it thinks them. In this perspective the *cogito* is neither more certain than the *cogitatum,* nor does it have a different kind of certainty. Both are possessed of ideal evidence. Descartes sometimes presented the *cogito* in this way—as, for example, in the *Regulae* when he placed one's own existence (*se esse*) among the most simple evidences. This supposes that the subject is perfectly transparent for itself, like an essence, and is incompatible with the idea of the hyperbolic doubt which even reaches to essences.

But there is a third meaning of the *cogito,* the only solid one: the act of doubting in which I put in question all possible objects of my experience. This act grasps itself in its own operation [*à l'oeuvre*] and thus cannot doubt itself. The very fact of doubting obturates doubt. The certitude I have of myself is here a veritable perception: I grasp myself, not as a constituting subject which is transparent to itself, and which constitutes the totality of every possible object of thought and experience, but as a particular thought, as a thought engaged with certain objects, as a thought in act; and it is in this sense that I am certain of myself. Thought is given to itself; I somehow find myself thinking and I become aware of it. In this sense I am certain that I am thinking this or that as well as being certain that I am simply thinking. Thus I can get outside the psychological *cogito*—without, however, taking myself to be a universal thinker. I am not simply a constituted happening; I am not a universal thinker [*naturant*].[2] I am a thought which recaptures itself as already possessing an ideal of truth (which it cannot at each moment wholly account for) and which is the horizon of its operations. This thought, which *feels* itself rather than *sees* itself, which searches after clarity rather than possesses it, and which creates truth rather than finds it, is described in a formerly celebrated text of Lagneau. Should we submit to life or create it, he asked. And he answered: "Once again this question does not pertain to the domain of the intellect; we are free and, in this sense, skepticism is true. But to answer negatively is to make the world and the self unintelligible; it is to decree chaos and above all to establish it in the self. But chaos is nothing. To be or not to be, the self and everything else, we must choose" (*Cours sur l'existence de dieu*). I find here, in an author who spent his whole life reflecting on Descartes, Spinoza, and Kant, the idea—sometimes considered barbarous— of a thought which remembers it began in time and then sovereignly recaptures itself and in which fact, reason, and freedom coincide.

Finally, let us ask what happens, from such a point of view, to rationality and experience, whether there can be any absolute affirmation already implied in experience.

The fact that my experiences hold together and that I experience the concordance of my own experiences with those of others is in no way compromised by what we have just said. On the contrary, this fact is put in relief, against skepticism. Something appears to me, as to anyone else, and these phenomena, which set the boundaries of everything thinkable or conceivable for us, are certain as phenomena. There is meaning. But rationality is neither a total nor an immediate guarantee. It is somehow open, which is to say that it is menaced.

Doubtless this thesis is open to two types of criticism, one from the psychological side and the other from the philosophical side.

The very psychologists who have described the perceived world as I did above, the Gestalt psychologists, have never drawn the philosophical conclusions of their description. In that respect they remain within the classical framework. Ultimately they consider the structures of the perceived world as the simple result of certain physical and physiological processes which take place in the nervous system and completely determine the *gestalten* and the experience of the *gestalten*. The organism and consciousness itself are only functions of external physical variables. Ultimately the real world is the physical world as science conceives it, and it engenders our consciousness itself.

But the question is whether Gestalt theory, after the work it has done in calling attention to the phenomena of the perceived world, can fall back on the classical notion of reality and objectivity and incorporate the world of the *gestalten* within this classical conception of reality. Without doubt one of the most important acquisitions of this theory has been its overcoming of the classical alternatives between objective psychology and introspective psychology. Gestalt psychology went beyond this alternative by showing that the object of psychology is the structure of behavior, accessible both from within and from without. In his book on the chimpanzees, Köhler applied this idea and showed that in order to describe the behavior of a chimpanzee it is necessary, in characterizing this behavior, to bring in notions such as the "melodic line" of behavior. These are anthropomorphic notions, but they can be utilized objectively because it is possible to agree on interpreting "melodic" and "non-melodic" behaviors in terms of "good solutions" and "bad solutions." The science of psychology thus is not something constructed outside the human world; it is, in fact, a property of the human world to make the distinction between the true and the false, the objective and the fictional. When, later on, Gestalt psychology tried to explain itself—in spite of its own discoveries—in terms of a scientistic or positivistic ontology, it was at the price of an internal contradiction which we have to reject.

Coming back to the perceived world as we have described it above, and basing our conception of reality on the phenomena, we do not in any way sacrifice objectivity to the interior life, as Bergson has been accused of doing. As Gestalt psychology has shown, structure, *Gestalt,* meaning are no less visible in objectively observable behavior than in the experience of ourselves—provided, of course, that objectivity is not confused with what is measurable. Is one truly objective with respect to man when he thinks he can take him as an object which can be explained as an intersection of processes and causalities? Is it not more objective to attempt to constitute a true science of human life based on the description of typical behaviors? Is it objective to apply tests to man which deal only with abstract aptitudes, or to attempt to grasp the situation of man as he is present to the world and to others by means of still more tests?

Psychology as a science has nothing to fear from a return to the perceived world, nor from a philosophy which draws out the consequences of this return. Far from hurting psychology, this attitude, on the contrary, clarifies the philosophical meaning of its discoveries. For there are not two truths; there is not an inductive psychology and an intuitive philosophy. Psychological induction is never more than the methodological means of bringing to light a certain typical behavior, and if induction includes intuition, conversely intuition does not occur in empty space. It exercises itself on the facts, on the material, on the phenomena brought to light by scientific research. There are not two kinds of knowledge, but two different degrees of clarification of the same knowledge. Psychology and philosophy are nourished by the same phenomena; it is only that the problems become more formalized at the philosophical level.

But the philosophers might say here that we are giving psychology too big a place, that we are compromising rationality by founding it on the texture of experience, as it is manifested in perceptual experience. But either the demand for an absolute rationality is only a wish, a personal preference which should not be confused with philosophy, or this point of view, to the extent that it is well-founded, satisfies it as well as, or even better than, any other. When philosophers wish to place reason above the vicissitudes of history they cannot purely and simply forget what psychology, sociology, ethnography, history, and psychiatry have taught us about the conditioning of human behavior. It would be a very romantic way of showing one's love for reason to base its reign on the disavowal of acquired knowledge. What can be validly demanded is that man never be submitted to the fate of an external nature or history and stripped of his consciousness. Now my philosophy satisfies this demand. In speaking of the primacy of perception, I have never, of course, meant to say (this would be a return to the theses of empiricism) that science, reflection, and philosophy are only transformed sensations or that values are deferred and calculated pleasures. By these words, the "primacy of perception," we mean that the experience of perception is our presence at the moment when things, truths, values are constituted for us; that perception is a nascent *logos*; that it teaches us, outside all dogmatism, the true conditions of objectivity itself; that it summons us to the tasks of knowledge and action. It is not a question of reducing human knowledge to sensation, but of assisting at the birth of this knowledge, to make it as sensible as the sensible, to recover the consciousness of rationality. This experience of rationality is lost when we take it for granted as self-evident, but is, on the contrary, rediscovered when it is made to appear against the background of non-human nature.

The work[3] which was the occasion for this paper is still, in this respect, only a preliminary study, since it hardly speaks of culture or of history. On the basis of perception—taken as a privileged realm of experience, since the perceived object is by definition present and living—this book attempts to define a method for getting closer to present and living reality, and which must then be applied to the relation of man to man in language, in knowledge, in society and religion, as it was applied in this work to man's relation to perceptible reality and with respect to man's relation to others on the level of perceptual experience. We call this level of experience "primordial"—not to assert that everything else derives from it by transformations and evolution (we have expressly said that man perceives in a way different from any animal) but rather that it reveals to us the permanent data of the problem which culture attempts to resolve. If we have not tied the subject to the determinism of an external nature and have only replaced it in the bed of the perceptible, which it transforms without ever quitting it, much less will we submit the subject to some impersonal history. History is other people; it is the interrelationships we establish with them, outside of which the realm of the ideal appears as an alibi.

This leads us . . . to draw certain conclusions from what has preceded as concerns the realm of the practical. If we admit that our life is inherent to the perceived world and the human world, even while it re-creates it and contributes to its making, then morality cannot consist in the private adherence to a system of values. Principles are mystifications unless they are put into practice; it is necessary that they animate our relations with others. Thus we cannot remain indifferent to the aspect in which our acts appear to others, and the question is posed whether intention suffices as moral justification. It is clear that the approval of such or such a group proves nothing, since, in looking for it, we choose our own judges—which comes down to saying that we are not yet thinking for ourselves. It is the very demand of rationality which imposes on us the need to act in such a way that our action cannot be considered by others as an act of aggression but, on the contrary, as generously meeting the other in the very particularity of a given situation. Now from the very moment when we start bringing the consequences of our actions for others into morality (and how can we avoid doing so if the universality of the act is to be anything more than a word?), it appears possible that our relations with others are involved in immorality, if perchance our perspectives are irreconcilable—if, for instance, the legitimate interests of one nation are incompatible with those of another. Nothing guarantees us that morality is possible, as Kant said in a passage which has not yet been fully understood. But even less is there any fatal assurance that morality is impossible. We observe it in an experience which is the perception of others, and, by sketching here the dangerous consequences which this position entails, we are very much aware of its difficulties—some of which we might wish to avoid. Just as the perception of a thing opens me up to being, by realizing the paradoxical synthesis of an infinity of perceptual aspects, in the same way the perception of the other founds morality by realizing the paradox of an *alter ego*, of a common situation, by placing my perspectives and my incommunicable solitude in the visual field of another and of all the others. Here as everywhere else the primacy of perception—the realization, at the very heart of our most personal experience, of a fecund contradiction which submits this experience to the regard of others—is the remedy to skepticism and pessimism. If we admit that sensibility is enclosed within itself, and if we do not seek communication with the truth and with others except on the level of a disembodied reason, then there is not much to hope for. Nothing is more pessimistic or skeptical than the famous text in which Pascal, asking himself what it is to love, remarks that one does not love a woman for her beauty, which is perishable, or for her mind, which she can lose, and then suddenly concludes: "One never loves anybody; one loves only qualities." Pascal is proceeding like the skeptic who asks *if* the world exists, remarks that the table is only a sum of sensations, the chair another sum of sensations, and finally concludes: one never sees anything; one sees only sensations.

If, on the contrary, as the primacy of perception requires, we call what we perceive "the world," and what we love "the person," there is a type of doubt concerning man, and a type of spite, which become impossible. Certainly, the world which we thus find is not absolutely reassuring. We weigh the hardihood of the love which promises beyond what it knows, which claims to be eternal when a sickness, perhaps an accident, will destroy it . . . But it is *true*, at the moment of this promise, that our love extends beyond *qualities,* beyond the body, beyond time, even though we could not love without qualities, bodies, and time. In order to safeguard the ideal unity of love, Pascal breaks human life into fragments at will and reduces the person to a discontinuous series of states. The absolute which he looks for beyond our experience is implied in it. Just as I grasp time through my present and by being present, I perceive others through my individual life, in the tension of an experience which transcends itself.

There is thus no destruction of the absolute or of rationality here, only of the absolute and the rationality separated from experience. To tell the truth, Christianity consists in replacing the separated absolute by the absolute in men. Nietzsche's idea that God is dead is already contained in the Christian idea of the death of God. God ceases to be an external object in order to mingle in human life, and this life is not simply a return to a non-temporal conclusion. God needs human history. As Malebranche said, the world is unfinished. My viewpoint differs from the Christian viewpoint to the extent that the Christian believes in another side of things where the *"renversement due pour au contre"* takes place. In my view this "reversal" takes place before our eyes. And perhaps some Christians would agree that the other side of things must already be visible in the environment in which we live. By advancing this thesis of the primacy of perception, I have less the feeling that I am proposing something completely new than the feeling of drawing out the conclusions of the work of my predecessors.

NOTES

1. The more usual term in Husserl is "passive synthesis," which designates the "syntheses" of perceptual consciousness as opposed to the "active syntheses" of imagination and categorial thought.—*Trans.*
2. The reference is to Spinoza's *natura naturans.*—*Trans.*
3. The *Phenomenology of Perception.*—*Trans.*

CLAUDE LÉVI-STRAUSS

"LANGUAGE AND THE ANALYSIS OF SOCIAL LAWS"

In a recent work, whose importance from the point of view of the future of the social sciences can hardly be overestimated, Wiener poses, and resolves in the negative, the question of a possible extension to the social sciences of the mathematical methods of prediction which have made possible the construction of the great modern electronic machines. He justifies his position by two arguments.[1]

In the first place, he maintains that the nature of the social sciences is such that it is inevitable that their very development have repercussions on the object of their investigation. The coupling of the observer with the observed phenomenon is well known to contemporary scientific thought, and, in a sense, it illustrates a universal situation. But it is negligible in fields which are ripe for the most advanced mathematical investigation; as, for example, in astrophysics, where the object has such vast dimensions that the influence of the observer need not be taken into account, or in atomic physics, where the object is so small that we are interested only in average mass effects in which the effect of bias on the part of the observer plays no role. In the field of the social sciences, on the contrary, the object of study is necessarily affected by the intervention of

"Language and the Analysis of Social Laws" from *Structural Anthropology, Volume 1* by Claude Lévi-Strauss. English translation copyright © 1963 by Basic Books, Inc. Reprinted by permission of Basic Books, a division of HarperCollins Publishers, Inc.

the observer, and the resulting modifications are *on the same scale* as the phenomena that are studied.

In the second place, Wiener observes that the phenomena subjected to sociological or anthropological inquiry are defined within our own sphere of interests; they concern questions of the life, education, career, and death of individuals. Therefore the statistical runs available for the study of a given phenomenon are always far too short to lay the foundation of a valid induction. Mathematical analysis in the field of social science, he concludes, can bring results which should be of as little interest to the social scientist as those of the statistical study of a gas would be to an individual about the size of a molecule.

These objections seem difficult to refute when they are examined in terms of the investigations toward which their author has directed them, the data of research monographs and of applied anthropology. In such cases, we are dealing with a study of individual behavior, directed by an observer who is himself an individual; or with a study of a culture, a national character, or a pattern, by an observer who cannot dissociate himself completely from his culture, or from the culture out of which his working hypotheses and his methods of observation, which are themselves cultural patterns, are derived.

There is, however, at least one area of the social sciences where Wiener's objections do not seem to be applicable, where the conditions which he sets as a requirement for a valid mathematical study seem to be rigorously met. This is the field of language, when studied in the light of structural linguistics, with particular reference to phonemics.

Language is a social phenomenon; and, of all social phenomena, it is the one which manifests to the greatest degree two fundamental characteristics which make it susceptible of scientific study. In the first place, much of linguistic behavior lies on the level of unconscious thought. When we speak, we are not conscious of the syntactic and morphological laws of our language. Moreover, we are not ordinarily conscious of the phonemes that we employ to convey different meanings; and we are rarely, if ever, conscious of the phonological oppositions which reduce each phoneme to a bundle of distinctive features. This absence of consciousness, moreover, still holds when we do become aware of the grammar or the phonemics of our language. For, while this awareness is the privilege of the scholar, language, as a matter of fact, lives and develops only as a collective construct; and even the scholar's linguistic knowledge always remains dissociated from his experience as a speaking agent, for his mode of speech is not affected by his ability to interpret his language on a higher level. We may say, then, that insofar as language is concerned we need not fear the influence of the observer on the observed phenomenon, because the observer cannot modify the phenomenon merely by becoming conscious of it.

Furthermore, as regards Wiener's second point, we know that language appeared very early in human history. Therefore, even if we can study it scientifically only when written documents are available, writing itself goes back a considerable distance and furnishes long enough runs to make language a valid subject for mathematical analysis. For example, the series we have at our disposal in studying Indo-European, Semitic, or Sino-Tibetan languages is about four or five thousand years old. And, where a comparable temporal dimension is lacking, the multiplicity of coexistent forms furnishes, for several other linguistic families, a spatial dimension that is no less valuable.

We thus find in language a social phenomenon that manifests both independence of the observer and long statistical runs, which would seem to indicate that language is a phenomenon fully qualified to satisfy the demands of mathematicians for the type of analysis Wiener suggests.

It is, in fact, difficult to see why certain linguistic problems could not be solved by modern calculating machines. With knowledge of the phonological structure of a language and the laws which govern the groupings of consonants and vowels, a student could easily use a machine to compute all the combinations of phonemes constituting the words of n syllables existing in the vocabulary, or even the number of combinations compatible with the structure of the language under consideration, such as previously defined. With a machine into which would be "fed" the equations regulating the types of structures with which phonemics usually deals, the repertory of sound which human speech organs can emit, and the minimal differential values, determined by psycho-physiological methods, which distinguish between the phonemes closest to one another, one would doubtless be able to obtain a computation of the totality of phonological structures for n oppositions (n being as high as one wished). One could thus construct a sort of periodic table of linguistic structures that would be comparable to the table of elements which Mendeleieff introduced into modern chemistry. It would then remain for us only to check the place of known languages in this table, to identify the positions and the relationships of the languages whose first-hand study is still too imperfect to give us a proper theoretical knowledge of them, and to discover the place of languages that have disappeared or are unknown, yet to come, or simply possible.

To add a last example: Jakobson has suggested that a language may possess several coexisting phonological structures, each of which may intervene in a different kind of grammatical operation.[2] Since there must obviously be a relationship between the different structural modalities of the same language, we arrive at the concept of a "metastructure" which would be something like the law of the group (loi du groupe) consisting of its modal structures. If all of these modalities could be analyzed by our machine, established mathematical methods would permit it to construct the "metastructure" of the language, which would in certain complex cases be so intricate as to make it difficult, if not impossible, to achieve on the basis of purely empirical investigation.

The problem under discussion here can, then, be defined as follows. Among all social phenomena, language alone has thus far been studied in a manner which permits it to serve as the object of truly scientific analysis, allowing us to understand its formative process and to predict its mode of change. This results from modern researches into the problems of phonemics, which have reached beyond the superficial conscious and historical expression of linguistic phenomena to attain fundamental and objective realities consisting of systems of relations which are the products of unconscious thought processes. The question which now arises is this: Is it possible to effect a similar reduction in the analysis of other forms of social phenomena? If so, would this analysis lead to the same result? And if the answer to this last question is in the affirmative, can we conclude that all forms of social life are substantially of the same nature—that is, do they consist of systems of behavior that represent the projection, on the level of conscious and socialized thought, of universal laws which regulate the unconscious activities of the mind? Obviously, no attempt can be made here to do more than to sketch this problem by indicating certain points of reference and projecting the principal lines along which its orientation might be effective.

Some of the researches of Kroeber appear to be of the greatest importance in suggesting approaches to our problem, particularly his work on changes in the styles of women's dress.[3] Fashion actually is, in the highest degree, a phenomenon that depends on the unconscious activity of the mind. We rarely take note of why a particular style pleases us or falls into disuse. Kroeber has demonstrated that this seemingly arbitrary evolution follows definite laws. These laws cannot be reached by purely empirical observation, or by intuitive consideration of phenomena, but result from measuring some basic relationships between the various elements of costume. The relationship thus obtained can be expressed in terms of mathematical functions, whose values, calculated at a given moment, make prediction possible.

Kroeber has thus shown how even such a highly arbitrary aspect of social behavior is susceptible of scientific study. His method may be usefully compared not only with that of structural linguistics, but also with that of the natural sciences. There is a remarkable analogy between these researches and those of a contemporary biologist, G. Teissier, on the growth of the organs of certain crustaceans.[4] Teissier has shown that, in order to formulate the laws of this growth, it is necessary to consider the relative dimensions of the component parts of the claws, and not the exterior forms of those organs. Here, relationships allow us to derive constants—termed parameters—from which it is possible to derive the laws which govern the development of these organisms. The object of a scientific zoology, in these terms, is thus not ultimately concerned with the forms of animals and their organs as they are usually perceived, but with the establishment of certain abstract and measurable relationships, which constitute the basic nature of the phenomena under study.

An analogous method has been followed in studying certain features of social organization, particularly marriage rules and kinship systems.[5] It has been shown that the complete set of marriage regulations operating in human societies, and usually classified under different headings, such as incest prohibitions, preferential forms of marriage, and the like, can be interpreted as being so many different ways of insuring the circulation of women within the social group or of substituting the mechanism of a sociologically determined affinity for that of a biologically determined consanguinity. Proceeding from this hypothesis, it would only be necessary to make a mathematical study of every possible type of exchange between *n* partners to enable one almost automatically to arrive at every type of marriage rule actually operating in living societies and, eventually, to discover other rules that are merely possible; one would also understand their function and the relationships between each type and the others.

This approach was fully validated by the demonstration, reached by pure deduction, that the mechanisms of reciprocity known to classical anthropology—namely, those based on dual organization and exchange-marriage between two partners or partners whose number is a multiple of two—are but a special instance of a wider kind of reciprocity between any number of partners. This fact has tended to remain unnoticed, because the partners in those matings, instead of giving and receiving from each other, do not give to those from whom they receive and do not receive from those to whom they give. They give to and receive from different partners to whom they are bound by a relationship that operates only in one direction.

This type of organization, no less important than the moiety system, has thus far been observed and described only imperfectly and incidentally. Starting with the results of mathematical study, data had to be compiled; thus, the real extension of the system was shown and its first theoretical analysis offered.[6] At the same time, it became possible to explain the more general features of marriage rules such as preferential marriage between bilateral cross-cousins or with only one kind of cross-cousin, on the father's side (patrilateral), or on that of the mother (matrilateral). Thus, for example, though such customs had been unintelligible to anthropologists,[7] they were perfectly clear when regarded as illustrating different modalities of the laws of exchange. In turn, these were reduced to a still more basic relationship between the rules of residence and the rules of descent.[8]

Now, these results can be achieved only by treating marriage regulations and kinship systems as a kind of language, a set of processes permitting the establishment, between individuals and groups, of a certain type of communication. That the mediating factor, in this case, should be the *women of the group,* who are *circulated* between clans, lineages, or families, in place of the *words of the group,* which are *circulated* between individuals, does not at all change the fact that the essential aspect of the phenomenon is identical in both cases.

We may now ask whether, in extending the concept of communication so as to make it include exogamy and the rules flowing from the prohibition of incest, we may not, reciprocally, achieve insight into a problem that is still very obscure, that of the origin of language. For marriage regulations, in relation to language, represent a much more crude and archaic complex. It is generally recognized that words are signs; but poets are practically the only ones who know that words were also once values. As against this, women are held by the social group to be values of the most essential kind, though we have difficulty in understanding how these values become integrated in systems endowed with a significant function. This ambiguity is clearly manifested in the reactions of persons who, on the basis of the analysis of social structures referred to,[9] have laid against it the charge of "anti-feminism," because women are referred to as objects.[10] Of course, it may be disturbing to some to have women conceived as mere parts of a meaningful system. However, one should keep in mind that the processes by which phonemes and words have lost—even though in an illusory manner—their character of value, to become reduced to pure signs, will never lead to the same results in matters concerning women. For words do not speak, while women do; as producers of signs, women can never be reduced to the status of symbols or tokens. But it is for this very reason that the position of women, as actually found in this system of communication between men that is made up of marriage regulations and kinship nomenclature, may afford us a workable image of the type of relationships that could have existed at a very early period in the development of language, between human beings and their words. As in the case of women, the original impulse which compelled men to exchange words must be sought for in that split representation that pertains to the symbolic function. For, since certain terms are simultaneously perceived as having a value both for the speaker and the listener, the only way to resolve this contradiction is in the exchange of complementary values, to which all social existence is reduced.

These speculations may be judged utopian. Yet, if one considers that the assumptions made here are legitimate, a very important consequence follows, one that is susceptible of immediate verification. That is, the question may be raised whether the different aspects of social life (including even art and religion) cannot only be studied by the methods of, and with the help of concepts similar to those employed in linguistics, but also whether they do not constitute phenomena whose inmost nature is the same as that of language. That is, in the words of Voegelin, we may ask whether there are not only "operational" but also "substantial comparabilities" between language and culture.[11]

How can this hypothesis be verified? It will be necessary to develop the analysis of the different features of social life, either for a given society or for a complex of societies, so that a deep enough level can be reached to make it possible to cross from one to the other; or to express the specific structure of each in terms of a sort of general language, valid for each system separately and for all of them taken together. It would thus be possible to ascertain if one had reached their inner nature and to determine if this pertained to the same kind of reality. In order to develop this point, an experiment can be attempted. It will consist, on the part of the anthropologist, in translating the basic features of the kinship systems from different parts of the world into terms general enough to be meaningful to the linguist, and thus be equally applicable by the linguist to the description of languages from the same regions. Both could thus ascertain whether or not different types of communication systems in the same societies—that is, kinship and language—are or are not caused by identical unconscious structures. Should this be the case, we could be assured of having reached a truly fundamental formulation.

If then, a substantial identity were assumed to exist between language structure and kinship systems, one should find, in the following regions of the world, languages whose structures would be of a type comparable to kinship systems in the following terms:

(1) *Indo-European:* As concerns the *kinship systems,* we find that the marriage regulations of our contemporary civilization are entirely based on the principle that, a few negative prescriptions being granted, the density and fluidity of the population will achieve by itself the same results which other societies have sought in more complicated sets of rules; i.e., social cohesion obtained by marriage in degrees far removed or even impossible to trace. This statistical solution has its origin in a typical feature of most ancient Indo-European systems. These belong, in the author's terminology, to a simple formula of generalized reciprocity (*formule simple de l'échange généralisé*).[12] However, instead of prevailing between lineages, this formula operates between more complex units of the *bratsvo* type, which actually are clusters of lineages, each of which enjoys a certain freedom within the rigid framework of general reciprocity effective at the cluster level. Therefore, it can be said that a characteristic feature of Indo-European kinship structure lies in the fact that a problem set in simple terms always admits of many solutions.

Should the linguistic structure be homologous with the kinship structure it would thus be possible to express the basic feature of Indo-European languages as follows: The languages have simple structures, utilizing numerous elements. The opposition between the *simplicity of the structure* and the *multiplicity of elements* is expressed in the fact that several elements compete to occupy the same positions in the structure.

(2) *Sino-Tibetan kinship systems* exhibit quite a different type of complexity. They belong to or derive directly from the simplest form of general reciprocity, namely, mother's brother's daughter marriage, so that, as has been shown,[13] while this type of marriage insures social cohesion in the simplest way, at the same time it permits this to be indefinitely extended so as to include any number of participants.

Translated into more general terms applicable to language that would correspond to the following linguistic pattern, we may say that the structure is complex, while the elements are few, a feature that may be related to the tonal structure of these languages.

(3) The typical feature of *African kinship systems* is the extension of the bride-wealth system, coupled with a rather frequent prohibition on marriage with the wife's brother's wife. The joint result is a system of general reciprocity more complex than the mother's brother's daughter system, while the types of unions resulting from the circulation of the marriage-price approaches, to some extent, the statistical mechanism operating in our own society.

Therefore one could say that African languages have several modalities corresponding in general to a position intermediate between (1) and (2).

(4) The widely recognized features of *Oceanic kinship systems* seem to lead to the following formulation of the basic characteristics of the linguistic pattern: simple structure and few elements.

(5) The originality of *American Indian kinship systems* lies in the so-called Crow-Omaha type, which should be carefully distinguished from other types showing the same disregard for generation levels.[14] The important point with the Crow-Omaha type is not that two kinds of cross-cousins are classified in different generation levels, but rather that they are classified with consanguineous kin instead of with affinal kin (as is the case, for instance, in the Miwok system). But systems of the Miwok type belong equally to the Old and the New World; while the differential systems just referred to as Crow-Omaha are, apart from a few exceptions, typical only for the New World. It can be shown that this quite exceptional feature of the Crow-Omaha system resulted from the simultaneous application of the two simple formulas of reciprocity, both special and general (*échange restreint* and *échange généralisé*),[15] which elsewhere in the world were generally considered to be incompatible. It thus became possible to achieve marriage within remote degrees by using simultaneously two simple formulas, each of which independently applied could have led only to different kinds of cross-cousin marriages.

The linguistic pattern corresponding to this situation is that certain of the American Indian languages offer a relatively high number of elements which succeed in becoming organized into relatively simple structures by the structures' assuming asymmetrical forms.

It should be kept in mind that in the above highly tentative experiment the anthropologist proceeds from what is known to him to what is unknown: namely, from kinship structures to linguistic structures. Whether or not the differential characteristics thus outlined have a meaning insofar as the respective languages are concerned remains for the linguist to decide. The author, being a social anthropologist and not a linguist, can only try to explain briefly to which specific features of kinship systems he is referring in this attempt toward a generalized formulation. Since the general lines of his interpretation have been fully developed elsewhere,[16] short sketches were deemed sufficient for the purpose of this paper.

If the general characteristics of the kinship systems of given geographical areas, which we have tried to bring into juxtaposition with equally general characteristics of the linguistic structures of those areas, are recognized by linguists as an approach to equivalences of their own observations, then it will be apparent, in terms of our preceding discussion, that we are much closer to understanding the fundamental characteristics of social life than we have been accustomed to think.

The road will then be open for a comparative structural analysis of customs, institutions, and accepted patterns of behavior. We shall be in a position to understand basic similarities between forms of social life, such as language, art, law, and religion, that on the surface seem to differ greatly. At the same time, we shall have the hope of overcoming the opposition between the collective nature of culture and its manifestations in the individual, since the so-called "collective consciousness" would, in the final analysis, be no more than the expression, on the level of individual thought and behavior, of certain time and space modalities of the universal laws which make up the unconscious activity of the mind.

NOTES

1. N. Wiener, *Cybernetics, or Control and Communication in the Animal and the Machine* (Paris-Cambridge-New York: 1948).
2. Roman Jakobson, "The Phonemic and Grammatical Aspects of Language in Their Interrelations," *Actes du VI⁶ Congrès International des Linguistes* (Paris: 1948).
3. J. Richardson and A.L. Kroeber, "Three Centuries of Women's Dress Fashions. A Quantitative Analysis," *Anthropological Records*, V, No. 2 (1940).
4. G. Teissier, "La Description mathématique des faits biologiques," *Revue de Métaphysique et de Morale* (January, 1936).
5. C. Lévi-Strauss, *Les Structures élémentaires de la parenté* (Paris: 1949), *passim*.
6. *Ibid.*, pp. 278–380.
7. *Ibid.*, pp. 558–66.
8. *Ibid.*, pp. 547–50.
9. *Ibid.*, p. 616.
10. *Ibid.*, p. 45 ff.
11. "Language and Culture: Substantial and Operational Comparabilities" was the title given by C.F. Voegelin to the symposium held at the Twenty-ninth International Congress of Americanists, New York, September 5–12, 1949, where these comments were first offered.
12. Lévi-Strauss, *op. cit.*, pp. 583–91.
13. *Ibid.*, pp. 291–380.
14. From this point of view, G.P. Murdock's suggestion (*Social Structure* [New York: 1949], pp. 224, 340) that the Crow-Omaha type be merged with the Miwok type should be categorically rejected.
15. Lévi-Strauss, *op. cit.*, pp. 228–33.
16. *Op. cit.*

JACQUES LACAN

"THE AGENCY OF THE LETTER IN THE UNCONSCIOUS OR REASON SINCE FREUD"

Of Children in Swaddling Clothes

O cities of the sea, I behold in you your citizens, women as well as men tightly bound with stout bonds around their arms and legs by folk who will not understand your language; and you will only be able to give vent to your griefs and sense of loss of liberty by making tearful complaints, and sighs, and lamentations one to another; for those who bind you will not understand your language nor will you understand them.

Leonardo da Vinci[1]

Although the nature of this contribution was determined by the theme of the third volume of *La Psychanalyse*,[2] I owe to what will be found there to insert it at a point somewhere between writing (*l'écrit*) and speech—it will be half-way between the two.

Writing is distinguished by a prevalence of the *text* in the sense that this factor of discourse will assume in this essay a factor that makes possible the kind of tightening up that I like in order to leave the reader no other way out than the way in, which I prefer to be difficult. In that sense, then, this will not be writing.

Because I always try to provide my seminars each time with something new, I have refrained so far from giving such a text, with one exception, which is not particularly outstanding in the context of the series, and which I refer to at all only for the general level of its argument.

For the urgency that I now take as a pretext for leaving aside such an aim only masks the difficulty that, in trying to maintain it at the level at which I ought to present my teaching here, I might push it too far from speech, whose very different techniques are essential to the formative effect I seek.

That is why I have taken the expedient offered me by the invitation to lecture to the philosophy group of the Fédération des étudiants ès lettres[3] to produce an adaptation suitable to what I have to say: its necessary generality matches the exceptional character of the audience, but its sole object encounters the collusion of their common training, a literary one, to which my title pays homage.

Indeed, how could we forget that to the end of his days Freud constantly maintained that such a training was the prime requisite in the formation of analysts, and that he designated the eternal *universitas litterarum* as the ideal place for its institution.[4]

Thus my recourse (in rewriting) to the movement of the (spoken) discourse, restored to its vitality, by showing whom I meant it for, marks even more clearly those for whom it is not intended.

I mean that it is not intended for those who, for any reason whatever, in psychoanalysis, allow their discipline to avail itself of some false identity—a fault of habit, but its effect on the mind is such that the true identity may appear as simply one alibi among others, a sort of refined reduplication whose implications will not be lost on the most subtle minds.

So one observes with a certain curiosity the beginnings of a new direction concerning symbolization and language in the *International Journal of Psychoanalysis,* with a great many sticky fingers leafing through the pages of Sapir and Jespersen. These exercises are still somewhat unpracticed, but it is above all the tone that is lacking. A certain "seriousness" as one enters the domain of veracity cannot fail to raise a smile.

And how could a psychoanalyst of today not realize that speech is the key to that truth, when his whole experience must find in speech alone its instrument, its context, its material, and even the background noise of its uncertainties.

I. THE MEANING OF THE LETTER

As my title suggests, beyond this "speech," what the psychoanalytic experience discovers in the unconscious is the whole structure of language. Thus from the outset I have alerted informed minds to the extent to which the notion that the unconscious is merely the seat of the instincts will have to be rethought.

But how are we to take this "letter" here? Quite simply, literally.[5]

By "letter" I designate that material support that concrete discourse borrows from language.

This simple definition assumes that language is not to be confused with the various psychical and somatic functions that serve it in the speaking subject—primarily because language and its structure exist prior to the moment at which each subject at a certain point in his mental development makes his entry into it.

Let us note, then, that aphasias, although caused by purely anatomical lesions in the cerebral apparatus that supplies the mental center for these functions, prove, on the whole, to distribute their deficits between the two sides of the signifying effect of what we call here "the letter" in the creation of signification.[6] A point that will be clarified later.

Thus the subject, too, if he can appear to be the slave of language is all the more so of a discourse in the universal movement in which his place is already inscribed at birth, if only by virtue of his proper name.

Reference to the experience of the community, or to the substance of this discourse, settles nothing. For this experience assumes its essential dimension in the tradition that this discourse itself establishes. This tradition, long before the drama of history is inscribed in it, lays down the elementary structures of culture. And these very structures reveal an ordering of possible exchanges which, even if unconscious, is inconceivable outside the permutations authorized by language.

With the result that the ethnographic duality of nature and culture is giving way to a ternary conception of the human condition—nature, society, and culture—the last term of which could well be reduced to language, or that which essentially distinguishes human society from natural societies.

But I shall not make of this distinction either a point or a point of departure, leaving to its own obscurity the question of the original relations between the signifier and labor. I shall be content, for my little jab at the general function of *praxis* in the genesis of history, to point out that the very society that wished to restore, along with the privileges of the producer, the causal hierarchy of the relations between production and the ideological superstructure to their full political rights, has none the less failed to give birth to an esperanto in which the relations of language to socialist realities would have rendered any literary formalism radically impossible.[7]

For my part, I shall trust only those assumptions that have already proven their value by virtue of the fact that language through them has attained the status of an object of scientific investigation.

For it is by virtue of this fact that linguistics[8] is seen to occupy the key position in this domain, and the reclassification of the sciences and a regrouping of them around it signals, as is usually the case, a revolution in knowledge; only the necessities of communication made me inscribe it at the head of this volume under the title "the sciences of man"—despite the confusion that is thereby covered over.[9]

To pinpoint the emergence of linguistic science we may say that, as in the case of all sciences in the modern sense, it is contained in the constitutive moment of an algorithm that is its foundation. This algorithm is the following:

$$\left\{ \frac{S}{s} \right.$$

which is read as: the signifier over the signified, "over" corresponding to the bar separating the two stages.

This sign should be attributed to Ferdinand de Saussure although it is not found in exactly this form in any of the numerous schemas, which none the less express it, to be found in the printed version of his lectures of the years 1906–7, 1908–9, and 1910–11, which the piety of a group of his disciples caused to be published under the title, *Cours de linguistique générale,* a work of prime importance for the transmission of a teaching worthy of the name, that is, that one can come to terms with only in its own terms.

That is why it is legitimate for us to give him credit for the formulation S/s by which, in spite of the differences among schools, the beginning of modern linguistics can be recognized.

The thematics of this science is henceforth suspended, in effect, at the primordial position of the signifier and the signified as being distinct orders separated initially by a barrier resisting signification. And that is what was to make possible an exact study of the connections proper to the signifier, and of the extent of their function in the genesis of the signified.

For this primordial distinction goes well beyond the discussion concerning the arbitrariness of the sign, as it has been elaborated since the earliest reflections of the ancients, and even beyond the impasse which, through the same period, has been encountered in every discussion of the bi-univocal correspondence between the word and the thing, if only in the mere act of naming. All this, of course, is quite contrary to the appearances suggested by the importance often imputed to the role of the index finger pointing to an object in the learning process of the *infans* subject learning his mother tongue, or the use in foreign language teaching of so-called "concrete" methods.

One cannot go further along this line of thought than to demonstrate that no signification can be sustained other than by reference to another signification[10]: in its extreme form this amounts to the proposition that there is no language (*langue*) in existence for which there is any question of its inability to cover the whole field of the signified, it being an effect of its existence as a language (*langue*) that it necessarily answers all needs. If we try to grasp in language the constitution of the object, we cannot fail to notice that this constitution is to be found only at the level of concept, a very different thing from a simple nominative, and that the *thing,* when reduced to the noun, breaks up into the double, divergent beam of the "cause" (*causa*) in which it has taken shelter in the French word *chose,* and the nothing *(rien)* to which it has abandoned its Latin dress *(rem).*

These considerations, important as their existence is for the philosopher, turn us away from the locus in which language questions us as to its very nature. And we will fail to pursue the question further as long as we cling to the illusion that the signifier answers to the function of representing the signified, or better, that the signifier has to answer for its existence in the name of any signification whatever.

For even reduced to this latter formulation, the heresy is the same—the heresy that leads logical positivism in search of the "meaning of meaning,"[11] as its objective is called in the language of its devotees. As a result, we can observe that even a text highly charged with meaning can be reduced, through this sort of analysis, to insignificant bagatelles, all that survives being mathematical algorithms that are, of course, without any meaning.[12]

To return to our formula S/s: if we could infer nothing from it but the notion of the parallelism of its upper and lower terms, each one taken in its globality, it would remain the enigmatic sign of a total mystery. Which of course is not the case.

In order to grasp its function I shall begin by reproducing the classic, yet faulty illustration by which its usage is normally introduced, and one can see how it opens the way to the kind of error referred to above.

TREE

In my lecture, I replaced this illustration with another, which has no greater claim to correctness than that it has been transplanted into that incongruous dimension that the psychoanalyst has not yet altogether renounced because of his quite justified feeling that his conformism takes its value entirely from it. Here is the other diagram:

LADIES   GENTLEMEN

where we see that, without greatly extending the scope of the signifier concerned in the experiment, that is, by doubling a noun through the mere juxtaposition of two terms whose complementary meanings ought apparently to reinforce each other, a surprise is produced by an unexpected precipitation of an unexpected meaning: the image of twin doors symbolizing, through the solitary confinement offered Western Man for the satisfaction of his natural needs away from home, the imperative that he seems to share with the great majority of primitive communities by which his public life is subjected to the laws of urinary segregation.

It is not only with the idea of silencing the nominalist debate with a low blow that I use this example, but rather to show how in fact the signifier enters the signified, namely, in a form which, not being immaterial, raises the question of its place in reality. For the blinking gaze of a short sighted person might be justified in wondering whether this was indeed the signifier as he peered closely at the little enamel signs that bore it, a signifier whose signified would in this call receive its final honors from the double and solemn procession from the upper nave.

But no contrived example can be as telling as the actual experience of truth. So I am happy to have invented the above, since it awoke in the person whose word I most trust a memory of childhood, which having thus happily come to my attention is best placed here.

A train arrives at a station. A little boy and a little girl, brother and sister, are seated in a compartment face to face next to the window through which the buildings along the station platform can be seen passing as the train pulls to a stop. "Look," says the brother, "we're at Ladies!"; "Idiot!" replies his sister, "Can't you see we're at Gentlemen."

Besides the fact that the rails in this story materialize the bar in the Saussurian algorithm (and in a form designed to suggest that its resistance may be other than dialectical), we should add that only someone who didn't have his eyes in front of the holes (it's the appropriate image here) could possibly confuse the place of the signifier and the signified in this story, or not see from what radiating center the signifier sends forth its light into the shadow of incomplete significations.

For this signifier will now carry a purely animal Dissension, destined for the usual oblivion of natural mists, to the unbridled power of ideological warfare, relentless for families, a torment to the Gods. For these children, Ladies and Gentlemen will be henceforth two countries towards which each of their souls will strive on divergent wings, and between which a truce will be the more impossible since they are actually the same country and neither can compromise on its own superiority without detracting from the glory of the other.

But enough. It is beginning to sound like the history of France. Which it is more human, as it ought to be, to evoke here than that of England, destined to tumble from the Large to the Small End of Dean Swift's egg.

It remains to be conceived what steps, what corridor, the S of the signifier, visible here in the plurals[13] in which it focuses its welcome beyond the window, must take in order to rest its elbows on the ventilators through which, like warm and cold air, indignation and scorn come hissing out below.

One thing is certain: if the algorithm S/s with its bar is appropriate, access from one to the other cannot in any case have a signification. For in so far as it is itself only pure function of the signifier, the algorithm can reveal only the structure of a signifier in this transfer.

Now the structure of the signifier is, as it is commonly said of language itself, that it should be articulated.

This means that no matter where one starts to designate their reciprocal encroachments and increasing inclusions, these units are subjected to the double condition of being reducible to ultimate differential elements and of combining them according to the laws of a closed order.

These elements, one of the decisive discoveries of linguistics, are *phonemes;* but we must not expect to find any *phonetic* constancy in the modulatory variability to which this term applies, but rather the synchronic system of differential couplings necessary for the discernment of sounds in a given language. Through this, one sees that an essential element of the spoken word itself was predestined to flow into the mobile characters which, in a jumble of lower-case Didots or Garamonds,[14] render validly present what we call the "letter," namely, the essentially localized structure of the signifier.

With the second property of the signifier, that of combining according to the laws of a closed order, is affirmed the necessity of the topological substratum of which the term I ordinarily use, namely, the signifying chain, gives an approximate idea: rings of a necklace that is a ring in another necklace made of rings.

Such are the structural conditions that define grammar as the order of constitutive encroachments of the signifier up to the level of the unit immediately superior to the sentence, and lexicology as the order of constitutive inclusions of the signifier to the level of the verbal locution.

In examining the limits by which these two exercises in the understanding of linguistic usage are determined, it is easy to see that only the correlations between signifier and signifier provide the standard for all research into signification, as is indicated by the notion of "usage" of a taxeme or semanteme which in fact refers to the context just above that of the units concerned.

But it is not because the undertakings of grammar and lexicology are exhausted within certain limits that we must think that beyond those limits signification reigns supreme. That would be an error.

For the signifier, by its very nature, always anticipates meaning by unfolding its dimension before it. As is seen at the level of the sentence when it is interrupted before the significant term: "I shall never . . . ," "All the same it is . . . ," "And yet there may be . . . ." Such sentences are not without meaning, a meaning all the more oppressive in that it is content to make us wait for it.[15]

But the phenomenon is no different which by the mere recoil of a "but" brings to the light, comely as the Shulamite, honest as the dew, the negress adorned for the wedding and the poor woman ready for the auction-block.[16]

From which we can say that it is in the chain of the signifier that the meaning "insists" but that none of its elements "consists" in the signification of which it is at the moment capable.

We are forced, then, to accept the notion of an incessant sliding of the signified under the signifier—which Ferdinand de Saussure illustrates with an image resembling the wavy lines of the upper and lower Waters in miniatures from manuscripts of *Genesis;* a double flux marked by fine streaks of rain, vertical dotted lines supposedly confining segments of correspondence.

All our experience runs counter to this linearity, which made me speak once, in one of my seminars on psychosis, of something more like "anchoring points" (*"points de capiton"*) as a schema for taking into account the dominance of the letter in the dramatic transformation that dialogue can effect in the subject.[17]

The linearity that Saussure holds to be constitutive of the chain of discourse, in conformity with its emission by a single voice and with its horizontal position in our writing—if this linearity is necessary, in fact, it is not sufficient. It applies to the chain of discourse only in the direction in which it is orientated in time, being taken as a signifying factor in all languages in which "Peter hits Paul" reverses its time when the terms are inverted.

But one has only to listen to poetry, which Saussure was no doubt in the habit of doing,[18] for a polyphony to be heard, for it to become clear that all discourse is aligned along the several staves of a score.

There is in effect no signifying chain that does not have, as if attached to the punctuation of each of its units, a whole articulation of relevant contexts suspended "vertically," as it were, from that point.

Let us take our word "tree" again, this time not as an isolated noun, but at the point of one of these punctuations, and see how it crosses the bar of the Saussurian algorithm. (The anagram of *"arbre"* and *"barre"* should be noted.)

For even broken down into the double spectre of its vowels and consonants, it can still call up with the robur and the plane tree the significations it takes on, in the context of our flora, of strength and majesty. Drawing on all the symbolic contexts suggested in the Hebrew of the Bible, it erects on a barren hill the shadow of the cross. Then reduces to the capital Y, the sign of dichotomy which, except for the illustration used by heraldry, would owe nothing to the tree however genealogical we may think it. Circulatory tree, tree of life of the cerebellum, tree of Saturn, tree of Diana, crystals formed in a tree struck by lightning, is it your figure that traces our destiny for us in the tortoise-shell cracked by the fire, or your lightning that causes that slow shift in the axis of being to surge up from an unnamable night into the Ἐυπάντα of language:

> No! says the Tree, it says No! in the shower of sparks
> Of its superb head

lines that require the harmonics of the tree just as much as their continuation:

> *Which the storm treats as universally*
> *As it does a blade of grass.*[19]

For this modern verse is ordered according to the same law of the parallelism of the signifier that creates the harmony governing the primitive Slavic epic or the most refined Chinese poetry.

As is seen in the fact that the tree and the blade of grass are chosen from the same mode of the existent in order for the signs of contradiction—saying "No!" and "treat as"—to affect them, and also so as to bring about, through the categorical contrast of the particularity of "superb" with the "universally" that reduces it, in the condensation of the "head" (*tête*) and the "storm" (*tempête*), the indiscernible shower of sparks of the eternal instant.

But this whole signifier can only operate, it may be said, if it is present in the subject. It is this objection that I answer by supposing that it has passed over to the level of the signified.

For what is important is not that the subject know anything whatsoever. (If LADIES and GENTLEMEN were written in a language unknown to the little boy and girl, their quarrel would simply be the more exclusively a quarrel over words, but no less ready to take on signification.)

What this structure of the signifying chain discloses is the possibility I have, precisely in so far as I have this language in common with other subjects, that is to say, in so far as it exists as a language, to use it in order to signify *something quite other* than what it says. This function of speech is more worth pointing out than that of "disguising the thought" (more often than not indefinable) of the subject; it is no less than the function of indicating the place of this subject in the search for the true.

I have only to plant my tree in a locution; climb the tree, even project on to it the cunning illumination a descriptive context gives to a word; raise it (*arborer*) so as not to let myself be imprisoned in some sort of *communiqué* of the facts, however official, and if I know the truth, make it heard, in spite of all the *between-the-lines* censures by the only signifier my acrobatics through the branches of the tree can constitute, provocative to the point of burlesque, or perceptible only to the practiced eye, according to whether I wish to be heard by the mob or by the few.

The properly signifying function thus depicted in language has a name. We learned this name in some grammar of our childhood, on the last page, where the shade of Quintilian, relegated to some phantom chapter concerning "final considerations on style," seemed suddenly to speed up his voice in an attempt to get in all he had to say before the end.

It is among the figures of style, or tropes—from which the verb "to find" (*trouver*) comes to us—that this name is found. This name is *metonymy*.

I shall refer only to the example given there: "thirty sails." For the disquietude I felt over the fact that the word "ship," concealed in this expression, seemed, by taking on its figurative sense, through the endless repetition of the same old example, only to increase its presence, obscured (*voilait*) not so much those illustrious sails (*voiles*) as the definition they were supposed to illustrate.

The part taken for the whole, we said to ourselves, and if the thing is to be taken seriously, we are left with very little idea of the importance of this fleet, which "thirty sails" is precisely supposed to give us: for each ship to have just one sail is in fact the least likely possibility.

By which we see that the connection between ship and sail is nowhere but in the signifier, and that it is in the *word-to-word* connection that metonymy is based.[20]

I shall designate as metonymy, then, the one side (*versant*) of the effective field constituted by the signifier, so that meaning can emerge there.

The other side is *metaphor*. Let us immediately find an illustration; Quillet's dictionary seemed an appropriate place to find a sample that would not seem to be chosen for my own purposes, and I didn't have to go any further than the well known line of Victor Hugo:

His sheaf was neither miserly nor spiteful . . .[21]

under which aspect I presented metaphor in my seminar on the psychoses.

It should be said that modern poetry and especially the Surrealist school have taken us a long way in this direction by showing that any conjunction of two signifiers would be equally sufficient to constitute a metaphor, except for the additional requirement of the greatest possible disparity of the images signified, needed for the production of the poetic spark, or in other words for metaphoric creation to take place.

It is true this radical position is based on the experiment known as automatic writing, which would not have been attempted if its pioneers had not been reassured by the Freudian discovery. But it remains a confused position because the doctrine behind it is false.

The creative spark of the metaphor does not spring from the presentation of two images, that is, of two signifiers equally actualized. It flashes between two signifiers one of which has taken the place of the other in the signifying chain, the occulted signifier remaining present through its (metonymic) connection with the rest of the chain.

One word for another: that is the formula for the metaphor and if you are a poet you will produce for your own delight a continuous stream, a dazzling tissue of metaphors. If the result is the sort of intoxication of the dialogue that Jean Tardieu wrote under this title, that is only because he was giving us a demonstration of the radical superfluousness of all signification in a perfectly convincing representation of a bourgeois comedy.

It is obvious that in the line of Hugo cited above, not the slightest spark of light springs from the proposition that the sheaf was neither miserly nor spiteful, for the reason that there is no question of the sheaf's having either the merit or demerit of these attributes, since the attributes, like the sheaf, belong to Booz, who exercises the former in disposing of the latter and without informing the latter of his sentiments in the case.

If, however, his sheaf does refer us to Booz, and this is indeed the case, it is because it has replaced him in the signifying chain at the very place where he was to be exalted by the sweeping away of greed and spite. But now Booz himself has been swept away by the sheaf, and hurled into the outer darkness where greed and spite harbor him in the hollow of their negation.

But once *his* sheaf has thus usurped his place, Booz can no longer return there; the slender thread of the little word *his* that binds him to it is only one more obstacle to his return in that it links him to the notion of possession that retains him at the heart of greed and spite. So *his* generosity, affirmed in the passage, is yet reduced to *less than nothing* by the munificence of the sheaf which, coming from nature, knows neither our reserve nor our rejections, and even in its accumulation remains prodigal by our standards.

But if in this profusion the giver has disappeared along with his gift, it is only in order to rise again in what surrounds the figure of speech in which he was annihilated. For it is the figure of the burgeoning of fecundity, and it is this that announces the surprise that the poem celebrates, namely, the promise that the old man will receive in the sacred context of his accession to paternity.

So, it is between the signifier in the form of the proper name of a man and the signifier that metaphorically abolishes him that the poetic spark is produced, and it is in this case all the more effective in realizing the signification of paternity in that it reproduces the mythical event in terms of which Freud reconstructed the progress, in the unconscious of all men, of the paternal mystery.

Modern metaphor has the same structure. So the line *Love is a pebble laughing in the sunlight*, recreates love in a dimension that seems to me most tenable in the face of its imminent lapse into the mirage of narcissistic altruism.

We see, then that, metaphor occurs at the precise point at which sense emerges from non-sense, that is, at that frontier which, as Freud discovered, when crossed the other way produces the word that in French is *the* word *par excellence*, the word that is simply the signifier "*esprit*";[22] it is at this frontier that we realize that man defies his very destiny when he derides the signifier.

But to come back to our subject, what does man find in metonymy if not the power to circumvent the obstacles of social censure? Does not this form, which gives its field to truth in its very oppression, manifest a certain servitude inherent in its presentation?

One may read with profit a book by Leo Strauss, from the land that traditionally offers asylum to those who choose freedom, in which the author reflects on the relation between the art of writing and persecution.[23] By pushing to its limits the sort of connaturality that links this art to that condition, he lets us glimpse a certain something which in this matter imposes its form, in the effect of truth on desire.

But haven't we felt for some time now that, having followed the ways of the letter in search of Freudian truth, we are getting very warm indeed, that it is burning all about us?

Of course, as it is said, the letter killeth while the spirit giveth life. We can't help but agree, having had to pay homage elsewhere to a noble victim of the error of seeking the spirit in the letter; but we should also like to know how the spirit could live without the letter. Even so, the pretentions of the spirit would remain unassailable if the letter had not shown us that it produces all the effects of truth in man without involving the spirit at all.

It is none other than Freud who had this revelation, and he called his discovery the unconscious.

II. THE LETTER IN THE UNCONSCIOUS

In the complete works of Freud, one out of every three pages is devoted to philological references, one out of every two pages to logical inferences, everywhere a dialectical apprehension of experience, the proportion of analysis of language increasing to the extent that the unconscious is directly concerned.

Thus in "The Interpretation of Dreams" every page deals with what I call the letter of the discourse, in its texture, its usage, its immanence in the matter in question. For it is with this work that the work of Freud begins to open the royal road to the unconscious. And Freud gave us notice of this; his confidence at the time of launching this book in the early days of this century[24] only confirms what he continued to proclaim to the end: that he had staked the whole of his discovery on this essential expression of his message.

The first sentence of the opening chapter announces what for the sake of the exposition could not be postponed: that the dream is a rebus. And Freud goes on to stipulate what I have said from the start, that it must be understood quite literally. This derives from the agency in the dream of that same literal (or phonematic) structure in which the signifier is articulated and analyzed in discourse. So the unnatural images of the boat on the roof, or the man with a comma for a head, which are specifically mentioned by Freud, are examples of dream-images that are to be taken only for their value as signifiers, that is to say, in so far as they allow us to spell out the "proverb" presented by the rebus of the dream. The linguistic structure that enables us to read dreams is the very principle of the "significance of the dream," the *Traumdeutung*.

Freud shows us in every possible way that the value of the image as signifier has nothing whatever to do with its signification, giving as an example Egyptian hieroglyphics in which it would be sheer buffoonery to pretend that in a given text the frequency of a vulture, which is an *aleph*, or of a chick, which is a *vau*, indicating a form of the verb "to be" or a plural, prove that the text has anything at all to do with these ornithological specimens. Freud finds in this writing certain uses of the signifier that are lost in ours, such as the use of determinatives, where a categorical figure is added to the literal figuration of a verbal term; but this is only to show us that even in this writing, the so-called "ideogram" is a letter.

But it does not require the current confusion on this last term for there to prevail in the minds of psychoanalysts lacking linguistic training the prejudice in favor of a symbolism deriving from natural analogy, or even of the image as appropriate to the instinct. And to such an extent that, outside the French school, which has been alerted, a distinction must be drawn between reading coffee grounds and reading hieroglyphics, by recalling to its own principles a technique that could not be justified were it not directed towards the unconscious.

It must be said that this is admitted only with difficulty and that the mental vice denounced above enjoys such favor that today's psychoanalyst can be expected to say that he decodes before he will come around to taking the necessary tour with Freud (turn at the statute of Champollion,[25] says the guide) that will make him understand that what he does is decipher; the distinction is that a cryptogram takes on its full dimension only when it is in a lost language.

Taking the tour is simply continuing in the *Traumdeutung*.

Entstellung, translated as "distortion" or "transposition," is what Freud shows to be the general precondition for the functioning of the dream, and it is what I designated above, following Saussure, as the sliding of the signified under the signifier, which is always active in discourse (its action, let us note, is unconscious).

But what we call the two "sides" of the effect of the signifier on the signified are also found here.

Verdichtung, or "condensation," is the structure of the superimposition of the signifiers, which metaphor takes as its field, and whose name, condensing in itself the word *Dichtung,* shows how the mechanism is connatural with poetry to the point that it envelops the traditional function proper to poetry.

In the case of *Verschiebung,* "displacement," the German term is closer to the idea of that veering off of signification that we see in metonymy, and which from its first appearance in Freud is represented as the most appropriate means used by the unconscious to foil censorship.

What distinguishes these two mechanisms, which play such a privileged role in the dream-work (*Traumarbeit*), from their homologous function in discourse? Nothing, except a condition imposed upon the signifying material, called *Rücksicht auf Darstellbarkeit,* which must be translated by "consideration of the means of representation." (The translation by "role of the possibility of figurative expression" being too approximative here.) But this condition constitutes a limitation operating *within* the system of writing; this is a long way from dissolving the system into a figurative semiology on a level with phenomena of natural expression. This fact could perhaps shed light on the problems involved in certain modes of pictography which, simply because they have been abandoned in writing as imperfect, are not therefore to be regarded as mere evolutionary stages. Let us say, then, that the dream is like the parlor-game in which one is supposed to get the spectators to guess some well known saying or variant of it solely by dumb-show. That the dream uses speech makes no difference since for the unconscious it is only one among several elements of the representation. It is precisely the fact that both the game and the dream run up against a lack of taxematic material for the representation of such logical articulations as causality, contradiction, hypothesis, etc., that proves they are a form of writing rather than of mime. The subtle processes that the dream is seen to use to represent these logical articulations, in a much less artificial way than games usually employ, are the object of a special study in Freud in which we see once more confirmed that the dream-work follows the laws of the signifier.

The rest of the dream-elaboration is designated as secondary by Freud, the nature of which indicates its value: they are phantasies or daydreams (*Tagtraum*) to use the term Freud prefers in order to emphasize their function of wish-fulfillment (*Wunscherfüllung*). Given the fact that these phantasies may remain unconscious, their distinctive feature is in this case their signification. Now, concerning these phantasies, Freud tells us that their place in the dream is either to be taken up and used as signifying elements for the statement of the unconscious thoughts (*Traumgedanke*), or to be used in the secondary elaboration just mentioned, that is to say, in a function not to be distinguished from our waking thought (*von unserem wachen Denken nicht zu unterschieden*). No better idea of the effects of this function can be given than by comparing it to areas of color which, when applied here and there to a stencilplate, can make the stencilled figures, rather forbidding in themselves, more reminiscent of hieroglyphics or of a rebus, look like a figurative painting.

Forgive me if I seem to have to spell out Freud's text; I do so not only to show how much is to be gained by not cutting it about, but also in order to situate the development of psychoanalysis according to its first guide-lines, which were fundamental and never revoked.

Yet from the beginning there was a general *méconnaissance* of the constitutive role of the signifier in the status that Freud from the first assigned to the unconscious and in the most precise formal manner.

There are two reasons for this, of which the least obvious, of course, is that this formalization was not sufficient in itself to bring about a recognition of the agency of the signifier because the *Traumdeutung* appeared long before the formalizations of linguistics for which one could no doubt show that it paved the way by the sheer weight of its truth.

The second reason, which is after all only the reverse side of the first, is that if psychoanalysts were fascinated exclusively by the significations revealed in the unconscious, it is because these significations derived their secret attraction from the dialectic that seemed to be immanent in them.

I have shown in my seminars that it is the need to counteract the continuously accelerating effects of this bias that alone explains the apparent changes of direction or rather changes of tack, which Freud, through his primary concern to preserve for posterity both his discovery and the fundamental revisions it effected in our knowledge, felt it necessary to apply to his doctrine.

For, I repeat, in the situation in which he found himself, having nothing that corresponded to the object of his discovery that was at the same level of scientific development—in this situation, at least he never failed to maintain this object on the level of its ontological dignity.

The rest was the work of the gods and took such a course that analysis today takes its bearings in those imaginary forms that I have just shown to be drawn "resist-style" (*en reserve*) on the text they mutilate—and the analyst tries to accommodate his direction to them, confusing them, in the interpretation of the dream, with the visionary liberation of the hieroglyphic aviary, and seeking generally the control of the exhaustion of the analysis in a sort of "scanning"[26] of these forms whenever they appear, in the idea that they are witnesses of the exhaustion of the regressions and of the remodelling of the object relation from which the subject is supposed to derive his "character-type."[27]

The technique that is based on such positions can be fertile in its various effects, and under the aegis of therapy, difficult to criticize. But an internal criticism must none the less arise from the flagrant disparity between the mode of operation by which the technique is justified—namely the analytic rule, all the instruments of which, beginning with "free association," depend on the conception of the unconscious of its inventor—and, on the other hand, the general *méconnaissance* that reigns regarding this conception of the unconscious. The most ardent adherents of this technique believe themselves to be freed of any need to reconcile the two by the merest pirouette: the analytic rule (they say) must be all the more religiously observed since it is only the result of a lucky accident. In other words, Freud never knew what he was doing.

A return to Freud's text shows on the contrary the absolute coherence between his technique and his discovery, and at the same time this coherence allows us to put all his procedures in their proper place.

That is why any rectification of psychoanalysis must inevitably involve a return to the truth of that discovery, which, taken in its original moment, is impossible to obscure.

For in the analysis of dreams, Freud intends only to give us the laws of the unconscious in their most general extension. One of the reasons why dreams were most propitious for this demonstration is exactly, Freud tells us, that they reveal the same laws whether in the normal person or in the neurotic.

But in either case, the efficacy of the unconscious does not cease in the waking state. The psychoanalytic experience does nothing other than establish that the unconscious leaves none of our actions outside its field. The presence of the unconscious in the psychological order, in other words in the relation-functions of the individual, should, however, be more precisely defined: it is not coextensive with that order, for we know that if unconscious motivation is manifest in conscious psychical effects, as well as in unconscious ones, conversely it is only elementary to recall to mind that a large number of psychical effects that are quite legitimately designated as unconscious, in the sense of excluding the characteristic of consciousness, are nonetheless without any relation whatever to the unconscious in the Freudian sense. So it is only by an abuse of the term that unconscious in that sense is confused with psychical, and that one may thus designate as psychical what is in fact an effect of the unconscious, as on the somatic for instance.

It is a matter, therefore, of defining the topography of this unconscious. I say that it is the very topography defined by the algorithm:

$$\left\{ \frac{S}{s} \right.$$

What we have been able to develop concerning the effects of the signifier on the signified suggests its transformation into:

$$\left\{ f(S)\frac{I}{s} \right.$$

We have shown the effects not only of the elements of the horizontal signifying chain, but also of its vertical dependencies in the signified, divided into two fundamental structures called metonymy and metaphor. We can symbolize them by, first:

$$\left\{ f(S \ldots S')S \cong S(-)s \right.$$

that is to say, the metonymic structure, indicating that it is the connection between signifier and signifier that permits the elision in which the signifier installs the lack-of-being in the object relation, using the value of "reference back" possessed by signification in order to invest it with the desire aimed at the very lack it supports. The sign — placed between ( ) represents here the maintenance of the bar — which, in the original algorithm, marked the irreducibility in which, in the relations between signifier and signified, the resistance of signification is constituted.[28]

Secondly,

$$\left\{ f\!\left(\frac{S'}{S}\right) S \cong S(+)s \right.$$

the metaphoric structure indicating that it is in the substitution of signifier for signifier that an effect of signification is produced that is creative or poetic, in other words, which is the advent of the signification in question.[29] The sign + between ( ) represents here the crossing of the bar — and the constitutive value of this crossing for the emergence of signification.

This crossing expresses the condition of passage of the signifier into the signified that I pointed out above, although provisionally confusing it with the place of the subject.

It is the function of the subject, thus introduced, that we must now turn to since it lies at the crucial point of our problem.

"I think, therefore I am" (cogito ergo sum) is not merely the formula in which is constituted, with the historical high point of reflection on the conditions of science, the link between the transparency of the transcendental subject and his existential affirmation.

Perhaps I am only object and mechanism (and so nothing more than phenomenon), but assuredly in so far as I think so, I am—absolutely. No doubt philosophers have brought important corrections to this formulation, notably that in that which thinks (cogitans), I can never constitute myself as anything but object (cogitatum). Nonetheless it remains true that by way of this extreme purification of the transcendental subject, my existential link to its project seems irrefutable, at least in its present form, and that: "cogito ergo sum" ubi cogito, ibi sum, overcomes this objection.

Of course, this limits me to being there in my being only in so far as I think that I am in my thought; just how far I actually think this concerns only myself and if I say it, interests no one.[30]

Yet to elude this problem on the pretext of its philosophical pretensions is simply to admit one's inhibition. For the notion of subject is indispensable even to the operation of a science such as strategy (in the modern sense) whose calculations exclude all "subjectivism."

It is also to deny oneself access to what might be called the Freudian universe—in the way that we speak of the Copernican universe. It was in fact the so-called Copernican revolution to which Freud himself compared his discovery, emphasizing that it was once again a question of the place man assigns to himself at the center of a universe.

Is the place that I occupy as the subject of a signifier concentric or excentric, in relation to the place I occupy as subject of the signified?—that is the question.

It is not a question of knowing whether I speak of myself in a way that conforms to what I am, but rather of knowing whether I am the same as that of which I speak. And it is not at all inappropriate to use the word "thought" here. For Freud uses the term to designate the elements involved in the unconscious, that is the signifying mechanisms that we now recognize as being there.

It is nonetheless true that the philosophical cogito is at the center of the mirage that renders modern man so sure of being himself even in his uncertainties about himself, and even in the mistrust he has learned to practice against the traps of self-love.

Furthermore, if, turning the weapon of metonymy against the nostalgia that it serves, I refuse to seek any meaning beyond tautology, if in the name of "war is war" and "a penny's a penny" I decide to be only what I am, how even here can I elude the obvious fact that I am in that very act?

And it is no less true if I take myself to the other, metaphoric pole of the signifying quest, and if I dedicate myself to becoming what I am, to coming into being, I cannot doubt that even if I lose myself in the process, I am in that process.

Now it is on these very points, where evidence will be subverted by the empirical, that the trick of the Freudian conversion lies.

This signifying game between metonymy and metaphor, up to and including the active edge that splits my desire between a refusal of the signifier and a lack of being, and links my fate to the question of my destiny, this game, in all its inexorable subtlety, is played until the match is called, there where I am not, because I cannot situate myself there.

That is to say, what is needed is more than these words with which, for a brief moment I disconcerted my audience: I think where I am not, therefore I am where I do not think. Words that render sensible to an ear properly attuned with what elusive ambiguity[31] the ring of meaning flees from our grasp along the verbal thread.

What one ought to say is: I am not wherever I am the plaything of my thought; I think of what I am where I do not think to think.

This two-sided mystery is linked to the fact that the truth can be evoked only in that dimension of alibi in which all "realism" in creative works takes its virtue from metonymy; it is likewise linked to this other fact that we accede to meaning only through the double twist of metaphor when we have the one and only key: the S and the s of the Saussurian algorithm are not on the same level, and man only deludes himself when he believes his true place is at their axis, which is nowhere.

Was nowhere, that is, until Freud discovered it; for if what Freud discovered isn't that, it isn't anything.

The contents of the unconscious with all their disappointing ambiguities give us no reality in the subject more consistent than the immediate; their virtue derives from the truth and in the dimension of being: *Kern unseres Wesen*[32] are Freud's own terms.

The double-triggered mechanism of metaphor is the very mechanism by which the symptom, in the analytic sense, is determined. Between the enigmatic signifier of the sexual trauma and the term that is substituted for it in an actual signifying chain there passes the spark that fixes in a symptom the signification inaccessible to the conscious subject in which that symptom may be resolved— a symptom being a metaphor in which flesh or function is taken as a signifying element.

And the enigmas that desire seems to pose for a "natural philosophy"—its frenzy mocking the abyss of the infinite, the secret collusion with which it envelops the pleasure of knowing and of dominating with *jouissance,* these amount to no other derangement of instinct than that of being caught in the rails— eternally stretching forth towards the *desire for something else*—of metonymy. Hence its "perverse" fixation at the very suspension-point of the signifying chain where the memory-screen is immobilized and the fascinating image of the fetish is petrified.

There is no other way of conceiving the indestructibility of unconscious desire—in the absence of a need which, when forbidden satisfaction, does not sicken and die, even if it means the destruction of the organism itself. It is in a memory, comparable to what is called by that name in our modern thinking-machines (which are in turn based on an electronic realization of the composition of signification), it is in this sort of memory that is found the chain that *insists* on reproducing itself in the transference, and which is the chain of dead desire.

It is the truth of what this desire has been in his history that the patient cries out through his symptom, as Christ said that the stones themselves would have cried out if the children of Israel had not lent them their voice.

And that is why only psychoanalysis allows us to differentiate within memory the function of recollection. Rooted in the signifier, it resolves the Platonic aporias of reminiscence through the ascendancy of history in man.

One has only to read the "Three Essays on Sexuality" to observe, in spite of the pseudo-biological glosses with which it is decked out for popular consumption, that Freud there derives all accession to the object from a dialectic of return.

Starting from Hölderlin's νοστος, Freud arrives less than twenty years later at Kierkegaard's repetition; that is, in submitting his thought solely to the humble but inflexible consequences of the "talking cure,"[33] he was unable ever to escape the living servitudes that led him from the sovereign principle of the Logos to re-thinking the Empedoclean antinomies of death.

And how else are we to conceive the recourse of a man of science to a *Deus ex machina* than on that "other scene" he speaks of as the locus of the dream, a *Deus ex machina* only less derisory for the fact that it is revealed to the spectator that the machine directs the director? How else can we imagine that a scientist of the nineteenth century, unless we realize that he had to bow before the force of evidence that went well beyond his prejudices, valued more highly than all his other works his *Totem and Taboo,* with its obscene, ferocious figure of the primordial father, not to be exhausted in the expiation of Oedipus' blindness, and before which the ethnologists of today bow as before the growth of an authentic myth?

So that imperious proliferation of particular symbolic creations, such as what are called the sexual theories of the child, which supply the motivation down to the smallest detail of neurotic compulsions, these reply to the same necessities as do myths.

Thus, to speak of the precise point we are treating in my seminars on Freud, little Hans, left in the lurch at the age of five by his symbolic environment, and suddenly forced to face the enigma of his sex and his existence, developed, under the direction of Freud and of his father, Freud's disciple, in mythic form, around the signifying crystal of his phobia, all the permutations possible on a limited number of signifiers.

The operation shows that even on the individual level the solution of the impossible is brought within man's reach by the exhaustion of all possible forms of the impossibilities encountered in solution by recourse to the signifying equation. It is a striking demonstration that illuminates the labyrinth of a case which so far has only been used as a source of demolished fragments. We should be struck, too, by the fact that it is in the coextensivity of the development of the symptom and of its curative resolution that the nature of the neurosis is revealed: whether phobic, hysterical, or obsessive, the neurosis is a question that being poses for the subject "from where it was before the subject came into the world" (Freud's phrase, which he used in explaining the Oedipal complex to little Hans).

The "being" referred to is that which appears in a lightning moment in the void of the verb "to be" and I said that it poses its question for the subject. What does that mean? It does not pose it *before* the subject, since the subject cannot come to the place where it is posed, but it poses it *in place* of the subject, that is to say, in that place it poses the question *with* the subject, as one poses a problem *with* a pen, or as Aristotle's man thought *with* his soul.

Thus Freud introduced the ego into his doctrine,[34] by defining it according to the resistances that are proper to it. What I have tried to convey is that these resistances are of an imaginary nature much in the same sense as those coaptative lures that the ethology of animal behavior shows us in display or combat, and that these lures are reduced in man to the narcissistic relation introduced by Freud, which I have elaborated in my essay on the mirror stage. I have tried to show that by situating in this ego the synthesis of the perceptual functions in which the sensorimotor selections are integrated, Freud seems to abound in that delegation that is traditionally supposed to represent reality for the ego, and that this reality is all the more included in the suspension of the ego.

For this ego, which is notable in the first instance for the imaginary inertias that it concentrates against the message of the unconscious, operates solely with a view to covering the displacement constituted by the subject with a resistance that is essential to the discourse as such.

That is why an exhaustion of the mechanisms of defense, which Fenichel the practitioner shows us so well in his studies of analytic technique (while his whole reduction on the theoretical level of neuroses and psychoses to genetic anomalies in libidinal development is pure platitude), manifests itself, without Fenichel's accounting for it or realizing it himself, as simply the reverse side of the mechanisms of the unconscious. Periphrasis, hyperbaton, ellipsis, suspension, anticipation, retraction, negation, digression, irony, these are the figures of style (Quintilian's *figurae sententiarum*); as catachresis, litotes, antonomasia, hypotyposis are the tropes, whose terms suggest themselves as the most proper for the labelling of these mechanisms. Can one really see these as mere figures of speech when it is the figures themselves that are the active principle of the rhetoric of the discourse that the analysand in fact utters?

By persisting in describing the nature of resistance as a permanent emotional state, thus making it alien to the discourse, today's psychoanalysts have simply shown that they have fallen under the blow of one of the fundamental truths that Freud rediscovered through psychoanalysis. One is never happy making way for a new truth, for it always means making our way into it: the truth is always disturbing. We cannot even manage to get used to it. We are used to the real. The truth we repress.

Now it is quite specially necessary to the scientist, to the seer, even to the quack, that he should be the only one to *know*. The idea that deep in the simplest (and even sickest) of souls there is something ready to blossom is bad enough! But if someone seems to know as much as they about what we ought to make of it . . . then the categories of primitive, prelogical, archaic, or even magical thought, so easy to impute to others, rush to our aid! It is not right that these nonentities keep us breathless with enigmas that prove to be only too unreliable.

To interpret the unconscious as Freud did, one would have to be as he was, an encyclopedia of the arts and muses, as well as an assiduous reader of the *Fliegende Blätter*.[35] And the task is made no easier by the fact that we are at the mercy of a thread woven with allusions, quotations, puns, and equivocations. And is that our profession, to be antidotes to trifles?

Yet that is what we must resign ourselves to. The unconscious is neither primordial nor instinctual; what it knows about the elementary is no more than the elements of the signifier.

The three books that one might call canonical with regard to the unconscious—"The Interpretation of Dreams," "The Psychopathology of Everyday Life," and "Jokes and their Relation to the Unconscious"—are simply a web of examples whose development is inscribed in the formulas of connection and substitution (though carried to the tenth degree by their particular complexity—diagrams of them are sometimes provided by Freud by way of illustration); these are the formulas we give to the signifier in its *transference*-function. For in "The Interpretation of Dreams" it is in the sense of such a function that the term *Übertragung*, or transference, is introduced, which later gave its name to the mainspring of the intersubjective link between analyst and analysand.

Such diagrams are not only constitutive of each of the symptoms in a neurosis, but they alone make possible the understanding of the thematic of its course and resolution. The great case-histories provided by Freud demonstrate this admirably.

To fall back on a more limited incident, but one more likely to provide us with the final seal on our proposition, let me cite the article on fetishism of 1927,[36] and the case Freud reports there of a patient who, to achieve sexual satisfaction, needed a certain shine on the nose (*Glanz auf der Nase*); analysis showed that his early, English-speaking years had seen the displacement of the burning curiosity that he felt for the phallus of his mother, that is to say, for that eminent *manque-à-être*, for that want-to-be, whose privileged signifier Freud revealed to us, into a *glance at the nose*[37] in the forgotten language of his childhood, rather than a *shine on the nose*.[37]

It is the abyss opened up at the thought that a thought should make itself heard in the abyss that provoked resistance to psychoanalysis from the outset. And not, as is commonly said, the emphasis on man's sexuality. This latter has after all been the dominant object in literature throughout the ages. And in fact the more recent evolution of psychoanalysis has succeeded by a bit of comical legerdemain in turning it into a quite moral affair, the cradle and trysting-place of oblativity and attraction. The Platonic setting of the soul, blessed and illuminated, rises straight to paradise.

The intolerable scandal in the time before Freudian sexuality was sanctified was that it was so "intellectual." It was precisely in that that it showed itself to be the worthy ally of all those terrorists whose plottings were going to ruin society.

At a time when psychoanalysts are busy remodelling psychoanalysis into a right-thinking movement whose crowning expression is the sociological poem of the *autonomous ego*, I would like to say, to all those who are listening to me, how they can recognize bad psychoanalysts; this is by the word they use to deprecate all technical or theoretical research that carries forward the Freudian experience along its authentic lines. That word is *"intellectualization"*—execrable to all those who, living in fear of being tried and found wanting by the wine of truth, spit on the bread of men, although their slaver can no longer have any effect other than that of leavening.

III. THE LETTER, BEING AND THE OTHER[38]

Is what thinks in my place, then, another I? Does Freud's discovery represent the confirmation, on the level of psychological experience, of Manicheism?[39]

In fact, there is no confusion on this point: what Freud's researches led us to is not a few more or less curious cases of split personality. Even at the heroic epoch I have been describing, when, like the animals in fairy stories, sexuality talked, the demonic atmosphere that such an orientation might have given rise to never materialized.[40]

The end that Freud's discovery proposes for man was defined by him at the apex of his thought in these moving terms: *Wo es war, soll Ich werden*. I must come to the place where that was.

This is one of reintegration and harmony, I could even say of reconciliation (*Versöhnung*).

But if we ignore the self's radical ex-centricity to itself with which man is confronted, in other words, the truth discovered by Freud, we shall falsify both the order and methods of psychoanalytic mediation; we shall make of it nothing more than the compromise operation that it has, in effect, become, namely, just what the letter as well as the spirit of Freud's work most repudiates. For since he constantly invoked the notion of compromise as supporting all the miseries that his analysis is supposed to assuage, we can say that any recourse to compromise, explicit or implicit, will necessarily disorient psychoanalytic action and plunge it into darkness.

But neither does it suffice to associate oneself with the moralistic tartufferies of our time or to be forever spouting something about the "total personality" in order to have said anything articulate about the possibility of mediation.

The radical heteronomy that Freud's discovery shows gaping within man can never again be covered over without whatever is used to hide it being profoundly dishonest.

Who, then, is this other to whom I am more attached than to myself, since, at the heart of my assent to my own identity it is still he who agitates me?

His presence can be understood only at a second degree of otherness, which already places him in the position of mediating between me and the double of myself, as it were with my counterpart.

If I have said that the unconscious is the discourse of the Other (with a capital O), it is in order to indicate the beyond in which the recognition of desire is bound up with the desire for recognition.

In other words this other is the Other that even my lie invokes as a guarantor of the truth in which it subsists.

By which we can also see that it is with the appearance of language the dimension of truth emerges.

Prior to this point, we can recognize in the psychological relation, which can be easily isolated in the observation of animal behavior, the existence of subjects, not by means of some projective mirage, the phantom of which a certain type of psychologist delights in hacking to pieces, but simply on account of the manifested presence of intersubjectivity. In the animal hidden in his lookout, in the well-laid trap of certain others, in the feint by which an apparent straggler leads a predator away from the flock, something more emerges than in the fascinating display of mating or combat ritual. Yet there is nothing even there that transcends the function of lure in the service of a need, or which affirms a presence in that beyond-the-veil where the whole of Nature can be questioned about its design.

For there even to be a question (and we know that it is one Freud himself posed in "Beyond the Pleasure Principle"), there must be language.

For I can lure my adversary by means of a movement contrary to my actual plan of battle, and this movement will have its deceiving effect only in so far as I produce it in reality and for my adversary.

But in the propositions with which I open peace negotiations with him, what my negotiations propose to him is situated in a third locus which is neither my speech nor my interlocutor.

This locus is none other than the locus of signifying convention, of the sort revealed in the comedy of the sad plaint of the Jew to his crony: "Why do you tell me you are going to Cracow so I'll believe you are going to Lvov, when you really are going to Cracow?"

Of course the flock-movement I just spoke of could be understood in the conventional context of game-strategy, where it is a rule that I deceive my adversary, but in that case my success is evaluated within the connotation of betrayal, that is to say, in relation to the Other who is the guarantor of Good Faith.

Here the problems are of an order the heteronomy of which is completely misconstrued (*méconnue*) if reduced to an "awareness of others," or whatever we choose to call it. For the "existence of the other" having once upon a time reached the ears of the Midas of psychoanalysis through the partition that separates him from the secret meetings of the phenomenologists, the news is now being whispered through the reeds: "Midas, King Midas, is the other of his patient. He himself has said it."

What sort of breakthrough is that? The other, what other?

The young André Gide, defying the landlady to whom his mother had confided him to treat him as a responsible person, opening with a key (false only in that it opened all locks of the same make) the lock that this lady took to be a worthy signifier of her educational intentions, and doing it quite obviously for her benefit—what "other" was he aiming at? She who was supposed to intervene and to whom he would then say: "Do you think my obedience can be secured with a ridiculous lock?" But by remaining out of sight and holding her peace until that evening in order, after primly greeting his return, to lecture him like a child, she showed him not just another with the face of anger, but another André Gide who is no longer sure, either then or later in thinking back on it, of just what he really meant to do—whose own truth has been changed by the doubt thrown on his good faith.

Perhaps it would be worth our while pausing a moment over this empire of confusion which is none other than that in which the whole human opera-buffa plays itself out, in order to understand the ways in which analysis can proceed not just to restore an order but to found the conditions for the possibility of its restoration.

Kern unseres Wesen, the nucleus of our being, but it is not so much that Freud commands us to seek it as so many others before him have with the empty adage "Know thyself"—as to reconsider the ways that lead to it, and which he shows us.

Or rather that which he proposes for us to attain is not that which can be the object of knowledge, but that (doesn't he tell us as much?) which creates our being and about which he teaches us that we bear witness to it as much and more in our whims, our aberrations, our phobias and fetishes, as in our more or less civilized personalities.

Madness, you are no longer the object of the ambiguous praise with which the sage decorated the impregnable burrow of his fear; and if after all he finds himself tolerably at home there, it is only because the supreme agent forever at work digging its tunnels is none other than reason, the very Logos that he serves.

So how do you imagine that a scholar with so little talent for the "commitments" that solicited him in his age (as they do in all ages), that a scholar such as Erasmus held such an eminent place in the revolution of a Reformation in which man has as much of a stake in each man as in all men?

The answer is that the slightest alteration in the relation between man and the signifier, in this case in the procedures of exegesis, changes the whole course of history by modifying the moorings that anchor his being.

It is precisely in this that Freudianism, however misunderstood it has been, and however confused its consequences have been, to anyone capable of perceiving the changes we have lived through in our own lives, is seen to have founded an intangible but radical revolution. There is no point in collecting witnesses to the fact:[41] everything involving not just the human sciences, but the destiny of man, politics, metaphysics, literature, the arts, advertising, propaganda, and through these even economics, everything has been affected.

Is all this anything more than the discordant effects of an immense truth in which Freud traced for us a clear path? What must be said, however, is that any technique that bases its claim on the mere psychological categorization of its object is not following this path, and this is the case of psychoanalysis today except in so far as we return to the Freudian discovery.

Furthermore, the vulgarity of the concepts by which it recommends itself to us, the embroidery of pseudo-Freudianism (frofreudisme) which is no longer anything but decoration, as well as the bad repute in which it seems to prosper, all bear witness to its fundamental betrayal of its founder.

By his discovery, Freud brought within the circle of science the boundary between the object and being that seemed to mark its outer limit.

That this is the symptom and the prelude of a re-examination of the situation of man in the existent such as has been assumed up to the present by all our postulates of knowledge—don't be content, I beg of you, to write this off as another case of Heideggerianism, even prefixed by a neo- that adds nothing to the dustbin style in which currently, by the use of his ready-made mental jetsam, one excuses oneself from any real thought.

When I speak of Heidegger, or rather when I translate him, I at least make the effort to leave the speech he proffers us its sovereign significance.

If I speak of being and the letter, if I distinguish the other and the Other, it is because Freud shows me that they are the terms to which must be referred the effects of resistance and transference against which, in the twenty years I have engaged in what we all call after him the impossible practice of psychoanalysis, I have done unequal battle. And it is also because I must help others not to lose their way there.

It is to prevent the field of which they are the inheritors from becoming barren, and for that reason to make it understood that if the symptom is a metaphor, it is not a metaphor to say so, any more than to say that man's desire is a metonymy. For the symptom *is* a metaphor whether one likes it or not, as desire *is* a metonymy, however funny people may find the idea.

Finally, if I am to rouse you to indignation over the fact that, after so many centuries of religious hypocrisy and philosophical bravado, nothing has yet been validly articulated as to what links metaphor to the question of being and metonymy to its lack, there must be an object there to answer to that indignation both as its instigator and its victim: that object is humanistic man and the credit, hopelessly affirmed, which he has drawn over his intentions.

14–26 May, 1957

NOTES

1. *Codice Atlantico* 145.
2. *Psychanalyse et sciences de l'homme.*
3. The lecture took place on 9 May, 1957, in the Amphithéâtre Descartes of the Sorbonne, and the discussion was continued afterwards over drinks.
4. *Die Frage der Laienanalyse*, G.W., XIV: 281–3.
5. "À la lettre" [Tr.].
6. This aspect of aphasia, so useful in overthrowing the concept of "psychological function," which only obscures every aspect of the question, becomes quite clear in the purely linguistic analysis of the two major forms of aphasia worked out by one of the leaders of modern linguistics, Roman Jakobson. See the most accessible of his works, the *Fundamentals of Language* (with Morris Halle), Mouton's, Gravenhage, part II, Chapters 1 to 4.
7. We may recall that the discussion of the need for a new language in communist society did in fact take place, and Stalin, much to the relief of those who adhered to his philosophy, put an end to it with the following formulation: language is not a superstructure.
8. By "linguistics" I mean the study of existing languages (*langues*) in their structure and in the laws revealed therein; this excludes any theory of abstract codes sometimes included under the heading of communication theory, as well as the theory, originating in the physical sciences, called information theory, or any semiology more or less hypothetically generalized.
9. *Psychanalyse et sciences de l'homme.*
10. Cf. the *De Magistro* of St. Augustine, especially the chapter "De significatione locutionis" which I analyzed in my seminar of 23 June, 1954.
11. English in the original [Tr.].
12. So, Mr. I.A. Richards, author of a work precisely in accord with such an objective, has in another work shown us its application. He took for his purposes a page from Mongtse (Mencius, to the Jesuits) and called the piece, *Mencius on the Mind.* The guarantees of the purity of the experiment are nothing to the luxury of the approaches. And

our expert on the traditional Canon that contains the text is found right on the spot in Peking where our demonstration-model mangle has been transported regardless of cost.

But we shall be no less transported, if less expensively, to see a bronze that gives out bell-tones at the slightest contact with thought, transformed into a rag to wipe the blackboard of the most dismaying British psychologism. And not without eventually being identified with the meninx of the author himself—all that remains of him or his object after having exhausted the meaning of the latter and the good sense of the former.

13. Not, unfortunately, the case in the English here—the plural of "gentleman" being indicated other than by the addition of an "s" [Tr.].

14. Names of different type-faces [Tr.].

15. To which verbal hallucination, when it takes this form, opens a communicating door with the Freudian structure of psychosis—a door until now unnoticed (cf. "On a Question Preliminary to any Possible Treatment of Psychosis," pp. 179–225).

16. The allusions are to the "I am black, but comely . . ." of the *Song of Solomon*, and to the nineteenth-century cliché of the "poor, but honest" woman [Tr.].

17. I spoke in my seminar of 6 June, 1956, of the first scene of *Athalie*, incited by an allusion—tossed off by a high-brow critic in the *New Statesman and Nation*—to the "high whoredom" of Racine's heroines, to renounce reference to the savage dramas of Shakespeare, which have become compulsional in analytic circles where they play the role of status-symbol for the Philistines.

18. The publication by Jean Starobinski, in *Le Mercure de France* (February 1964) of Saussure's notes on anagrams and their hypogrammatical use, from the Saturnine verses to the writings of Cicero, provide the corroboration that I then lacked (note 1966).

19. "*Non! dit l'Arbre, il dit: Non! dans*
    l'étincellement
    De sa tête superbe
    Que la tempête traite universellement
    Comme elle fait une herbe."
    (Paul Valéry, "Au Platane," *Les Charmes*)

20. I pay homage here to the works of Roman Jakobson—to which I owe much of this formulation; works to which a psychoanalyst can constantly refer in order to structure his own experience, and which render superfluous the "personal communications" of which I could boast as much as the next fellow.

Indeed, one recognizes in this oblique form of allegiance the style of that immortal couple, Rosencrantz and Guildenstern, who are virtually indistinguishable, even in the imperfection of their destiny, for it survives by the same method as Jeannot's knife, and for the same reason for which Goethe praised Shakespeare for presenting the character in double form: they represent, in themselves alone, the whole *Gesellschaft*, the Association itself (*Wilhelm Meisters Lehrjahre*, ed. Trunz, Christian Wegner Verlag, Hamburg, V (5): 299)—I mean the International Psychoanalytical Association.

We should savour the passage from Goethe as a whole: "*Dieses leise Auftreten dieses Schmiegen und Biegen, dies Jasagen, Streicheln und Schmeicheln, dieses Behendigkeit, dies Schwänzein, diese Allheit und Leerheit, diese rechtliche Schurkerei, diese Unfähigkeit, wie kann sie durch einen Menschen ausgedruckt werden? Es sollten ihrer wenigstens ein Dutzend sein, wenn man sie haben könnte; denn sie bloss in Gesellschaft etwas, sie sind die Gesellschaft . . .*"

Let us thank also, in this context, the author R.M. Loewenstein of "Some Remarks on the Role of Speech in Psychoanalytic Technique" (*I.J.P.*, Nov.–Dec., 1956, XXXVII (6): 467) for taking the trouble to point out that his remarks are "based on" work dating from 1952. This is no doubt the explanation for the fact that he has learned nothing from work done since then, yet which he is not ignorant of, as he cites me as their "editor" (sic).

21. "Sa gerbe n'était pas avare ni haineuse," a line from "Booz endormi" [Tr.].
22. "*Mot*," in the broad sense, means "word." In the narrower sense, however, it means "a witticism." The French "*esprit*" is translated, in this context, as "wit," the equivalent of Freud's *Witz* [Tr.].

"*Esprit*" is certainly the equivalent of the German *Witz* with which Freud marked the approach of his third fundamental work on the unconscious. The much greater difficulty of finding this equivalent in English is instructive: "wit," burdened with all the discussion of which it was the object from Davenant and Hobbes to Pope and Addison, abandoned its essential virtues to "humour," which is something else. There only remains the "pun," but this word is too narrow in its connotation.

23. Leo Strauss, *Persecution and the Art of Writing*, The Free Press, Glencoe, Illinois.
24. Cf. the correspondence, namely letters 107 and 109.
25. Jean-François Champollion (1790–1832), the first scholar to decipher the Ancient Egyptian hieroglyphics [Tr.].
26. That is the process by which the results of a piece of research are assured through a mechanical exploration of the entire extent of the field of its object.
27. By referring only to the development of the organism, the typology fails to recognize (*méconnaît*) the structure in which the subject is caught up respectively in phantasy, in drive, in sublimation. I am at present developing the theory of this structure (note 1966).
28. The sign ≅ here designates congruence.
29. S′ designating here the term productive of the signifying effect (or significance); one can see that the term is latent in metonymy, patent in metaphor.
30. It is quite otherwise if by posing a question such as "Why philosophers?" I become more candid than nature, for then I am asking not only the question that philosophers have been asking themselves for all time, but also the one in which they are perhaps most interested.
31. "*Ambiguïté de furet*"— literally, "ferret-like ambiguity." This is one of a number of references in Lacan to the game "hunt-the-slipper" (*jeu du furet*) [Tr.].
32. "The nucleus of our being" [Tr.].
33. English in the original [Tr.].
34. This and the next paragraph were rewritten solely with a view to greater clarity of expression (note 1968).
35. A German comic newspaper of the late nineteenth and early twentieth centuries [Tr.].
36. *Fetischismus*, G.W. XIV: 311; "Fetishism," *Collected Papers*, **V:** 198; *Standard Edition* XXI: 149.
37. English in the original [Tr.].
38. *La lettre l'être et l'autre*.
39. One of my colleagues went so far in this direction as to wonder if the id (*Es*) of the last phase wasn't in fact the "bad ego." (It should now be obvious whom I am referring to—1966.)

40. Note, nonetheless, the tone with which one spoke in that period of the "elfin pranks" of the unconscious; a work of Silberer's is called *Der Zufall und die Koboldstreiche des Unbewussten* (Chance and the Elfin Tricks of the Unconscious)—completely anachronistic in the context of our present soul-managers.

41. To pick the most recent in date, François Mauriac, in the *Figaro littéraire* of 25 May, apologizes for refusing "to tell the story of his life." If no one these days can undertake to do that with the old enthusiasm, the reason is that, "a half century since, Freud, whatever we think of him" has already passed that way. And after being briefly tempted by the old saw that this is only the "history of our body," Mauriac returns to the truth that his sensitivity as a writer makes him face: to write the history of oneself is to write the confession of the deepest part of our neighbors' souls as well.

MAX HORKHEIMER AND THEODOR ADORNO

"THE CONCEPT OF ENLIGHTENMENT" FROM *DIALECTIC* OF ENLIGHTENMENT

In the most general sense of progressive thought, the Enlightenment has always aimed at liberating men from fear and establishing their sovereignty. Yet the fully enlightened earth radiates disaster triumphant. The program of the Enlightenment was the disenchantment of the world; the dissolution of myths and the substitution of knowledge for fancy. Bacon, the "father of experimental philosophy,"[1] had defined its motives. He looked down on the masters of tradition, the "great reputed authors" who first "believe that others know that which they know not; and after themselves know that which they know not. But indeed facility to believe, impatience to doubt, temerity to answer, glory to know, doubt to contradict, end to gain, sloth to search, seeking things in words, resting in part of nature; these and the like have been the things which have forbidden the happy match between the mind of man and the nature of things; and in place thereof have married it to vain notions and blind experiments: and what the posterity and issue of so honorable a match may be, it is not hard to consider. Printing, a gross invention; artillery, a thing that lay not far out of the way; the needle, a thing partly known before: what a change have these three things made in the world in these times; the one in state of learning, the other in the state of war, the third in the state of treasure, commodities, and navigation!

And those, I say, were but stumbled upon and lighted upon by chance. Therefore, no doubt, the sovereignty of man lieth hid in knowledge; wherein many things are reserved, which kings with their treasure cannot buy, nor with their force command; their spials and intelligencers can give no news of them, their seamen and discoverers cannot sail where they grow: now we govern nature in opinions, but we are thrall unto her in necessity: but if we would be led by her in invention, we should command her by action."[2]

Despite his lack of mathematics, Bacon's view was appropriate to the scientific attitude that prevailed after him. The concordance between the mind of man and the nature of things that he had in mind is patriarchal: the human mind, which overcomes superstition, is to hold sway over a disenchanted nature. Knowledge, which is power, knows no obstacles: neither in the enslavement of men nor in compliance with the world's rulers. As with all the ends of bourgeois economy in the factory and on the battlefield, origin is no bar to the dictates of the entrepreneurs: kings, no less directly than businessmen, control technology; it is as democratic as the economic system with which it is bound up. Technology is the essence of this knowledge. It does not work by concepts and images, by the fortunate insight, but refers to method, the exploitation of others' work, and capital. The "many things" which, according to Bacon, "are reserved," are themselves no more than instrumental: the radio as a sublimated printing press, the dive bomber as a more effective form of artillery, radio control as a more reliable compass. What men want to learn from nature is how to use it in order wholly to dominate it and other men. That is the only aim. Ruthlessly, in despite of itself, the Enlightenment has extinguished any trace of its own self-consciousness. The only kind of thinking that is sufficiently hard to shatter myths is ultimately self-destructive. In face of the present triumph of the factual mentality, even Bacon's nominalist credo would be suspected of a metaphysical bias and come under the same verdict of vanity that he pronounced on scholastic philosophy. Power and knowledge are synonymous.[3] For Bacon as for Luther, "knowledge that tendeth but to satisfaction, is but a courtesan, which is for pleasure, and not for fruit or generation." Not "satisfaction, which men call truth," but "operation," "to do the business," is the "right mark": for ". . . what is the true end, scope, or office of knowledge, which I have set down to consist not in any plausible, delectable, reverend or admired discourse, or any satisfactory arguments, but in effecting and working, and in discovery of particulars not revealed before, for the better endowment and help of man's life."[4] There is to be no mystery—which means, too, no wish to reveal mystery.

The disenchantment of the world is the extirpation of animism. Xenophanes derides the multitude of deities because they are but replicas of the men who produced them, together with all that is contingent and evil in mankind; and the most recent school of logic denounces—for the impressions they bear— the words of language, holding them to be false coins better replaced by neutral counters. The world becomes chaos, and synthesis salvation. There is said to be no difference between the totemic animal, the dreams of the ghost-seer, and the absolute Idea. On the road to modern science, men renounce any claim to meaning. They substitute formula for concept, rule and probability for cause and motive. Cause was only the last philosophic concept which served as a yardstick for scientific criticism: so to speak because it alone among the old ideas still seemed to offer itself to scientific criticism, the latest secularization of the creative principle. Substance and quality, activity and suffering, being and existence: to define these concepts in a way appropriate to the times was a concern of philosophy after Bacon—but science managed without such categories. They were abandoned as *idola theatri* of the old metaphysics, and assessed as being even then memorials of the elements and powers of the prehistory for which life and death disclosed their nature in myths and became interwoven in them. The categories by which Western philosophy defined its everlasting natural order marked the spots once occupied by Oncus and Persephone, Ariadne and Nereus. The pre-Socratic cosmologies preserve the moment of transition. The moist, the indivisible, air, and fire, which they hold to be the primal matter of nature, are already rationalizations of the mythic mode of apprehension. Just as the images of generation from water and earth, which came from the Nile to the Greeks, became here hylozoistic principles, or elements, so all the equivocal multitude of mythical demons were intellectualized in the pure form of ontological essences. Finally, by means of the Platonic ideas, even the patriarchal gods of Olympus were absorbed in the philosophical *logos*. The Enlightenment, however, recognized the old powers in the Platonic and Aristotelian aspects of metaphysics, and opposed as superstition the claim that truth is predicable of universals. It asserted that in the authority of universal concepts, there was still discernible fear of the demonic spirits which men sought to portray in magic rituals, hoping thus to influence nature. From now on, matter would at last be mastered without any illusion of ruling or inherent powers, of hidden qualities. For the Enlightenment, whatever does not conform to the rule of computation and utility is suspect. So long as it can develop undisturbed by any outward repression, there is no holding it. In the process, it treats its own ideas of human rights exactly as it does the older universals. Every spiritual resistance it encounters serves merely to increase its strength.[5] Which means that enlightenment still recognizes itself even in myths. Whatever myths the resistance may appeal to, by virtue of the very fact that they become arguments in the process of opposition, they acknowledge the principle of dissolvent rationality for which they reproach the Enlightenment. Enlightenment is totalitarian.

Enlightenment has always taken the basic principle of myth to be anthropomorphism, the projection onto nature of the subjective.[6] In this view, the supernatural, spirits and demons, are mirror images of men who allow themselves to be frightened by natural phenomena. Consequently the many mythic figures can all be brought to a common denominator, and reduced to the human subject. Oedipus' answer to the Sphinx's riddle: "It is man!" is the Enlightenment stereotype repeatedly offered as information, irrespective of whether it is faced with a piece of objective intelligence, a bare schematization, fear of evil powers, or hope of redemption. In advance, the Enlightenment recognizes as being and occurrence only what can be apprehended in unity: its ideal is the system from which all and everything follows. Its rationalist and empiricist versions do not part company on that point. Even though the individual schools may interpret the axioms differently, the structure of scientific unity has always been the same. Bacon's postulate of *una scientia universalis*,[7] whatever the number of fields of research, is as inimical to the unassignable as Leibniz's *mathesis universalis* is to discontinuity. The multiplicity of forms is reduced to position and arrangement, history to fact, things to matter. According to Bacon, too, degrees of universality provide an unequivocal logical connection between first principles and observational judgments. De Maistre mocks him for harboring *"une idole d'échelle."*[8] Formal logic was the major school of unified science. It provided the Enlightenment thinkers with the schema of the calculability of the world. The mythologizing equation of Ideas with numbers in Plato's last writings expresses the longing of all demythologization: number became the canon of the Enlightenment. The same equations dominate bourgeois justice and commodity exchange. "Is not the rule, *'Si inaequalibus aequalia addas, omnia erunt inaequalia,'* an axiom of justice as well as of the mathematics? And is there not a true coincidence between commutative and distributive justice, and arithmetical and geometrical proportion?"[9] Bourgeois society is ruled by equivalence. It makes the dissimilar comparable by reducing it to abstract quantities. To the Enlightenment, that which does not reduce to numbers, and ultimately to the one, becomes illusion; modern positivism writes it off as literature. Unity is the slogan from Parmenides to Russell. The destruction of gods and qualities alike is insisted upon.

Yet the myths which fell victim to the Enlightenment were its own products. In the scientific calculation of occurrence, the computation is annulled which thought had once transferred from occurrence into myths. Myth intended report, naming, the narration of the Beginning; but also presentation, confirmation, explanation: a tendency that grew stronger with the recording and collection of myths. Narrative became didactic at an early stage. Every ritual includes the idea of activity as a determined process which magic can nevertheless influence. This theoretical element in ritual won independence in the earliest national epics. The myths, as the tragedians came upon them, are already characterized by the discipline and power that Bacon celebrated as the "right mark." In place of the local spirits and demons there appeared heaven and its hierarchy; in place of the invocations of the magician and the tribe the distinct gradation of sacrifice and the labor of the unfree mediated through the word of command. The Olympic deities are no longer directly identical with elements, but signify them. In Homer, Zeus represents the sky and the weather, Apollo controls the sun, and Helios and Eos are already shifting to an allegorical function. The gods are distinguished from material elements as their quintessential concepts. From now on, being divides into the *logos* (which with the progress of philosophy contracts to the monad, to a mere point of reference), and into the mass of all things and creatures without.

This single distinction between existence proper and reality engulfs all others. Without regard to distinctions, the world becomes subject to man. In this the Jewish creation narrative and the religion of Olympia are at one: ". . . and let them have dominion over the fish of the sea, and over the fowl of the air, and over the cattle, and over all the earth, and over every creeping thing that creepeth upon the earth."[10] "O Zeus, Father Zeus, yours is the dominion of the heavens, and you oversee the works of man, both wicked and just, and even the wantonness of the beasts; and righteousness is your concern."[11] For so it is that one atones straight-away, and another later; but should one escape and the threatening decree of the gods not reach him, yet it will certainly be visited at last, if not upon him then upon his children or another generation."[12] Only he who always submits survives in the face of the gods. The awakening of the self is paid for by the acknowledgement of power as the principle of all relations. In view of the unity of this *ratio,* the divorcement between God and man dwindles to the degree of irrelevancy to which unswervable reason has drawn attention since even the earliest critique of Homer. The creative god and the systematic spirit are alike as rulers of nature. Man's likeness to God consists in sovereignty over existence, in the countenance of the lord and master, and in command.

Myth turns into enlightenment, and nature into mere objectivity. Men pay for the increase of their power with alienation from that over which they exercise their power. Enlightenment behaves toward things as a dictator toward men. He knows them in so far as he can manipulate them. The man of science knows things in so far as he can make them. In this way their potentiality is turned to his own ends. In the metamorphosis the nature of things, as a substratum of domination, is revealed as always the same. This identity constitutes the unity of nature. It is a presupposition of the magical invocation as little as the unity of the subject. The shaman's rites were directed to the wind, the rain, the serpent without, or the demon in the sick man, but not to materials or specimens. Magic was not ordered by one, identical spirit: it changed like the cultic masks which were supposed to accord with the various spirits. Magic is utterly untrue, yet in it domination is not yet negated by transforming itself into the pure truth and acting as the very ground of the world that has become subject to it. The magician imitates demons; in order to frighten them or to appease them, he behaves frighteningly or makes gestures of appeasement. Even though his task is impersonation, he never conceives of himself as does the civilized man for whom the unpretentious preserves of the happy hunting-grounds become the unified cosmos, the inclusive concept for all possibilities of plunder. The magician never interprets himself as the image of the invisible power; yet this is the very image in which man attains to the identity of self that cannot disappear through identification with another, but takes possession of itself once and for all as an impenetrable mask. It is the identity of the spirit and its correlate, the unity of nature, to which the multiplicity of qualities falls victim. Disqualified nature becomes the chaotic matter of mere classification, and the all-powerful self becomes mere possession—abstract identity. In magic there is specific representation. What happens to the enemy's spear, hair or name, also happens to the individual; the sacrificial animal is massacred instead of the god. Substitution in the course of sacrifice marks a step toward discursive logic. Even though the hind offered up for the daughter, and the lamb for the first-born, still had to have specific qualities, they already represented the species. They already exhibited the non-specificity of the example. But the holiness of the *hic et nunc,* the uniqueness of the chosen one into which the representative enters, radically marks it off, and makes it unfit for exchange. Science prepares the end of this state of affairs. In science there is no specific representation: and if there are no sacrificial animals there is no god. Representation is exchanged for the fungible—universal interchangeability. An atom is smashed not in representation but as a specimen of matter, and the rabbit does not represent but, as a mere example, is virtually ignored by the zeal of the laboratory. Because the distinctions in functional science are so fluid that everything is subsumed in the same matter, the scientific object is petrified, and the fixed ritual of former times appears flexible because it attributed the other to the one. The world of magic retained distinctions whose traces have disappeared even in linguistic form.[13] The multitudinous affinities between existents are suppressed by the single relation between the subject who bestows meaning and the meaningless object, between rational significance and the chance vehicle of significance. On the magical plane, dream and image were not mere signs for the thing in question, but were bound up with it by similarity or names. The relation is one not of intention but of relatedness. Like science, magic pursues aims, but seeks to achieve them by mimesis—not by progressively distancing itself from the object. It is not grounded in the "sovereignty of ideas," which the primitive, like the neurotic, is said to ascribe to himself;[14] there can be no "over-evaluation of mental processes as against reality" where there is no radical distinction between thoughts and reality. The "unshakable confidence in the possibility of world domination,"[15] which Freud anachronistically ascribes to magic, corresponds to realistic world domination only in terms of a more skilled science. The replacement of the milieu-bound practices of the medicine man by all-inclusive industrial technology required first of all the autonomy of ideas in regard to objects that was achieved in the reality-adjusted ego.

As a linguistically expressed totality, whose claim to truth suppresses the older mythic belief, the national religion or patriarchal solar myth is itself an Enlightenment with which the philosophic form can compare itself on the same level. And now it has its requital. Mythology itself set off the unending process of enlightenment in which ever and again, with the inevitability of necessity, every specific theoretic view succumbs to the destructive criticism that it is only a belief—until even the very notions of spirit, of truth and, indeed, enlightenment itself, have become animistic magic. The principle of fatal necessity, which brings low the heroes of myth and derives as a logical consequence from the pronouncement of the oracle, does not merely, when refined to the stringency of formal logic, rule in every rationalistic system of Western philosophy, but itself dominates the series of systems which begins with the hierarchy of the gods and, in a permanent twilight of the idols, hands down an identical content: anger against insufficient righteousness. Just as the myths already realize enlightenment, so enlightenment with every step becomes more deeply engulfed in mythology. It receives all its matter from the myths, in order to destroy them; and even as a judge it comes under the mythic curse. It wishes to extricate itself from the process of fate and retribution, while exercising retribution on that process. In the myths everything that happens must atone for having happened. And so it is in enlightenment: the fact becomes null and void, and might as well not have happened. The doctrine of the equivalence of action and reaction asserted the power of repetition over reality, long after men had renounced the illusion that by repetition they could identify themselves with the repeated reality and thus escape its power. But as the magical illusion fades away, the more relentlessly in the name of law repetition imprisons man in the cycle—that cycle whose objectification in the form of natural law he imagines will ensure his action as a free subject. The principle of immanence, the explanation of every event as repetition, that the Enlightenment upholds against mythic imagination, is the principle of myth itself. That arid wisdom that holds there is nothing new under the sun, because all the pieces in the meaningless game have been played, and all the great thoughts have already been thought, and because all possible discoveries can be construed in advance and all men are decided on adaptation as the means to self-preservation—that dry sagacity merely reproduces the fantastic wisdom that it supposedly rejects: the sanction of fate that in retribution relentlessly remakes what has already been. What was different is equalized. That is the verdict which critically determines the limits of possible experience. The identity of everything with everything else is paid for in that nothing may at the same time be identical with itself. Enlightenment dissolves the injustice of the old inequality—unmediated lordship and mastery—but at the same time perpetuates it in universal mediation, in the relation of any one existent to any other. It does what Kierkegaard praises his Protestant ethic for, and what in the Heraclean epic cycle is one of the primal images of mythic power; it excises the incommensurable. Not only are qualities dissolved in thought, but men are brought to actual conformity. The blessing that the market does not enquire after one's birth is paid for by the barterer, in that he models the potentialities that are his by birth on the production of the commodities that can be bought in the market. Men were given their individuality as unique in each case, different to all others, so that it might all the more surely be made the same as any other. But because the unique self never wholly disappeared, even after the liberalistic epoch, the Enlightenment has always sympathized with the social impulse. The unity of the manipulated collective consists in the negation of each individual: for individuality makes a mockery of the kind of society which would turn all individuals to the one collectivity. The horde which so assuredly appears in the organization of the Hitler Youth is not a return to barbarism but the triumph of repressive equality, the disclosure through peers of the parity of the right to injustice. The phony Fascist mythology is shown to be the genuine myth of antiquity, insofar as the genuine one saw retribution, whereas the false one blindly doles it out to the sacrifices. Every attempt to break the natural thralldom, because nature is broken, enters all the more deeply into that natural enslavement. Hence the course of European civilization. Abstraction, the tool of enlightenment, treats its objects as did fate, the notion of which it rejects: it liquidates them. Under the leveling domination of abstraction (which makes everything in nature repeatable), and of industry (for which abstraction ordains repetition), the freedom themselves finally came to form that "herd" which Hegel[16] has declared to be the result of the Enlightenment.

The distance between subject and object, a presupposition of abstraction, is grounded in the distance from the thing itself which the master achieved through the mastered. The lyrics of Homer and the hymns of the Rig-Veda date from the time of territorial dominion and the secure locations in which a dominant warlike race established themselves over the mass of vanquished natives.[17] The first god among the gods arose with this civil society in which the king, as chieftain of the arms-bearing nobility, holds down the conquered to the earth, whereas physicians, soothsayers, craftsmen and merchants see to social intercourse. With the end of a nomadic existence, the social order is created on a basis of fixed property. Mastery and labor are divided. A proprietor like Odysseus "manages from a distance a numerous, carefully gradated staff of cowherds, shepherds, swineherds and servants. In the evening, when he has seen from his castle that the countryside is illumined by a thousand fires, he can compose himself for sleep with a quiet mind: he knows that his upright servants are keeping watch lest wild animals approach, and to chase thieves from the preserves which they are there to protect."[18] The universality of ideas as developed by discursive logic, domination in the conceptual sphere, is raised up on the basis of actual domination. The dissolution of the magical heritage, of the old diffuse ideas, by conceptual unity, expresses the hierarchical constitution of life determined by those who are free. The individuality that learned order and subordination in the subjection of the world, soon wholly equated truth with the regulative thought without whose fixed distinctions universal truth cannot exist. Together with mimetic magic, it tabooed the knowledge which really concerned the object. Its hatred was extended to the image of the vanquished former age and its imaginary happiness. The chthonic gods of the original inhabitants are banished to the hell to which, according to the sun and light religion of Indra and Zeus, the earth is transformed.

Heaven and hell, however, hang together. Just as the name of Zeus, in nonexclusive cults, was given to a god of the underworld as well as to a god of light;[19] just as the Olympian gods had every kind of commerce with the chthonic deities: so the good and evil powers, salvation and disaster, were not unequivocally distinct. They were linked together like coming up and passing away, life and death, summer and winter. The gloomy and indistinct religious principle that was honored as *mana* in the earliest known stages of humanity, lives on in the radiant world of Greek religion. Everything unknown and alien is primary and undifferentiated: that which transcends the confines of experience; whatever in things is more than their previously known reality. What the primitive experiences in this regard is not a spiritual as opposed to a material substance, but the intricacy of the Natural in contrast to the individual. The gasp of surprise which accompanies the experience of the unusual becomes its name. It fixes the transcendence of the unknown in relation to the known, and therefore terror as sacredness. The dualization of nature as appearance and sequence, effort and power, which first makes possible both myth and science, originates in human fear, the expression of which becomes explanation. It is not the soul which is transposed to nature, as psychologism would have it; *mana,* the moving spirit, is no projection, but the echo of the real supremacy of nature in the weak souls of primitive men. The separation of the animate and the inanimate, the occupation of certain places by demons and deities, first arises from this pre-animism, which contains the first lines of the separation of subject and object. When the tree is no longer approached merely as tree, but as evidence for an Other, as the location of *mana,* language expresses the contradiction that something is itself, identical and not identical.[20] Through the deity, language is transformed from tautology to language. The concept, which some would see as the sign-unit for whatever is comprised under it, has from the beginning been instead the product of dialectical thinking in which everything is always that which it is, only because it becomes that which it is not. That was the original form of objectifying definition, in which concept and thing are separated. The same form which is already far advanced in the Homeric epic and confounds itself in modern positivist science. But this dialectic remains impotent to the extent that it develops from the cry of terror which is the duplication, the tautology, of terror itself. The gods cannot take fear away from man, for they bear its petrified sound with them as they bear their names. Man imagines himself free from fear when there is no longer anything unknown. That determines the course of demythologization, of enlightenment, which compounds the animate with the inanimate just as myth compounds the inanimate with the animate. Enlightenment is mythic fear turned radical. The pure immanence of positivism, its ultimate product, is no more than a so to speak universal taboo. Nothing at all may remain outside, because the mere idea of outsideness is the very source of fear. The revenge of the primitive for death, when visited upon one of his kin, was sometimes appeased by reception of the murderer into his own family;[21] this, too, signified the infusion of alien blood into one's own, the generation of immanence. The mythic dualism does not extend beyond the environs of existence. The world permeated by *mana* and even the world of Indian and Greek myth know no exits, and are eternally the same. Every birth is paid for with death, every fortune with misfortune. Men and gods may try in their short space to assess fate in other terms than the blind course of destiny, but in the end existence triumphs over them. Even their justice, which is wrested from fatality, bears the marks of fatality: it corresponds to the look which men—primitives, Greeks and barbarians alike—cast from a society of pressure and misery on the circumambient world. Hence, for mythic and en-lightened justice, guilt and atonement, happiness and unhappiness were sides of an equation. Justice is subsumed in law. The shaman wards off danger by means of its image. Equivalence is his instrument; and equivalence regulates punish-ment and reward in civilization. The mythic representations can also be traced back in their entirety to natural conditions. Just as the Gemini—the constellation of Castor and Pollux—and all other symbols of duality refer to the inevitable cy-cle of nature, which itself has its ancient sign in the symbol of the egg from which they came, so the balance held by Zeus, which symbolizes the justice of the entire patriarchal world, refers back to mere nature. The step from chaos to civiliza-tion, in which natural conditions exert their power no longer directly but through the medium of the human consciousness, has not changed the principle of equivalence. Indeed, men paid for this very step by worshipping what they were once in thrall to only in the same way as all other creatures. Before, the fetishes were subject to the law of equivalence. Now equivalence itself has be-come a fetish. The blindfold over Justitia's eyes does not only mean that there should be no assault upon justice, but that justice does not originate in freedom.

The doctrine of the priests was symbolic in the sense that in it sign and im-age were one. Just as hieroglyphs bear witness, so the word too originally had a pictorial function, which was transferred to myths. Like magical rites, myths signify self-repetitive nature, which is the core of the symbolic: a state of being or a process that is presented as eternal, because it incessantly becomes actual once more by being realized in symbolic form. Inexhaustibility, unending re-newal and the permanence of the signified are not mere attributes of all sym-bols, but their essential content. The representations of creation in which the world comes forth from the primal mother, the cow, or the egg, are symbolic—unlike the Jewish Genesis. The elders' mockery of the all-too-human gods left the core untouched. The gods were not wholly individual. They still had some-thing of *mana* in them, for they embodied nature as universal power. With their pre-animistic characteristics they are prominent in the Enlightenment. Beneath the coy veil of the Olympian *chronique scandaleuse*, there was already apparent the doctrine of the mixture, pressure, and impact of the elements, which presently established itself as science and turned the myths into fantastic im-ages. With the clean separation of science and poetry, the division of labor it had already helped to effect was extended to language. For science the word is a sign: as sound, image, and word proper it is distributed among the different arts, and is not permitted to reconstitute itself by their addition, by synesthesia, or in the composition of the *Gesamtkunstwerk*. As a system of signs, language is required to resign itself to calculation in order to know nature, and must dis-card the claim to be like her. As image, it is required to resign itself to mirror-imagery in order to be nature entire, and must discard the claim to know her. With the progress of enlightenment, only authentic works of art were able to avoid the mere imitation of that which already is. The practicable antithesis of art and science, which tears them apart as separate areas of culture in order to make them both manageable as areas of culture ultimately allows them, by dint of their own tendencies, to blend with one another even as exact contraries. In its neo-positivist version, science becomes aestheticism, a system of detached signs devoid of any intention that would transcend the system: it becomes the game which mathematicians have for long proudly asserted is their concern. But the art of integral representability, even in its techniques, subscribed to positive science, and in fact adapts to the world yet again, becoming ideological duplication, partisan reproduction. The separation of sign and image is irremediable. Should unconscious self-satisfaction cause it once again to become hypostatized, then each of the two isolated principles tends toward the destruction of truth.

In the relationship of intuition (i.e. direct perception) and concept, philosophy already discerned the gulf which opened with that separation, and again tries in vain to close it: philosophy, indeed, is defined by this very attempt. For the most part it has stood on the side from which it derives its name. Plato banned poetry with the same gesture that positivism used against the theory of ideas (*Ideenlehre*). With his much-renowned art, Homer carried out no public or private reforms, and neither won a war nor made any discovery. We know of no multitude of followers who might have honored or adored him. Art must first prove its utility.[22] For art, as for the Jews, imitation is proscribed. Reason and religion deprecate and condemn the principle of magic enchantment. Even in resigned self-distancing from real existence, as art, it remains dishonest; its practitioners become travelers, latterday nomads who find no abiding home under the established what-has-come-to-be. Nature must no longer be influenced by approximation, but mastered by labor. The work of art still has something in common with enchantment: it posits its own, self-enclosed area, which is withdrawn from the context of profane existence, and in which special laws apply. Just as in the ceremony the magician first of all marked out the limits of the area where the sacred powers were to come into play, so every work of art describes its own circumference which closes it off from actuality. This very renunciation of influence, which distinguishes art from magical sympathy, retains the magic heritage all the more surely. It places the pure image in contrast to animate existence, the elements of which it absorbs. It is in the nature of the work of art, or aesthetic semblance, to be what the new, terrifying occurrence became in the primitive's magic: the appearance of the whole in the particular. In the work of art that duplication still occurs by which the thing appeared as spiritual, as the expression of *mana*. This constitutes its aura. As an expression of totality art lays claim to the dignity of the absolute. This sometimes causes philosophy to allow it precedence to conceptual knowledge. According to Schelling, art comes into play where knowledge forsakes mankind. For him it is "the prototype of science, and only where there is art may science enter in."[23] In his theory, the separation of image and sign is "wholly canceled by every single artistic representation."[24] The bourgeois world was but rarely open to such confidence in art. Where it restricted knowledge, it usually did so not for the sake of art, but in order to make room for faith. Through faith the militant religiousness of the new age hoped to reconcile Torquemada, Luther, Mohammed, spirit and real life. But faith is a privative concept: it is destroyed as faith if it does not continually display its contradistinction to, or conformity with, knowledge. Since it is always set upon the restriction of knowledge, it is itself restricted. The attempt of Protestant faith to find, as in prehistory, the transcendental principle of truth (without which belief cannot exist) directly in the world itself, and to reinvest this with symbolic power, has been paid for with obedience to the word, and not to the sacred. As long as faith remains unhesitatingly tied—as friend or foe—to knowledge, it perpetuates the separation in the very course of the struggle to overcome it: its fanaticism is the occasion of its untruth, the objective admission that he who only has faith, for that very reason no longer has it. Bad conscience is its second nature. In the secret consciousness of the deficiency—necessarily inherent in faith—of its immanent contradiction in making reconciliation a vocation, lies the reason why the integrity of all believers has always been a sensitive and dangerous thing. The atrocities of fire and sword, counter-Reformation and Reformation, have occurred not as exaggerations but as realizations of the principle of faith itself. Faith constantly reveals itself to be of the same cut as the world-history which it would dictate to—in modern times, indeed, it becomes its favorite instrument, its particular stratagem. It is not merely the Enlightenment of the eighteenth century that, as Hegel confirmed, is relentless but—as no one knew better than he—the advance of thought itself. The lowest and the highest insight alike manifest that distance from truth which makes apologists liars. The paradoxical nature of faith ultimately degenerates into a swindle, and becomes the myth of the twentieth century; and its irrationality turns it into an instrument of rational administration by the wholly enlightened as they steer society toward barbarism.

When language enters history its masters are priests and sorcerers. Whoever harms the symbols is, in the name of the supernatural powers, subject to their earthly counterparts, whose representatives are those chosen organs of society. What happened previously is hid in darkness. The dread which gives to *mana*, wherever it is met with in ethnology, is always sanctioned—at least by the tribal elders. Unidentified, volatile *mana* was rendered consistent by men and forcibly materialized. Soon the magicians peopled every spot with emanations and made a multiplicity of sacred rites concordant with the variety of sacred places. They expanded their professional knowledge and their influence with the expansion of the spirit world and its characteristics. The nature of the sacred being transferred itself to the magicians, who were privy to it. In the first stages of nomadic life the members of the tribe still took an individual part in the process of influencing the course of nature. Men hunted game, while women did the work which could be produced without strict command. It is impossible to determine to what extent habit contributed to so simple an arrangement. In it, the world is already divided into the territory of power and the profane area; as the emanation of *mana*, the course of nature is elevated to become the norm, and submission to it is required. But even though, despite all submission, the savage nomad still participated in the magic which determined the lines of that submission, and clothed himself as his quarry in order to stalk it, in later times intercourse with spirits and submission were assigned to different classes: the power is on the one side, and obedience on the other. For the vanquished (whether by alien tribes or by their own cliques), the recurrent, eternally similar natural processes become the rhythm of labor according to the beat of cudgel and whip which resounds in every barbaric drum and every monotonous ritual. The symbols undertake a fetishistic function. In the process, the recurrence of nature which they signify is always the permanence of the social pressure which they represent. The dread objectified as a fixed image becomes the sign of the established domination of the privileged. Such is the fate of universal concepts, even when they have discarded everything pictorial. Even the deductive form of science reflects hierarchy and coercion. Just as the first categories represented the organized tribe and its power over the individual, so the whole logical order, dependency, connection, progression, and union of concepts is grounded in the corresponding conditions of social reality—that is, of the division of labor.[25] But of course this social character of categories of thought is not, as Durkheim asserts, an expression of social solidarity, but evidence of the inscrutable unity of society and domination. Domination lends increased consistency and force to the social whole in which it establishes itself. The division of labor to which domination tends serves the dominated whole for the end of self-preservation. But then the whole as whole, the manifestation of its immanent reason, necessarily leads to the execution of the particular. To the individual, domination appears to be the universal: reason in actuality. Through the division of labor imposed on them, the power of all the members of society—for whom as such there is no other course—amounts over and over again to the realization of the whole, whose rationality is reproduced in this way. What is done to all by the few, always occurs as the subjection of individuals by the many: social repression always exhibits the masks of repression by a collective. It is this unity of the collectivity and domination, and not direct social universality, solidarity, which is expressed in thought forms. By virtue of the claim to universal validity, the philosophic concepts with which Plato and Aristotle represented the world, elevated the conditions they were used to substantiate to the level of true reality. These concepts originated, as Vico puts it,[26] in the marketplace of Athens; they reflected with equal clarity the laws of physics, the equality of full citizens and the inferiority of women, children and slaves. Language itself gave what was asserted, the conditions of domination, the universality that they had assumed as the means of intercourse of a bourgeois society. The metaphysical emphasis, and sanction by means of ideas and norms, were no more than a hypostatization of the rigidity and exclusiveness which concepts were generally compelled to assume wherever language united the community of rulers with the giving of orders. As a mere means of reinforcing the social power of language, ideas became all the more superfluous as this power grew, and the language of science prepared the way for their ultimate desuetude. The suggestion of something still akin to the terror of the fetish did not inhere in conscious justification; instead the unity of collectivity and domination is revealed in the universality necessarily assumed by the bad content of language, both metaphysical and scientific. Metaphysical apology betrayed the injustice of the *status quo* least of all in the incongruence of concept and actuality. In the impartiality of scientific language, that which is powerless has wholly lost any means of expression, and only the given finds its neutral sign. This kind of neutrality is more metaphysical than metaphysics. Ultimately, the Enlightenment consumed not just the symbols but their successors, universal concepts, and spared no remnant of metaphysics apart from the abstract fear of the collective from which it arose. The situation of concepts in the face of the Enlightenment is like that of men of private means in regard to industrial trusts: none can feel safe. Even if logical positivism still allowed leeway to probability, ethnological positivism puts it in its place: "Our vague ideas of chance and quintessence are pale shadows of this much richer notion"[27]—that is, of magical substance.

As a nominalist movement, the Enlightenment calls a halt before the *nomen,* the exclusive, precise concept, the proper name. Whether—as some assert[28]—proper names were originally species names as well, can no longer be ascertained, yet the former have not shared the fate of the latter. The substantial ego refuted by Hume and Mach is not synonymous with the name. In Jewish religion, in which the idea of the patriarchate culminates in the destruction of myth, the bond between name and being is still recognized in the ban on pronouncing the name of God. The disenchanted world of Judaism conciliates magic by negating it in the idea of God. Jewish religion allows no word that would alleviate the despair of all that is mortal. It associates hope only with the prohibition against calling on what is false as God, against invoking the finite as the infinite, lies as truth. The guarantee of salvation lies in the rejection of any belief that would replace it: it is knowledge obtained in the denunciation of illusion. Admittedly, the negation is not abstract. The contesting of every positive without distinction, the stereotype formula of vanity, as used by Buddhism, sets itself above the prohibition against naming the Absolute with names: just as far above as its contrary, pantheism; or its caricature, bourgeois skepticism. Explanations of the world as all or nothing are mythologies, and guaranteed roads to redemption are sublimated magic practices. The self-satisfaction of knowing in advance and the transfiguration of negativity into redemption are untrue forms of resistance against deception. The justness of the image is preserved in the faithful pursuit of its prohibition. This pursuit, "determinate negativity"[29] does not receive from the sovereignty of the abstract concept any immunity against corrupting intuition, as does skepticism, to which both true and false are equally vain. Determinate negation rejects the defective ideas of the absolute, the idols, differently than does rigorism, which confronts them with the Idea that they cannot match up to. Dialectic, on the contrary, interprets every image as writing. It shows how the admission of its falsity is to be read in the lines of its features—a confession that deprives it of its power and appropriates it for truth. With the notion of determinate negativity, Hegel revealed an element that distinguishes the Enlightenment from the positivist degeneracy to which he attributes it. By ultimately making the conscious result of the whole process of negation—totality in system and in history—into an absolute, he of course contravened the prohibition and himself lapsed into mythology.

This did not happen merely to his philosophy as the apotheosis of progressive thought, but to the Enlightenment itself, as the sobriety which it thought distinguished it from Hegel and from metaphysics. For enlightenment is as totalitarian as any system. Its untruth does not consist in what its romantic enemies have always reproached it for: analytical method, return to elements, dissolution through reflective thought; but instead in the fact that for enlightenment the process is always decided from the start. When in mathematical procedure the unknown becomes the unknown quantity of an equation, this marks it as the well-known even before any value is inserted. Nature, before and after the quantum theory, is that which is to be comprehended mathematically; even what cannot be made to agree, indissolubility and irrationality, is converted by means of mathematical theorems. In the anticipatory identification of the wholly conceived and mathematized world with truth, enlightenment intends to secure itself against the return of the mythic. It confounds thought and mathematics. In this way the latter is, so to speak, released and made into an absolute instance. "An infinite world, in this case a world of idealities, is conceived as one whose objects do not accede singly, imperfectly, and as if by chance to our cognition, but are attained by a rational, systematically unified method—in a process of infinite progression—so that each object is ultimately apparent according to its full inherent being . . . In the Galilean mathematization of the world, however, *this selfness* is idealized under the guidance of the new mathematics: in modern terms, it becomes itself a mathematical multiplicity."[30] Thinking objectifies itself to become an automatic, self-activating process; an impersonation of the machine that it produces itself so that ultimately the machine can replace it. Enlightenment[31] has put aside the classic requirement of thinking about thought—Fichte is its extreme manifestation—because it wants to avoid the precept of dictating practice that Fichte himself wished to obey. Mathematical procedure became, so to speak, the ritual of thinking. In spite of the axiomatic self-restriction, it establishes itself as necessary and objective: it turns thought into a thing, an instrument—which is its own term for it. But this kind of mimesis, in which universal thought is equalized, so turns the actual into the unique, that even atheism itself is subjected to the ban on metaphysics. For positivism, which represents the court of judgment of enlightened reason, to digress into intelligible worlds is no longer merely forbidden, but meaningless prattle. It does not need—fortunately—to be atheistic, because objectified thinking cannot even raise the problem. The positivist censor lets the established cult escape as willingly as art—as a cognition-free special area of social activity; but he will never permit that denial of it which itself claims to be knowledge. For the scientific mind, the separation of thought from business for the purpose of adjusting actuality, departure from the privileged area of real existence, is as insane and self-destructive as the primitive magician would consider stepping out of the magic circle he has prepared for his invocation; in both cases the offense against the taboo will actually result in the malefactor's ruin. The mastery of nature draws the circle into which the criticism of pure reason banished thought. Kant joined the theory of its unceasingly laborious advance into infinity with an insistence on its deficiency and everlasting limitation. His judgment is an oracle. There is no form of being in the world that science could not penetrate, but what can be penetrated by science is not being. According to Kant, philosophic judgment aims at the new; and yet it recognizes nothing new, since it always merely recalls what reason has always deposited in the object. But there is a reckoning for this form of thinking that considers itself secure in the various departments of science—secure from the dreams of a ghost-seer: world domination over nature turns against the thinking subject himself; nothing is left of him but that eternally same *I think* that must accompany all my ideas. Subject and object are both rendered ineffectual. The abstract self, which justifies record-making and systematization, has nothing set over against it but the abstract material which possesses no other quality than to be a substrate of such possession. The equation of spirit and world arises eventually, but only with a mutual restriction of both sides. The reduction of thought to a mathematical apparatus conceals the sanction of the world as its own yardstick. What appears to be the triumph of subjective rationality, the subjection of all reality to logical formalism, is paid for by the obedient subjection of reason to what is directly given. What is abandoned is the whole claim and approach of knowledge: to comprehend the given as such; not merely to determine the abstract spatio-temporal relations of the facts which allow them just to be grasped, but on the contrary to conceive them as the superficies, as mediated conceptual moments which come to fulfillment only in the development of their social, historical, and human significance. The task of cognition does not consist in mere apprehension, classification, and calculation, but in the determinate negation of each im-mediacy. Mathematical formalism, however, whose medium is number, the most abstract form of the immediate, instead holds thinking firmly to mere immediacy. Factuality wins the day; cognition is restricted to its repetition; and thought becomes mere tautology. The more the machinery of thought subjects existence to itself, the more blind its resignation in reproducing existence. Hence enlightenment returns to mythology, which it never really knew how to elude. For in its figures mythology had the essence of the *status quo:* cycle, fate, and domination of the world reflected as the truth and deprived of hope. In both the pregnancy of the mythical image and the clarity of the scientific formula, the everlastingness of the factual is confirmed and mere existence pure and simple expressed as the meaning which it forbids. The world as a gigantic analytic judgment, the only one left over from all the dreams of science, is of the same mold as the cosmic myth which associated the cycle of spring and autumn with the kidnapping of Persephone. The uniqueness of the mythic process, which tends to legitimize factuality, is deception. Originally the carrying off of the goddess was directly synonymous with the dying of nature. It repeated itself every autumn, and even the repetition was not the result of the buried one but the same every time. With the rigidification of the consciousness of time, the process was fixed in the past as a unique one, and in each new cycle of the seasons an attempt was made ritually to appease fear of death by recourse to what was long past. But the separation is ineffective. Through the establishment of a unique past, the cycle takes on the character of inevitability, and dread radiates from the age-old occurrence to make every event its mere repetition. The absorption of factuality, whether into legendary prehistory or into mathematical formalism, the symbolical relation of the contemporary to the mythic process in the rite or to the abstract category in science, makes the new appear as the predetermined, which is accordingly the old. Not existence but knowledge is without hope, for in the pictorial or mathematical symbol it appropriates and perpetuates existence as a schema.

In the enlightened world, mythology has entered into the profane. In its blank purity, the reality which has been cleansed of demons and their conceptual descendants assumes the numinous character which the ancient world attributed to demons. Under the title of brute facts, the social injustice from which they proceed is now as assuredly sacred a preserve as the medicine man was sacrosanct by reason of the protection of his gods. It is not merely that domination is paid for by the alienation of men from the objects dominated: with the objectification of spirit, the very relations of men—even those of the individual to himself—were bewitched. The individual is reduced to the nodal point of the conventional responses and modes of operation expected of him. Animism spiritualized the object, whereas industrialism objectifies the spirits of men. Automatically, the economic apparatus, even before total planning, equips commodities with the values which decide human behavior. Since, with the end of free exchange, commodities lost all their economic qualities except for fetishism, the latter has extended its arthritic influence over all aspects of social life. Through the countless agencies of mass production and its culture the conventionalized modes of behavior are impressed on the individual as the only natural, respectable, and rational ones. He defines himself only as a thing, as a static element, as success or failure. His yardstick is self-preservation, successful or unsuccessful approximation to the objectivity of his function and the models established for it. Everything else, idea and crime, suffers the force of the collective, which monitors it from the classroom to the trade union. But even the threatening collective belongs only to the deceptive surface, beneath which are concealed the powers which manipulate it as the instrument of power. Its brutality, which keeps the individual up to scratch, represents the true quality of men as little as value represents the things which he consumes. The demonically distorted form which things and men have assumed in the light of unprejudiced cognition, indicates domination, the principle which effected the specification of *mana* in spirits and gods and occurred in the jugglery of magicians and medicine men. The fatality by means of which prehistory sanctioned the incomprehensibility of death is transferred to wholly comprehensible real existence. The noontide panic fear in which men suddenly became aware of nature as totality has found its like in the panic which nowadays is ready to break out at every moment: men expect that the world, which is without any issue, will be set on fire by a totality which they themselves are and over which they have no control.

The mythic terror feared by the Enlightenment accords with myth. Enlightenment discerns it not merely in unclarified concepts and words, as demonstrated by semantic language-criticism, but in any human assertion that has no place in the ultimate context of self-preservation. Spinoza's *"Conatus sese conservandi primum et unicum virtutis est fundamentum"*[32] contains the true maxim of all Western civilization, in which the religious and philosophical differences of the middle class are reconciled. The self (which, according to the methodical extirpation of all natural residues because they are mythological, must no longer be either body or blood, or soul, or even the natural I), once sublimated into the transcendental or logical subject, would form the reference point of reason, of the determinative instance of action. Whoever resigns himself to life without any rational reference to self-preservation would, according to the Enlightenment—and Protestantism—regress to prehistory. Impulse as such is as mythic as superstition; to serve the god not postulated by the self is as idiotic as drunkenness. Progress has prepared the same fate for both adoration and descent into a state of directly natural being, and has anathematized both the self-abandonment of thought and that of pleasure. The social work of every individual in bourgeois society is mediated through the principle of self; for one, labor will bring an increased return on capital; for others, the energy for extra labor. But the more the process of self-preservation is effected by the bourgeois division of labor, the more it requires the self-alienation of the individuals who must model their body and soul according to the technical apparatus. This again is taken into account by enlightened thought: in the end the transcendental subject of cognition is apparently abandoned as the last reminiscence of subjectivity and replaced by the much smoother work of automatic control mechanisms. Subjectivity has given way to the logic of the allegedly indifferent rules of the game, in order to dictate all the more unrestrainedly. Positivism, which finally did not spare thought itself, the chimera in a cerebral form, has removed the very last insulating instance between individual behavior and the social norm. The technical process, into which the subject has objectified itself after being removed from the consciousness, is free of the ambiguity of mythic thought as of all meaning altogether, because reason itself has become the mere instrument of the all-inclusive economic apparatus. It serves as a general tool, useful for the manufacture of all other tools, firmly directed toward its end, as fateful as the precisely calculated movement of material production, whose result for mankind is beyond all calculation. At last its old ambition, to be a pure organ of ends, has been realized. The exclusiveness of logical laws originates in this unique functional significance, and ultimately in the compulsive nature of self-preservation. And self-preservation repeatedly culminates in the choice between survival and destruction, apparent again in the principle that of two contradictory propositions only one can be true and only one false. The formalism of this principle, and of the entire logic in which form it is established, derives from the opacity and complexity of interests in a society in which the maintenance of forms and the preservation of individuals coincide only by chance. The derivation of thought from logic ratifies in the lecture room the reification of man in the factory and the office. In this way the taboo encroaches upon the anathematizing power, and enlightenment upon the spirit which it itself comprises. Then, however, nature as true self-preservation is released by the very process which promised to extirpate it, in the individual as in the collective destiny of crisis and armed conflict. If the only norm that remains for theory is the ideal of unified science, practice must be subjected to the irrepressible process of world history. The self that is wholly comprehended by civilization resolves itself in an element of the inhumanity which from the beginning has aspired to evade civilization. The primordial fear of losing one's own name is realized. For civilization, pure natural existence, animal and vegetative, was the absolute danger. One after the other, mimetic, mythic and metaphysical modes of behavior were taken as superseded eras, any reversion to which was to be feared as implying a reversion of the self to that mere state of nature from which it had estranged itself with so huge an effort, and which therefore struck such terror into the self. In every century, any living reminiscence of olden times, not only of nomadic antiquity but all the more of the pre-patriarchal stages, was most rigorously punished and extirpated from human consciousness. The spirit of enlightenment replaced the fire and the rack by the stigma it attached to all irrationality, because it led to corruption. Hedonism was moderate, finding the extreme no less odious than did Aristotle. The bourgeois ideal of naturalness intends not amorphous nature, but the virtuous mean. Promiscuity and asceticism, excess and hunger, are directly identical, despite the antagonism, as powers of disintegration. By subjecting the whole of life to the demands of its maintenance, the dictatorial minority guarantees, together with its own security, the persistence of the whole. From Homer to modern times, the dominant spirit wishes to steer between the Scylla of a return to mere reproduction and the Charybdis of unfettered fulfillment; it has always mistrusted any star other than that of the lesser evil. The new German pagans and warmongers want to set pleasure free once more. But under the pressure of labor, through the centuries, pleasure has learned self-hatred, and therefore in the state of totalitarian emancipation remains mean and disabled by self-contempt. It remains in the grip of the self-preservation to which it once trained reason—deposed in the meantime. At the turning points of Western civilization, from the transition to Olympian religion up to the Renaissance, Reformation, and bourgeois atheism, whenever new nations and classes more firmly repressed myth, the fear of uncomprehended, threatening nature, the consequence of its very materialization and objectification, was reduced to animistic superstition, and the subjugation of nature was made the absolute purpose of life within and without. If in the end self-preservation has been automated, so reason has been abandoned by those who, as administrators of production, entered upon its inheritance and now fear it in the persons of the disinherited. The essence of enlightenment is the alternative whose ineradicability is that of domination. Men have always had to choose between their subjection to nature or the subjection of nature to the Self. With the extension of the bourgeois commodity economy, the dark horizon of myth is illumined by the sun of calculating reason, beneath whose cold rays the seed of the new barbarism grows to fruition. Under the pressure of domination human labor has always led away from myth—but under domination always returns to the jurisdiction of myth.

The entanglement of myth, domination, and labor is preserved in one of the Homeric narratives. Book XII of the Odyssey tells of the encounter with the Sirens. Their allurement is that of losing oneself in the past. But the hero to whom the temptation is offered has reached maturity through suffering. Throughout the many mortal perils he has had to endure, the unity of his own life, the identity of the individual, has been confirmed for him. The regions of time part for him as do water, earth, and air. For him, the flood of that-which-was has retreated from the rock of the present, and the future lies cloudy on the horizon. What Odysseus left behind him entered into the nether world; for the self is still so close to prehistoric myth, from whose womb it tore itself, that its very own experienced past becomes mythic prehistory. And it seeks to encounter that myth through the fixed order of time. The three-fold schema is intended to free the present moment from the power of the past by referring that power behind the absolute barrier of the unrepeatable and placing it at the disposal of the present as practicable knowledge. The compulsion to rescue what is gone as what is living instead of using it as the material of progress was appeased only in art, to which history itself appertains as a presentation of past life. So long as art declines to pass as cognition and is thus separated from practice, social practice tolerates it as it tolerates pleasure. But the Sirens' song has not yet been rendered powerless by reduction to the condition of art. They know "everything that ever happened on this so fruitful earth,"[33] including the events in which Odysseus himself took part, "all those things that Argos' sons and the Trojans suffered by the will of the gods on the plains of Troy."[34] While they directly evoke the recent past, with the irresistible promise of pleasure as which their song is heard, they threaten the patriarchal order which renders to each man his life only in return for his full measure of time. Whoever falls for their trickery must perish, whereas only perpetual presence of mind forces an existence from nature. Even though the Sirens know all that has happened, they demand the future as the price of that knowledge, and the promise of the happy return is the deception with which the past ensnares the one who longs for it. Odysseus is warned by Circe, that divinity of reversion to the animal, whom he resisted and who therefore gives him strength to resist other powers of disintegration. But the allurement of the Sirens remains superior; no one who hears their song can escape. Men had to do fearful things to themselves before the self, the identical, purposive, and virile nature of man, was formed, and something of that recurs in every childhood. The strain of holding the I together adheres to the I in all stages; and the temptation to lose it has always been there with the blind determination to maintain it. The narcotic intoxication which permits the atonement of deathlike sleep for the euphoria in which the self is suspended, is one of the oldest social arrangements which mediate between self-preservation and self-destruction—an attempt of the self to survive itself. The dread of losing the self and of abrogating together with the self the barrier between oneself and other life, the fear of death and destruction, is intimately associated with a promise of happiness which threatened civilization in every moment. Its road was that of obedience and labor, over which fulfillment shines forth perpetually—but only as illusive appearance, as devitalized beauty. The mind of Odysseus, inimical both to his own death and to his own happiness, is aware of this. He knows only two possible ways to escape. One of them he prescribes for his men. He plugs their ears with wax, and they must row with all their strength. Whoever would survive must not hear the temptation of that which is unrepeatable, and he is able to survive only by being unable to hear it. Society has always made provision for that. The laborers must be fresh and concentrate as they look ahead, and must ignore whatever lies to one side. They must doggedly sublimate in additional effort the drive that impels to diversion. And so they become practical.—The other possibility Odysseus, the seigneur who allows the others to labor for themselves, reserves to himself. He listens, but while bound impotently to the mast; the greater the temptation the more he has his bonds tightened—just as later the burghers would deny themselves happiness all the more doggedly as it drew closer to them with the growth of their own power. What Odysseus hears is without consequence for him; he is able only to nod his head as a sign to be set free from his bonds; but it is too late; his men, who do not listen, know only the song's danger but nothing of its beauty, and leave him at the mast in order to save him and themselves. They reproduce the oppressor's life together with their own, and the oppressor is no longer able to escape his social role. The bonds with which he has irremediably tied himself to practice, also keep the Sirens away from practice: their temptation is neutralized and becomes a mere object of contemplation—becomes art. The prisoner is present at a concert, an inactive eavesdropper like later concertgoers, and his spirited call for liberation fades like applause. Thus the enjoyment of art and manual labor break apart as the world of prehistory is left behind. The epic already contains the appropriate theory. The cultural material is in exact correlation to work done according to command; and both are grounded in the inescapable compulsion to social domination of nature.

Measures such as those taken on Odysseus' ship in regard to the Sirens form presentient allegory of the dialectic of enlightenment. Just as the capacity of representation is the measure of domination, and domination is the most powerful thing that can be represented in most performances, so the capacity of representation is the vehicle of progress and regression at one and the same time. Under the given conditions, exemption from work—not only among the unemployed but even at the other end of the social scale—also means disablement. The rulers experience existence, with which they need no longer concern themselves, only as a substratum, and hence wholly ossify into the condition of the commanding self. Primitive man experienced the natural thing merely as the evasive object of desire. "But the master, who has interposed the servant between it and himself, in this way relates himself only to the dependence of the thing and enjoys it pure; however, he leaves the aspect of [its] independence to the servant, who works upon it."[25] Odysseus is represented in labor. Just as he cannot yield to the temptation to self-abandonment, so, as proprietor, he finally renounces even participation in labor, and ultimately even its management, whereas his men—despite their closeness to things—cannot enjoy their labor because it is performed under pressure, in desperation, with senses stopped by force. The servant remains enslaved in body and soul; the master regresses. No authority has yet been able to escape paying this price, and the apparent cyclical nature of the advance of history is partly explained by this debilitation, the equivalent of power. Mankind, whose versatility and knowledge become differentiated with the division of labor, is at the same time forced back to anthropologically more primitive stages, for with the technical easing of life the persistence of domination brings about a fixation of the instincts by means of heavier repression. Imagination atrophies. The disaster is not merely that individuals might remain behind society or its material production. Where the evolution of the machine has already turned into that of the machinery of domination (so that technical and social tendencies, always interwoven, converge in the total schematization of men), untruth is not represented merely by the outdistanced. As against that, adaptation to the power of progress involves the progress of power, and each time anew brings about those degenerations which show not unsuccessful but successful progress to be its contrary. The curse of irresistible progress is irresistible regression.

This regression is not restricted to the experience of the sensuous world bound up with the circumambient animate, but at the same time affects the self-dominant intellect, which separates from sensuous experience in order to subjugate it. The unification of intellectual functions by means of which domination over the senses is achieved, the resignation of thought to the rise of unanimity, means the impoverishment of thought and of experience: the separation of both areas leaves both impaired. The restriction of thought to organization and administration, practiced by rulers from the cunning Odysseus to the naïve managing directors of today, necessarily implies the restriction which comes upon the great as soon as it is no longer merely a question of manipulating the small. Hence the spirit becomes the very apparatus of domination and self-domination which bourgeois thought has always mistakenly supposed it to be. The stopped ears which the pliable proletarians have retained ever since the time of myth have no advantage over the immobility of the master. The over-maturity of society lives by the immaturity of the dominated. The more complicated and precise the social, economic, and scientific apparatus with whose service the production system has long harmonized the body, the more impoverished the experiences which it can offer. The elimination of qualities, their conversion into functions, is translated from science by means of rationalized modes of labor to the experiential world of nations, and tends to approximate it once more to that of the amphibians. The regression of the masses today is their inability to hear the unheard-of with their own ears, to touch the unapprehended with their own hands—the new form of delusion which deposes every conquered mythic form. Through the mediation of the total society which embraces all relations and emotions, men are once again made to be that against which the evolutionary law of society, the principle of self, had turned: mere species beings, exactly like one another through isolation in the forcibly united collectivity. The oarsmen, who cannot speak to one another, are each of them yoked in the same rhythm as the modern worker in the factory, movie theater, and collective. The actual working conditions in society compel conformism—not the conscious influences which also made the suppressed men dumb and separated them from truth. The impotence of the worker is not merely a stratagem of the rulers, but the logical consequence of the industrial society into which the ancient Fate—in the very course of the effort to escape it—has finally changed.

But this logical necessity is not conclusive. It remains tied to domination, as both its reflection and its tool. Therefore its truth is no less questionable than its evidence is irrefutable. Of course thought has always sufficed concretely to characterize its own equivocation. It is the servant that the master cannot check as he wishes. Domination, ever since men settled down, and later in the commodity society, has become objectified as law and organization and must therefore restrict itself. The instrument achieves independence: the mediating instance of the spirit, independently of the will of the master, modifies the directness of economic injustice. The instruments of domination, which would encompass all—language, weapons, and finally machines—must allow themselves to be encompassed by all. Hence in domination the aspect of rationality prevails as one that is also different from it. The "objectivity" of the means, which makes it universally available, already implies the criticism of that domination as whose means thought arose. On the way from mythology to logistics, thought has lost the element of self-reflection, and today machinery disables men even as it nurtures them. But in the form of machines the alienated *ratio* moves toward a society which reconciles thought in its fixed form as a material and intellectual apparatus with free, live, thought, and refers to society itself as the real subject of thought. The specific origin of thought and its universal perspective have always been inseparable. Today, with the transformation of the world into industry, the perspective of universality, the social realization of thought, extends so far that in its behalf the rulers themselves disavow thought as mere ideology. The bad conscience of cliques which ultimately embody economic necessity is betrayed in that its revelations, from the intuitions of the Leader to the dynamic *Weltanschauung,* no longer recognize (in marked contrast to earlier bourgeois apologetics) their own misdeeds as necessary consequences of statutory contexts. The mythological lies of mission and destiny which they use as substitutes never declare the whole truth: gone are the objective laws of the market which ruled in the actions of the entrepreneurs and tended toward catastrophe. Instead the conscious decision of the managing directors executes as results (which are more obligatory than the blindest price-mechanisms) the old law of value and hence the destiny of capitalism. The rulers themselves do not believe in any objective necessity, even though they sometimes describe their concoctions thus. They declare themselves to be the engineers of world history. Only the ruled accept as unquestionable necessity the course of development that with every decreed rise in the standard of living makes them so much more powerless. When the standard of living of those who are still employed to service the machines can be assured with a minimal part of the working time available to the rulers of society, the superfluous remainder, the vast mass of the population, is drilled as yet another battalion—additional material to serve the present and future great plans of the system. The masses are fed and quartered as the army of the unemployed. In their eyes, their reduction to mere objects of the administered life, which preforms every sector of modern existence including language and perception, represents objective necessity, against which they believe there is nothing they can do. Misery as the antithesis of power and powerlessness grows immeasurably, together with the capacity to remove all misery permanently. Each individual is unable to penetrate the forest of cliques and institutions which, from the highest levels of command to the last professional rackets, ensure the boundless persistence of status. For the union boss, let alone the director, the proletarian (should he ever come face to face with him) is nothing but a supernumerary example of the mass, while the boss in his turn has to tremble at the thought of his own liquidation.

The absurdity of a state of affairs in which the enforced power of the system over men grows with every step that takes it out of the power of nature, denounces the rationality of the rational society as obsolete. Its necessity is illusive, no less than the freedom of the entrepreneurs who ultimately reveal their compulsive nature in their inevitable wars and contracts. This illusion, in which a wholly enlightened mankind has lost itself, cannot be dissolved by a philosophy which, as the organ of domination, has to choose between command and obedience. Without being able to escape the confusion which still ensnares it in prehistory, it is nevertheless able to recognize the logic of either-or, of consequence and antimony, with which it radically emancipated itself from nature, as this very nature, unredeemed and self-alienated. Thinking, in whose mechanism of compulsion nature is reflected and persists, inescapably reflects its very own self as its own forgotten nature—as a mechanism of compulsion. Ideation is only an instrument. In thought, men distance themselves from nature in order thus imaginatively to present it to themselves—but only in order to determine how it is to be dominated. Like the thing, the material tool, which is held on to in different situations as the same thing, and hence divides the world as the chaotic, manysided, and disparate from the known, one, and identical, the concept is the ideal tool, fit to do service for everything, wherever it can be applied. And so thought becomes illusionary whenever it seeks to deny the divisive function, distancing and objectification. All mystic unification remains deception, the impotently inward trace of the absolved revolution. But while enlightenment maintains its justness against any hypostatization of utopia and unfailingly proclaims domination to be disunion, the dichotomy between subject and object that it will not allow to be obscured becomes the index of the untruth of that dichotomy and of truth. The proscription of superstition has always signified not only the progress of domination but its compromise. Enlightenment is more than enlightenment—the distinct representation of nature in its alienation. In the self-cognition of the spirit as nature in disunion with itself, as in prehistory, nature calls itself to account; no longer directly, as *mana*—that is, with the alias that signifies omnipotence—but as blind and lame. The decline, the forfeiture, of nature consists in the subjugation of nature without which spirit does not exist. Through the decision in which spirit acknowledges itself to be domination and retreats into nature, it abandons the claim to domination which makes it a vassal of nature. Even though in the flight from necessity, in progress and civilization, mankind cannot hold the course without abandoning knowledge itself, at least it no longer mistakes the ramparts that it erects against necessity (the institutions and practices of subjection that have always redounded on society from the subjugation of nature) for guarantees of the freedom to come. Every progress made by civilization has renewed together with domination that prospect of its removal. Whereas, however, real history is woven out of a real suffering that is not lessened in proportion to the growth of means for its abrogation, the realization of the prospect is referred to the notion, the concept. For it does not merely, as science, distance men from nature, but, as the self-consideration of thought that in the form of science remains tied to blind economic tendency, allows the distance perpetuating injustice to be measured. By virtue of this remembrance of nature in the subject, in whose fulfillment the unacknowledged truth of all culture lies hidden, enlightenment is universally opposed to domination; and the call to check enlightenment resounded even in the time of Vanini[36] less out of fear of exact science than out of that hatred of undisciplined ideas which emerges from the jurisdiction of nature even as it acknowledges itself to be nature's very dread of its own self. The priests always avenged *mana* on the prophet of enlightenment, who propitiated *mana* by a terror-stricken attitude to what went by the name of terror, and the augurs of the Enlightenment were one with the priests in their hybris. In its bourgeois form, the Enlightenment had lost itself in its positivistic aspect long before Turgot and d'Alembert. It was never immune to the exchange of freedom for the pursuit of self-preservation. The suspension of the concept, whether in the name of progress or of culture—which had already long before tacitly leagued themselves against the truth—opened the way for falsehood. And this in a world that verified only evidential propositions, and preserved thought—degraded to the achievement of great thinkers—as a kind of stock of superannuated clichés, no longer to be distinguished from truth neutralized as a cultural commodity.

But to recognize domination, even in thought itself, as unreconciled nature, would mean a slackening of the necessity whose perpetuity socialism itself prematurely confirmed as a concession to reactionary common sense. By elevating necessity to the status of the basis for all time to come, and by idealistically degrading the spirit for ever to the very apex, socialism held on all too surely to the legacy of bourgeois philosophy. Hence the relation of necessity to the realm of freedom would remain merely quantitative and mechanical, and nature, posited as wholly alien—just as in the earliest mythology—would become totalitarian and absorb freedom together with socialism. With the abandonment of thought, which in its reified form of mathematics, machine, and organization avenges itself on the men who have forgotten it, enlightenment has relinquished its own realization. By taking everything unique and individual under its tutelage, it left the uncomprehended whole the freedom, as domination, to strike back at human existence and consciousness by way of things. But true revolutionary practice depends on the intransigence of theory in the face of the insensibility with which society allows thought to ossify. It is not the material prerequisites of fulfillment—liberated technology as such—which jeopardize fulfillment. That is asserted by those sociologists who are again searching for an antidote, and—should it be a collectivist measure—to master the antidote.[37] Guilt is a context of social delusion. The mythic scientific respect of the peoples of the earth for the *status quo* that they themselves unceasingly produce, itself finally becomes positive fact: the oppressor's fortress in regard to which even revolutionary imagination despises itself as utopism and decays to the condition of pliable trust in the objective tendency of history. As the organ of this kind of adaptation, as a mere construction of means, the Enlightenment is as destructive as its romantic enemies accuse it of being. It comes into its own only when it surrenders the last remaining concordance with the latter and dares to transcend the false absolute, the principle of blind domination. The spirit of this kind of unrelenting theory would turn even the mind of relentless progress to its end. Its herald Bacon dreamed of the many things "which kings with their treasure cannot buy, nor with their force command," of which "their spials and intelligencers can give no news." As he wished, they fell to the burghers, the enlightened heirs of those kings. While bourgeois economy multiplied power though the mediation of the market, it also multiplied its objects and powers to such an extent that for their administration not just the kings, not even the middle classes are no longer necessary, but all men. They learn from the power of things to dispense at last with power. Enlightenment is realized and reaches its term when the nearest practical ends reveal themselves as the most distant goal now attained, and the lands of which "their spials and intelligencers can give no news," that is, those of the nature despised by dominant science, are recognized as the lands of origin. Today, when Bacon's utopian vision that we should "command nature by action"—that is, in practice—has been realized on a tellurian scale, the nature of the thralldom that he ascribed to unsubjected nature is clear. It was domination itself. And knowledge, in which Bacon was certain the "sovereignty of man lieth hid," can now become the dissolution of domination. But in the face of such a possibility, and in the service of the present age, enlightenment becomes wholesale deception of the masses.

NOTES

1. Voltaire, *Lettres Philosophiques, XII, Œuvres Complètes* (Garnier: Paris, 1879), Vol. XXII, p. 118.
2. Bacon, "In Praise of Human Knowledge" (*Miscellaneous Tracts upon Human Knowledge*), *The Works of Francis Bacon*, ed. Basil Montagu (London, 1825), Vol. I, pp. 254ff.
3. Cf. Bacon, *Novum Organum, Works*, Vol. XIV, p. 31.
4. Bacon, "Valerius Terminus: Of the Interpretation of Nature" (*Miscellaneous Tracts upon Human Knowledge*), *Works*, Vol. I, p. 281.
5. Cf. Hegel, *Phänomenologie des Geistes (The Phenomenology of Spirit), Werke*, Vol. II, pp. 410ff.
6. Xenophanes, Montaigne, Hume, Feuerbach, and Salomon Reinach are at one here. See, for Reinach: *Orpheus*, trans. F. Simmons (London & New York, 1909), pp. 9ff.
7. Bacon, *De Augmentis Scientiarum, Works*, Vol. VIII, p. 152.
8. *Les Soirées de Saint-Pétersbourg* (5ième entretien), *Œuvres Complètes* (Lyon, 1891), Vol. IV, p. 256.
9. Bacon, *Advancement of Learning, Works*, Vol. II, p. 126.
10. Genesis I. 26 (AV).
11. Archilochos, fr. 87; quoted by Deussen, *Allgemeine Geschichte der Philosophie*, Vol. II, Pt. 1 (Leipzig, 1911), p. 18.
12. Solon, fr. 13.25 *et seq.*, quoted by Deussen, p. 20.
13. See, for example: Robert H. Lowie, *An Introduction to Cultural Anthropology* (New York, 1940), pp. 344ff.
14. Cf. Freud, *Totem und Tabu (Totem and Taboo), Gesammelte Werke*, Vol. IX, pp. 106ff.
15. *Totem und Tabu*, p. 110.
16. *Phänomenologie des Geistes*, p. 424.
17. Cf. W. Kirfel, *Geschichte Indiens*, in: *Propyläenweltgeschichte*, Vol. III, pp. 261ff; and G. Glotz, *Histoire Grècque*, Vol. I, in: *Histoire Ancienne* (Paris, 1938), pp. 137ff.
18. Glotz, p. 140.
19. See Kurt Eckermann, *Jahrbuch der Religionsgeschichte und Mythologie* (Halle, 1845), Vol. I, p. 241; and O. Kern, *Die Religion der Griechen* (Berlin, 1926), Vol. I, pp. 181ff.
20. This is how Hubert and Mauss interpret "sympathy," or *mimesis: "L'un est le tout, est dans l'un, la nature triomphe de la nature."* H. Hubert and M. Mauss, *"Théorie générale de la Magie,"* in: *L'Année Sociologique*, 1902–3, p. 100.

21. Cf. Westermarck, *Ursprung der Moralbegriffe* (Leipzig, 1913), Vol. I, p. 402.
22. Cf. Plato, *Republic*, Book X.
23. *Erster Entwurf eines Systems der Naturphilosophie*, S. 5, *Werke*, Abt. 1, Vol. II, p. 623.
24. *Ibid.*, p. 626.
25. See E. Durkheim, *"De Quelques Formes Primitives de Classification,"* in: *L'Année Sociologique*, Vol. IV, 1903, pp. 66ff.
26. Giambattista Vico, *Scienza Nuova* (*Principles of a New Science of the Common Nature of Nations*).
27. Hubert and Mauss, *op. cit.*, p. 118.
28. See Tönnies, *"Philosophische Terminologie,"* in: *Psychologisch-Soziologische Ansicht* (Leipzig, 1980), p. 31.
29. *Phänomenologie des Geistes*, p. 65.
30. Edmund Husserl, *"Die Krisis der europäischen Wissenschaften und die transzendentale Phänomenologie,"* in: *Philosophia* (Belgrade, 1936), pp. 95ff.
31. Cf. Schopenhauer, *Parerga und Paralipomena*, Vol. II, S. 356; *Werke*, ed. Deussen, Vol. V, p. 671.
32. *Ethica*, Pars., IV. Propos, XXII. Coroll.
33. *Odyssey* 12.191. (Since the authors' translation differs at certain concise points from the best-known English versions, this and other passages quoted here are near-literal prose renderings of the German.—TR.).
34. *Odyssey* 12.189–90.
35. *Phänomenologie des Geistes*, p. 146.
36. Lucilio Vanini, a quasi-pantheistic Italian philosopher (1584–1619) sentenced and burned for blasphemy by the Inquisition.—TR.
37. "The supreme question which confronts our generation today—the question to which all other problems are merely corollaries—is whether technology can be brought under control . . . Nobody can be sure of the formula by which this end can be achieved . . . We must draw on all the resources to which access can be had . . ." (*The Rockefeller Foundation. A Review for 1943* [New York, 1944], pp. 33ff.).

HANS-GEORG GADAMER

"THE UNIVERSALITY OF THE HERMENEUTICAL PROBLEM"

Why has the problem of language come to occupy the same central position in current philosophical discussions that the concept of thought, or "thought thinking itself," held in philosophy a century and a half ago? By answering this question, I shall try to give an answer indirectly to the central question of the modern age—a question posed for us by the existence of modern science. It is the question of how our natural view of the world—the experience of the world that we have as we simply live out our lives—is related to the unassailable and anonymous authority that confronts us in the pronouncements of science. Since the seventeenth century, the real task of philosophy has been to mediate this new employment of man's cognitive and constructive capacities with the totality of our experience of life. This task has found expression in a variety of ways, including our own generation's attempt to bring the topic of language to the center of philosophical concern. Language is the fundamental mode of operation of our being-in-the-world and the all-embracing form of the constitution of the world. Hence we always have in view the pronouncements of the sciences, which are fixed in nonverbal signs. And our task is to reconnect the objective world of technology, which the sciences place at our disposal and discretion, with those fundamental orders of our being that are neither arbitrary nor manipulable by us, but rather simply demand our respect.

I want to elucidate several phenomena in which the universality of this question becomes evident. I have called the point of view involved in this theme "hermeneutical," a term developed by Heidegger. Heidegger was continuing a perspective stemming originally from Protestant theology and transmitted into our own century by Wilhelm Dilthey.

What is hermeneutics? I would like to start from two experiences of alienation that we encounter in our concrete existence: the experience of alienation of the aesthetic consciousness and the experience of alienation of the historical consciousness. In both cases what I mean can be stated in a few words. The aesthetic consciousness realizes a possibility that as such we can neither deny nor diminish in its value, namely, that we relate ourselves, either negatively or affirmatively, to the quality of an artistic form. This statement means we are related in such a way that the judgment we make decides in the end regarding the expressive power and validity of what we judge. What we reject has nothing to say to us—or we reject it because it has nothing to say to us. This characterizes our relation to art in the broadest sense of the word, a sense that, as Hegel has shown, includes the entire religious world of the ancient Greeks, whose religion of beauty experienced the divine in concrete works of art that man creates in response to the gods. When it loses its original and unquestioned authority, this whole world of experience becomes alienated into an object of aesthetic judgment. At the same time, however, we must admit that the world of artistic tradition—the splendid contemporaneousness that we gain through art with so many human worlds—is more than a mere object of our free acceptance or rejection. Is it not true that when a work of art has seized us it no longer leaves us the freedom to push it away from us once again and to accept or reject it on our own terms? And is it not also true that these artistic creations, which come down through the millennia, were not created for such aesthetic acceptance or rejection? No artist of the religiously vital cultures of the past ever produced his work of art with any other intention than that his creation should be received in terms of what it says and presents and that it should have its place in the world where men live together. The consciousness of art—the aesthetic consciousness—is always secondary to the immediate truth-claim that proceeds from the work of art itself. To this extent, when we judge a work of art on the basis of its aesthetic quality, something that is really much more intimately familiar to us is alienated. This alienation into aesthetic judgment always takes place when we have withdrawn ourselves and are no longer open to the immediate claim of that which grasps us. Thus one point of departure for my reflections in *Truth and Method* was that the aesthetic sovereignty that claims its rights in the experience of art represents an alienation when compared to the authentic experience that confronts us in the form of art itself.

About thirty years ago, this problem cropped up in a particularly distorted form when National Socialist politics of art, as a means to its own ends, tried to criticize formalism by arguing that art is bound to a people. Despite its misuse by the National Socialists, we cannot deny that the idea of art being bound to a people involves a real insight. A genuine artistic creation stands within a particular community, and such a community is always distinguishable from the cultured society that is informed and terrorized by art criticism.

The second mode of the experience of alienation is the historical consciousness—the noble and slowly perfected art of holding ourselves at a critical distance in dealing with witnesses to past life. Ranke's celebrated description of this idea as the extinguishing of the individual provided a popular formula for the ideal of historical thinking: the historical consciousness has the task of understanding all the witnesses of a past time out of the spirit of that time, of extricating them from the preoccupations of our own present life, and of knowing, without moral smugness, the past as a human phenomenon. In his well-known essay *The Use and Abuse of History,* Nietzsche formulated the contradiction between this historical distancing and the immediate will to shape things that always cleaves to the present. And at the same time he exposed many of the consequences of what he called the "Alexandrian," weakened form of the will, which is found in modern historical science. We might recall his indictment of the weakness of evaluation that has befallen the modern mind because it has become so accustomed to considering things in ever different and changing lights that it is blinded and incapable of arriving at an opinion of its own regarding the objects it studies. It is unable to determine its own position vis-à-vis what confronts it. Nietzsche traces the value-blindness of historical objectivism back to the conflict between the alienated historical world and the life-powers of the present.

To be sure, Nietzsche is an ecstatic witness. But our actual experience of the historical consciousness in the last one hundred years has taught us most emphatically that there are serious difficulties involved in its claim to historical objectivity. Even in those masterworks of historical scholarship that seem to be the very consummation of the extinguishing of the individual demanded by Ranke, it is still an unquestioned principle of our scientific experience that we can classify these works with unfailing accuracy in terms of the political tendencies of the time in which they were written. When we read Mommsen's *History of Rome,* we know who alone could have written it, that is, we can identify the political situation in which this historian organized the voices of the past in a meaningful way. We know it too in the case of Treitschke or of Sybel, to choose only a few prominent names from Prussian historiography. This clearly means, first of all, that the whole reality of historical experience does not find expression in the mastery of historical method. No one disputes the fact that controlling the prejudices of our own present to such an extent that we do not misunderstand the witnesses of the past is a valid aim, but obviously such control does not completely fulfill the task of understanding the past and its transmissions. Indeed, it could very well be that only *insignificant* things in historical scholarship permit us to approximate this ideal of totally extinguishing individuality, while the great productive achievements of scholarship always preserve something of the splendid magic of immediately mirroring the present in the past and the past in the present. Historical science, the second experience from which I begin, expresses only one part of our actual experience—our actual encounter with historical tradition—and it knows only an alienated form of this historical tradition.

We can contrast the hermeneutical consciousness with these examples of alienation as a more comprehensive possibility that we must develop. But, in the case of this hermeneutical consciousness also, our initial task must be to overcome the epistemological truncation by which the traditional "science of hermeneutics" has been absorbed into the idea of modern science. If we consider Schleiermacher's hermeneutics, for instance, we find his view of this discipline peculiarly restricted by the modern idea of science. Schleiermacher's hermeneutics shows him to be a leading voice of historical romanticism. But at the same time, he kept the concern of the Christian theologian clearly in mind, intending his hermeneutics, as a general doctrine of the art of understanding, to be of value in the special work of interpreting Scripture. Schleiermacher defined hermeneutics as the art of avoiding misunderstanding. To exclude by controlled, methodical consideration whatever is alien and leads to misunderstanding—misunderstanding suggested to us by distance in time, change in linguistic usages, or in the meanings of words and modes of thinking—that is certainly far from an absurd description of the hermeneutical endeavor. But the question also arises as to whether the phenomenon of understanding is defined appropriately when we say that to understand is to avoid misunderstanding. Is it not, in fact, the case that every misunderstanding presupposes a "deep common accord"?

I am trying to call attention here to a common experience. We say, for instance, that understanding and misunderstanding take place between I and thou. But the formulation "I and thou" already betrays an enormous alienation. There is nothing like an "I and thou" at all—there is neither the I nor the thou as isolated, substantial realities. I may say "thou" and I may refer to myself over against a thou, but a common understanding [Verständigung] always precedes these situations. We all know that to say "thou" to someone presupposes a deep common accord [tiefes Einverständnis]. Something enduring is already present when this word is spoken. When we try to reach agreement on a matter on which we have different opinions, this deeper factor always comes into play, even if we are seldom aware of it. Now the science of hermeneutics would have us believe that the opinion we have to understand is something alien that seeks to lure us into misunderstanding, and our task is to exclude every element through which a misunderstanding can creep in. We accomplish this task by a controlled procedure of historical training, by historical criticism, and by a controllable method in connection with powers of psychological empathy. It seems to me that this description is valid in one respect, but yet it is only a partial description of a comprehensive life-phenomenon that constitutes the "we" that we all are. Our task, it seems to me, is to transcend the prejudices that underlie the aesthetic consciousness, the historical consciousness, and the hermeneutical consciousness that has been restricted to a technique for avoiding misunderstandings and to overcome the alienations present in them all.

What is it, then, in these three experiences that seemed to us to have been left out, and what makes us so sensitive to the distinctiveness of these experiences? What is the *aesthetic* consciousness when compared to the fullness of what has already addressed us—what we call "classical" in art? Is it not always already determined in this way what will be expressive for us and what we will find significant? Whenever we say with an instinctive, even if perhaps erroneous, certainty (but a certainty that is initially valid for our consciousness) "this is classical; it will endure," what we are speaking of has already preformed our possibility for aesthetic judgment. There are no purely formal criteria that can claim to judge and sanction the formative level simply on the basis of its artistic virtuosity. Rather, our sensitive-spiritual existence is an aesthetic resonance chamber that resonates with the voices that are constantly reaching us, preceding all explicit aesthetic judgment.

The situation is similar with the historical consciousness. Here, too, we must certainly admit that there are innumerable tasks of historical scholarship that have no relation to our own present and to the depths of its historical consciousness. But it seems to me there can be no doubt that the great horizon of the past, out of which our culture and our present live, influences us in everything we want, hope for, or fear in the future. History is only present to us in light of our futurity. Here we have all learned from Heidegger, for he exhibited precisely the primacy of futurity for our possible recollection and retention, and for the whole of our history.

Heidegger worked out this primacy in his doctrine of the productivity of the hermeneutical circle. I have given the following formulation to this insight: It is not so much our judgments as it is our prejudices that constitute our being.[1] This is a provocative formulation, for I am using it to restore to its rightful place a positive concept of prejudice that was driven out of our linquistic usage by the French and the English Enlightenment. It can be shown that the concept of prejudice did not originally have the meaning we have attached to it. Prejudices are not necessarily unjustified and erroneous, so that they inevitably distort the truth. In fact, the historicity of our existence entails that prejudices, in the literal sense of the word, constitute the initial directedness of our whole ability to experience. Prejudices are biases of our openness to the world. They are simply conditions whereby we experience something—whereby what we encounter says something to us. This formulation certainly does not mean that we are enclosed within a wall of prejudices and only let through the narrow portals those things that can produce a pass saying, "Nothing new will be said here." Instead we welcome just that guest who promises something new to our curiosity. But how do we know the guest whom we admit is one who has something *new* to say to us? Is not our expectation and our readiness to hear the new also necessarily determined by the old that has already taken possession of us? The concept of prejudice is closely connected to the concept of authority, and the above image makes it clear that it is in need of hermeneutical rehabilitation. Like every image, however, this one too is misleading. The nature of the hermeneutical experience is not that something is outside and desires admission. Rather, we are possessed by something and precisely by means of it we are opened up for the new, the different, the true. Plato made this clear in his beautiful comparison of bodily foods with spiritual nourishment: while we can refuse the former (e.g., on the advice of a physician), we have always taken the latter into ourselves already.

But now the question arises as to how we can legitimate this hermeneutical conditionedness of our being in the face of modern science, which stands or falls with the principle of being unbiased and prejudiceless. We will certainly not accomplish this legitimation by making prescriptions for science and recommending that it toe the line—quite aside from the fact that such pronouncements always have something comical about them. Science will not do us this favor. It will continue along its own path with an inner necessity beyond its control, and it will produce more and more breathtaking knowledge and controlling power. It can be no other way. It is senseless, for instance, to hinder a genetic researcher because such research threatens to breed a superman. Hence the problem cannot appear as one in which our human consciousness ranges itself over against the world of science and presumes to develop a kind of anti-science. Nevertheless, we cannot avoid the question of whether what we are aware of in such apparently harmless examples as the aesthetic consciousness and the historical consciousness does not represent a problem that is also present in modern natural science and our technological attitude toward the world. If modern science enables us to erect a new world of technological purposes that transforms everything around us, we are not thereby suggesting that the researcher who gained the knowledge decisive for this state of affairs even considered technical applications. The genuine researcher is motivated by a desire for knowledge and by nothing else. And yet, over against the whole of our civilization that is founded on modern science, we must ask repeatedly if something has not been omitted. If the presuppositions of these possibilities for knowing and making remain half in the dark, cannot the result be that the hand applying this knowledge will be destructive?

The problem is really universal. The hermeneutical question, as I have characterized it, is not restricted to the areas from which I began in my own investigations. My only concern there was to secure a theoretical basis that would enable us to deal with the basic factor of contemporary culture, namely, science and its industrial, technological utilization. Statistics provide us with a useful example of how the hermeneutical dimension encompasses the entire procedure of science. It is an extreme example, but it shows us that science always stands under definite conditions of methodological abstraction and that the successes of modern sciences rest on the fact that other possibilities for questioning are concealed by abstraction. This fact comes out clearly in the case of statistics, for the anticipatory character of the questions statistics answer make it particularly suitable for propaganda purposes. Indeed, effective propaganda must always try to influence initially the judgment of the person addressed and to restrict his possibilities of judgment. Thus what is established by statistics seems to be a language of facts, but which questions these facts answer and which facts would begin to speak if other questions were asked are hermeneutical questions. Only a hermeneutical inquiry would legitimate the meaning of these facts and thus the consequences that follow from them.

But I am anticipating, and have inadvertently used the phrase, "which answers to which questions fit the facts." This phrase is in fact the hermeneutical *Urphänomen:* No assertion is possible that cannot be understood as an answer to a question, and assertions can only be understood in this way. It does not impair the impressive methodology of modern science in the least. Whoever wants to learn a science has to learn to master its methodology. But we also know that methodology as such does not guarantee in any way the productivity of its application. Any experience of life can confirm the fact that there is such a thing as methodological sterility, that is, the application of a method to something not really worth knowing, to something that has not been made an object of investigation on the basis of a genuine question.

The methodological self-consciousness of modern science certainly stands in opposition to this argument. A historian, for example, will say in reply: It is all very nice to talk about the historical tradition in which alone the voices of the past gain their meaning and through which the prejudices that determine the present are inspired. But the situation is completely different in questions of serious historical research. How could one seriously mean, for example, that the clarification of the taxation practices of fifteenth-century cities or of the marital customs of Eskimos somehow first receive their meaning from the consciousness of the present and its anticipations? These are questions of historical knowledge that we take up as tasks quite independently of any relation to the present.

In answering this objection, one can say that the extremity of this point of view would be similar to what we find in certain large industrial research facilities, above all in America and Russia. I mean the so-called random experiment in which one simply covers the material without concern for waste or cost, taking the chance that some day one measurement among the thousands of measurements will finally yield an interesting finding; that is, it will turn out to be the answer to a question from which someone can progress. No doubt modern research in the humanities also works this way to some extent. One thinks, for instance, of the great editions and especially of the ever more perfect indexes. It must remain an open question, of course, whether by such procedures modern historical research increases the chances of actually noticing the interesting fact and thus gaining from it the corresponding enrichment of our knowledge. But even if they do, one might ask: Is this an ideal, that countless research projects (i.e., determinations of the connection of facts) are extracted from a thousand historians, so that the 1001st historian can find something interesting? Of course I am drawing a caricature of genuine scholarship. But in every caricature there is an element of truth, and this one contains an indirect answer to the question of what it is that really makes the productive scholar. That he has learned the methods? The person who never produces anything new has also done that. It is imagination [*Phantasie*] that is the decisive function of the scholar. Imagination naturally has a hermeneutical function and serves the sense for what is questionable. It serves the ability to expose real, productive questions, something in which, generally speaking, only he who masters all the methods of his science succeeds.

As a student of Plato, I particularly love those scenes in which Socrates gets into a dispute with the Sophist virtuosi and drives them to despair by his questions. Eventually they can endure his questions no longer and claim for themselves the apparently preferable role of the questioner. And what happens? They can think of nothing at all to ask. Nothing at all occurs to them that is worthwhile going into and trying to answer.

I draw the following inference from this observation. The real power of hermeneutical consciousness is our ability to see what is questionable. Now if what we have before our eyes is not only the artistic tradition of a people, or historical tradition, or the principle of modern science in its hermeneutical preconditions but rather the whole of our experience, then we have succeeded, I think, in joining the experience of science to our own universal and human experience of life. For we have now reached the fundamental level that we can call (with Johannes Lohmann) the "linguistic constitution of the world."[2] It presents itself as the consciousness that is effected by history [*wirkungsgeschichtliches Bewusstsein*] and that provides an initial schematization for all our possibilities of knowing. I leave out of account the fact that the scholar—even the natural scientist—is perhaps not completely free of custom and society and from all possible factors in his environment. What I mean is that precisely *within* his scientific experience it is not so much the "laws of ironclad inference" (Helmholz) that present fruitful ideas to him, but rather unforseen constellations that kindle the spark of scientific inspiration (e.g., Newton's falling apple or some other incidental observation).

The consciousness that is effected by history has its fulfillment in what is linguistic. We can learn from the sensitive student of language that language, in its life and occurrence, must not be thought of as merely changing, but rather as something that has a teleology operating within it. This means that the words that are formed, the means of expression that appear in a language in order to say certain things, are not accidentally fixed, since they do not once again fall altogether into disuse. Instead, a definite articulation of the world is built up—a process that works as if guided and one that we can always observe in children who are learning to speak.

We can illustrate this by considering a passage in Aristotle's *Posterior Analytics* that ingeniously describes one definite aspect of language formation.[3] The passage treats what Aristotle calls the *epagoge*, that is, the formation of the universal. How does one arrive at a universal? In philosophy we say: how do we arrive at a general concept, but even words in this sense are obviously general. How does it happen that they are "words," that is, that they have a general meaning? In his first apperception, a sensuously equipped being finds himself in a surging sea of stimuli, and finally one day he begins, as we say, to know something. Clearly we do not mean that he was previously blind. Rather, when we say "to know" [erkennen] we mean "to recognize" [wiedererkennen], that is, to pick something out [herauserkennen] of the stream of images flowing past as being identical. What is picked out in this fashion is clearly retained. But how? When does a child know its mother for the first time? When it sees her for the first time? No. Then when? How does it take place? Can we really say at all that there is a single event in which a first knowing extricates the child from the darkness of not knowing? It seems obvious to me that we cannot. Aristotle has described this wonderfully. He says it is the same as when an army is in flight, driven by panic, until at last someone stops and looks around to see whether the foe is still dangerously close behind. We cannot say that the army stops when one soldier has stopped. But then another stops. The army does not stop by virtue of the fact that two soldiers stop. When does it actually stop, then? Suddenly it stands its ground again. Suddenly it obeys the command once again. A subtle pun is involved in Aristotle's description, for in Greek "command" means arche, that is, principium. When is the principle present as a principle? Through what capacity? This question is in fact the question of the occurrence of the universal.

If I have not misunderstood Johannes Lohmann's exposition, precisely this same teleology operates constantly in the life of language. When Lohmann speaks of linguistic tendencies as the real agents of history in which specific forms expand, he knows of course that it occurs in these forms of realization, of "coming to a stand" [Zum-Stehen-Kommen], as the beautiful German word says. What is manifest here, I contend, is the real mode of operation of our whole human experience of the world. Learning to speak is surely a phase of special productivity, and in the course of time we have all transformed the genius of the three-year-old into a poor and meager talent. But in the utilization of the linguistic interpretation of the world that finally comes about, something of the productivity of our beginnings remains alive. We are all acquainted with this, for instance, in the attempt to translate, in practical life or in literature or wherever; that is, we are familiar with the strange, uncomfortable, and tortuous feeling we have as long as we do not have the right word. When we have found the right expression (it need not always be one word), when we are certain that we have it, then it "stands," then something has come to a "stand." Once again we have a halt in the midst of the rush of the foreign language, whose endless variation makes us lose our orientation. What I am describing is the mode of the whole human experience of the world. I call this experience hermeneutical, for the process we are describing is repeated continually throughout our familiar experience. There is always a world already interpreted, already organized in its basic relations, into which experience steps as something new, upsetting what has led our expectations and undergoing reorganization itself in the up-heaval. Misunderstanding and strangeness are not the first factors, so that avoiding misunderstanding can be regarded as the specific task of hermeneutics. Just the reverse is the case. Only the support of familiar and common under-standing makes possible the venture into the alien, the lifting up of something out of the alien, and thus the broadening and enrichment of our own experience of the world.

This discussion shows how the claim to universality that is appropriate to the hermeneutical dimension is to be understood. Understanding is language-bound. But this assertion does not lead us into any kind of linguistic relativism. It is indeed true that we live within a language, but language is not a system of signals that we send off with the aid of a telegraphic key when we enter the of-fice or transmission station. That is not speaking, for it does not have the infin-ity of the act that is linguistically creative and world experiencing. While we live wholly within a language, the fact that we do so does not constitute linguistic relativism because there is absolutely no captivity within a language—not even within our native language. We all experience this when we learn a foreign lan-guage, especially on journeys insofar as we master the foreign language to some extent. To master the foreign language means precisely that when we engage in speaking it in the foreign land, we do not constantly consult inwardly our own world and its vocabulary. The better we know the language, the less such a side glance at our native language is perceptible, and only because we never know foreign languages well enough do we always have something of this feeling. But it is nevertheless already speaking, even if perhaps a stammering speaking, for stammering is the obstruction of a desire to speak and is thus opened into the infinite realm of possible expression. Any language in which we live is infinite in this sense, and it is completely mistaken to infer that reason is fragmented because there are various languages. Just the opposite is the case. Precisely through our finitude, the particularity of our being, which is evident even in the variety of languages, the infinite dialogue is opened in the direction of the truth that we are.

If this is correct, then the relation of our modern industrial world, founded by science, which we described at the outset, is mirrored above all on the level of language. We live in an epoch in which an increasing leveling of all life-forms is taking place—that is the rationally necessary requirement for maintaining life on our planet. The food problem of mankind, for example, can only be over-come by the surrender of the lavish wastefulness that has covered the earth. Un-avoidably, the mechanical, industrial world is expanding within the life of the individual as a sort of sphere of technical perfection. When we hear modern lovers talking to each other, we often wonder if they are communicating with words or with advertising labels and technical terms from the sign language of the modern industrial world. It is inevitable that the leveled life-forms of the industrial age also affect language, and in fact the impoverishment of the vocab-ulary of language is making enormous progress, thus bringing about an approximation of language to a technical sign-system. Leveling tendencies of this kind are irresistible. Yet in spite of them the simultaneous building up of our own world in language still persists whenever we want to say something to each other. The result is the actual relationship of men to each other. Each one is at first a kind of linguistic circle, and these linguistic circles come into contact with each other, merging more and more. Language occurs once again, in vocabulary and grammar as always, and never without the inner infinity of the dialogue that is in progress between every speaker and his partner. That is the fundamental dimension of hermeneutics. Genuine speaking, which has something to say and hence does not give prearranged signals, but rather seeks words through which one reaches the other person, is the universal human task—but it is a special task for the theologian, to whom is commissioned the saying-further (*Weitersagen*) of a message that stands written.

NOTES

1. Cf. *WM*, p. 261.
2. Cf. Johannes Lohmann, *Philosophie und Sprachwissenschaft* (Berlin: Duncker & Humbolt, 1963).
3. Aristotle, *Posterior Analytics*, 100a 11–13.

PAUL RICOEUR

SELECTION FROM "PHENOMENOLOGY AND HERMENEUTICS"

This study does not aim to be a contribution to the history of phenomenology, to its archaeology, but rather an inquiry into the destiny of phenomenology today. And if I have chosen the general theory of interpretation or hermeneutics as a touchstone, that does not mean either that I would replace a historical monograph by a chapter on the comparative history of modern philosophy. For with hermeneutics as well, I do not wish to proceed as a historian, even as a historian of the present day. Whatever may be the dependence of the following meditation on Heidegger and above all on Gadamer, what is at stake is the possibility of continuing to do philosophy with them and after them—without forgetting Husserl. Thus my essay will seek to be a debate about the ways in which philosophy can still be pursued.[1]

I propose the following two theses for discussion. *First thesis:* what hermeneutics has ruined is not phenomenology but one of its interpretations, namely, its *idealistic* interpretation by Husserl himself; accordingly, I shall speak henceforth of Husserlian idealism. I shall take the "Nachwort" to the *Ideas* as a reference and a guide, submitting its principal theses to the hermeneutical critique.[2] The first part of the essay will thus be purely and simply *antithetical.*

Reprinted from *From Text to Action: Essays in Hermeneutics, II*, tr. Kathleen Blamey and John B. Thompson. Evanston: Northwestern University Press, 1991, pp. 25–43. (Essay tr. John B. Thompson) Used with permission of Blackwell Publishers.

Second thesis: beyond the simple opposition there exists, between phenomenology and hermeneutics, a mutual belonging that it is important to make explicit. This belonging can be recognized from either position. On the one hand, hermeneutics is erected on the basis of phenomenology and thus preserves something of the philosophy from which it nevertheless differs: *phenomenology remains the unsurpassable presupposition of hermeneutics.* On the other hand, phenomenology cannot constitute itself without a *hermeneutical presupposition.* The hermeneutical condition of phenomenology is linked to the role of *Auslegung* [explication] in the fulfillment of its philosophical project.

I. THE HERMENEUTICAL CRITIQUE OF HUSSERLIAN IDEALISM

The first part of this essay seeks to disclose the gap, if not the gulf, that separates the project of hermeneutics from all idealistic expressions of phenomenology. The antithetical position of the two philosophical projects will alone be developed. We shall nevertheless reserve the possibility that phenomenology as such is not wholly exhausted by one of its interpretations, even that of Husserl himself. It is, in my view, Husserlian idealism that succumbs to the hermeneutical critique.

1. The Schematic Theses of Husserlian Idealism

For the purposes of a necessarily schematic discussion, I have taken the 1930 "Nachwort" to the *Ideas* as a typical document of Husserlian idealism. It constitutes, together with the *Cartesian Meditations,* the most advanced expression of this idealism. I have extracted from it the following theses, which I shall subsequently submit to the critique of hermeneutics.

(a) The ideal of scientificity proclaimed by phenomenology is not in continuity with the sciences, their axioms and their foundational enterprise: the "ultimate justification" that constitutes phenomenology is of a different order (*Hua* 5:138ff., 159ff.).

This thesis, which expresses phenomenology's claim to radicality, is asserted in a polemical style; it is the thesis of a combatant philosophy that always has an enemy in view, whether that enemy be objectivism, naturalism, vitalistic philosophy, or anthropology. Phenomenology begins with a radical move that cannot be framed in a demonstrative argument, for whence would it be deduced? Hence the self-assertive style of the claim to radicality, which is attested to only by the denial of what could deny it. The expression *aus letzter Begründung* [ultimate grounding] is most typical in this respect. It recalls the Platonic tradition of the anhypothetical as well as the Kantian tradition of the autonomy of the critical act; it also marks, in the sense of *Rückfrage* [questioning back] (*Hua* 5:139), a

certain continuity with the question of principle that the sciences ask of themselves. And yet the process of returning to the foundations is absolutely discontinuous with regard to any foundation internal to a science: for a science of
foundations, "there can be no more obscure and problematic concepts, nor any
paradoxes" (*Hua* 5:160). That does not mean there have not been *several*
"ways" answering to this unique Idea; the idea of foundation is rather that
which secures the equivalence and convergence of the ways (logical, Cartesian,
psychological, historicoteleological, etc.). There are "real beginnings," or rather
"paths toward the beginning," elicited by "the absolute absence of presuppositions." It is thus fruitless to inquire into the motivation for such a radical beginning; there is no reason internal to a domain for raising the question of origin. It
is in this sense that justification is a *Selbst-Begründung* [self-grounding].

(b) The foundation in principle is of the order of intuition; to found is to
see. The "Nachwort" thereby confirms the priority, asserted by the sixth *Logical Investigation,* of intentional fulfillment as opposed to any philosophy of deduction or construction (*Hua* 5:141 ff., 143ff.).

The key concept in this respect is that of an *Erfahrungsfeld* [field of experi-
ence]. The strangeness of phenomenology lies entirely therein: from the outset,
the principle is a "field" and the first truth an "experience." In contrast to all
"speculative constructions," every question of principle is resolved through vision. I just spoke of strangeness: for is it not astonishing that in spite of (and
thanks to) the critique of empiricism, experience in the strict empirical sense is
surpassed only in an "experience"? This synonymy of *Erfahrung* signifies that
phenomenology is not situated elsewhere, in another world, but rather is concerned with natural experience itself, insofar as the latter is unaware of its
meaning. Consequently, however much the emphasis may be placed on the a
priori character, on the reduction to the *eidos,* on the role of imaginative variations, and even on the notion of "possibility," it is still and always the character
of experience that is underlined (one has only to consider the expression "intuitive possibilities"; *Hua* 5:142).

(c) The place of plenary intuition is subjectivity. All transcendence is doubtful; immanence alone is indubitable.

This is the central thesis of Husserlian idealism. All transcendence is doubtful
because it proceeds by *Abschattungen,* by "sketches" or "profiles"; because the
convergence of these *Abschattungen* is always presumptive; because the presumption can be disappointed by some discordance; and finally, because consciousness
can form the hyperbolic hypothesis of a radical discordance of appearances,
which is the very hypothesis of the "destruction of the world." Immanence is not
doubtful, because it is not given by "profiles" and hence involves nothing presumptive, allowing only the coincidence of reflection with what "has just" been
experienced.

(d) The subjectivity thus promoted to the rank of the transcendental is not
empirical consciousness, the object of psychology. Nevertheless, phenomenol-

ogy and phenomenological psychology are parallel and constitute a "doublet" that constantly leads to the confusion of the two disciplines, one transcendental and the other empirical. Only the reduction distinguishes and separates them.

Here phenomenology must struggle against a misunderstanding that constantly reappears and that phenomenology itself provokes. For the phenomenological "field of experience" has a structural analogy with nonreduced experience; the reason for this isomorphism lies in the very nature of intentionality (Brentano had discovered intentionality without being aware of the reduction, and the fifth *Logical Investigation* still defined it in terms that are as compatible with intentional psychology as with phenomenology). Moreover, the reduction proceeds "from the natural attitude"; transcendental phenomenology thus presupposes, in a certain way, that which it surpasses and which it reiterates as *the same*, although *in another attitude*. So the difference does not consist in descriptive features but in ontological indices, in *Seinsgeltung* [validity of being]; validity *als Reales* must be "lost,"[3] psychological realism must be shattered. Now that would be no small task, if phenomenology is not to be understood as the necessity of losing the world, the body and nature, thereby enclosing itself within an acosmic realm. The paradox is that it is only through this loss that the world is revealed as "pregiven," the body as "existing," and nature as "being" [*étant*]. So the reduction does not take place between me and the world, between the soul and the body, between the spirit and nature, but through the pregiven, the existing, and the being, which cease to be self-evident and to be assumed in the blind and opaque *Seinsglaube* [belief in being], becoming instead *meaning: meaning* of the pregiven, *meaning* of the existing, *meaning* of the being. Thus the phenomenological radicality, which severs the transcendental subjectivity from the empirical self, is the same as that radicality that transforms the *Seinsglaube* into the noematic correlate of the noesis. A noetics or no-ology is therefore distinct from a psychology. Their "content" (*Gehalt*) is the same, but the phenomenological is the psychological "reduced." Therein lies the principle of the "parallelism," or better of the "correspondence," between the two. Therein lies also the principle of their difference: for a "conversion"—*the* philosophical conversion—separates them.

(e) The awareness that sustains the work of reflection develops its own ethical implications: reflection is thus the immediately self-responsible act.

The ethical nuance, which the expression *aus letzter Selbstver-antwortung* [ultimate self-responsibility] (*Hua* 5:139) seems to introduce into the foundational thematic, is not the practical complement of an enterprise that as such would be purely epistemological: the inversion by which reflection tears itself away from the natural attitude is at the same time—in the same breath, so to speak—epistemological and ethical. The philosophical conversion is the supremely autonomous act. What we have called the ethical nuance is thus immediately implied in the foundational act, insofar as the latter can only be self-positing. It is in this sense that it is ultimately self-responsible.

The self-assertive character of the foundation constitutes the philosophical subject as responsible subject. This is the philosophizing subject as such.

2. Hermeneutics against Husserlian Idealism

It is possible to oppose hermeneutics, thesis by thesis, not perhaps to phenomenology as a whole and as such, but to Husserlian idealism. This "antithetical" approach is the necessary path to the establishment of a genuinely "dialectical" relation between the two.

(a) The ideal of scientificity, construed by Husserlian idealism as ultimate justification, encounters its fundamental limit in the ontological condition of understanding.

This ontological condition can be expressed as finitude. This is not, however, the concept I shall regard as primary; for it designates, in negative terms, an entirely positive condition that would be better expressed by the concept of belonging. The latter directly designates the unsurpassable condition of any enterprise of justification and foundation, namely, that it is always preceded by a relation that supports it. Is this a relation to an object? That is precisely what it is not. The aspect of Husserlian idealism that hermeneutics questions first is the way in which the immense and unsurpassable discovery of intentionality is couched in a conceptuality that weakens its scope, namely, the conceptuality of the subject-object relation. It is the latter that gives rise to the necessity of searching for something that unifies the meaning of the object and the necessity of founding this unity in a constituting subjectivity. The first declaration of hermeneutics is to say that the problematic of objectivity presupposes a prior relation of inclusion that encompasses the allegedly autonomous subject and the allegedly adverse object. This inclusive or encompassing relation is what I call belonging. The ontological priority of belonging implies that the question of foundation can no longer simply coincide with that of ultimate justification. Of course, Husserl is the first to underline the discontinuity, instituted by the *epochē,* between the transcendental enterprise of foundation and the internal work, proper to each science, whereby it seeks to elaborate its own grounds. Moreover, he always distinguishes the demand for justification raised by transcendental phenomenology from the preestablished model of the *mathesis universalis.* In this way, as we shall see later, he lays down the phenomenological conditions of hermeneutics. But hermeneutics seeks precisely to radicalize the Husserlian thesis of the discontinuity between transcendental foundation and epistemological grounding.

For hermeneutics, the problem of ultimate foundation still belongs to the sphere of objectifying thought, so long as the ideal of scientificity is not questioned as such. The radicality of such questioning leads from the idea of scientificity back to the ontological condition of belonging, whereby he who questions shares in the very thing about which he questions.

It is the relation of belonging that is subsequently apprehended as the finitude of knowledge. The negative nuance conveyed by the very word *finitude* is introduced into the totally positive relation of belonging—*which is the hermeneutical experience itself*—only because subjectivity has already raised its claim to be the ultimate ground. This claim, this immoderate pretension, this *hubris*, makes the relation of belonging appear by contrast as finitude.

Belonging is expressed by Heidegger in the language of being-in-the-world. The two notions are equivalent. The term *being-in-the-world* expresses better the primacy of care over the gaze, and the horizontal character of that to which we are bound. It is indeed being-in-the-world that precedes reflection. At the same time, the term attests to the priority of the ontological category of the *Dasein* that we are over the epistemological and psychological category of the subject that posits itself. Despite the density of meaning in the expression "being-in-the-world," I prefer, following Gadamer, to use the notion of belonging, which immediately raises the problem of the subject-object relation and prepares the way for the subsequent introduction of the concept of distanciation.

(b) The Husserlian demand for the return to intuition is countered by the necessity for all understanding to be mediated by an interpretation.

There is no doubt that this principle is borrowed from the epistemology of the historical sciences. As such, it belongs to the epistemological field delimited by Schleiermacher and Dilthey. However, if interpretation were only a historical-hermeneutic concept, it would remain as regional as the human sciences themselves. But the usage of interpretation in the historical-hermeneutic sciences is only the anchoring point for a universal concept of interpretation which has the same extension as that of understanding and, in the end, as that of belonging. Hence it goes beyond the mere methodology of exegesis and philology, designating the work of explication which adheres to all hermeneutical experience. According to Heidegger's remark in *Being and Time*, the *Auslegung* is the "development of understanding" in terms of the structure of the "as" (*als*).[4] In thereby effecting the mediation of the "as," "explication does not transform understanding into something else, but makes it become itself" (*SZ*, 148; *BT*, 188, modified).

The dependence of interpretation on understanding explains why explication as well always precedes reflection and comes before any constitution of the object by a sovereign subject. This antecedence is expressed at the level of explication by the "structure of anticipation," which prevents explication from ever being a presuppositionless grasp of a pregiven being [*étant*]; explication precedes its object in the mode of the *Vor-habe*, the *Vor-sicht*, the *Vor-Griff*, the *Vor-Meinung* (*SZ*, 150; *BT*, 191). I shall not comment here on these well-known expressions of Heidegger. What is important to emphasize is that it is not possible to implement the structure of the "as" without also implementing the structure of anticipation. The notion of "meaning" obeys this double condition of the *als* and the *Vor-*: "Meaning, which is structured by fore-having, fore-sight and fore-conception, forms for any project the horizon in terms of which something can be understood as something" (*SZ,* 151; *BT,* 193, modified). Thus the field of interpretation is as vast as that of understanding, which covers all projection of meaning in a situation.

The universality of interpretation is attested to in several ways. The most ordinary application is the use of natural languages in the conversational situation. In contrast to well-formed languages, constructed according to the exigencies of mathematical logic and in which all basic terms are defined in an axiomatic way, the use of natural languages rests on the polysemic value of words. The latter contain a semantic potential which is not exhausted by any particular use, but which must be constantly sifted and determined by the context. It is with this selective function of context that interpretation, in the most primitive sense of the word, is connected. Interpretation is the process by which, in the interplay of question and answer, the interlocutors collectively determine the contextual values that structure their conversion. So before any *Kunstlehre,* which would establish exegesis and philology as an autonomous discipline, there is a spontaneous process of interpretation which is part of the most primitive exercise of understanding in any given situation.

But conversation rests upon a relation that is too limited to cover the whole field of explication. Conversation, that is, ultimately the dialogical relation, is contained within the limits of a vis-à-vis which is a face-à-face. The historical connection that encompasses it is singularly more complex. The "short" intersubjective relation is intertwined, in the interior of the historical connection, with various "long" intersubjective relations, mediated by diverse social institutions, social roles, and collectivities (groups, classes, nations, cultural traditions, etc.). The long intersubjective relations are sustained by a historical tradition, of which dialogue is only a segment. Explication therefore extends much further than dialogue, coinciding with the broadest historical connection.[5]

Mediation by the text, that is, by expressions fixed in writing but also by all the documents and monuments that have a fundamental feature in common with writing, is connected with the use of explication on the scale of the transmission of historical tradition. This common feature, which constitutes the text as a text, is that the meaning contained therein is rendered *autonomous* with respect to the intention of the author, the initial situation of discourse, and the original addressee. Intention, situation, and original addressee constitute the *Sitz-im-Leben* [site-in-life] of the text. The possibility of multiple interpretations is opened up by a text that is thus freed from its *Sitz-im-Leben.* Beyond the polysemy of words in a conversation is the polysemy of a text that invites multiple readings. This is the moment of interpretation in the technical sense of *textual exegesis.* It is also the moment of the hermeneutical circle between the understanding initiated by the reader and the proposals of meaning offered by the text. The most fundamental condition of the hermeneutical circle lies in the structure of preunderstanding which relates all explication to the understanding that precedes and supports it.

In what sense is the development of all understanding in interpretation opposed to the Husserlian project of *ultimate* foundation? Essentially in the sense that all interpretation places the interpreter in medias res and never at the beginning or the end. We suddenly arrive, as it were, in the middle of a conversation which has already begun and in which we try to orientate ourselves in order to be able to contribute to it. Now the ideal of an intuitive foundation is the ideal of an interpretation that, at a certain point, would pass into full vision. This is what Gadamer calls the hypothesis of "total mediation." Only a total mediation would be equivalent to an intuition that is both first and final. Idealist phenomenology can therefore sustain its pretension to ultimate foundation only by adopting, in an intuitive rather than a speculative mode, the Hegelian claim to absolute knowledge. But the key hypothesis of hermeneutic philosophy is that interpretation is an open process that no single vision can conclude.

(c) That the place of ultimate foundation is subjectivity, that all transcendence is doubtful and only immanence indubitable—this in turn becomes eminently doubtful, from the moment that the cogito as well seems susceptible to the radical critique that phenomenology otherwise applies to all appearances.

The ruses of self-consciousness are more subtle than those of the thing. Recall the doubt that, in Heidegger's work, accompanies the question, who is *Dasein*?

> Is it then obvious *a priori* that access to Dasein must be gained only by mere reflective awareness of the "I" of actions? What if this kind of "giving-itself" on the part of Dasein should lead our existential analytic astray and do so, indeed, in a manner grounded in the Being of Dasein itself? Perhaps when Dasein addresses itself in the way which is closest to itself, it always says "I am this entity," and in the long run says this loudest when it is "not" this entity. What if the aforementioned approach, starting with the givenness of the "I" to Dasein itself, and with a rather patent self-interpretation of Dasein, should lead the existential analytic, as it were, into a pitfall? If that which is accessible by mere "giving" can be determined, there is presumably an ontological horizon for determining it; but what if this horizon should remain in principle undetermined? (SZ, 115; BT, 151)

Here, as elsewhere, I shall not adhere to the letter of Heidegger's philosophy but shall develop it for my own purposes. It is in the *critique of ideology,* as much as and perhaps more than in psychoanalysis, that I would look for documentation of the doubt contained in Heidegger's question, who is *Dasein?* The critiques of ideology and psychoanalysis provide us today with the means to complement the critique of the object by a critique of the subject. In Husserl's work, the critique of the object is coextensive with *Dingkonstitution* [constitution of the thing]; it rests, as we have said, on the presumptive character of schematic synthesis. But Husserl believed that self-knowledge could not be presumptive because it does not proceed by "sketches" or "profiles." Self-knowledge can, however, be presumptive for other reasons. Insofar as self-knowledge is a dialogue of the soul with itself, and insofar as the dialogue can be systematically distorted by violence and by the intrusion of structures of domination into those of communication, self-knowledge as internalized communication can be as doubtful as knowledge of the object, although for different and quite specific reasons.

Could it be said that, through the reduction, the *ego meditans* of phenomenology escapes from the distortions of empirical self-knowledge? This would be to forget that the Husserlian *ego* is not the Kantian *I think,* whose individuality is at least problematic if not devoid of sense. It is because the ego can be and must be reduced to the "sphere of belonging"—in a different sense, to be sure, of the word *belonging,* which no longer means belonging to the world but belonging to oneself—that it is necessary to found the objectivity of nature and the objectivity of historical communities on intersubjectivity and not on an impersonal subject. Consequently, the distortions of communication directly concern the constitution of the intersubjective network in which a common nature and common historical entities can be formed, entities such as the "personalities of a higher order" discussed in §58 of the *Cartesian Meditations.* Egology must take the fundamental distortions of communication into account, in the same way as it considers the illusions of perception in the constitution of the thing.

It seems to me that only a hermeneutics of communication can assume the task of incorporating the critique of ideology into self-understanding.[6] It can do this in two complementary ways. On the one hand, it can demonstrate the insurmountable character of the ideological phenomenon through its meditation on the role of "preunderstanding" in the apprehension of any cultural object. Hermeneutics has simply to raise this notion of understanding, initially applied to the exegesis of texts, to the level of a general theory of prejudices, which would be coextensive with the historical connection itself. Just as misunderstanding is a fundamental structure of exegesis (Schleiermacher), so too prejudice is a fundamental structure of communication in its social and institutional forms. On the other hand, hermeneutics can demonstrate the necessity of a critique of ideology, even if, in virtue of the very structure of preunderstanding, this critique can never be total. Critique rests on the moment of *distanciation,* which belongs to the historical connection as such.

The concept of distanciation is the dialectical counterpart of the notion of belonging, in the sense that we belong to a historical tradition through a relation of distance which oscillates between remoteness and proximity. To interpret is to render near what is far (temporally, geographically, culturally, spiritually). In this respect, mediation by the text is the model of a distanciation which would not be simply alienating, like the *Verfremdung* that Gadamer combats throughout his work (WM, 11, 80, 156, 364ff.; TM, 15, 75, 145, 348ff.), but which would be genuinely creative. The text is, par excellence, the basis for communication in and through distance.

If that is so, then hermeneutics has the means to account for both the insurmountable character of the ideological phenomenon and the possibility of beginning, without ever being able to finish, a critique of ideology. Hermeneutics can do this because, in contrast to phenomenological idealism, the subject of which it speaks is always open to the efficacy of history (to make an allusion to Gadamer's famous notion of *wirkungsgeschichtliches Bewusstsein* [WM, 284; TM, 267]). Since distanciation is a moment of belonging, the critique of ideology can be incorporated, as an objective and explanatory segment, in the project of enlarging and restoring communication and self-understanding. The extension of understanding through textual exegesis and its constant rectification through the critique of ideology are properly part of the process of *Auslegung*. Textual exegesis and critique of ideology are the two privileged routes along which understanding is developed into interpretation and thus becomes itself.

(d) A radical way of placing the primacy of subjectivity in question is to take the theory of the text as the hermeneutical axis. Insofar as the meaning of a text is rendered autonomous with respect to the subjective intention of its author, the essential question is not to recover, behind the text, the lost intention but to unfold, in front of the text, the "world" it opens up and discloses.

In other words, the hermeneutical task is to discern the "matter" of the text (Gadamer) and not the psychology of the author. The matter of the text is to its structure as, in the proposition, the reference is to the sense (Frege). Just as in the proposition we are not content with the sense that is its ideal object but inquire further into its reference, that is, into its claim to truth, so too with the text we cannot stop at the immanent structure, at the internal system of dependencies arising from the crossing of the "codes" the text employs; we wish moreover to explicate the world the text projects. In saying that, I am not unaware that an important category of texts that we call *literature*—namely, narrative fiction, drama, poetry—appears to abolish all reference to everyday reality, to the point where language seems destined to supreme dignity, as if glorifying itself at the expense of the referential function of ordinary discourse. But it is precisely insofar as fictional discourse "suspends" its first-order referential function that it releases a second-order reference, where the world is manifested no longer as the totality of manipulable objects but as the horizon of our life and our project, in short as *Lebens-welt* [life-world], as being-in-the-world. It is this referential dimension, attaining its full development only with works of fiction and poetry, which raises the fundamental hermeneutical problem. Hermeneutics can no longer be defined as an inquiry into the psychological intentions that are hidden beneath the text, but rather as the explication of the being-in-the-world displayed by the text. What is to be interpreted in the text is a proposed world which I could inhabit and in which I could project my ownmost possibilities. Recalling the principle of distanciation mentioned above, it could be said that the fictional or poetic text not only places the meaning of the text at a *distance* from the intention of the author but also places the reference of the text at a *distance* from the *world* articulated by everyday language. Reality is, in this way, metamorphosed by means of what I shall call the "imaginative variations" that literature carries out on the real.

What is the consequence for Husserlian idealism of the hermeneutical focus on the matter of the text? Essentially this: the phenomenology that arose with the discovery of the universal character of intentionality has not remained faithful to its own discovery, namely, that the meaning of consciousness lies outside of itself. The idealist theory of the constitution of meaning in consciousness has thus culminated in the hypostasis of subjectivity. The price of this hypostasis is indicated by the above-mentioned difficulties in the "parallelism" between phenomenology and psychology. Such difficulties attest that phenomenology is always in danger of reducing itself to a transcendental subjectivism. The radical way of putting an end to this constantly recurring confusion is to shift the axis of interpretation from the problem of subjectivity to that of the world. That is what the theory of the text attempts to do, by subordinating the question of the author's intention to that of the matter of the text.

(e) In opposition to the idealist thesis of the ultimate self-responsibility of the mediating subject, hermeneutics proposes to make subjectivity the final, and not the first, category of a theory of understanding. Subjectivity must be lost as radical origin if it is to be recovered in a more modest role.

Here again, the theory of the text is a good guide. For it shows that the act of subjectivity is not so much what initiates understanding as what terminates it. The terminal act can be characterized as appropriation (*Zueignung*) (*SZ*, 150; *BT,* 191). It does not purport, as in Romantic hermeneutics, to rejoin the original subjectivity that would support the meaning of the text. Rather it *responds* to the matter of the text, and hence to the proposals of meaning the text unfolds. It is thus the counterpart of the distanciation that establishes the autonomy of the text with respect to its author, its situation, and its original addressee. It is also the counterpart of that other distanciation by which a new being-in-the-world, projected by the text, is freed from the false evidences of everyday reality. Appropriation is the *response* to this double distanciation, which is linked to the matter of the text, as regards its sense and as regards its reference. Thus appropriation can be integrated into the theory of interpretation without surreptitiously reintroducing the primacy of subjectivity which the four preceding theses have destroyed.

That appropriation does not imply the secret return of the sovereign subject can be attested to in the following way: if it remains true that hermeneutics terminates in self-understanding, then the subjectivism of this proposition must be rectified by saying that to understand *oneself* is to understand oneself *in front of the text.* Consequently, what is appropriation from one point of view is disappropriation from another. To appropriate is to make what was alien become one's own. What is appropriated is indeed the matter of the text. But the matter of the text becomes my own only if I disappropriate myself, in order to let the matter of the text be. So I exchange the *me, master* of itself, for the *self, disciple* of the text.

The process could also be expressed as a *distanciation of self from itself* within the interior of appropriation. This distanciation implements all the strategies of suspicion, among which the critique of ideology is a principal modality. Distanciation, in all its forms and figures, constitutes par excellence the critical moment in understanding.

This final and radical form of distanciation is the ruin of the ego's pretension to constitute itself as ultimate origin. The ego must assume for itself the "imaginative variations" by which it could *respond* to the "imaginative variations" on reality that literature and poetry, more than any other form of discourse, engender. It is this style of *"response to . . ."* that hermeneutics opposes to the idealism of ultimate *self*-responsibility.

II. TOWARD A HERMENEUTIC PHENOMENOLOGY

The hermeneutical critique of Husserlian idealism is, in my view, only the negative side of a positive research program that I shall place under the provisional and exploratory title of *hermeneutic phenomenology*. The present essay does not claim to work out—"to do"—this hermeneutic phenomenology. It seeks only to show its possibility by establishing, on the one hand, that beyond the critique of Husserlian idealism, phenomenology remains the unsurpassable presupposition of hermeneutics; and on the other hand, that phenomenology cannot carry out its program of *constitution* without constituting itself in the *interpretation* of the experience of the ego.

1. The Phenomenological Presupposition of Hermeneutics

(a) The most fundamental phenomenological presupposition of a philosophy of interpretation is that every question concerning any sort of "being" [*étant*] is a question about the meaning of that "being."

Thus, in the first few pages of *Being and Time*, we read that the forgotten question is the question of the *meaning* of being. In that respect, the ontological question is a phenomenological question. It is a hermeneutical problem only insofar as the meaning is concealed, not of course in itself, but by everything that forbids access to it. However, in order to become a hermeneutical problem—a problem about concealed meaning—the central question of phenomenology must be recognized as a question about meaning. Thereby the phenomenological attitude is already placed above the naturalistic-objectivistic attitude. *The choice in favor of meaning is thus the most general presupposition of any hermeneutics.*

It may be objected that hermeneutics is older than phenomenology. Even before the word *hermeneutics* was restored to dignity in the eighteenth century, there existed a biblical exegesis and a classical philology, both of which had already "stood up for meaning." That is indeed true; but hermeneutics becomes a philosophy of interpretation—and not simply a methodology of exegesis and philology—only if, going back to the conditions of possibility of exegesis and philology, going beyond even a general theory of the text, it addresses itself to the lingual condition—the *Sprachlichkeit*—of all experience (*WM*, 367ff.; *TM*, 345ff.).

This lingual condition has its own presupposition in a general theory of "meaning." It must be supposed that experience, in all its fullness (such as Hegel conceived it, as may be seen in Heidegger's famous text entitled "Hegel's Concept of Experience")[7] has an expressibility in principle. Experience can be said, it demands to be said. To bring it to language is not to change it into something else but, in articulating and developing it, to make it become itself.

Such is the presupposition of "meaning" which exegesis and philology employ at the level of a certain category of texts, those that have contributed to our historical tradition. Exegesis and philology may well be historically prior to phenomenological awareness, but the latter precedes them in the order of foundation.

It is difficult, admittedly, to formulate this presupposition in a nonidealist language. The break between the phenomenological attitude and the naturalistic attitude—or as we said, the choice in favor of meaning—seems to amount to nothing more than an opting for the consciousness "in" which meaning occurs. Is it not by "suspending" all *Seinsglaube* that the dimension of meaning is attained? Is not the *epoché* of being-in-itself therefore presupposed by the choice in favor of meaning? Is not every philosophy of meaning idealist?

These implications, it seems to me, are not at all compelling, neither in fact nor in principle. They are not compelling in fact—I mean from a plainly historical point of view; for if we return from Husserl's *Ideas* and *Cartesian Meditations* to his *Logical Investigations*, we rediscover a state of phenomenology where the notions of expression and meaning, of consciousness and intentionality, of intellectual intuition, are elaborated without the "reduction" being introduced in its idealist sense. On the contrary, the thesis of intentionality explicitly states that if all meaning is for a consciousness, then no consciousness is self-consciousness before being consciousness *of* something *toward* which it surpasses itself, or as Sartre said in a remarkable article, of something toward which it "explodes."[8] That consciousness is outside of itself, that it is *toward meaning* before meaning is for it and, above all, before consciousness is *for itself*: is this not what the central discovery of phenomenology implies? Thus to return to the nonidealist sense of the reduction is to remain faithful to the major discovery of the *Logical Investigations*, namely, that the logical notion of signification—such as Frege, for example, had introduced—is carved out of a broader notion of meaning which is coextensive with the concept of intentionality. Hence the right to speak of the "meaning" of perception, the "meaning" of imagination, the "meaning" of the will, and so on. This subordination of the logical notion of signification to the universal notion of meaning, under the guidance of the concept of intentionality, in no way implies that a transcendental subjectivity has sovereign mastery of the meaning toward which it orients itself. On the contrary, phenomenology could be drawn in the opposite direction, namely, toward the thesis of the priority of meaning over self-consciousness.

(b) Hermeneutics comes back to phenomenology in another way, namely, by its recourse to distanciation at the very heart of the experience of belonging. Hermeneutical distanciation is not unrelated to the phenomenological *epoché*, that is, to an *epoché* interpreted in a nonidealist sense as an aspect of the intentional movement of consciousness toward meaning. For all consciousness of meaning involves a moment of distanciation, a distancing from "lived experience" as purely and simply adhered to. Phenomenology begins when, not content to "live" or "relive," we interrupt lived experience in order to signify it. Thus the *epoché* and the meaning-intention [*visée de sens*] are closely linked.

This relation is easy to discern in the case of language. The linguistic sign can *stand* for something only if it is *not* the thing. In this respect, the sign possesses a specific negativity. Everything happens as if, in order to enter the symbolic universe, the speaking subject must have at his disposal an "empty space" from which the use of signs can begin. The *epoché* is the virtual event, the imaginary act that inaugurates the whole game by which we exchange signs for things and signs for other signs. Phenomenology is like the explicit revival of this virtual event, which it raises to the dignity of the act, the philosophical gesture. It renders thematic what was only operative, and thereby makes meaning appear as meaning.

Hermeneutics extends this philosophical gesture into its own domain, which is that of the historical and, more generally, the human sciences. The "lived experience" that it is concerned to bring to language and raise to meaning is the historical connection, mediated by the transmission of written documents, works, institutions, and monuments which render present the historical past. What we have called "belonging" is nothing other than the adherence to this historical lived experience, what Hegel called the "substance" of moral life. The "lived experience" of phenomenology corresponds, on the side of hermeneutics, to consciousness exposed to historical efficacy. Hence hermeneutical distanciation is to belonging as, in phenomenology, the *epoché* is to lived experience. Hermeneutics similarly begins when, not content to belong to transmitted tradition, we interrupt the relation of belonging in order to signify it.

This parallel is of considerable importance if indeed hermeneutics must incorporate a critical moment, a moment of suspicion, from which the critique of ideology, psychoanalysis, and so on, can proceed. The critical moment can be integrated with the relation of belonging only if distanciation is consubstantial with belonging. Phenomenology shows that this is possible when it elevates to a philosophical decision the virtual act of instituting the "empty space" that enables a subject to signify his lived experience and his belonging to a historical tradition.

(c) Hermeneutics also shares with phenomenology the thesis of the derivative character of linguistic meaning.

It is easy, in this respect, to return to the phenomenological roots of some well-known hermeneutical theses. Beginning with the most recent theses, those of Gadamer, it can be seen that the secondary character of the problematic of language is reflected in the very composition of *Truth and Method*. Even if it is true that all experience has a "lingual dimension" and that this *Sprachlichkeit* imprints and pervades all experience, nevertheless it is not with *Spachlichkeit* that hermeneutic philosophy must begin. It is necessary to say first what comes to language. Hence hermeneutic philosophy begins with the experience of art, which is not necessarily linguistic. Moreover it accentuates, in this experience, the more ontological aspects of the experience of *play*—in the playful [*ludique*] as well as the theatrical sense of the word (*WM*, 97ff.; *TM*, 91ff.). For it is in the participation of players in a game that we find the first experience of belonging susceptible of being examined by the philosopher. And it is in the game that the constitution of the function of exhibition or presentation (*Darstellung*) can be seen, a function that doubtlessly summons the linguistic medium, but that in principle precedes and supports it. Nor is discourse dominant in the second group of experiences interpreted in *Truth and Method*. Consciousness of being exposed to the effects of history, which precludes a total reflection on prejudices and precedes any objectification of the past by the historian, is not reducible to the properly lingual aspects of the transmission of the past. Texts, documents, and monuments represent only one mediation among others, however exemplary it may be for the reasons mentioned above. The interplay of distance and proximity, constitutive of the historical connection, is what comes to language rather than what language produces.

This way of subordinating *Sprachlichkeit* to the experience that comes to language is perfectly faithful to Heidegger's gesture in *Being and Time*. Recall how the Analytic of *Dasein* subordinates the level of the assertion (*Aussage*), which is also that of logical signification, of signification in the strict sense (*Bedeutung*), to the level of discourse (*Rede*); and the latter, according to Heidegger, is "equiprimordial" with state-of-mind (*Befindlichkeit*) and *understanding* (*Verstehen*) (*SZ*, §34). The logical order is thus preceded by a "saying" that is interwoven with a "finding oneself" and an "understanding." The level of assertion can therefore claim no autonomy; it refers back to the existential structures constitutive of being-in-the-world.

The reference of the linguistic order back to the structure of experience (which comes to language in the assertion) constitutes, in my view, the most important phenomenological presupposition of hermeneutics.

Since the period of the *Logical Investigations*, a development can be discerned which enables logical signification to be situated within a general theory of intentionality. This development implied the displacement of the intentional model from the logical plane toward the perceptive plane, where our first signifying relation with things is formed. At the same time, phenomenology drew back from the predicative and apophantic level of signification—the level of the *Logical Investigations*—to the properly pre-predicative level, where noematic analysis precedes linguistic inquiry. Thus, in *Ideas*, vol. 1, Husserl goes so far as to say that the layer of expression is an essentially "unproductive" layer (*Hua* 3, §124); and indeed, the analysis of noetic-noematic correlations can be carried very far without linguistic articulation being considered as such. The strategic level proper to phenomenology is therefore the *noema*, with its modifications (presence, memory, fantasy, etc.), its modes of belief (certitude, doubt, supposition, etc.), and its degrees of actuality and potentiality. The constitution of the *complete noema* precedes the properly linguistic plane upon which the functions of denomination, predication, syntactic liaison, and so on come to be articulated.

This way of subordinating the linguistic plane to the prelinguistic level of noematic analysis is, it seems to me, exemplary for hermeneutics. When the latter subordinates lingual experience to the whole of our aesthetic and historical experience, it continues, on the level of the human sciences, the movement initiated by Husserl on the plane of perceptive experience.

(d) The kinship between the pre-predicative of phenomenology and that of hermeneutics is all the closer in that Husserlian phenomenology itself began to develop the phenomenology of perception in the direction of a hermeneutics of historical experience.

It is well known how, on the one hand, Husserl continued to develop the properly *temporal* implications of perceptual experience. He was thus led, by his own analyses, toward the historicity of human experience as a whole. In particular, it became increasingly evident that the presumptive, inadequate, unfinished character that perceptual experience acquires from its temporal structure could be applied step-by-step to the whole of historical experience. A new model of truth could thus be elicited from the phenomenology of perception and transposed into the domain of the historical-hermeneutic sciences. Such is the consequence that Merleau-Ponty drew from Husserlian phenomenology.

On the other hand, perceptual experience appeared more and more like an artificially isolated segment of a relation to the "life-world," itself directly endowed with historical and cultural features. Here I shall not emphasize this philosophy of the *Lebenswelt* which characterized the period of the *Crisis,* and which was contemporaneous with Heidegger's Analytic of *Dasein*. It will suffice to say that the return from a nature objectified and mathematicized by Galilean and Newtonian science to the *Lebenswelt* is the very same principle of return that hermeneutics seeks to implement elsewhere, on the plane of the human sciences; for hermeneutics similarly wishes to withdraw from the objectifications and explanations of historical science and sociology to the artistic, historical, and lingual experience that precedes and supports these objectifications and explanations. The return to the *Lebenswelt* can more effectively play this paradigmatic role for hermeneutics if the *Lebenswelt* is not confused with some sort of ineffable immediacy and is not identified with the vital and emotional envelope of human experience, but rather is construed as designating the reservoir of meaning, the surplus of sense in living experience, which renders the objectifying and explanatory attitude possible.

These last remarks have already brought us to the point where phenomenology can be the presupposition of hermeneutics only insofar as phenomenology, in turn, incorporates a hermeneutical presupposition.

NOTES

1. This essay reflects the changes of method implied by my own evolution, from an eidetic phenomenology in *Freedom and Nature* (1950) to *Freud and Philosophy* (1965) and *The Conflict of Interpretations* (1969).
2. The "Nachwort" first appeared in the *Jahrbuch für Philosophie und phänome-nologische Forschung* (1930); it was subsequently published in *Husserliana*, vol. 5, ed. H.L. van Breda (The Hague: Martinus Nijhoff, 1952; hereafter cited in the text as *Hua* 5), pp. 138–62.
3. The word *"verliert"* reappears three times: *Hua* 5:145.
4. Martin Heidegger, *Sein und Zeit* (Tübingen: Max Niemeyer, 1927; hereafter cited in the text as *SZ*), p. 149 [*Being and Time*, trans. John Macquarrie and Edward Robinson (Oxford: Basil Blackwell, 1978; hereafter cited in the text as *BT*), p. 189].
5. Hans-Georg Gadamer, *Wahrheit und Methode* (Tübingen: J.C.B. Mohr, 1960; hereafter cited in the text as *WM*), pp. 250ff. [*Truth and Method* (London: Sheed & Ward, 1975; hereafter cited in the text as *TM*), pp. 235ff.].
6. See "Hermeneutics and the Critique of Ideology."
7. Martin Heidegger, "Hegels Begriff der Erfahrung," in *Holzwege* (Frankfurt: Vittoria Klostermann, 1950) [*Hegel's Concept of Experience* (New York: Harper & Row, 1970)].
8. Jean-Paul Sartre, "Une idée fondamentale de la phénoménologie de Husserl: l'intentionnalité," in *Situations 1* (Paris: Gallimard, 1947) ["Intentionality: A Fundamental Idea of Husserl's Phenomenology," trans. Joseph P. Fell, *Journal of the British Society for Phenomenology* 1, no. 2 (1970): 4–5].

JEAN-FRANÇOIS LYOTARD

"ANSWERING THE QUESTION: WHAT IS POSTMODERNISM?"

A DEMAND

This is a period of slackening—I refer to the color of the times. From every direction we are being urged to put an end to experimentation, in the arts and elsewhere. I have read an art historian who extols realism and is militant for the advent of a new subjectivity. I have read an art critic who packages and sells "Transavantgardism" in the marketplace of painting. I have read that under the name of postmodernism, architects are getting rid of the Bauhaus project, throwing out the baby of experimentation with the bathwater of functionalism. I have read that a new philosopher is discovering what he drolly calls Judaeo-Christianism, and intends by it to put an end to the impiety which we are supposed to have spread. I have read in a French weekly that some are displeased with *Mille Plateaux* [by Deleuze and Guattari] because they expect, especially when reading a work of philosophy, to be gratified with a little sense. I have read from the pen of a reputable historian that writers and thinkers of the 1960 and 1970 avant-gardes spread a reign of terror in the use of language, and that the conditions for a fruitful exchange must be restored by imposing on the intel-

Jean-François Lyotard. "Answering the Question: What Is Postmodernism?" Translated by Regis Durand. From Ihab Hassan and Sally Hassan, eds. *Innovation/Rennovation: New Perspectives on the Humanities.* © 1983. (Madison: The University of Wisconsin Press.) Reprinted by permission of The University of Wisconsin Press.

lectuals a common way of speaking, that of the historians. I have been reading a young philosopher of language who complains that Continental thinking, under the challenge of speaking machines, has surrendered to the machines the concern for reality, that it has substituted for the referential paradigm that of "adlinguisticity" (one speaks about speech, writes about writing, intertexuality), and who thinks that the time has now come to restore a solid anchorage of language in the referent. I have read a talented theatrologist for whom postmodernism, with its games and fantasies, carries very little weight in front of political authority, especially when a worried public opinion encourages authority to a politics of totalitarian surveillance in the face of nuclear warfare threats.

I have read a thinker of repute who defends modernity against those he calls the neoconservatives. Under the banner of postmodernism, the latter would like, he believes, to get rid of the uncompleted project of modernism, that of the Enlightenment. Even the last advocates of *Aufklärung,* such as Popper or Adorno, were only able, according to him, to defend the project in a few particular spheres of life—that of politics for the author of *The Open Society,* and that of art for the author of *Ästhetische Theorie.* Jürgen Habermas (everyone has recognized him) thinks that if modernity has failed, it is in allowing the totality of life to be splintered into independent specialties which are left to the narrow competence of experts, while the concrete individual experiences "desublimated meaning" and "destructured form," not as a liberation but in the mode of that immense *ennui* which Baudelaire described over a century ago.

Following a prescription of Albrecht Wellmer, Habermas considers that the remedy for this splintering of culture and its separation from life can only come from "changing the status of aesthetic experience when it is no longer primarily expressed in judgments of taste," but when it is "used to explore a living historical situation," that is, when "it is put in relation with problems of existence." For this experience then "becomes a part of a language game which is no longer that of aesthetic criticism"; it takes part "in cognitive processes and normative expectations"; "it alters the manner in which those different moments *refer* to one another." What Habermas requires from the arts and the experiences they provide is, in short, to bridge the gap between cognitive, ethical, and political discourses, thus opening the way to a unity of experience.

My question is to determine what sort of unity Habermas has in mind. Is the aim of the project of modernity the constitution of sociocultural unity within which all the elements of daily life and of thought would take their places as in an organic whole? Or does the passage that has to be charted between heterogeneous language games—those of cognition, of ethics, of politics—belong to a different order from that? And if so, would it be capable of effecting a real synthesis between them?

The first hypothesis, of a Hegelian inspiration, does not challenge the notion of a dialectically totalizing *experience;* the second is closer to the spirit of Kant's *Critique of Judgment;* but must be submitted, like the *Critique,* to that severe reexamination which postmodernity imposes on the thought of the Enlightenment, on the idea of a unitary end of history and of a subject. It is this critique which not only Wittgenstein and Adorno have initiated, but also a few other thinkers (French or other) who do not have the honor to be read by Professor Habermas—which at least saves them from getting a poor grade for their neoconservatism.

REALISM

The demands I began by citing are not all equivalent. They can even be contradictory. Some are made in the name of postmodernism, others in order to combat it. It is not necessarily the same thing to formulate a demand for some referent (and objective reality), for some sense (and credible transcendence), for an addressee (and audience), or an addressor (and subjective expressiveness) or for some communicational consensus (and a general code of exchanges, such as the genre of historical discourse). But in the diverse invitations to suspend artistic experimentation, there is an identical call for order, a desire for unity, for identity, for security, or popularity (in the sense of *Offentlichkeit,* of "finding a public"). Artists and writers must be brought back into the bosom of the community, or at least, if the latter is considered to be ill, they must be assigned the task of healing it.

There is an irrefutable sign of this common disposition: it is that for all those writers nothing is more urgent than to liquidate the heritage of the avant-gardes. Such is the case, in particular, of the so-called transavantgardism. The answers given by Achille Bonito Oliva to the questions asked by Bernard Lamarche-Vadel and Michel Enric leave no room for doubt about this. By putting the avant-gardes through a mixing process, the artist and critic feel more confident that they can suppress them than by launching a frontal attack. For they can pass off the most cynical eclecticism as a way of going beyond the fragmentary character of the preceding experiments; whereas if they openly turned their backs on them, they would run the risk of appearing ridiculously neoacademic. The *Salons* and the *Académies,* at the time when the bourgeoisie was establishing itself in history, were able to function as purgation and to grant awards for good plastic and literary conduct under the cover of realism. But capitalism inherently possesses the power to derealize familiar objects, social roles, and institutions to such a degree that the so-called realistic representations can no longer evoke reality except as nostalgia or mockery, as an occasion for suffering rather than for satisfaction. Classicism seems to be ruled out in a world in which reality is so destabilized that it offers no occasion for experience but one for ratings and experimentation.

This theme is familiar to all readers of Walter Benjamin. But it is necessary to assess its exact reach. Photography did not appear as a challenge to painting from the outside, any more than industrial cinema did to narrative literature.

The former was only putting the final touch to the program of ordering the visible elaborated by the quattrocento; while the latter was the last step in rounding off diachronies as organic wholes, which had been the ideal of the great novels of education since the eighteenth century. That the mechanical and the industrial should appear as substitutes for hand or craft was not in itself a disaster—except if one believes that art is in its essence the expression of an individuality of genius assisted by an elite craftsmanship.

The challenge lay essentially in that photographic and cinematographic processes can accomplish better, faster, and with a circulation a hundred thousand times larger than narrative or pictorial realism, the task which academicism had assigned to realism: to preserve various consciousnesses from doubt. Industrial photography and cinema will be superior to painting and the novel whenever the objective is to stabilize the referent, to arrange it according to a point of view which endows it with a recognizable meaning, to reproduce the syntax and vocabulary which enable the addressee to decipher images and sequences quickly, and so to arrive easily at the consciousness of his own identity as well as the approval which he thereby receives from others—since such structures of images and sequences constitute a communication code among all of them. This is the way the effects of reality, or if one prefers, the fantasies of realism, multiply.

If they too do not wish to become supporters (of minor importance at that) of what exists, the painter and novelist must refuse to lend themselves to such therapeutic uses. They must question the rules of the art of painting or of narrative as they have learned and received them from their predecessors. Soon those rules must appear to them as a means to deceive, to seduce, and to reassure, which makes it impossible for them to be "true." Under the common name of painting and literature, an unprecedented split is taking place. Those who refuse to reexamine the rules of art pursue successful careers in mass conformism by communicating, by means of the "correct rules," the endemic desire for reality with objects and situations capable of gratifying it. Pornography is the use of photography and film to such an end. It is becoming a general model for the visual or narrative arts which have not met the challenge of the mass media.

As for the artists and writers who question the rules of plastic and narrative arts and possibly share their suspicions by circulating their work, they are destined to have little credibility in the eyes of those concerned with "reality" and "identity"; they have no guarantee of an audience. Thus it is possible to ascribe the dialectics of the avant-gardes to the challenge posed by the realisms of industry and mass communication to painting and the narrative arts. Duchamp's "ready made" does nothing but actively and parodistically signify this constant process of dispossession of the craft of painting or even of being an artist. As Thierry de Duve penetratingly observes, the modern aesthetic question is not "What is beautiful?" but "What can be said to be art (and literature)?"

Realism, whose only definition is that it intends to avoid the question of reality implicated in that of art, always stands somewhere between academicism and kitsch. When power assumes the name of a party, realism and its neoclassical complement triumph over the experimental avant-garde by slandering and banning it—that is, provided the "correct" images, the "correct" narratives, the "correct" forms which the party requests, selects, and propagates can find a public to desire them as the appropriate remedy for the anxiety and depression that public experiences. The demand for reality—that is, for unity, simplicity, communicability, etc.—did not have the same intensity nor the same continuity in German society between the two world wars and in Russian society after the Revolution: this provides a basis for a distinction between Nazi and Stalinist realism.

What is clear, however, is that when it is launched by the political apparatus, the attack on artistic experimentation is specifically reactionary: aesthetic judgment would only be required to decide whether such or such work is in conformity with the established rules of the beautiful. Instead of the work of art having to investigate what makes it an art object and whether it will be able to find an audience, political academicism possesses and imposes a priori criteria of the beautiful, which designate some works and a public at a stroke and forever. The use of categories in aesthetic judgment would thus be of the same nature as in cognitive judgment. To speak like Kant, both would be determining judgments: the expression is "well formed" first in the understanding, then the only cases retained in experience are those which can be subsumed under this expression.

When power is that of capital and not that of a party, the "transavant-gardist" or "postmodern" (in Jencks's sense) solution proves to be better adapted than the antimodern solution. Eclecticism is the degree zero of contemporary general culture: one listens to reggae, watches a western, eats McDonald's food for lunch and local cuisine for dinner, wears Paris perfume in Tokyo and "retro" clothes in Hong Kong; knowledge is a matter for TV games. It is easy to find a public for eclectic works. By becoming kitsch, art panders to the confusion which reigns in the "taste" of the patrons. Artists, gallery owners, critics, and public wallow together in the "anything goes," and the epoch is one of slackening. But this realism of the "anything goes," is in fact that of money; in the absence of aesthetic criteria, it remains possible and useful to assess the value of works of art according to the profits they yield. Such realism accommodates all tendencies, just as capital accommodates all "needs," providing that the tendencies and needs have purchasing power. As for taste, there is no need to be delicate when one speculates or entertains oneself.

Artistic and literary research is doubly threatened, once by the "cultural policy" and once by the art and book market. What is advised, sometimes through one channel, sometimes through the other, is to offer works which, first, are relative to subjects which exist in the eyes of the public they address,

228 Jean-François Lyotard

and second, works so made ("well made") that the public will recognize what they are about, will understand what is signified, will be able to give or refuse its approval knowingly, and if possible, even to derive from such work a certain amount of comfort.

The interpretation which has just been given of the contact between the industrial and mechanical arts, and literature and the fine arts is correct in its outline, but it remains narrowly sociologizing and historicizing—in other words, one-sided. Stepping over Benjamin's and Adorno's reticences, it must be recalled that science and industry are no more free of the suspicion which concerns reality than are art and writing. To believe otherwise would be to entertain an excessively humanistic notion of the mephistophelian functionalism of sciences and technologies. There is no denying the dominant existence today of techno-science, that is, the massive subordination of cognitive statements to the finality of the best possible performance, which is the technological criterion. But the mechanical and the industrial, especially when they enter fields traditionally reserved for artists, are carrying with them much more than power effects. The objects and the thoughts which originate in scientific knowledge and the capitalist economy convey with them one of the rules which supports their possibility: the rule that there is no reality unless testified by a consensus between partners over a certain knowledge and certain commitments.

This rule is of no little consequence. It is the imprint left on the politics of the scientist and the trustee of capital by a kind of flight of reality out of the metaphysical, religious, and political certainties that the mind believed it held. This withdrawal is absolutely necessary to the emergence of science and capitalism. No industry is possible without a suspicion of the Aristotelian theory of motion, no industry without a refutation of corporatism, of mercantilism, and of physiocracy. Modernity, in whatever age it appears, cannot exist without a shattering of belief and without discovery of the "lack of reality" of reality, together with the invention of other realities.

What does this "lack of reality" signify if one tries to free it from a narrowly historicized interpretation? The phrase is of course akin to what Nietzsche calls nihilism. But I see a much earlier modulation of Nietzschean perspectivism in the Kantian theme of the sublime. I think in particular that it is in the aesthetic of the sublime that modern art (including literature) finds its impetus and the logic of avant-gardes finds its axioms.

The sublime sentiment, which is also the sentiment of the sublime, is, according to Kant, a strong and equivocal emotion: it carries with it both pleasure and pain. Better still, in it pleasure derives from pain. Within the tradition of the subject, which comes from Augustine and Descartes and which Kant does not radically challenge, this contradiction, which some would call neurosis or masochism, develops as a conflict between the faculties of a subject, the faculty to conceive of something and the faculty to "present" something. Knowledge exists if, first, the statement is intelligible, and second, if "cases" can be derived from the experience which "corresponds" to it. Beauty exists if a certain "case" (the work of art), given first by the sensibility without any conceptual determination, the sentiment of pleasure independent of any interest the work may elicit, appeals to the principle of a universal consensus (which may never be attained).

Taste, therefore, testifies that between the capacity to conceive and the capacity to present an object corresponding to the concept, an undetermined agreement, without rules, giving rise to a judgment which Kant calls reflective, may be experienced as pleasure. The sublime is a different sentiment. It takes place, on the contrary, when the imagination fails to present an object which might, if only in principle, come to match a concept. We have the Idea of the world (the totality of what is), but we do not have the capacity to show an example of it. We have the Idea of the simple (that which cannot be broken down, decomposed), but we cannot illustrate it with a sensible object which would be a "case" of it. We can conceive the infinitely great, the infinitely powerful, but every presentation of an object destined to "make visible" this absolute greatness of power appears to us painfully inadequate. Those are Ideas of which no presentation is possible. Therefore, they impart no knowledge about reality (experience); they also prevent the free union of the faculties which gives rise to the sentiment of the beautiful; and they prevent the formation and the stabilization of taste. They can be said to be unpresentable.

I shall call modern the art which devotes its "little technical expertise" (*son "petit technique"*), as Diderot used to say, to present the fact that the unpresentable exists. To make visible that there is something which can be conceived and which can neither be seen nor made visible: this is what is at stake in modern painting. But how to make visible that there is something which cannot be seen? Kant himself shows the way when he names "formlessness, the absence of form," as a possible index to the unpresentable. He also says of the empty "abstraction" which the imagination experiences when in search for a presentation of the infinite (another unpresentable): this abstraction itself is like a presentation of the infinite, its "negative presentation." He cites the commandment, "Thou shalt not make graven images" (*Exodus*), as the most sublime passage in the Bible in that it forbids all presentation of the Absolute. Little needs to be added to those observations to outline an aesthetic of sublime paintings. As painting, it will of course "present" something though negatively; it will therefore avoid figuration or representation. It will be "white" like one of Malevitch's squares; it will enable us to see only by making it impossible to see; it will please only by causing pain. One recognizes in those instructions the axioms of avant-gardes in painting, inasmuch as they devote themselves to making an allusion to the unpresentable by means of visible presentations. The systems in the name of which, or with which, this task has been able to support or to justify itself deserve the greatest attention; but they can originate only in the vocation of the sublime in order to legitimize it, that is, to conceal it. They remain inexplicable without the incommensurability of reality to concept which is implied in the Kantian philosophy of the sublime.

230 Jean-François Lyotard

It is not my intention to analyze here in detail the manner in which the various avant-gardes have, so to speak, humbled and disqualified reality by examining the pictorial techniques which are so many devices to make us believe in it. Local tone, drawing, the mixing of colors, linear perspective, the nature of the support and that of the instrument, the treatment, the display, the museum: the avant-gardes are perpetually flushing out artifices of presentation which make it possible to subordinate thought to the gaze and to turn it away from the unpresentable. If Habermas, like Marcuse, understands this task of derealization as an aspect of the (repressive) "desublimation" which characterizes the avant-garde, it is because he confuses the Kantian sublime with Freudian sublimation, and because aesthetics has remained for him that of the beautiful.

THE POSTMODERN

What, then, is the postmodern? What place does it or does it not occupy in the vertiginous work of the questions hurled at the rules of image and narration? It is undoubtedly a part of the modern. All that has been received, if only yesterday (*modo, modo,* Petronius used to say), must be suspected. What space does Cézanne challenge? The Impressionists'. What object do Picasso and Braque attack? Cézanne's. What presupposition does Duchamp break with in 1912? That which says one must make a painting, be it cubist. And Buren questions that other presupposition which he believes had survived untouched by the work of Duchamp: the place of presentation of the work. In an amazing acceleration, the generations precipitate themselves. A work can become modern only if it is first postmodern. Postmodernism thus understood is not modernism at its end but in the nascent state, and this state is constant.

Yet I would like not to remain with this slightly mechanistic meaning of the word. If it is true that modernity takes place in the withdrawal of the real and according to the sublime relation between the presentable and the conceivable, it is possible, within this relation, to distinguish two modes (to use the musician's language). The emphasis can be placed on the powerlessness of the faculty of presentation, on the nostalgia for presence felt by the human subject, on the obscure and futile will which inhabits him in spite of everything. The emphasis can be placed, rather, on the power of the faculty to conceive, on its "inhumanity" so to speak (it was the quality Apollinaire demanded of modern artists), since it is not the business of our understanding whether or not human sensibility or imagination can match what it conceives. The emphasis can also be placed on the increase of being and the jubilation which result from the invention of new rules of the game, be it pictorial, artistic, or any other. What I have in mind will become clear if we dispose very schematically a few names on the chessboard of the history of avant-gardes: on the side of melancholia, the German Expressionists, and on the side of *novatio,* Braque and Picasso, on the former Malevitch and on the latter Lissitzky, on the one Chirico and on the other Duchamp. The nuance which distinguishes these two modes may be infinitesimal; they often coexist in the same piece, are almost indistinguishable; and yet they testify to a difference (*un différend*) on which the fate of thought depends and will depend for a long time, between regret and assay.

The work of Proust and that of Joyce both allude to something which does not allow itself to be made present. Allusion, to which Paolo Fabbri recently called my attention, is perhaps a form of expression indispensable to the works which belong to an aesthetic of the sublime. In Proust, what is being eluded as the price to pay for this allusion is the identity of consciousness, a victim to the excess of time (*au trop de temps*). But in Joyce, it is the identity of writing which is the victim of an excess of the book (*au trop de livre*) or of literature.

Proust calls forth the unpresentable by means of a language unaltered in its syntax and vocabulary and of a writing which in many of its operators still belongs to the genre of novelistic narration. The literary institution, as Proust inherits it from Balzac and Flaubert, is admittedly subverted in that the hero is no longer a character but the inner consciousness of time, and in that the diegetic diachrony, already damaged by Flaubert, is here put in question because of the narrative voice. Nevertheless, the unity of the book, the odyssey of that consciousness, even if it is deferred from chapter to chapter, is not seriously challenged: the identity of the writing with itself throughout the labyrinth of the interminable narration is enough to connote such unity, which has been compared to that of *The Phenomenology of Mind*.

Joyce allows the unpresentable to become perceptible in his writing itself, in the signifier. The whole range of available narrative and even stylistic operators is put into play without concern for the unity of the whole, and new operators are tried. The grammar and vocabulary of literary language are no longer accepted as given; rather, they appear as academic forms, as rituals originating in piety (as Nietzsche said) which prevent the unpresentable from being put forward.

Here, then, lies the difference: modern aesthetics is an aesthetic of the sublime, though a nostalgic one. It allows the unpresentable to be put forward only as the missing contents; but the form, because of its recognizable consistency, continues to offer to the reader or viewer matter for solace and pleasure. Yet these sentiments do not constitute the real sublime sentiment, which is in an intrinsic combination of pleasure and pain: the pleasure that reason should exceed all presentation, the pain that imagination or sensibility should not be equal to the concept.

The postmodern would be that which, in the modern, puts forward the unpresentable in presentation itself; that which denies itself the solace of good forms, the consensus of a taste which would make it possible to share collectively the nostalgia for the unattainable; that which searches for new presentations, not in order to enjoy them but in order to impart a stronger sense of the unpresentable. A postmodern artist or writer is in the position of a philosopher: the text he writes, the work he produces are not in principle governed by preestablished rules, and they cannot be judged according to a determining judgment, by applying familiar categories to the text or to the work. Those rules and categories are what the work of art itself is looking for. The artist and the writer, then, are working without rules in order to formulate the rules of what *will have been done*. Hence the fact that work and text have the characters of an *event*; hence also, they always come too late for their author, or, what amounts to the same thing, their being put into work, their realization (*mise en oeuvre*) always begin too soon. *Post modern* would have to be understood according to the paradox of the future (*post*) anterior (*modo*).

It seems to me that the essay (Montaigne) is postmodern, while the fragment (*The Athaeneum*) is modern.

Finally, it must be clear that it is our business not to supply reality but to invent allusions to the conceivable which cannot be presented. And it is not to be expected that this task will effect the last reconciliation between language games (which, under the name of faculties, Kant knew to be separated by a chasm), and that only the transcendental illusion (that of Hegel) can hope to totalize them into a real unity. But Kant also knew that the price to pay for such an illusion is terror. The nineteenth and twentieth centuries have given us as much terror as we can take. We have paid a high enough price for the nostalgia of the whole and the one, for the reconciliation of the concept and the sensible, of the transparent and the communicable experience. Under the general demand for slackening and for appeasement, we can hear the mutterings of the desire for a return of terror, for the realization of the fantasy to seize reality. The answer is: Let us wage a war on totality; let us be witnesses to the unpresentable; let us activate the differences and save the honor of the name.

MICHEL FOUCAULT

NIETZSCHE, GENEALOGY, HISTORY

1. Genealogy is gray, meticulous, and patiently documentary. It operates on a field of entangled and confused parchments, on documents that have been scratched over and recopied many times.

On this basis, it is obvious that Paul Ree[1] was wrong to follow the English tendency in describing the history of morality in terms of a linear development—in reducing its entire history and genesis to an exclusive concern for utility. He assumed that words had kept their meaning, that desires still pointed in a single direction, and that ideas retained their logic; and he ignored the fact that the world of speech and desires has known invasions, struggles, plundering, disguises, ploys. From these elements, however, genealogy retrieves an indispensable restraint: it must record the singularity of events outside of any monotonous finality; it must seek them in the most unpromising places, in what we tend to feel is without history—in sentiments, love, conscience, instincts; it

This essay first appeared in *Hommage à Jean Hyppolite* (Paris: Presses Universitaires de France, 1971), pp. 145–72. Along with "Réponse au cercle d'épistémologie," which became the introductory chapter of *The Archaeology of Knowledge*, this essay represents Foucault's attempt to explain his relationship to those sources which are fundamental to his development. Its importance, in terms of understanding Foucault's objectives, cannot be exaggerated. It appears here by permission of Presses Universitaires de France.

Reprinted with permission from *Language, Counter-Memory, Practice: Selected Essays and Interviews*, Cornell University Press, 1977, ed. Donald F. Bouchard, tr. Donald F. Bouchard and Sherry Simon.

must be sensitive to their recurrence, not in order to trace the gradual curve of their evolution, but to isolate the different scenes where they engaged in different roles. Finally, genealogy must define even those instances where they are absent, the moment when they remained unrealized (Plato, at Syracuse, did not become Mohammed).

Genealogy, consequently, requires patience and a knowledge of details and it depends on a vast accumulation of source material. Its "cyclopean monuments"[2] are constructed from "discreet and apparently insignificant truths and according to a rigorous method"; they cannot be the product of "large and well-meaning errors."[3] In short, genealogy demands relentless erudition. Genealogy does not oppose itself to history as the lofty and profound gaze of the philosopher might compare to the molelike perspective of the scholar; on the contrary, it rejects the metahistorical deployment of ideal significations and indefinite teleologies. It opposes itself to the search for "origins."

2. In Nietzsche, we find two uses of the word *Ursprung*. The first is unstressed, and it is found alternately with other terms such as *Entstehung, Herkunft, Abkunft, Geburt*. In *The Genealogy of Morals*, for example, *Entstehung* or *Ursprung* serve equally well to denote the origin of duty or guilty conscience;[4] and in the discussion of logic or knowledge in *The Gay Science*, their origin is indiscriminately referred to as *Ursprung, Entstehung, or Herkunft*.[5]

The other use of the word is stressed. On occasion, Nietzsche places the term in opposition to another: in the first paragraph of *Human, All Too Human* the miraculous origin (*Wunderursprung*) sought by metaphysics is set against the analyses of historical philosophy, which poses questions *über Herkunft und Anfang. Ursprung* is also used in an ironic and deceptive manner. In what, for instance, do we find the original basis (*Ursprung*) of morality, a foundation sought after since Plato? "In detestable, narrowminded conclusions. *Pudenda origo*."[6] Or in a related context, where should we seek the origin of religion (*Ursprung*), which Schopenhauer located in a particular metaphysical sentiment of the hereafter? It belongs, very simply, to an invention (*Erfindung*), a sleight-of-hand, an artifice (*Kunststück*), a secret formula, in the rituals of black magic, in the work of the *Schwarzkünstler*.[7]

One of the most significant texts with respect to the use of all these terms and to the variations in the use of *Ursprung* is the preface to the *Genealogy*. At the beginning of the text, its objective is defined as an examination of the origin of moral preconceptions and the term used is *Herkunft*. Then, Nietzsche proceeds by retracing his personal involvement with this question: he recalls the period when he "calligraphied" philosophy, when he questioned if God must be held responsible for the origin of evil. He now finds this question amusing and properly characterizes it as a search for *Ursprung* (he will shortly use the same term to summarize Paul Ree's activity).[8] Further on, he evokes the analyses that are characteristically Nietzschean and that began with *Human, All Too Human*. Here, he speaks of *Herkunfthypothesen*. This use of the word *Herkunft* cannot be arbitrary, since it serves to designate a number of texts, beginning with

Human, All Too Human, which deal with the origin of morality, asceticism, justice, and punishment. And yet, the word used in all these works had been *Ursprung*.[9] It would seem that at this point in the *Genealogy* Nietzsche wished to validate an opposition between *Herkunft* and *Ursprung* that did not exist ten years earlier. But immediately following the use of the two terms in a specific sense, Nietzsche reverts, in the final paragraphs of the preface, to a usage that is neutral and equivalent.[10]

Why does Nietzsche challenge the pursuit of the origin (*Ursprung*), at least on those occasions when he is truly a genealogist? First, because it is an attempt to capture the exact essence of things, their purest possibilities, and their carefully protected identities, because this search assumes the existence of immobile forms that precede the external world of accident and succession. This search is directed to "that which was already there," the image of a primordial truth fully adequate to its nature, and it necessitates the removal of every mask to ultimately disclose an original identity. However, if the genealogist refuses to extend his faith in metaphysics, if he listens to history, he finds that there is "something altogether different" behind things: not a timeless and essential secret, but the secret that they have no essence or that their essence was fabricated in a piecemeal fashion from alien forms. Examining the history of reason, he learns that it was born in an altogether "reasonable" fashion—from chance;[11] devotion to truth and the precision of scientific methods arose from the passion of scholars, their reciprocal hatred, their fanatical and unending discussions, and their spirit of competition—the personal conflicts that slowly forged the weapons of reason.[12] Further, genealogical analysis shows that the concept of liberty is an "invention of the ruling classes"[13] and not fundamental to man's nature or at the root of his attachment to being and truth. What is found at the historical beginning of things is not the inviolable identity of their origin; it is the dissension of other things. It is disparity.[14]

History also teaches how to laugh at the solemnities of the origin. The lofty origin is no more than "a metaphysical extension which arises from the belief that things are most precious and essential at the moment of birth."[15] We tend to think that this is the moment of their greatest perfection, when they emerged dazzling from the hands of a creator or in the shadowless light of a first morning. The origin always precedes the Fall. It comes before the body, before the world and time; it is associated with the gods, and its story is always sung as a theogony. But historical beginnings are lowly: not in the sense of modest or discreet like the steps of a dove, but derisive and ironic, capable of undoing every infatuation. "We wished to awaken the feeling of man's sovereignty by showing his divine birth: this path is now forbidden, since a monkey stands at the entrance."[16] Man originated with a grimace over his future development; and Zarathustra himself is plagued by a monkey who jumps along behind him, pulling on his coattails.

The final postulate of the origin is linked to the first two in being the site of truth. From the vantage point of an absolute distance, free from the restraints of positive knowledge, the origin makes possible a field of knowledge whose function is to recover it, but always in a false recognition due to the excesses of its own speech. The origin lies at a place of inevitable loss, the point where the truth of things corresponded to a truthful discourse, the site of a fleeting articulation that discourse has obscured and finally lost. It is a new cruelty of history that compels a reversal of this relationship and the abandonment of "adolescent" quests: behind the always recent, avaricious, and measured truth, it posits the ancient proliferation of errors. It is now impossible to believe that "in the rending of the veil, truth remains truthful; we have lived long enough not to be taken in."[17] Truth is undoubtedly the sort of error that cannot be refuted because it was hardened into an unalterable form in the long baking process of history.[18] Moreover, the very question of truth, the right it appropriates to refute error and oppose itself to appearance,[19] the manner in which it developed (initially made available to the wise, then withdrawn by men of piety to an unattainable world where it was given the double role of consolation and imperative, finally rejected as a useless notion, superfluous, and contradicted on all sides)—does this not form a history, the history of an error we call truth? Truth, and its original reign, has had a history from which we are barely emerging "in the time of the shortest shadow," when light no longer seems to flow from the depths of the sky or to arise from the first moments of the day.[20]

A genealogy of values, morality, asceticism, and knowledge will never confuse itself with a quest for their "origins," will never neglect as inaccessible the vicissitudes of history. On the contrary, it will cultivate the details and accidents that accompany every beginning; it will be scrupulously attentive to their petty malice; it will await their emergence, once unmasked, as the face of the other. Wherever it is made to go, it will not be reticent—in "excavating the depths," in allowing time for these elements to escape from a labyrinth where no truth had ever detained them. The genealogist needs history to dispel the chimeras of the origin, somewhat in the manner of the pious philosopher who needs a doctor to exorcise the shadow of his soul. He must be able to recognize the events of history, its jolts, its surprises, its unsteady victories and unpalatable defeats—the basis of all beginnings, atavisms, and heredities. Similarly, he must be able to diagnose the illnesses of the body, its conditions of weakness and strength, its breakdown and resistances, to be in a position to judge philosophical discourse. History is the concrete body of a development, with its moments of intensity, its lapses, its extended periods of feverish agitation, its fainting spells; and only a metaphysician would seek its soul in the distant ideality of the origin.

3. *Entstehung* and *Herkunft* are more exact than *Ursprung* in recording the true objective of genealogy; and, while they are ordinarily translated as "origin," we must attempt to reestablish their proper use.

Herkunft is the equivalent of stock or *descent*; it is the ancient affiliation to a group, sustained by the bonds of blood, tradition, or social class. The analysis of *Herkunft* often involves a consideration of race[21] or social type.[22] But the traits it attempts to identify are not the exclusive generic characteristics of an individual, a sentiment, or an idea, which permit us to qualify them as "Greek" or "English"; rather, it seeks the subtle, singular, and subindividual marks that might possibly intersect in them to form a network that is difficult to unravel. Far from being a category of resemblance, this origin allows the sorting out of different traits: the Germans imagined that they had finally accounted for their complexity by saying they possessed a double soul; they were fooled by a simple computation, or rather, they were simply trying to master the racial disorder from which they had formed themselves.[23] Where the soul pretends unification or the self fabricates a coherent identity, the genealogist sets out to study the beginning—numberless beginnings whose faint traces and hints of color are readily seen by an historical eye. The analysis of descent permits the dissociation of the self, its recognition and displacement as an empty synthesis, in liberating a profusion of lost events.[24]

An examination of descent also permits the discovery, under the unique aspect of a trait or a concept, of the myriad events through which—thanks to which, against which—they were formed. Genealogy does not pretend to go back in time to restore an unbroken continuity that operates beyond the dispersion of forgotten things; its duty is not to demonstrate that the past actively exists in the present, that it continues secretly to animate the present, having imposed a predetermined form to all its vicissitudes. Genealogy does not resemble the evolution of a species and does not map the destiny of a people. On the contrary, to follow the complex course of descent is to maintain passing events in their proper dispersion; it is to identify the accidents, the minute deviations—or conversely, the complete reversals—the errors, the false appraisals, and the faulty calculations that gave birth to those things that continue to exist and have value for us; it is to discover that truth or being do not lie at the root of what we know and what we are, but the exteriority of accidents.[25] This is undoubtedly why every origin of morality from the moment it stops being pious—and *Herkunft* can never be—has value as a critique.[26]

Deriving from such a source is a dangerous legacy. In numerous instances, Nietzsche associates the terms *Herkunft* and *Erbschaft*. Nevertheless, we should not be deceived into thinking that this heritage is an acquisition, a possession that grows and solidifies; rather, it is an unstable assemblage of faults, fissures, and heterogeneous layers that threaten the fragile inheritor from within or from underneath: "injustice or instability in the minds of certain men, their disorder and lack of decorum, are the final consequences of their ancestors' numberless logical inaccuracies, hasty conclusions, and superficiality."[27] The search for descent is not the erecting of foundations: on the contrary, it disturbs what was previously considered immobile; it fragments what was thought unified; it shows the heterogeneity of what was imagined consistent with itself. What convictions and, far more decisively, what knowledge can resist it? If a genealogical analysis of a scholar were made—of one who collects facts and carefully accounts for them—his *Herkunft* would quickly divulge the official papers of the scribe and the pleadings of the lawyer—their father[28]—in their apparently disinterested attention, in the "pure" devotion to objectivity.

Finally, descent attaches itself to the body.[29] It inscribes itself in the nervous system, in temperament, in the digestive apparatus; it appears in faulty respiration, in improper diets, in the debilitated and prostate body of those whose ancestors committed errors. Fathers have only to mistake effects for causes, believe in the reality of an "afterlife," or maintain the value of eternal truths, and the bodies of their children will suffer. Cowardice and hypocrisy, for their part, are the simple offshoots of error: not in a Socratic sense, not that evil is the result of a mistake, not because of a turning away from an original truth, but because the body maintains, in life as in death, through its strength or weakness, the sanction of every truth and error, as it sustains, in an inverse manner, the origin—descent. Why did men invent the contemplative life? Why give a supreme value to this form of existence? Why maintain the absolute truth of those fictions which sustain it? "During barbarous ages . . . if the strength of an individual declined, if he felt himself tired or sick, melancholy or satiated and, as a consequence, without desire or appetite for a short time, he became relatively a better man, that is, less dangerous. His pessimistic ideas could only take form as words or reflections. In this frame of mind, he either became a thinker and prophet or used his imagination to feed his superstitions."[30] The body—and everything that touches it: diet, climate, and soil—is the domain of the *Herkunft*. The body manifests the stigmata of past experience and also gives rise to desires, failings, and errors. These elements may join in a body where they achieve a sudden expression, but as often, their encounter is an engagement in which they efface each other, where the body becomes the pretext of their insurmountable conflict.

The body is the inscribed surface of events (traced by language and dissolved by ideas), the locus of a dissociated Self (adopting the illusion of a substantial unity), and a volume in perpetual disintegration. Genealogy, as an analysis of descent, is thus situated within the articulation of the body and history. Its task is to expose a body totally imprinted by history and the process of history's destruction of the body.

4. *Entstehung* designates *emergence*, the moment of arising. It stands as the principle and the singular law of an apparition. As it is wrong to search for descent in an uninterrupted continuity, we should avoid thinking of emergence as the final term of an historical development; the eye was not always intended for contemplation, and punishment has had other purposes than setting an example. These developments may appear as a culmination, but they are merely the current episodes in a series of subjugations: the eye initially responded to the requirements of hunting and warfare; and punishment has been subjected, throughout its history, to a variety of needs—revenge, excluding an aggressor, compensating a victim, creating fear. In placing present needs at the origin, the metaphysician would convince us of an obscure purpose that seeks its realiza-

tion at the moment it arises. Genealogy, however, seeks to reestablish the various systems of subjection: not the anticipatory power of meaning, but the hazardous play of dominations.

Emergence is always produced through a particular stage of forces. The analysis of the *Entstehung* must delineate this interaction, the struggle these forces wage against each other or against adverse circumstances, and the attempt to avoid degeneration and regain strength by dividing these forces against themselves. It is in this sense that the emergence of a species (animal or human) and its solidification are secured "in an extended battle against conditions which are essentially and constantly unfavorable." In fact, "the species must realize itself as a species, as something—characterized by the durability, uniformity, and simplicity of its form—which can prevail in the perpetual struggle against outsiders or the uprising of those it oppresses from within." On the other hand, individual differences emerge at another stage of the relationship of forces, when the species has become victorious and when it is no longer threatened from outside. In this condition, we find a struggle "of egoisms turned against each other, each bursting forth in a splintering of forces and a general striving for the sun and for the light."[31] There are also times when force contends against itself, and not only in the intoxication of an abundance, which allows it to divide itself, but at the moment when it weakens. Force reacts against its growing lassitude and gains strength; it imposes limits, inflicts torments and mortifications; it masks these actions as a higher morality, and, in exchange, regains its strength. In this manner, the ascetic ideal was born, "in the instinct of a decadent life which . . . struggles for its own existence."[32] This also describes the movement in which the Reformation arose, precisely where the church was least corrupt;[33] German Catholicism, in the sixteenth century, retained enough strength to turn against itself, to mortify its own body and history, and to spiritualize itself into a pure religion of conscience.

Emergence is thus the entry of forces; it is their eruption, the leap from the wings to center stage, each in its youthful strength. What Nietzsche calls the *Entstehungsherd*[34] of the concept of goodness is not specifically the energy of the strong or the reaction of the weak, but precisely this scene where they are displayed superimposed or face-to-face. It is nothing but the space that divides them, the void through which they exchange their threatening gestures and speeches. As descent qualifies the strength or weakness of an instinct and its inscription on a body, emergence designates a place of confrontation but not as a closed field offering the spectacle of a struggle among equals. Rather, as Nietzsche demonstrates in his analysis of good and evil, it is a "non-place," a pure distance, which indicates that the adversaries do not belong to a common space. Consequently, no one is responsible for an emergence; no one can glory in it, since it always occurs in the interstice.

In a sense, only a single drama is ever staged in this "non-place," the endlessly repeated play of dominations. The domination of certain men over others leads to the differentiation of values;[35] class domination generates the idea of liberty;[36] and the forceful appropriation of things necessary to survival and the imposition of a duration not intrinsic to them account for the origin of logic.[37] This relationship of domination is no more a "relationship" than the place where it occurs is a place; and, precisely for this reason, it is fixed, throughout its history, in rituals, in meticulous procedures that impose rights and obligations. It establishes marks of its power and engraves memories on things and even within bodies. It makes itself accountable for debts and gives rise to the universe of rules, which is by no means designed to temper violence, but rather to satisfy it. Following traditional beliefs, it would be false to think that total war exhausts itself in its own contradictions and ends by renouncing violence and submitting to civil laws. On the contrary, the law is a calculated and relentless pleasure, delight in the promised blood, which permits the perpetual instigation of new dominations and the staging of meticulously repeated scenes of violence. The desire for peace, the serenity of compromise, and the tacit acceptance of the law, far from representing a major moral conversion or a utilitarian calculation that gave rise to the law, are but its result and, in point of fact, its perversion: "guilt, conscience, and duty had their threshold of emergence in the right to secure obligations; and their inception, like that of any major event on earth, was saturated in blood."[38] Humanity does not gradually progress from combat to combat until it arrives at universal reciprocity, where the rule of law finally replaces warfare; humanity installs each of its violences in a system of rules and thus proceeds from domination to domination.

The nature of these rules allows violence to be inflicted on violence and the resurgence of new forces that are sufficiently strong to dominate those in power. Rules are empty in themselves, violent and unfinalized; they are impersonal and can be bent to any purpose. The successes of history belong to those who are capable of seizing these rules, to replace those who had used them, to disguise themselves so as to pervert them, invert their meaning, and redirect them against those who had initially imposed them; controlling this complex mechanism, they will make it function so as to overcome the rulers through their own rules.

The isolation of different points of emergence does not conform to the successive configurations of an identical meaning; rather, they result from substitutions, displacements, disguised conquests, and systematic reversals. If interpretation were the slow exposure of the meaning hidden in an origin, then only metaphysics could interpret the development of humanity. But if interpretation is the violent or surreptitious appropriation of a system of rules, which in itself has no essential meaning, in order to impose a direction, to bend it to a new will, to force its participation in a different game, and to subject it to secondary rules, then the development of humanity is a series of interpretations. The role of genealogy is to record its history: the history of morals, ideals, and metaphysical concepts, the history of the concept of liberty or of the ascetic life; as they stand for the emergence of different interpretations, they must be made to appear as events on the stage of historical process.

5. How can we define the relationship between genealogy, seen as the exam- ination of *Herkunft* and *Entstehung*, and history in the traditional sense? We could, of course, examine Nietzsche's celebrated apostrophes against history, but we will put these aside for the moment and consider those instances when he conceives of genealogy as "wirkliche Historie," or its more frequent charac- terization as historical "spirit" or "sense."[39] In fact, Nietzsche's criticism, be- ginning with the second of the *Untimely Meditations*, always questioned the form of history that reintroduces (and always assumes) a suprahistorical per- spective: a history whose function is to compose the finally reduced diversity of time into a totality fully closed upon itself; a history that always encourages subjective recognitions and attributes a form of reconciliation to all the dis- placements of the past; a history whose perspective on all that precedes it im- plies the end of time, a completed development. The historian's history finds its support outside of time and pretends to base its judgments on an apocalyptic objectivity. This is only possible, however, because of its belief in eternal truth, the immortality of the soul, and the nature of consciousness as always identical to itself. Once the historical sense is mastered by a suprahistorical perspective, metaphysics can bend it to its own purpose and, by aligning it to the demands of objective science, it can impose its own "Egyptianism." On the other hand, the historical sense can evade metaphysics and become a privileged instrument of genealogy if it refuses the certainty of absolutes. Given this, it corresponds to the acuity of a glance that distinguishes, separates, and disperses, that is capable of liberating divergence and marginal elements—the kind of dissociating view that is capable of decomposing itself, capable of shattering the unity of man's being through which it was thought that he could extend his sovereignty to the events of his past.

Historical meaning becomes a dimension of "wirkliche Historie" to the ex- tent that it places within a process of development everything considered im- mortal to man. We believe that feelings are immutable, but every sentiment, particularly the noblest and most disinterested, has a history. We believe in the dull constancy of instinctual life and imagine that it continues to exert its force indiscriminately in the present as it did in the past. But a knowledge of history easily disintegrates this unity, depicts its wavering course, locates its moments of strength and weakness, and defines its oscillating reign. It easily seizes the slow elaboration of instincts and those movements where, in turning upon themselves, they relentlessly set about their self-destruction.[40] We believe, in any event, that the body obeys the exclusive laws of physiology and that it es- capes the influence of history, but this too is false. The body is molded by a great many distinct regimes; it is broken down by the rhythms of work, rest, and holidays; it is poisoned by food or values, through eating habits or moral laws; it constructs resistances.[41] "Effective" history differs from traditional his- tory in being without constants. Nothing in man—not even his body—is suffi- ciently stable to serve as the basis for self-recognition or for understanding other men. The traditional devices for constructing a comprehensive view of history and for retracing the past as a patient and continuous development must be systematically dismantled. Necessarily, we must dismiss those tendencies that encourage the consoling play of recognitions. Knowledge, even under the banner of history, does not depend on "rediscovery," and it emphatically excludes the "rediscovery of ourselves."[42] History becomes "effective" to the degree that it introduces discontinuity into our very being—as it divides our emotions, dramatizes our instincts, multiplies our body and sets it against itself. "Effective" history deprives the self of the reassuring stability of life and nature, and it will not permit itself to be transported by a voiceless obstinacy toward a millenial ending. It will uproot its traditional foundations and relentlessly disrupt its pretended continuity. This is because knowledge is not made for understanding; it is made for cutting.[43]

From these observations, we can grasp the particular traits of historical meaning as Nietzsche understood it—the sense which opposes "wirkliche Historie" to traditional history. The former transposes the relationship ordinarily established between the eruption of an event and necessary continuity. An entire historical tradition (theological or rationalistic) aims at dissolving the singular event into an ideal continuity—as a teleological movement or a natural process. "Effective" history, however, deals with events in terms of their most unique characteristics, their most acute manifestations. An event, consequently, is not a decision, a treaty, a reign, or a battle, but the reversal of a relationship of forces, the usurpation of power, the appropriation of a vocabulary turned against those who had once used it, a feeble domination that poisons itself as it grows lax, the entry of a masked "other." The forces operating in history are not controlled by destiny or regulative mechanisms, but respond to haphazard conflicts.[44] They do not manifest the successive forms of a primordial intention and their attraction is not that of a conclusion, for they always appear through the singular randomness of events. The inverse of the Christian world, spun entirely by a divine spider, and different from the world of the Greeks, divided between the realm of will and the great cosmic folly, the world of effective history knows only one kingdom, without providence or final cause, where there is only "the iron hand of necessity shaking the dice-box of chance."[45] Chance is not simply the drawing of lots, but raising the stakes in every attempt to master chance through the will to power, and giving rise to the risk of an even greater chance.[46] The world we know is not this ultimately simple configuration where events are reduced to accentuate their essential traits, their final meaning, or their initial and final value. On the contrary, it is a profusion of entangled events. If it appears as a "marvelous motley, profound and totally meaningful," this is because it began and continues its secret existence through a "host of errors and phantasms."[47] We want historians to confirm our belief that the present rests upon profound intentions and immutable necessities. But the true historical sense confirms our existence among countless lost events, without a landmark or a point of reference.

Effective history can also invert the relationship that traditional history, in its dependence on metaphysics, establishes between proximity and distance. The latter is given to a contemplation of distances and heights: the noblest periods, the highest forms, the most abstract ideas, the purest individualities. It accomplishes this by getting as near as possible, placing itself at the foot of its mountain peaks, at the risk of adopting the famous perspective of frogs. Effective history, on the other hand, shortens its vision to those things nearest to it—the body, the nervous system, nutrition, digestion, and energies; it unearths the periods of decadence and if it chances upon lofty epochs, it is with the suspicion—not vindictive but joyous—of finding a barbarous and shameful confusion. It has no fear of looking down, so long as it is understood that it looks from above and descends to seize the various perspectives, to disclose dispersions and differences, to leave things undisturbed in their own dimension and intensity.[48] It reverses the surreptitious practice of historians, their pretension to examine things furthest from themselves, the grovelling manner in which they approach this promising distance (like the metaphysicians who proclaim the existence of an afterlife, situated at a distance from this world, as a promise of their reward). Effective history studies what is closest, but in an abrupt dispossession, so as to seize it at a distance (an approach similar to that of a doctor who looks closely, who plunges to make a diagnosis and to state its difference). Historical sense has more in common with medicine than philosophy; and it should not surprise us that Nietzsche occasionally employs the phrase "historically and physiologically,"[49] since among the philosopher's idiosyncrasies is a complete denial of the body. This includes, as well, "the absence of historical sense, a hatred for the idea of development, Egyptianism," the obstinate "placing of conclusions at the beginning," of "making last things first."[50] History has a more important task than to be a handmaiden to philosophy, to recount the necessary birth of truth and values; it should become a differential knowledge of energies and failings, heights and degenerations, poisons and antidotes. Its task is to become a curative science.[51]

The final trait of effective history is its affirmation of knowledge as perspective. Historians take unusual pains to erase the elements in their work which reveal their grounding in a particular time and place, their preferences in a controversy—the unavoidable obstacles of their passion. Nietzsche's version of historical sense is explicit in its perspective and acknowledges its system of injustice. Its perception is slanted, being a deliberate appraisal, affirmation, or negation; it reaches the lingering and poisonous traces in order to prescribe the best antidote. It is not given to a discreet effacement before the objects it observes and does not submit itself to their processes; nor does it seek laws, since it gives equal weight to its own sight and to its objects. Through this historical sense, knowledge is allowed to create its own genealogy in the act of cognition; and "wirkliche Historie" composes a genealogy of history as the vertical projection of its position.

6. In this context, Nietzsche links historical sense to the historian's history. They share a beginning that is similarly impure and confused, share the same sign in which the symptoms of sickness can be recognized as well as the seed of an exquisite flower.[52] They arose simultaneously to follow their separate ways, but our task is to trace their common genealogy.

The descent (*Herkunft*) of the historian is unequivocal: he is of humble birth. A characteristic of history is to be without choice: it encourages thorough understanding and excludes qualitative judgments—a sensitivity to all things without distinction, a comprehensive view excluding differences. Nothing must escape it and, more importantly, nothing must be excluded. Historians argue that this proves their tact and discretion. After all, what right have they to impose their tastes and preferences when they seek to determine what actually occurred in the past? Their mistake is to exhibit a total lack of taste, the kind of crudeness that becomes smug in the presence of the loftiest elements and finds satisfaction in reducing them to size. The historian is insensitive to the most disgusting things; or rather, he especially enjoys those things that should be repugnant to him. His apparent serenity follows from his concerted avoidance of the exceptional and his reduction of all things to the lowest common denominator. Nothing is allowed to stand above him; and underlying his desire for total knowledge is his search for the secrets that belittle everything: "base curiosity." What is the source of history? It comes from the plebs. To whom is it addressed? To the plebs. And its discourse strongly resembles the demagogue's refrain: "No one is greater than you and anyone who presumes to get the better of you—you who are good—is evil." The historian, who functions as his double, can be heard to echo: "No past is greater than your present, and, through my meticulous erudition, I will rid you of your infatuations and transform the grandeur of history into pettiness, evil, and misfortune." The historian's ancestry goes back to Socrates.

This demagogy, of course, must be masked. It must hide its singular malice under the cloak of universals. As the demagogue is obliged to invoke truth, laws of essences, and eternal necessity, the historian must invoke objectivity, the accuracy of facts, and the permanence of the past. The demagogue denies the body to secure the sovereignty of a timeless idea and the historian effaces his proper individuality so that others may enter the stage and reclaim their own speech.[53] He is divided against himself: forced to silence his preferences and overcome his distaste, to blur his own perspective and replace it with the fiction of a universal geometry, to mimic death in order to enter the kingdom of the dead, to adopt a faceless anonymity. In this world where he has conquered his individual will, he becomes a guide to the inevitable law of a superior will. Having curbed the demands of his individual will in his knowledge, he will disclose the form of an eternal will in his object of study. The objectivity of historians inverts the relationships of will and knowledge and it is, in the same stroke, a necessary belief in Providence, in final causes and teleology—the beliefs that place the historian in the family of ascetics. "I can't stand these lustful eunuchs of history, all the seductions of an ascetic ideal; I can't stand these whited sepulchres producing life or those tired and indifferent beings who dress up in the part of wisdom and adopt an objective point of view."[54]

The *Entstehung* of history is found in nineteenth-century Europe: the land of interminglings and bastardy, the period of the "man-of-mixture." We have become barbarians with respect to those rare moments of high civilization: cities in ruin and enigmatic monuments are spread out before us; we stop before gaping walls; we ask what gods inhabited these empty temples. Great epochs lacked this curiosity, lacked our excessive deference; they ignored their predecessors: the classical period ignored Shakespeare. The decadence of Europe presents an immense spectacle (while stronger periods refrained from such exhibitions), and the nature of this scene is to represent a theater; lacking monuments of our own making, which properly belong to us, we live among crowded scenes. But there is more. Europeans no longer know themselves; they ignore their mixed ancestries and seek a proper role. They lack individuality. We can begin to understand the spontaneous historical bent of the nineteenth century: the anemia of its forces and those mixtures that effaced all its individual traits produced the same results as the mortifications of asceticism; its inability to create, its absence of artistic works, and its need to rely on past achievements forced it to adopt the base curiosity of plebs.

If this fully represents the genealogy of history, how could it become, in its own right, a genealogical analysis? Why did it not continue as a form of demagogic or religious knowledge? How could it change roles on the same stage? Only by being seized, dominated, and turned against its birth. And it is this movement which properly describes the specific nature of the *Entstehung*: it is not the unavoidable conclusion of a long preparation, but a scene where forces are risked in the chance of confrontations, where they emerge triumphant, where they can also be confiscated. The locus of emergence for metaphysics was surely Athenian demagogy, the vulgar spite of Socrates and his belief in immortality, and Plato could have seized this Socratic philosophy to turn it against itself. Undoubtedly, he was often tempted to do so, but his defeat lies in its consecration. The problem was similar in the nineteenth century: to avoid doing for the popular asceticism of historians what Plato did for Socrates. This historical trait should not be founded upon a philosophy of history, but dismantled beginning with the things it produced; it is necessary to master history so as to turn it to genealogical uses, that is, strictly anti-Platonic purposes. Only then will the historical sense free itself from the demands of a suprahistorical history.

7. The historical sense gives rise to three uses that oppose and correspond to the three Platonic modalities of history. The first is parodic, directed against reality, and opposes the theme of history as reminiscence or recognition; the second is dissociative, directed against identity, and opposes history given as continuity or representative of a tradition; the third is sacrificial, directed against truth, and opposes history as knowledge. They imply a use of history that severs its connection to memory, its metaphysical and anthropological model, and

constructs a counter-memory—a transformation of history into a totally different form of time.

First, the parodic and farcical use. The historian offers this confused and anonymous European, who no longer knows himself or what name he should adopt, the possibility of alternate identities, more individualized and substantial than his own. But the man with historical sense will see that this substitution is simply a disguise. Historians supplied the Revolution with Roman prototypes, romanticism with knight's armor, and the Wagnerian era was given the sword of a German hero—ephemeral props that point to our own unreality. No one kept them from venerating these religions, from going to Bayreuth to commemorate a new afterlife; they were free, as well, to be transformed into street-vendors of empty identities. The new historian, the genealogist, will know what to make of this masquerade. He will not be too serious to enjoy it; on the contrary, he will push the masquerade to its limit and prepare the great carnival of time where masks are constantly reappearing. No longer the identification of our faint individuality with the solid identities of the past, but our "unrealization" through the excessive choice of identities—Frederick of Hohenstaufen, Caesar, Jesus, Dionysus, and possibly Zarathustra. Taking up these masks, revitalizing the buffoonery of history, we adopt an identity whose unreality surpasses that of God who started the charade. "Perhaps, we can discover a realm where originality is again possible as parodists of history and buffoons of God."[55] In this, we recognize the parodic double of what the second of the *Untimely Meditations* called "monumental history": a history given to reestablishing the high points of historical development and their maintenance in a perpetual presence, given to the recovery of works, actions, and creations through the monogram of their personal essence. But in 1874, Nietzsche accused this history, one totally devoted to veneration, of barring access to the actual intensities and creations of life. The parody of his last texts serves to emphasize that "monumental history" is itself a parody. Genealogy is history in the form of a concerted carnival.

The second use of history is the systematic dissociation of identity. This is necessary because this rather weak identity, which we attempt to support and to unify under a mask, is in itself only a parody: it is plural; countless spirits dispute its possession; numerous systems intersect and compete. The study of history makes one "happy, unlike the metaphysicians, to possess in oneself not an immortal soul but many mortal ones."[56] And in each of these souls, history will not discover a forgotten identity, eager to be reborn, but a complex system of distinct and multiple elements, unable to be mastered by the powers of synthesis: "it is a sign of superior culture to maintain, in a fully conscious way, certain phases of its evolution which lesser men pass through without thought. The initial result is that we can understand those who resemble us as completely determined systems and as representative of diverse cultures, that is to say, as necessary and capable of modification. And in return, we are able to separate the phases of our own evolution and consider them individually."[57] The purpose of history, guided by genealogy, is not to discover the roots of our identity but to commit itself to its dissipation. It does not seek to define our unique threshold of emergence, the homeland to which metaphysicians promise a return; it seeks to make visible all of those discontinuities that cross us. "Antiquarian history," according to the *Untimely Meditations*, pursues opposite goals. It seeks the continuities of soil, language, and urban life in which our present is rooted and, "by cultivating in a delicate manner that which existed for all time, it tries to conserve for posterity the conditions under which we were born."[58] This type of history was objected to in the *Meditations* because it tended to block creativity in support of the laws of fidelity. Somewhat later—and already in *Human, All Too Human*—Nietzsche reconsiders the task of the antiquarian, but with an altogether different emphasis. If genealogy in its own right gives rise to questions concerning our native land, native language, or the laws that govern us, its intention is to reveal the heterogenous systems which, masked by the self, inhibit the formation of any form of identity.

The third use of history is the sacrifice of the subject of knowledge. In appearance, or rather, according to the mask it bears, historical consciousness is neutral, devoid of passions, and committed solely to truth. But if it examines itself and if, more generally, it interrogates the various forms of scientific consciousness in its history, it finds that all these forms and transformations are aspects of the will to knowledge: instinct, passion, the inquisitor's devotion, cruel subtlety, and malice. It discovers the violence of a position that sides against those who are happy in their ignorance, against the effective illusions by which humanity protects itself, a position that encourages the dangers of research and delights in disturbing discoveries.[59] The historical analysis of this rancorous will to knowledge[60] reveals that all knowledge rests upon injustice (that there is no right, not even in the act of knowing, to truth or a foundation for truth) and that the instinct for knowledge is malicious (something murderous, opposed to the happiness of mankind). Even in the greatly expanded form it assumes today, the will to knowledge does not achieve a universal truth; man is not given an exact and serene mastery of nature. On the contrary, it ceaselessly multiplies the risks, creates dangers in every area; it breaks down illusory defences; it dissolves the unity of the subject; it releases those elements of itself that are devoted to its subversion and destruction. Knowledge does not slowly detach itself from its empirical roots, the initial needs from which it arose, to become pure speculation subject only to the demands of reason; its development is not tied to the constitution and affirmation of a free subject; rather, it creates a progressive enslavement in its instinctive violence. Where religions once demanded the sacrifice of bodies, knowledge now calls for experimentation on ourselves,[61] calls us to the sacrifice of the subject of knowledge. "The desire for knowledge has been transformed among us into a passion which fears no sacrifice, which fears nothing but its own extinction. It may be that mankind will eventually perish from this passion for knowledge. If not through passion, then through weakness. We must be prepared to state our choice: do we wish humanity to end in fire and light or to end on the sands?"[62] We should now replace the two great problems of nineteenth-century philosophy, passed on by Fichte and Hegel (the reciprocal basis of truth and liberty and the possibility of absolute knowledge), with the theme that "to perish through absolute knowledge may well form a part of the basis of being."[63] This does not mean, in terms of a critical procedure, that the will to truth is limited by the intrinsic finitude of cognition, but that it loses all sense of limitations and all claim to truth in its unavoidable sacrifice of the subject of knowledge. "It may be that there remains one prodigious idea which might be made to prevail over every other aspiration, which might overcome the most victorious: the idea of humanity sacrificing itself. It seems indisputable that if this new constellation appeared on the horizon, only the desire for truth, with its enormous prerogatives, could direct and sustain such a sacrifice. For to knowledge, no sacrifice is too great. Of course, this problem has never been posed."[64]

The *Untimely Meditations* discussed the critical use of history: its just treatment of the past, its decisive cutting of the roots, its rejection of traditional attitudes of reverence, its liberation of man by presenting him with other origins than those in which he prefers to see himself. Nietzsche, however, reproached critical history for detaching us from every real source and for sacrificing the very movement of life to the exclusive concern for truth. Somewhat later, as we have seen, Nietzsche reconsiders this line of thought he had at first refused, but directs it to altogether different ends. It is no longer a question of judging the past in the name of a truth that only we can possess in the present; but risking the destruction of the subject who seeks knowledge in the endless deployment of the will to knowledge.

In a sense, genealogy returns to the three modalities of history that Nietzsche recognized in 1874. It returns to them in spite of the objections that Nietzsche raised in the name of the affirmative and creative powers of life. But they are metamorphosized; the veneration of monuments becomes parody; the respect for ancient continuities becomes systematic dissociation; the critique of the injustices of the past by a truth held by men in the present becomes the destruction of the man who maintains knowledge by the injustice proper to the will to knowledge.

NOTES

1. See Nietzsche's Preface to *The Genealogy of Morals*, 4, 7—ED. (Donald Bouchard).
2. *The Gay Science*, 7.
3. *Human, All Too Human*, 3.
4. *The Genealogy*, II, 6, 8.
5. *The Gay Science*, 110, 111, 300.
6. *The Dawn*, 102 ("Shameful origin"—ED.).
7. *The Gay Science*, 151, 353; and also *The Dawn*, 62; *The Genealogy*, I, 14; *Twilight of the Idols*, "The Great Errors," 7. (*Schwarzkünstler* is a black magician—ED.)

8. Paul Ree's text was entitled *Ursprung der Moralischen Empfindungen*.
9. In *Human, All Too Human*, aphorism 92 was entitled *Ursprung der Gerechtigkeit*.
10. In the main body of *The Genealogy*, *Ursprung* and *Herkunft* are used interchangeably in numerous instances (I, 2; II, 8, 11, 12, 16, 17).
11. *The Dawn*, 123.
12. *Human, All Too Human*, 34.
13. *The Wanderer and His Shadow*, 9.
14. A wide range of key terms, found in *The Archaeology of Knowledge*, are related to this theme of "disparity": the concepts of series, discontinuity, division, and difference. If the *same* is found in the realm and movement of dialectics, the *disparate* presents itself as an "event" in the world of chance. For a more detailed discussion, see below, "Theatrum Philosophicum," pp. 180, 193–196—Ed.
15. *The Wanderer and His Shadow*, 3.
16. *The Dawn*, 49.
17. *Nietzsche contra Wagner*, p. 99.
18. *The Gay Science*, 265 and 110.
19. See "Theatrum Philosophicum," pp. 167–168, for a discussion of the development of truth; and also "History of Systems of Thought: Summary of a Course at the Collège de France—1970–1971," pp. 202–204—Ed.
20. *Twilight of the Idols*, "How the world of truth becomes a fable."
21. For example, *The Gay Science*, 135; *Beyond Good and Evil*, 200, 242, 244; *The Genealogy*, I, 5.
22. *The Gay Science*, 348–349; *Beyond Good and Evil*, 260.
23. *Beyond Good and Evil*, 244.
24. See "Theatrum Philosophicum," pp. 172–176—Ed.
25. *The Genealogy*, III, 17. The *abkunft* of feelings of depression.
26. *Twilight*, "Reasons for philosophy."
27. *The Dawn*, 247.
28. *The Gay Science*, 348–349.
29. Ibid., 200.
30. *The Dawn*, 42.
31. *Beyond Good and Evil*, 262.
32. *The Genealogy*, III, 13.
33. *The Gay Science*, 148. It is also to an anemia of the will that one must attribute the *Entstehung* of Buddhism and Christianity, 347.
34. *The Genealogy*, I, 2.
35. *Beyond Good and Evil*, 260; cf. also *The Genealogy*, II, 12.
36. *The Wanderer*, 9.
37. *The Gay Science*, 111.
38. *The Genealogy*, II, 6.
39. *The Genealogy*, Preface, 7; and I, 2. *Beyond Good and Evil*, 224.
40. *The Gay Science*, 7.
41. Ibid.
42. See "What Is an Author?" p. 134, on rediscoveries—Ed.
43. This statement is echoed in Foucault's discussion of "differentiations" in *The Archaeology of Knowledge*, pp. 130–131, 206; or the use of the word "division" in "A Preface to Transgression," p. 36—Ed.
44. *The Genealogy*, II, 12.

45. *The Dawn*, 130.

46. *The Genealogy*, II, 12.

47. *Human, All Too Human*, 16.

48. See "Theatrum Philosophicum", p. 183, for an analysis of Deleuze's thought as intensity of difference—ED.

49. *Twilight*, 44.

50. *Twilight*, "Reason within philosophy," 1 and 4.

51. *The Wanderer*, 188. (This conception underlies the task of *Madness and Civilization* and *The Birth of the Clinic* even though it is not found as a conscious formulation until *The Archaeology of Knowledge*; for a discussion of archaeology as "diagnosis," see especially p. 131—ED.)

52. *The Gay Science*, 337.

53. See "Intellectuals and Power," p. 211—ED.

54. *The Genealogy*, III, 26.

55. *Beyond Good and Evil*, 223.

56. *The Wanderer* (Opinions and Mixed Statements), 17.

57. *Human, All Too Human*, 274.

58. *Untimely Meditations*, II, 3.

59. Cf. *The Dawn*, 429 and 432; *The Gay Science*, 333; *Beyond Good and Evil*, 229–230.

60. "Vouloir-savoir": the phrase in French means both the will to knowledge and knowledge as revenge—ED.

61. *The Dawn*, 501.

62. Ibid., 429.

63. *Beyond Good and Evil*, 39.

64. *The Dawn*, 45.

LUCE IRIGARAY

"THIS SEX WHICH IS NOT ONE"

Female sexuality has always been conceptualized on the basis of masculine parameters. Thus the opposition between "masculine" clitoral activity and "feminine" vaginal passivity, an opposition which Freud—and many others—saw as stages, or alternatives, in the development of a sexually "normal" woman, seems rather too clearly required by the practice of male sexuality. For the clitoris is conceived as a little penis pleasant to masturbate so long as castration anxiety does not exist (for the boy child), and the vagina is valued for the "lodging" it offers the male organ when the forbidden hand has to find a replacement for pleasure-giving.

In these terms, woman's erogenous zones never amount to anything but a clitoris-sex that is not comparable to the noble phallic organ, or a hole-envelope that serves to sheathe and massage the penis in intercourse: a non-sex, or a masculine organ turned back upon itself, self-embracing.

About woman and her pleasure, this view of the sexual relation has nothing to say. Her lot is that of "lack," "atrophy" (of the sexual organ), and "penis envy," the penis being the only sexual organ of recognized value. Thus she attempts by every means available to appropriate that organ for herself: through her somewhat servile love of the father-husband capable of giving her one, through her desire for a child-penis, preferably a boy, through access to the cultural values still reserved by right to males alone and therefore always masculine, and so on. Woman lives her own desire only as the expectation that she may at last come to possess an equivalent of the male organ.

Yet all this appears quite foreign to her own pleasure, unless it remains within the dominant phallic economy. Thus, for example, woman's autoeroticism is very different from man's. In order to touch himself, man needs an instrument: his hand, a woman's body, language ... And this self-caressing requires at least a minimum of activity. As for woman, she touches herself in and of herself without any need for mediation, and before there is any way to distinguish activity from passivity. Woman "touches herself" all the time, and moreover no one can forbid her to do so, for her genitals are formed of two lips in continuous contact. Thus, within herself, she is already two—but not divisible into one(s)—that caress each other.

This autoeroticism is disrupted by a violent break-in: the brutal separation of the two lips by a violating penis, an intrusion that distracts and deflects the woman from this "self-caressing" she needs if she is not to incur the disappearance of her own pleasure in sexual relations. If the vagina is to serve *also*, but *not only*, to take over for the little boy's hand in order to assure an articulation between autoeroticism and heteroeroticism in intercourse (the encounter with the totally other always signifying death), how, in the classic representation of sexuality, can the perpetuation of autoeroticism for woman be managed? Will woman not be left with the impossible alternative between a defensive virginity, fiercely turned in upon itself, and a body open to penetration that no longer knows, in this "hole" that constitutes its sex, the pleasure of its own touch? The more or less exclusive—and highly anxious—attention paid to erection in Western sexuality proves to what extent the imaginary that governs it is foreign to the feminine. For the most part, this sexuality offers nothing but imperatives dictated by male rivalry: the "strongest" being the one who has the best "hard-on," the longest, the biggest, the stiffest penis, or even the one who "pees the farthest" (as in little boys' contests). Or else one finds imperatives dictated by the enactment of sadomasochistic fantasies, these in turn governed by man's relation to his mother: the desire to force entry, to penetrate, to appropriate for himself the mystery of this womb where he has been conceived, the secret of his begetting, of his "origin." Desire/need, also to make blood flow again in order to revive a very old relationship—intrauterine, to be sure, but also prehistoric—to the maternal.

Woman, in this sexual imaginary, is only a more or less obliging prop for the enactment of man's fantasies. That she may find pleasure there in that role, by proxy, is possible, even certain. But such pleasure is above all a masochistic prostitution of her body to a desire that is not her own, and it leaves her in a familiar state of dependency upon man. Not knowing what she wants, ready for anything, even asking for more, so long as he will "take" her as his "object" when he seeks his own pleasure. Thus she will not say what she herself wants; moreover, she does not know, or no longer knows, what she wants. As Freud admits, the beginnings of the sexual life of a girl child are so "obscure," so "faded with time," that one would have to dig down very deep indeed to discover beneath the traces of this civilization, of this history, the vestiges of a more archaic civilization that might give some clue to woman's sexuality. That extremely ancient civilization would undoubtedly have a different alphabet, a different language . . . Woman's desire would not be expected to speak the same language as man's; woman's desire has doubtless been submerged by the logic that has dominated the West since the time of the Greeks.

Within this logic, the predominance of the visual, and of the discrimination and individualization of form, is particularly foreign to female eroticism. Woman takes pleasure more from touching than from looking, and her entry into a dominant scopic economy signifies, again, her consignment to passivity: she is to be the beautiful object of contemplation. While her body finds itself thus eroticized, and called to a double movement of exhibition and of chaste retreat in order to stimulate the drives of the "subject," her sexual organ represents *the horror of nothing to see*. A defect in this systematics of representation and desire. A "hole" in its scoptophilic lens. It is already evident in Greek statuary that this nothing-to-see has to be excluded, rejected, from such a scene of representation. Woman's genitals are simply absent, masked, sewn back up inside their "crack."

This organ which has nothing to show for itself also lacks a form of its own. And if woman takes pleasure precisely from this incompleteness of form which allows her organ to touch itself over and over again, indefinitely, by itself, that pleasure is denied by a civilization that privileges phallomorphism. The value granted to the only definable form excludes the one that is in play in female autoeroticism. The *one* of form, of the individual, of the (male) sexual organ, of the proper name, of the proper meaning . . . supplants, while separating and dividing, that contact of *at least two* (lips) which keeps woman in touch with herself, but without any possibility of distinguishing what is touching from what is touched.

Whence the mystery that woman represents in a culture claiming to count everything, to number everything by units, to inventory everything as individualities. *She is neither one nor two.* Rigorously speaking, she cannot be identified either as one person, or as two. She resists all adequate definition. Further, she has no "proper" name. And her sexual organ, which is not *one* organ, is counted as *none*. The negative, the underside, the reverse of the only visible and morphologically designatable organ (even if the passage from erection to detumescence does pose some problems): the penis.

But the "thickness" of that "form," the layering of its volume, its expansions and contractions and even the spacing of the moments in which it produces itself as form—all this the feminine keeps secret. Without knowing it. And if woman is asked to sustain, to revive, man's desire, the request neglects to spell out what it implies as to the value of her own desire. A desire of which she is not aware, moreover, at least not explicitly. But one whose force and continuity are capable of nurturing repeatedly and at length all the masquerades of "feminity" that are expected of her.

It is true that she still has the child, in relation to whom her appetite for touch, for contact, has free rein, unless it is already lost, alienated by the taboo against touching of a highly obsessive civilization. Otherwise her pleasure will find, in the child, compensations for and diversions from the frustrations that she too often encounters in sexual relations per se. Thus maternity fills the gaps in a repressed female sexuality. Perhaps man and woman no longer caress each other except through that mediation between them that the child—preferably a boy—represents? Man, identified with his son, rediscovers the pleasure of maternal fondling; woman touches herself again by caressing that part of her body: her baby-penis-clitoris.

What this entails for the amorous trio is well known. But the Oedipal interdiction seems to be a somewhat categorical and factitious law—although it does provide the means for perpetuating the authoritarian discourse of fathers—when it is promulgated in a culture in which sexual relations are impracticable because man's desire and woman's are strangers to each other. And in which the two desires have to try to meet through indirect means, whether the archaic one of a sense-relation to the mother's body, or the present one of active or passive extension of the law of the father. These are regressive emotional behaviors, exchanges of words too detached from the sexual arena not to constitute an exile with respect to it: "mother" and "father" dominate the interactions of the couple, but as social roles. The division of labor prevents them from making love. They produce or reproduce. Without quite knowing how to use their leisure. Such little as they have, such little indeed as they wish to have. For what are they to do with leisure? What substitute for amorous resource are they to invent? Still . . .

Perhaps it is time to return to that repressed entity, the female imaginary. So woman does not have a sex organ? She has at least two of them, but they are not identifiable as ones. Indeed, she has many more. Her sexuality, always at least double, goes even further: it is *plural*. Is this the way culture is seeking to characterize itself now? Is this the way texts write themselves/are written now? Without quite knowing what censorship they are evading? Indeed, woman's pleasure does not have to choose between clitoral activity and vaginal passivity, for example. The pleasure of the vaginal caress does not have to be substituted for that of the clitoral caress. They each contribute, irreplaceably, to woman's pleasure. Among other caresses . . . Fondling the breasts, touching the vulva, spreading the lips, stroking the posterior wall of the vagina, brushing against the mouth of the uterus, and so on. To evoke only a few of the most specifically female pleasures. Pleasures which are somewhat misunderstood in sexual difference as it is imagined—or not imagined, the other sex being only the indispensable complement to the only sex.

But *woman has sex organs more or less everywhere.* She finds pleasure almost anywhere. Even if we refrain from invoking the hystericization of her entire body, the geography of her pleasure is far more diversified, more multiple in its differences, more complex, more subtle, than is commonly imagined—in an imaginary rather too narrowly focused on sameness.

"She" is indefinitely other in herself. This is doubtless why she is said to be whimsical, incomprehensible, agitated, capricious . . . not to mention her language, in which "she" sets off in all directions leaving "him" unable to discern the coherence of any meaning. Hers are contradictory words, somewhat mad from the standpoint of reason, inaudible for whoever listens to them with ready-made grids, with a fully elaborated code in hand. For in what she says, too, at least when she dares, woman is constantly touching herself. She steps ever so slightly aside from herself with a murmur, an exclamation, a whisper, a sentence left unfinished . . . When she returns, it is to set off again from elsewhere. From another point of pleasure, or of pain. One would have to listen with another ear, as if hearing an *"other meaning" always in the process of weaving itself, of embracing itself with words, but also of getting rid of words in order not to become fixed, congealed in them.* For if "she" says something, it is not, it is already no longer, identical with what she means. What she says is never identical with anything, moreover; rather, it is contiguous. *It touches (upon).* And when it strays too far from that proximity, she breaks off and starts over at "zero": her body-sex.

It is useless, then, to trap women in the exact definition of what they mean, to make them repeat (themselves) so that it will be clear; they are already elsewhere in that discursive machinery where you expected to surprise them. They have returned within themselves. Which must not be understood in the same way as within yourself. They do not have the interiority that you have, the one you perhaps suppose they have. Within themselves means *within the intimacy of that silent, multiple, diffuse touch.* And if you ask them insistently what they are thinking about, they can only reply: Nothing. Everything.

Thus what they desire is precisely nothing, and at the same time everything. Always something more and something else besides that *one*—sexual organ, for example—that you give them, attribute to them. Their desire is often interpreted, and feared, as a sort of insatiable hunger, a voracity that will swallow you whole. Whereas it really involves a different economy more than anything else, one that upsets the linearity of a project, undermines the goal-object of a desire, diffuses the polarization toward a single pleasure, disconcerts fidelity to a single discourse . . .

Must this multiplicity of female desire and female language be understood as shards, scattered remnants of a violated sexuality? A sexuality denied? The question has no simple answer. The rejection, the exclusion of a female imaginary certainly puts woman in the position of experiencing herself only fragmentarily, in the little-structured margins of a dominant ideology, as waste, or excess, what is left of a mirror invested by the (masculine) "subject" to reflect himself, to copy himself. Moreover, the role of "femininity" is prescribed by this masculine specula(riza)tion and corresponds scarcely at all to woman's desire, which may be recovered only in secret, in hiding, with anxiety and guilt.

But if the female imaginary were to deploy itself, if it could bring itself into play otherwise than as scraps, uncollected debris, would it represent itself, even so, in the form of *one* universe? Would it even be volume instead of surface? No. Not unless it were understood, yet again, as a privileging of the maternal over the feminine. Of a phallic maternal, at that. Closed in upon the jealous possession of its valued product. Rivaling man in his esteem for productive excess. In such a race for power, woman loses the uniqueness of her pleasure. By closing herself off as volume, she renounces the pleasure that she gets from the *nonsuture of her lips:* she is undoubtedly a mother, but a virgin mother; the role was assigned to her by mythologies long ago. Granting her a certain social power to the extent that she is reduced, with her own complicity, to sexual impotence.

(Re-)discovering herself, for a woman, thus could only signify the possibility of sacrificing no one of her pleasures to another, of identifying herself with none of them in particular, *of never being simply one.* A sort of expanding universe to which no limits could be fixed and which would not be incoherence nonetheless—nor that polymorphous perversion of the child in which the erogenous zones would lie waiting to be regrouped under the primacy of the phallus.

Woman always remains several, but she is kept from dispersion because the other is already within her and is autoerotically familiar to her. Which is not to say that she appropriates the other for herself, that she reduces it to her own property. Ownership and property are doubtless quite foreign to the feminine. At least sexually. But not *nearness.* Nearness so pronounced that it makes all discrimination of identity, and thus all forms of property, impossible. Woman derives pleasure from what is *so near that she cannot have it, nor have herself.* She herself enters into a ceaseless exchange of herself with the other without any possibility of identifying either. This puts into question all prevailing economies: their calculations are irremediably stymied by woman's pleasure, as it increases indefinitely from its passage in and through the other.

However, in order for woman to reach the place where she takes pleasure as woman, a long detour by way of the analysis of the various systems of oppression brought to bear upon her is assuredly necessary. And claiming to fall back on the single solution of pleasure risks making her miss the process of going back through a social practice that *her* enjoyment requires.

For woman is traditionally a use-value for man, an exchange value among men; in other words, a commodity. As such, she remains the guardian of material substance, whose price will be established, in terms of the standard of their work and of their need/desire, by "subjects": workers, merchants, consumers. Women are marked phallically by their fathers, husbands, procurers. And this branding determines their value in sexual commerce. Woman is never anything but the locus of a more or less competitive exchange between two men, including the competition for the possession of mother earth.

How can this object of transaction claim a right to pleasure without removing her/itself from established commerce? With respect to other merchandise in the marketplace, how could this commodity maintain a relationship other than one of aggressive jealousy? How could material substance enjoy her/itself without provoking the consumer's anxiety over the disappearance of his nurturing ground? How could that exchange—which can in no way be defined in terms "proper" to woman's desire—appear as anything but a pure mirage, mere foolishness, all too readily obscured by a more sensible discourse and by a system of apparently more tangible values?

A woman's development, however radical it may seek to be, would thus not suffice to liberate woman's desire. And to date no political theory or political practice has resolved, or sufficiently taken into consideration, this historical problem, even though Marxism has proclaimed its importance. But women do not constitute, strictly speaking, a class, and their dispersion among several classes makes their political struggle complex, their demands sometimes contradictory.

There remains, however, the condition of underdevelopment arising from women's submission by and to a culture that oppresses them, uses them, makes of them a medium of exchange, with very little profit to them. Except in the quasi monopolies of masochistic pleasure, the domestic labor force, and reproduction. The powers of slaves? Which are not negligible powers, moreover. For where pleasure is concerned, the master is not necessarily well served. Thus to reverse the relation, especially in the economy of sexuality, does not seem a desirable objective.

But if women are to preserve and expand their autoeroticism, their homosexuality, might not the renunciation of heterosexual pleasure correspond once again to that disconnection from power that is traditionally theirs? Would it not involve a new prison, a new cloister, built of their own accord? For women to undertake tactical strikes, to keep themselves apart from men long enough to learn to defend their desire, especially through speech, to discover the love of other women while sheltered from men's imperious choices that put them in the position of rival commodities, to forge for themselves a social status that compels recognition, to earn their living in order to escape from the condition of prostitute . . . these are certainly indispensable stages in the escape from their proletarization on the exchange market. But if their aim were simply to reverse the order of things, even supposing this to be possible, history would repeat itself in the long run, would revert to sameness: to phallocratism. It would leave room neither for women's sexuality, nor for women's imaginary, nor for women's language to take (their) place.

JULIA KRISTEVA

"FROM ONE IDENTITY TO AN OTHER"

I shall attempt, within the ritual limits of a one-hour seminar, to posit (if not to demonstrate) that every language theory is predicated upon a conception of the subject that it explicitly posits, implies, or tries to deny. Far from being an "epistemological perversion," a definite subject is present as soon as there is consciousness of signification. Consequently, I shall need to outline an epistemological itinerary: taking three stages in the recent history of linguistic theory, I shall indicate the variable position these may have required of the speaking subject-support within their object language. This—on the whole, technical—foray into the epistemology of linguistic science will lead us to broach and, I hope, elucidate a problem whose ideological stakes are considerable but whose banality is often ignored. Meaning, identified either within the unity or the multiplicity of subject, structure, or theory, necessarily guarantees a certain transcendence, if not a theology; this is precisely why all human knowledge, whether it be that of an individual subject or of a meaning structure, retains religion as its blind

Originally a paper read at a seminar organized by Jean-Marie Benoist and directed by Claude Lévi-Strauss at the Collège de France, January 27, 1975; first published in *Tel Quel* (Summer 1975), no. 62; reprinted in *Polylogue* (Paris: Seuil, 1977), pp. 149–72. "D'une identité l'autre," the original title of Kristeva's essay reflects and makes use of the title of Céline's novel *D'un château l'autre*. Although this has been translated as *Castle to Castle*, the more literal "From One Identity to an Other" has been chosen in order to keep the ambiguous feeling of the French as well as the word "other," an important one in philosophy since Hegel and also in Kristeva's work.

boundaries, or at least, as an internal limit, and at best, can just barely "explain and validate religious sentiment" (as Lévi-Strauss observed, in connection with structuralism).[1]

Second, I shall deal with a particular signifying practice, which, like the Russian Formalists, I call "poetic language," in order to demonstrate that this kind of language, through the particularity of its signifying operations, is an unsettling process—when not an outright destruction—of the identity of meaning and speaking subject,[2] and consequently, of transcendence or, by derivation, of "religious sensibility." On that account, it accompanies crises within social structures and institutions—the moments of their mutation, evolution, revolution, or disarray. For if mutation within language and institutions finds its code through this signifying practice and its questionable subject in process that constitutes poetic language, then that practice and subject are walking a precarious tightrope. Poetic language, the only language that uses up transcendence and theology to sustain itself; poetic language, knowingly the enemy of religion, by its very economy borders on psychosis (as for its subject) and totalitarianism or fascism (as for the institutions it implies or evokes). I could have spoken of Vladimir Mayakovsky or Antonin Artaud; I shall speak of Louis-Ferdinand Céline.

Finally, I shall try to draw a few conclusions concerning the possibility of a *theory* in the sense of an *analytical discourse* on signifying systems, which would take into account these crises of meaning, subject, and structure. This for two reasons: first, such crises, far from being accidents, are inherent in the signifying function and, consequently, in sociality; secondly, situated at the forefront of twentieth-century politics, these phenomena (which I consider within poetic language, but which may assume other forms in the West as well as in other civilizations) could not remain outside the so-called human sciences without casting suspicion on their ethic. I shall therefore and in conclusion argue in favor of an analytical theory of signifying systems and practices that would search within the signifying phenomenon for the *crisis* or the *unsettling process* of meaning and subject rather than for the coherence or identity of either *one* or a *multiplicity* of structures.

Without referring back to the stoic sage, who guaranteed both the sign's triad and the inductive conditional clause, let us return to the congruence between conceptions of language and of subject where Ernest Renan left them. We are all aware of the scandal he caused among nineteenth-century minds when he changed a theological discourse (the Gospels) not into a *myth* but into the *history* of a man and a people. This conversion of *theological* discourse into *historical* discourse was possible thanks to a tool (for him, scientific) whose omnipotence he never ceased praising—philology. As used by Renan or Eugene Burnouf in Avestic Studies, for example, philology incorporates the *comparativism* of philologists Franz Bopp or August Schleicher. Whatever the difference between comparativists seeking those *laws* unique to *families* of languages and philologists deciphering the *meaning* of *one* language, a common conception of language as an *organic identity* unites them. Little does it matter that, as comparativists believed, this organic identity articulates itself thanks to *a law* that crosses national and historical language borders making of them one family (cf. Jacob Grimm's phonetic laws); or that, as philologists believed, this organic identity articulates itself thanks to *one meaning*—singular and unique—inscribed into a text still undeciphered or whose decipherability is debatable. In both cases this *organic identity* of law or meaning implies that language is the possession of a *homo loquens* within history. As Renan writes in *Averoés et l'Averroïsme*, "for the philologist, a text has only one meaning" even if it is through "a kind of necessary misinterpretation" that "the philosophical and religious development of humanity" proceeds.[3] Closer to the objectivity of the Hegelian "consciousness of self" for the comparativists, embodied into a singularity that, be it concrete, individual, or national, still owes something to Hegel for the philologists; language is always *one* system, perhaps even one "structure," always *one meaning*, and, therefore, it necessarily implies a subject (collective or individual) to bear witness to its history. If one has difficulty following Renan when he affirms that "rationalism is based on philology"—for it is obvious that the two are interdependent—it is no less obvious that philological reasoning is maintained through the identity of a historical subject: a subject in becoming. Why? Because, far from dissecting the internal logic of sign, predication (sentence grammar), or syllogism (logic), as did the universal grammar of Port Royal, the comparativist and philological reason that Renan exemplifies considers the signifying unit in itself (sign, sentence, syllogism) as an unanalyzable given. This signifying unit remains implicit within each description of law or text that philologists and comparativists undertake: linear, unidimensional descriptions—with no analysis of the sign's density, the logical problematic of meaning, etc.—but which, once technically completed, restore structural identity (for the comparativists) or meaning (for the philologists); in so doing they reveal the initial presupposition of the specifically linguistic undertaking as an ideology that posits either the people or an exceptional individual as appropriating this structure or this meaning. Because it is in itself unanalyzable (like the sign, sentence, and syllogism, it has no density, no economy), this subject-support of comparativist laws or of philological analysis does not lend itself to change, that is to say, to shifting from one law to another, from one structure to another, or from one meaning to another, except by postulating the movement of becoming, that is, of history. In the analysis of a signifying function (language or any "human," social phenomenon), what is censured at the level of semantic complexity reemerges in the form of a becoming: that obliteration of the density that constitutes sign, sentence, and syllogism (and consequently, the speaking subject), is compensated for by historical reasoning; the reduction of the complex signifying economy of the speaking subject (though obliquely perceived by Port Royal) produces without fail an opaque "I" that makes history. Thus, philological reasoning, while founding history, becomes a deadlock for language sciences, even though there actually is in

Renan, beyond countless contradictions, an appreciation of universal grammar, a call for the constitution of a linguistics for an isolated language (in the manner of the ancient Indian grammarian Pāṇini), and even surprisingly modern proposals that advocate the study of crisis rather than normality, and in his semitic studies the remarks on "that delirious vision transcribed in a barbaric and undecipherable style" as he calls the Christian gnostic texts, or on the texts of John the Apostle.[4]

Linguistic reasoning, which, through Saussure, succeeded philological reasoning, works its revolution precisely by affecting the constitutive unity of a particular language; a language is not a system, it is a system of signs, and this vertically opens up the famous gap between signifier and signified, thus allowing linguistics to claim a logical, mathematical formalization on the one hand, but on the other, it definitely prevents reducing a language or text to one law or one meaning. Structural linguistics and the ensuing structural movement seem to explore this epistemological space by eliminating the speaking subject. But, on a closer look, we see that the subject they legitimately do without is nothing but the subject (individual or collective) of historico-philological discourse I just discussed, and in which the Hegelian consciousness of self became stranded as it was concretized, embodied into philology and history; this subject, which linguistics and the corollary human sciences do without, is the "personal identity, miserable treasure."[5] Nevertheless, a subject of enunciation takes shape within the gap opened up between signifier and signified that admits both structure and interplay within; and structural linguistics ignores such a subject. Moreover, because it left its place vacant, structural linguistics could not become a linguistics of speech or discourse; it lacked a grammar, for in order to move from sign to sentence the place of the subject had to be acknowledged and no longer kept vacant. Of course, generative grammar does reinstate it by rescuing universal grammar and the Cartesian subject from oblivion, using that subject to justify the generative, recursive functions of syntactic trees. But in fact, generative grammar is evidence of what structural linguistics omitted, rather than a new beginning; whether structural or generative, linguistics since Saussure adheres to the same presuppositions, implicit within the structuralist current, explicit in the generative tendency that can be found summed up in the philosophy of Husserl.

I refer modern linguistics and the modes of thought which it oversees within the so-called human sciences back to this founding father from another field, but not for conjunctural reasons, though they are not lacking. Indeed, Husserl was invited to and discussed by the Circle of Prague; indeed, Jakobson explicitly recognized in him a philosophical mentor for post-Saussurian linguists; indeed, several American epistemologists of generative grammar recognize in Husserlian phenomenology, rather than in Descartes, the foundations of the generative undertaking. But it is possible to detect in Husserl the basis of linguistic reasoning (structural or generative) to the extent that, after the reduction of the Hegelian consciousness of self into philological or historical identity,

Husserl masterfully understood and posited that any signifying act, insofar as it remains capable of elucidation by knowledge, does not maintain itself by a "me, miserable treasure" but by the "*transcendental ego.*"

If it is true that the division of the Saussurian sign (signifier/signified), unknown to Husserl, also introduces the heretofore unrecognized possibility of envisioning language as a free play, forever without closure, it is also true that this possibility was not developed by Saussure except in the very problematic *Anagrammes.*[6] Moreover, this investigation has no linguistic followers, but rather, philosophical (Heideggerian discourse) and psychoanalytic (Lacan's signifier) contemporaries or successors, who today effectively enable us to appreciate and circumscribe the contribution of phenomenological linguistics from a Husserlian perspective. For post-Saussurian structural linguistics still encloses the signifier, even if nonmotivated, within patterns of a signification originally destined for faultless communication, either coinciding with the explicit signified or set off a short distance from it, but still fastened to the unalterable presence of meaning and, similarly, tributary to phenomenological reason.

It is therefore impossible to take up the congruence between conceptions of language and of subject where Renan left off without recalling how Husserl shifted ground by raising it above empiricism, psychologism, and incarnation theories typical of Renan. Let us examine for a moment the signifying act and the Husserlian transcendental ego, keeping in mind that linguistic reason (structural or generative) is to Husserl what philological reason was to Hegel: reduction perhaps, but also concrete realization, that is, failure made manifest.

As early as *Logical Investigations* of 1901, Husserl situates the sign (of which one could have naively thought that it had no subject) within the act of expressing meaning, constituted by a judgment on something: "The articulate sound-complex, the written sign, etc., first becomes a spoken word or communicative bit of speech, when a speaker produces it with the intention of 'expressing himself about something' through its means."[7]

Consequently, the thin sheath of the sign (signifier/signified) opens onto a complex architecture where intentional life-experience captures material (hylic) multiplicities, endowing them first with noetic meaning, then with noematic meaning, so that finally the result for the judging consciousness is the formation of an *object* once and for all signified as real. The important point here is that this real *object*, first signified by means of hylic data, through noesis and noemis, if it exists, can only be transcendental in the sense that it is elaborated in its identity by the judging consciousness of transcendental ego. The signified is transcendent as it is posited by means of certain concatenations within an experience that is always confined to judgment; for if the phenomenologist distinguishes between intuiting and endowing with meaning, then perception is already *cogitation* and the *cogitation* is transcendent to perception.[8] So much so that if the world were annihilated, the signified "*res*" would remain because they are transcendental: they "refer entirely to a consciousness" insofar as they are signified *res*. The *predicative* (syntactic) operation constitutes this judging consciousness, positing at the

same time the signified *Being* (and therefore, the object of meaning and signification) and the *operating consciousness* itself. The ego as support of the predicative
act therefore does not operate as the ego-cogito, that is, as the ego of a logically
conceived consciousness and "fragment of the world"; rather, the transcendental
ego belongs to the constituting operating consciousness, which means that it
takes shape within the predicative operation. This operation is *thetic* because it
simultaneously posits the thesis (position) of both Being *and* ego. Thus, for every
signified transcendental object, there is a transcendental ego, both of which are
givens by virtue of thetic operation—predication of judgment.

"Transcendental egology"[9] thus reformulates the question of the signifying
act's subject: (1) the operating consciousness, through predication, simultaneously constitutes Being, the (transcendent) signified real object, and the ego (in
so far as it is transcendental); the problematic of the sign is also bound up in
this question; (2) even if intentionality, and with it, the judging consciousness, is
already a given in material data and perceptions, as it "resembles" them (which
allows us to say that the transcendental ego is always already in a way given), *in
fact*, the ego constitutes itself only through the operating consciousness at the
time of predication; the subject is merely the subject of predication, of judgment, of the sentence; (3) "belief" and "judgment" are closely interdependent
though not identical: "The synthesis of belief (Glaubenssynthesen) find their
'expression' in the forms of stated meaning."[10]

Neither a historical individual nor a logically conceived consciousness, the
subject is henceforth the operating thetic consciousness positing correlatively
the transcendental Being and ego. Thus, Husserl makes clear that any linguistic
act, insofar as it sets up a signified that can be communicated in a sentence (and
there is no sign or signifying structure that is not already part of a sentence), is
sustained by the transcendental ego.

It is perhaps not unimportant that the rigor of Judaism and the persecution
it has been subjected to in our time underlie Husserl's extraordinarily firm elucidation of the transcendental ego, just as they are the foundation of the human
sciences.

For the purposes of our discussion, we can draw two conclusions from this
brief review:
1. It is impossible to treat problems of signification seriously, in linguistics
or semiology, without including in these considerations *the subject thus formulated as operating consciousness*. This phenomenological conception of the
speaking subject is made possible in modern linguistics by the introduction of
logic into generative grammar and, in a much more lucid manner, through a linguistics (developing in France after Benveniste) which is attuned to the *subject
of enunciation* and which includes in the latter's operating consciousness not
only logical modalities, but also interlocutory relationships.
2. If it is true, consequently, that the question of signification and therefore
of modern linguistics is dominated by Husserl, the attempts to criticize or "de-

construct" phenomenology bear concurrently on Husserl, meaning, the still transcendental subject of enunciation, and linguistic methodology. These criticisms circumscribe the metaphysics inherent in the sciences of signification and therefore in the human sciences—an important epistemological task in itself. But they reveal their own shortcomings not so much, as some believe, in that they prevent serious, theoretical or scientific research, but in that such "deconstructions" refuse (through discrediting the signified and with it the transcendental ego) what constitutes one function of language though not the only one: to express meaning in a communicable sentence between speakers. This function harbors coherence (which is indeed transcendental) or, in other words, social identity. Let us first acknowledge, with Husserl, this thetic character of the signifying act, which establishes the transcendent object and the transcendental ego of communication (and consequently of sociability), before going beyond the Husserlian problematic to search for that which produces, shapes, and exceeds the operating consciousness (this will be our purpose when confronting poetic language). Without that acknowledgement, which is also that of the episteme underlying structuralism, any reflection on significance, by refusing its thetic character, will continually ignore its constraining, legislative, and socializing elements: under the impression that it is breaking down the metaphysics of the signified or the transcendental ego, such a reflection will become lodged in a negative theology that denies their limitations.

Finally, even when the researcher in the field, beginning with what is now a descriptive if not scientific perspective, thinks he has discovered givens that may escape the *unity* of the transcendental ego (because each identity would be as if flaked into a multiplicity of qualities or appurtenances, the discourse of knowledge that delivers this multiplied identity to us remains a prisoner of phenomenological reason for which the multiplicities, inasmuch as they signify, are givens of consciousness, predicates within the same eidetic unity: the unity of an object signified by and for a transcendental ego. In an interpretive undertaking for which there is no domain heterogeneous to meaning, all material diversities, as multiple attributes, revert to a real (transcendental) object. Even apparently psychoanalytic interpretations (relationship to parents, et cetera), from the moment they are posited by the structuring learning as particularities of the transcendental real object, are false multiplicities; deprived of what is heterogeneous to meaning, these multiplicities can only produce a plural identity—but an identity all the same, since it is eidetic, transcendental. Husserl therefore stands on the threshold not only of modern linguistics concerned with a subject of enunciation, but of any science of man as signified phenomenon, whose objecthood, even if multiple, is to be restored.

To the extent that poetic language operates with and communicates meaning, it also shares particularities of the signifying operations elucidated by Husserl (correlation between signified object and the transcendental ego, operating consciousness, which constitutes itself by predication—by syntax—as thetic: thesis of Being, thesis of the object, thesis of the ego). Meaning and signification, however, do not exhaust the poetic function. Therefore, the thetic predicative operation and its correlatives (signified object and transcendental ego), though valid for the signifying economy of poetic language, are only one of its *limits:* certainly constitutive, but not all-encompassing. While poetic language can indeed be studied through its meaning and signification (by revealing, depending on the method, either structures or process), such a study would, in the final analysis, amount to reducing it to the phenomenological perspective and, hence, failing to see what in the poetic function departs from the signified and the transcendental ego and makes of what is known as "literature" something other than knowledge: the very place where social code is destroyed and renewed, thus providing, as Artaud writes, "A release for the anguish of its time" by "animating, attracting, lowering onto its shoulders the wandering anger of a particular time for the discharge of its psychological evil-being."[11]

Consequently, one should begin by positing that there is within poetic language (and therefore, although in a less pronounced manner, within any language) a *heterogeneousness* to meaning and signification. This *heterogeneousness,* detected genetically in the first echolalias of infants as rhythms and intonations anterior to the first phonemes, morphemes, lexemes, and sentences; this heterogeneousness, which is later reactivated as rhythms, intonations, glossalalias in psychotic discourse, serving as ultimate support of the speaking subject threatened by the collapse of the signifying function; this heterogeneousness to signification operates through, despite, and in excess of it and produces in poetic language "musical" but also nonsense effects that destroy not only accepted beliefs and significations, but, in radical experiments, syntax itself, that guarantee of thetic consciousness (of the signified object and ego)—for example, carnivalesque discourse, Artaud, a number of texts by Mallarmé, certain Dadaist and Surrealist experiments. The notion of *heterogeneity* is indispensable, for though articulate, precise, organized, and complying with constraints and rules (especially, like the rule of *repetition,* which articulates the units of a particular rhythm or intonation), this signifying disposition is not that of meaning or signification: no sign, no predication, no signified object and therefore no operating consciousness of a transcendental ego. We shall call this disposition *semiotic (le sémiotique),* meaning, according to the etymology of the Greek *sémeion* (σημεῖον), a distinctive mark, trace, index, the premonitory sign, the proof, engraved mark, imprint—in short, a *distinctiveness* admitting of an uncertain and indeterminate articulation because it does not yet refer (for young children) or no longer refers (in psychotic discourse) to a signified object for a thetic consciousness (this side of, or through, both object and consciousness). Plato's *Timeus* speaks of a *chora* (χώρα), receptacle (ὑποδοχεῖον), unnamable, improbable, hybrid, anterior to naming, to the One, to the father, and consequently, maternally connoted to such an extent that it merits "not even the rank of syllable." One can describe more precisely than did philosophical intuition the particularities of this signifying disposition that I have just named semiotic—a term which quite clearly designates that we are dealing with a disposition that is definitely heterogeneous to meaning but always in sight of it or in either a negative or surplus relationship to it. Research I have recently undertaken on child language acquisition in the prephonological, one could say prepredicative stages, or anterior to the "mirror stage," as well as another concomitant study on particularities of psychotic discourse aim notably at describing as precisely as possible—with the help of, for example, modern phono-acoustics—these semiotic operations (rhythm, intonation) and their dependence vis-à-vis the body's drives observable through muscular contractions and the libidinal or sublimated cathexis that accompany vocalizations. It goes without saying that, concerning a *signifying practice*, that is, a socially communicable discourse like poetic language, this semiotic heterogeneity posited by theory is inseparable from what I shall call, to distinguish it from the latter, the *symbolic* function of significance. The symbolic (*le symbolique*), as opposed to the semiotic, is this inevitable attribute of meaning, sign, and the signified object for the consciousness of Husserl's transcendental ego. Language as social practice necessarily presupposes these two dispositions, though combined in different ways to constitute *types of discourse,* types of signifying practices. Scientific discourse, for example, aspiring to the status of metalanguage, tends to reduce as much as possible the semiotic component. On the contrary, the signifying economy of poetic language is specific in that the semiotic is not only a constraint as is the symbolic, but it tends to gain the upper hand at the expense of the thetic and predicative constraints of the ego's judging consciousness. Thus in any poetic language, not only do the rhythmic constraints, for example, perform an organizing function that could go so far as to violate certain grammatical rules of a national language and often neglect the importance of an ideatory message, but in recent texts, these semiotic constraints (rhythm, phonic, vocalic timbres in Symbolist work, but also graphic disposition on the page) are accompanied by nonrecoverable syntactic elisions; it is impossible to reconstitute the particular elided syntactic category (object or verb), which makes the meaning of the utterance undecidable (for example, the nonrecoverable elisions in *Un Coup de Dés*).[12] However elided, attacked, or corrupted the symbolic function might be in poetic language, due to the impact of semiotic processes, the symbolic function nonetheless maintains its presence. It is for this reason that it is a language. First, it persists as an internal limit of this bipolar economy, since a multiple and sometimes even uncomprehensible signified is nevertheless communicated; secondly, it persists also because the semiotic processes themselves, far from being set adrift (as they would be in insane discourse), set up a new formal construct: a so-called new formal or ideological "writer's universe," the never-finished, undefined production of a new space of significance. Husserl's "thetic function" of the signifying act is thus re-assumed, but in different form: though poetic language unsettled the position of the signified and the transcendental ego, it nonetheless posits a thesis, not of a particular being or meaning, but of a signifying apparatus; it posits its own process as an undecidable process between sense and nonsense, between *language* and *rhythm* (in the sense of linkage that the word "rhythm" had for Aeschylus's *Prometheus* according to Heidegger's reading), between the symbolic and semiotic.

For a theory attuned to this kind of functioning, the language object itself appears quite differently than it would from a phenomenological perspective. Thus, a phoneme, as distinctive element of meaning, belongs to language as symbolic. But this same phoneme is involved in rhythmic, intonational repetitions; it thereby tends towards autonomy from meaning so as to maintain itself in a semiotic disposition near the instinctual drives' body; it is a sonorous distinctiveness, which therefore is no longer either a phoneme or a part of the symbolic system— one might say that its belonging to the set of the language is indefinite, between zero and one. Nevertheless, the set to which it thus belongs exists with this indefinition, with this fuzziness.

It is poetic language that awakens our attention to this undecidable character of any so-called natural language, a feature that univocal, rational, scientific discourse tends to hide—and this implies considerable consequences for its subject. The support of this signifying economy could not be the transcendental ego alone. If it is true that there would unavoidably be a speaking *subject* since the signifying set exists, it is nonetheless evident that this subject, in order to tally with its heterogeneity, must be, let us say, a questionable *subject-in-process*. It is of course Freud's theory of the unconscious that allows the apprehension of such a subject; for through the surgery it practiced in the operating consciousness of the transcendental ego, Freudian and Lacanian psychoanalysis did allow, not for (as certain simplifications would have it) a few typologies or structures that might accommodate the same phenomenological reason, but rather for heterogeneity, which, known as the unconscious, shapes the signifying function. In light of these statements, I shall now make a few remarks on the questionable subject-in-process of poetic language.

1. The semiotic activity, which introduces wandering or fuzziness into language and, *a fortiori*, into poetic language is, from a synchronic point of view, a mark of the workings of drives (appropriation/rejection, orality/anality, love/hate, life/death) and, from a diachronic point of view, stems from the archaisms of the semiotic body. Before recognizing itself as identical in a mirror and, consequently, as signifying, this body is dependent vis-à-vis the mother. At the same time instinctual and maternal, semiotic processes prepare the future speaker for entrance into meaning and signification (the symbolic). But the symbolic (i.e., language as nomination, sign, and syntax) constitutes itself only by breaking with this anteriority, which is retrieved as "signifier," "primary processes," displacement and condensation, metaphor and metonomy, rhetorical figures—but which always remains subordinate—subjacent to the principal function of naming-predicating. Language as symbolic function constitutes itself at the cost of repressing instinctual drive and continuous relation to the mother. On the contrary, the unsettled and questionable subject of poetic language (for whom the word is never uniquely sign) maintains itself at the cost of reactivating this repressed instinctual, maternal element. If it is true that the prohibition of incest constitutes, at the same time, language as communicative

code and women as exchange objects in order for a society to be established, *poetic language would be* for its questionable subject-in-process the *equivalent of incest*: it is within the economy of signification itself that the questionable subject-in-process appropriates to itself this archaic, instinctual, and maternal territory; thus it simultaneously prevents the word from becoming mere sign and the mother from becoming an object like any other—forbidden. This passage into and through the forbidden, which constitutes the sign and is correlative to the prohibition of incest, is often explicit as such (Sade: "Unless he becomes his mother's lover from the day she has brought him into the world, let him not bother to write, for we shall not read him,"—*Idée sur les romans;* Artaud, identifying with his "daughters"; Joyce and his daughter at the end of *Finnegans Wake;* Céline who takes as pseudonym his grandmother's first name; and innumerable identifications with women, or dancers, that waver between fetishization and homosexuality). I stress this point for three reasons:

(a) To emphasize that the dominance of semiotic constraint in poetic language cannot be solely interpreted, as formalist poetics would have it, as a preoccupation with the "sign," or with the "signifier" at the expense of the "message"; rather, it is more deeply indicative of the instinctual drives' activity relative to the first structurations (constitution of the body as self) and identifications (with the mother).

(b) To elucidate the intrinsic connection between literature and breaking up social concord; because it utters incest, poetic language is linked with "evil"; "literature and evil" (I refer to a title by Georges Bataille) should be understood, beyond the resonances of Christian ethics, as the social body's self-defense against the discourse of incest as destroyer and generator of any language and sociality. This applies all the more as "great literature," which has mobilized unconsciousnesses for centuries, has nothing to do with the hypostasis of incest (a petty game of fetishists at the end of an era, priesthood of a would-be enigma—the forbidden mother); on the contrary, this incestuous relation, exploding in language, embracing it from top to bottom in such a *singular* fashion that it defies *generalizations,* still has this common feature in all outstanding cases: it presents itself as demystified, even disappointed, deprived of its hallowed function as support of the law, in order to become the cause of a permanent trial of the speaking subject, a cause of that agility, of that analytic "competency" that legend attributes to Ulysses.

(c) It is of course possible, as Lévi-Strauss pointed out to Dr. André Green, to ignore the mother-child relationship within a given anthropological vision of society; now, given not only the thematization of this relationship, but especially the mutations in the very economy of discourse attributable to it, one must, in discussing poetic language, consider what this presymbolic and transsymbolic relationship to the mother introduces as aimless wandering within the identity of the speaker and the economy of its very discourse. Moreover, this relationship of the speaker to the mother is probably one of the most important

factors producing interplay within the structure of meaning as well as a questioning process of subject and history.

2. And yet, this reinstatement of maternal territory into the very economy of language does not lead its questioned subject-in-process to repudiate its symbolic disposition. Formulator—logothete, as Roland Barthes would say—the subject of poetic language continually but never definitively assumes the thetic function of naming, establishing meaning and signification, which the paternal function represents within reproductive relation. Son permanently at war with father, not in order to take his place, nor even to endure it, erased from reality, as a symbolic, divine menace and salvation in the manner of *Senatspräsident* Schreber. But rather, to signify what is untenable in the symbolic, nominal, paternal function. If symbolic and social cohesion are maintained by virtue of a sacrifice (which makes of a *soma* a sign towards an unnamable transcendence, so that only thus are signifying and social structures clinched even though they are ignorant of this sacrifice) and if the paternal function represents this sacrificial function, then it is not up to the poet to adjust to it. Fearing its rule but sufficiently aware of the legislation of language not to be able to turn away from this sacrificial-paternal function, he takes it by storm and from the flank. In *Maldoror,* Lautréamont struggles against the Omnipotent. After the death of his son Anatole, Mallarmé writes a *Tombeau,* thanks to which a book replaces not only the dead son, his own father, mother, and fiancée at the same time, but also hallowed humanism and the "instinct of heaven" itself. The most analytical of them all, the Marquis de Sade, gives up this battle with, or for, the symbolic legislation represented by the father, in order to attack the power represented by a woman, Madame de Montreuil, visible figurehead of a dynasty of matrons toward whom he usurps, through writing, the role of father and incestuous son; here, the transgression is carried out and the transsymbolic, transpaternal function of poetic language reaches its thematic end by staging a simultaneously impossible, sacrificial, and orgastic society—never one without the other.

Here we must clearly distinguish two positions: that of the rhetorician and that of the writer in the strongest sense of the word; that is, as Céline puts it, one who has "style." The rhetorician does not invent a language; fascinated by the symbolic function of paternal discourse, he *seduces* it in the Latin sense of the verb—he "leads it astray," inflicts it with a few anomalies generally taken from writers of the past, thus miming a father who remembers having been a son and even a daughter of his father, but not to the point of leaving cover. This is indeed what is happening to the discourse of contemporary philosophers, in France particularly, when, hemmed in by the breakthroughs in social sciences on the one hand, and social upheavals on the other, the philosopher begins performing literary tricks, thus arrogating to himself a power over imaginations: a power which, though minor in appearance, is more fetching than that of the transcendental consciousness. The stylist's adventure is totally different; he no longer needs to seduce the father by rhetorical affectations. As winner of the battle, he may even drop the name of the father to take a pseudonym (Céline signs with his grand-mother's first name), and thus, in the place of the father, assume a different discourse; neither imaginary discourse of the self, nor discourse of transcendental knowledge, but a permanent go-between from one to the other, a pulsation of sign and rhythm, of consciousness and instinctual drive. "I am the father of my imaginative creations," writes Mallarmé at the birth of Geneviève. "I am my father, my mother, my son, and me," Artaud claims. Stylists all, they sound a dissonance within the thetic, paternal function of language.

3. Psychosis and fetishism represent the two abysses that threaten the unstable subject of poetic language, as twentieth-century literature has only too clearly demonstrated. As to *psychosis,* symbolic legality is wiped out in favor of arbitrariness of an instinctual drive without meaning and communication; panicking at the loss of all reference, the subject goes through fantasies of omnipotence or identification with a totalitarian leader. On the other hand, where *fetishism* is concerned, constantly dodging the paternal, sacrificial function produces an objectification of the pure signifier, more and more emptied of meaning—an insipid formalism. Nevertheless, far from thus becoming an unpleasant or negligible accident within the firm progress of symbolic process (which, in the footsteps of science, would eventually find signified elements for all signifiers, as rationalists believe), these borderline experiences, which contemporary poetic language has undergone, perhaps more dramatically than before or elsewhere, show not only that the Saussurian cleavage (signifier/signified) is forever unbridgeable, but also that it is reinforced by another, even more radical one between an instinctual, semioticizing body, heterogeneous to signification, and this very signification based on prohibition (of incest), sign, and thetic signification establishing signified object and transcendental ego. Through the permanent contradiction between these two dispositions (semiotic/symbolic), of which the internal setting off of the sign (signifier/signified) is merely a witness, poetic language, in its most disruptive form (unreadable for meaning, dangerous for the subject), shows the constraints of a civilization dominated by transcendental rationality. Consequently, it is a means of overriding this constraint. And if in so doing it sometimes falls in with deeds brought about by the same rationality, as is, for example, the instinctual determination of fascism—demonstrated as such by Wilhelm Reich—poetic language is also there to forestall such translations into action.

This means that if poetic economy has always borne witness to crises and impossibilities of transcendental symbolics, in our time it is coupled with crises of social institutions (state, family, religion), and, more profoundly, a turning point in the relationship of man to meaning. Transcendental mastery over discourse is possible, but repressive; such a position is necessary, but only as a limit open to constant challenge; this relief with respect to repression—establishing meaning—is no longer possible under the incarnate appearance of a providential, historical, or even rationalist, humanist ego (in the manner of Renan), but through a *discordance* in the symbolic function and consequently within the identity of the transcendental ego itself: this is what the literary experience of our century intimates to theoretical reason, thereby taking its place with other phenomena of symbolic and social unrest (youth, drugs, women).

Without entering into a technical analysis of the economy specific to poetic language (an analysis too subtle and specious, considering the purpose of this specific paper), I shall extract from Céline, first, several procedures and, second, several themes, which illustrate the position of the unsettled, questionable subject-in-process of poetic language. I shall not do this without firmly underlining that these themes are not only inseparable from "style," but that they are produced by it; in other words, it is not necessary "to know" them, one could have heard them by simply listening to Céline's staccato, rhythmic discourse, stuffed with jargon and obscenity.

Thus, going beyond semantic themes and their distributions, one ought to examine the functioning of poetic language and its questionable subject-in-process, beginning with constitutive linguistic operations: syntax and semantics. Two phenomena, among others, will become the focus of our attention in Céline's writing: *sentential rhythms* and *obscene words*. These are of interest not only because they seem to constitute a particularity of his discourse, but also because, though they function differently, both of them involve constitutive operations of the judging consciousness (therefore of identity) by simultaneously perturbing its clarity and the designation of an object (objecthood). Moreover, if they constitute a network of constraints that is added to denotative signification, such a network has nothing to do with classic poeticness (rhythm, meter, conventional rhetorical figures) because it is drawn from the drives' register of a desiring body, both identifying with and rejecting a community (familial or folk). Therefore, even if the so-called poetic codes are not recognizable within poetic language, a constraint that I have termed semiotic functions in addition to the judging consciousness, provokes its lapses, or compensates for them; in so doing, it refers neither to a literary convention (like our poetic canons, contemporary with the major national epics and the constitution of nations themselves) nor even to the body *itself*, but rather, to a signifying disposition, pre- or transsymbolic, which fashions any judging consciousness so that any ego recognizes its crisis within it. It is a jubilant recognition that, in "modern" literature, replaces petty aesthetic pleasure.

Sentential rhythms. Beginning with *Death on the Installment Plan,* the sentence is condensed: not only does Céline avoid coordination and embeddings, but when different "object-phrases" are for example numerous and juxtaposed with a verb, they are separated by the characteristic "three dots." This procedure divides the sentence into its constitutive phrases; they thus tend to become independent of the central verb, to detach themselves from the sentence's own signification, and to acquire a meaning initially incomplete and consequently capable of taking on multiple connotations that no longer depend on the framework of the sentence, but on a free context (the entire book, but also, all the addenda of which the reader is capable). Here, there are no syntactic anomalies (as in the *Coup de Dés* or the glossalalias of Artaud). The predicative thesis, constitutive of the judging consciousness, is maintained. By using three dots to space the phrases making up a sentence, thus giving them rhythm, he causes connotation to rush through a predication that has been striated in that manner; the denoted object of the utterance, the transcendental object, loses its clear contours. The elided object in the sentence relates to a hesitation (if not an erasure) of the *real object* for the speaking subject. That literature is witness to this kind of deception involving the object (object of love or transcendental object); that the existence of the object is more than fleeting and indeed impossible: this is what Céline's rhythms and syntactic elisions have recently evidenced within the stern humor of an experiment and with all its implications for the subject. This is also true of Beckett, whose recent play, *Not I,* spoken by a dying woman, sets forth in elided sentences and floating phrases the impossibility of God's existence for a speaking subject lacking any object of signification and/or love. Moreover, beyond and with connotation, with the blurred or erased object, there flows through meaning this "emotion" of which Céline speaks—the nonsemanticized instinctual drive that precedes and exceeds meaning.

The exclamation marks alternating with three dots even more categorically point to this surge of instinctual drive: a panting, a breathlessness, an acceleration of verbal utterance, concerned not so much with finally reaching a global summing up of the world's meaning, as, to the contrary, with revealing, within the interstices of predication, the rhythm of a drive that remains forever unsatisfied—in the vacancy of judging consciousness and sign—because it could not find an other (an addressee) so as to obtain meaning in this exchange. We must also listen to Céline, Artaud, or Joyce, and read their texts in order to understand that the aim of this practice, which reaches us as a language, is, through the signification of the nevertheless transmitted message, not only to impose a music, a rhythm—that is, a polyphony—but also to wipe out sense through nonsense and laughter. This is a difficult operation that obliges the reader not so much to combine significations as to shatter his own judging consciousness in order to grant passage through it to this rhythmic drive constituted by repression and, once filtered by language and its meaning, experienced as jouissance. Could the resistance against modern literature be evidence of an obsession with meaning, of an unfitness for such jouissance?

Obscene words. Semantically speaking, these pivotal words in the Célinian lexicon exercise a *desemanticization* function analogous to the fragmentation of syntax by rhythm. Far from referring, as do all signs, to an object exterior to discourse and identifiable as such by consciousness, the obscene word is the minimal mark of a situation of desire where the identity of the signifying subject, if not destroyed, is exceeded by a conflict of instinctual drives linking one subject to another. There is nothing better than an obscene word for perceiving the limits of a phenomenological linguistics faced with the heterogeneous and complex architectonics of significance. The obscene word, lacking an objective referent, is also the contrary of an autonym—which involves the function of a word or utterance as sign; the obscene word mobilizes the signifying resources of the subject, permitting it to cross through the membrane of meaning where consciousness holds it, connecting it to gesturality, kinesthesia, the drives' body, the movement of rejection and appropriation of the other. Then, it is neither object, transcendental signified, nor signifier available to a neutralized consciousness: around the object denoted by the obscene word, and that object provides a scanty delineation, more than a simple context asserts itself— the drama of a questioning process heterogeneous to the meaning that precedes and exceeds it. Childrens' counting-out rhymes, or what one calls the "obscene folklore of children," utilize the same rhythmic and semantic resources; they maintain the subject close to these jubilatory dramas that run athwart the repression that a univocal, increasingly pure signifier vainly attempts to impose upon the subject. By reconstituting them, and this on the very level of language, literature achieves its cathartic effects.

Several themes in Céline bring to light the relationships of force, at first within the family triangle, and then in contemporary society, that produce, promote, and accompany the particularities of poetic language to which I have just referred.

In *Death on the Installment Plan,* the most "familial" of Céline's writings, we find a paternal figure, Auguste: a man "of instruction," "a mind," sullen, a prohibitor, prone to scandal, full of obsessional habits like, for example, cleaning the flagstones in front of his shop. His anger explodes spectacularly once, when he shuts himself up in the basement and shoots his pistol for hours, not without explaining in the face of general disapproval, "I have my conscience on my side," just before falling ill. "My mother wrapped the weapon in several layers of newspaper and then in a cashmere shawl . . . 'Come, child . . . come!' she said when we were alone [. . .] We threw the package in the drink."[13]

Here is an imposing and menacing father, strongly emphasizing the enviable necessity of his position, but spoiling it by his derisive fury: undermined power whose weapon one could only take away in order to engulf it at the end of a journey between mother and son.

In an interview, Céline compares himself to a "society woman" who braves the nevertheless maintained family prohibition, and who has the right to her own desire, "a choice in a drawing room": "the whore's trade doesn't interest me"; before defining himself, at the end: "I am the son of a woman who restored old lace . . . [I am] one of those rare men who knows how to distinguish batiste from valencienne . . . I do not need to be taught. I know it."

This fragile delicacy, heritage of the mother, supports the language—or if you wish, the identity—of him who unseated what Céline calls the "heaviness" of men, of fathers, in order to flee it. The threads of instinctual drive, exceeding the law of the paternal word's own mastery, are nonetheless woven with scrupulous precision. One must therefore conceive of another disposition of the law, through signified and signifying identity and confronting the semiotic network: a disposition closer to the Greek *gnomon* ("one that knows," "carpenter's square") than to the Latin *lex,* which necessarily implies the act of logical and legal judgment. A device, then, a regulated discrimination, weaves the semiotic network of instinctual drives; if it thus fails to conform to signifying identity, it nevertheless constitutes another identity closer to repressed and gnomic archaisms, susceptible of a psychosis-inducing explosion, where we decipher the relationship of the speaker to a desiring and desired mother.

In another interview, this maternal reference to old lacework is explicitly thought of as an archeology of the word: "No! In the beginning was emotion. The Word came next to replace emotion as the trot replaces the gallop [. . .] They pulled man out of emotive poetry in order to plunge him into dialectics, that is, into gibberish, right?" Anyway, what is *Rigodon* if not a popular dance which obliges language to bow to the rhythm of its emotion.

A speech thus slatted by instinctual drive—Diderot would have said "musicated"—could not describe, narrate, or theatricalize "objects": by its composition and signification it also goes beyond the accepted categories of lyric, epic, dramatic, or tragic. The last writings of Céline, plugged in live to an era of war, death, and genocide, are what he calls in *North,* "the vivisection of the wounded," "the circus," "the three hundred years before Christ."

While members of the Resistance sing in alexandrine verse, it is Céline's language that records not only the institutional but also the profoundly symbolic jolt involving meaning and the identity of transcendental reason; fascism inflicted this jolt on our universe and the human sciences have hardly begun to figure out its consequences. I am saying that this literary discourse enunciates through its formal decentering, more apparent in Artaud's glossalalias, but also through the rhythms and themes of violence in Céline, better than anything else, the faltering of transcendental consciousness: this does not mean that such a discourse is aware of such a faltering or interprets it. As proof, writing that pretends to agree with "circus" and "vivisection" will nonetheless find its idols, even if only provisional; though dissolved in laughter and dominant non-sense, they are nevertheless posited as idols in Hitlerian ideology. A reading of any one of Céline's anti-semitic tracts is sufficient to show the crudely exhibited phantasms of an analysand struggling against a desired and frustrating, castrating, and sodomizing father; sufficient also to understand that it is not enough to allow what is repressed by the symbolic structure to emerge in a "musicated" language to avoid its traps. Rather, we must in addition dissolve its sexual determinations. Unless poetic work can be linked to analytical interpretation, the discourse that undermines the judging consciousness and releases its repressed instinctual drive as rhythm always turns out to be at fault from the viewpoint of an ethic that remains with the transcendental ego—whatever joys or negations might exist in Spinoza's or Hegel's.

Since at least Hölderlin, poetic language has deserted beauty and meaning to become a laboratory where, facing philosophy, knowledge, and the transcendental ego of all signification, the impossibility of a signified or signifying identity is being sustained. If we took this venture seriously—if we could hear the burst of black laughter it hurls at all attempts to master the human situation, to master language by language—we would be forced to reexamine "literary history," to rediscover beneath rhetoric and poetics its unchanging but always different polemic with the symbolic function. We could not avoid wondering about the possibility, or simultaneously, the legitimacy of a theoretical discourse on this practice of language whose stakes are precisely to render impossible the transcendental bounding that supports the discourse of knowledge.

Faced with this poetic language that defies knowledge, many of us are rather tempted to leave our shelter to deal with literature only by miming its meanderings, rather than by positing it as an object of knowledge. We let ourselves be taken in by this mimeticism: fictional, para-philosophical, para-scientific writings. It is probably necessary to be a woman (ultimate guarantee of sociality beyond the wreckage of the paternal symbolic function, as well as the inexhaustible generator of its renewal, of its expansion) not to renounce theoretical reason but to compel it to increase its power by giving it an object beyond its limits. Such a position, it seems to me, provides a possible basis for a theory of signification, which, confronted with poetic language, could not in any way account for it, but would rather use it as an indication of what is heterogeneous to meaning (to sign and predication): instinctual economies, always and at the same time open to bio-physiological sociohistorical constraints.

This kind of heterogeneous economy and its questionable subject-in-process thus calls for a linguistics other than the one descended from the phenomenological heavens; a linguistics capable, within its language object, of accounting for a nonetheless articulated *instinctual drive,* across and through the constitutive and insurmountable frontier of *meaning.* This instinctual drive, however, located in the matrix of the sign, refers back to an instinctual body (to which psychoanalysis has turned its attention), which ciphers the language with rhythmic, intonational, and other arrangements, nonreducible to the position of the transcendental ego even though always within sight of its thesis.

The development of this theory of signification is in itself regulated by Husserlian precepts, because it inevitably makes an *object* even of that which departs from meaning. But, even though abetting the law of signifying structure as well as of all sociality, this expanded theory of signification cannot give itself new objects except by positing itself as nonuniversal: that is, by presupposing that a questionable subject-in-process exists in an economy of discourse other than that of thetic consciousness. And this requires that subjects of the theory must be themselves subjects in infinite analysis; this is what Husserl could not imagine, what Céline could not know, but what a woman, among others, can finally admit, aware as she is of the inanity of Being.

When it avoids the risks that lie in wait for it, literary experience remains nevertheless something other than this analytical theory, which it never stops challenging. Against knowing thought, poetic language pursues an effect of *singular truth*, and thus accomplishes, perhaps, for the modern community, this solitary practice that the materialists of antiquity unsuccessfully championed against the ascendance of theoretical reason.

NOTES

1. Claude Lévi-Strauss, *l'Homme nu* (Paris: Plon, 1971), p. 615.
2. Kristeva's French phrase is *mise en procès*, which, like *le sujet en procès*, refers to an important, recurring concept—that of a constantly changing subject whose identity is open to question.
3. Ernest Renan, *Oeuvres Complètes*, (Paris: Calmann-Lévy, 1947–58) 3:322.
4. Ernest Renan, *The Future of Science* (Boston: Roberts Brothers, 1891), p. 402.
5. Lévi-Strauss, *L'Homme nu*, p. 614.
6. See Jean Starobinski, *Les Mots sous les mots* (Paris: Gallimard, 1971). [Ed.]
7. Edmund Husserl, *Logical Investigations*, J.N. Findlay, trans. (London: Routledge & Kegan Paul, 1970), pp. 276–77.
8. Edmund Husserl, *Ideas: General Introduction to Pure Phenomenology*. W.R. Boyce Gibson, trans. (London: Collier-MacMillan, 1962), pp. 93–94 and 101.
9. Edmund Husserl, *Erste Philosophie*, VIII, in *Husserliana* (The Hague: Hrsg. von R. Boehm, 1956).
10. Husserl, *Ideas*, p. 313.
11. Antonin Artaud, "l'Anarchie sociale de l'art," in *Oeuvres complètes* (Paris: Gallimard), 8:287.
12. See Kristeva, *La Révolution du language poétique* (Paris: Seuil, 1974), pp. 274ff. [Ed.]
13. Louis-Ferdinand Céline, *Death on the Installment Plan*. Ralph Manheim, trans. (New York: New Directions, 1966), p. 78.

JACQUES DERRIDA

"DIFFERANCE"

The verb "to differ" [*différer*] seems to differ from itself. On the one hand, it indicates difference as distinction, inequality, or discernibility; on the other, it expresses the interposition of delay, the interval of a *spacing* and *temporalizing* that puts off until "later" what is presently denied, the possible that is presently impossible. Sometimes the *different* and sometimes the *deferred* correspond [in French] to the verb "to differ." This correlation, however, is not simply one between act and object, cause and effect, or primordial and derived.

In the one case "to differ" signifies nonidentity; in the other case it signifies the order of the *same*. Yet there must be a common, although entirely differant[1] [*différante*], root within the sphere that relates the two movements of differing to one another. We provisionally give the name *differance* to this *sameness* which is not *identical:* by the silent writing of its *a*, it has the desired advantage of referring to differing, *both* as spacing/temporalizing and as the movement that structures every dissociation.

This essay appeared originally in the *Bulletin de la Société française de philosophie*, LXII, No. 3 (July–September, 1968), 73–101. Derrida's remarks were delivered as a lecture at a meeting of the Société at the Sorbonne, in the Amphithéâtre Michelet, on January 27, 1968, with Jean Wahl presiding. Professor Wahl's introductory and closing remarks have not been translated. The essay was reprinted in *Théorie d'ensemble*, a collection of essays by Derrida and others, published by Editions Seuil in 1968.

As distinct from difference, differance thus points out the irreducibility of temporalizing (which is also temporalization—in transcendental language which is no longer adequate here, this would be called the constitution of primordial temporality—just as the term "spacing" also includes the constitution of primordial spatiality). Differance is not simply active (any more than it is a subjective accomplishment); it rather indicates the middle voice, it precedes and sets up the opposition between passivity and activity. With its *a*, differance more properly refers to what in classical language would be called the origin or production of differences and the differences between differences, the *play* [*jeu*] of differences. Its locus and operation will therefore be seen wherever speech appeals to difference.

Differance is neither a *word* nor a *concept*. In it, however, we shall see the juncture—rather than the summation—of what has been most decisively inscribed in the thought of what is conveniently called our "epoch": the difference of forces in Nietzsche, Saussure's principle of semiological difference, differing as the possibility of [neurone] facilitation,[2] impression and delayed effect in Freud, difference as the irreducibility of the trace of the other in Levinas, and the ontic-ontological difference in Heidegger.

Reflection on this last determination of difference will lead us to consider differance as the *strategic* note or connection—relatively or provisionally *privileged*—which indicates the closure of presence, together with the closure of the conceptual order and denomination, a closure that is effected in the functioning of traces.

I shall speak, then, of a letter—the first one, if we are to believe the alphabet and most of the speculations that have concerned themselves with it.

I shall speak then of the letter *a*, this first letter which it seemed necessary to introduce now and then in writing the word "difference." This seemed necessary in the course of writing about writing, and of writing within a writing whose different strokes all pass, in certain respects, through a gross spelling mistake, through a violation of the rules governing writing, violating the law that governs writing and regulates its conventions of propriety. In fact or theory we can always erase or lessen this spelling mistake, and, in each case, while these are analytically different from one another but for practical purposes the same, find it grave, unseemly, or, indeed, supposing the greatest ingenuousness, amusing. Whether or not we care to quietly overlook this infraction, the attention we give it beforehand will allow us to recognize, as though prescribed by some mute irony, the inaudible but displaced character of this literal permutation. We can always act as though this makes no difference. I must say from the start that my account serves less to justify this silent spelling mistake, or still less to excuse it, than to aggravate its obtrusive character.

On the other hand, I must be excused if I refer, at least implicitly, to one or another of the texts that I have ventured to publish. Precisely what I would like to attempt to some extent (although this is in principle and in its highest degree impossible, due to essential *de jure* reasons) is to bring together an *assemblage* of the different ways I have been able to utilize—or, rather, have allowed to be imposed on me—what I will provisionally call the word or concept of differance in its new spelling. It is literally neither a word nor a concept, as we shall see. I insist on the word "assemblage" here for two reasons: on the one hand, it is not a matter of describing a history, of recounting the steps, text by text, context by context, each time showing which scheme has been able to impose this graphic disorder, although this could have been done as well; rather, we are concerned with the *general system of all these schemata.* On the other hand, the word "assemblage" seems more apt for suggesting that the kind of bringing-together proposed here has the structure of an interlacing, a weaving, or a web, which would allow the different threads and different lines of sense or force to separate again, as well as being ready to bind others together.

In a quite preliminary way, we now recall that this particular graphic intervention was conceived in the writing-up of a question about writing; it was not made simply to shock the reader or grammarian. Now, in point of fact, it happens that this graphic difference (the *a* instead of the *e*), this marked difference between two apparently vocalic notations, between vowels, remains purely graphic: it is written or read, but it is not heard. It cannot be heard, and we shall see in what respects it is also beyond the order of understanding. It is put forward by a silent mark, by a tacit monument, or, one might even say, by a pyramid—keeping in mind not only the capital form of the printed letter but also that passage from Hegel's *Encyclopaedia* where he compares the body of the sign to an Egyptian pyramid. The *a* of differance, therefore, is not heard; it remains silent, secret, and discreet, like a tomb.[3]

It is a tomb that (provided one knows how to decipher its legend) is not far from signaling the death of the king.

It is a tomb that cannot even be made to resonate. For I cannot even let you know, by my talk, now being spoken before the Société Française de Philosophie, which difference I am talking about at the very moment I speak of it. I can only talk about this graphic difference by keeping to a very indirect speech about writing, and on the condition that I specify each time that I am referring to difference with an *e* or differance with an *a*. All of which is not going to simplify matters today, and will give us all a great deal of trouble when we want to understand one another. In any event, when I do specify which difference I mean—when I say "with an *e*" or "with an *a*"—this will refer irreducibly to a *written text,* a text governing my talk, a text that I keep in front of me, that I will read, and toward which I shall have to try to lead your hands and eyes. We cannot refrain here from going by way of a written text, from ordering ourselves by the disorder that is produced therein—and this is what matters to me first of all.

Doubtless this pyramidal silence of the graphic difference between the *e* and the *a* can function only within the system of phonetic writing and within a language or grammar historically tied to phonetic writing and to the whole culture which is inseparable from it. But I will say that it is just this—this silence that functions only within what is called phonetic writing—that points out or reminds us in a very opportune way that, contrary to an enormous prejudice, there is no phonetic writing. There is only purely and strictly phonetic writing. What is called phonetic writing can only function—in principle and *de jure,* and not due to some factual and technical inadequacy—by incorporating nonphonetic "signs" (punctuation, spacing, etc.); but when we examine their structure and necessity, we will quickly see that they are ill described by the concept of signs. Saussure had only to remind us that the play of difference was the functional condition, the condition of possibility, for every sign; and it is itself silent. The difference between two phonemes, which enables them to exist and to operate, is inaudible. The inaudible opens the two present phonemes to hearing, as they present themselves. If, then, there is no purely phonetic writing, it is because there is no purely phonetic phone. The difference that brings out phonemes and lets them be heard and understood [*entendre*] itself remains inaudible.

It will perhaps be objected that, for the same reasons, the graphic difference itself sinks into darkness, that it never constitutes the fullness of a sensible term, but draws out an invisible connection, the mark of an inapparent relation between two spectacles. That is no doubt true. Indeed, since from this point of view the difference between the *e* and the *a* marked in "differance" eludes vision and hearing, this happily suggests that we must here let ourselves be referred to an order that no longer refers to sensibility. But we are not referred to intelligibility either, to an ideality not fortuitously associated with the objectivity of *theōrein* or understanding. We must be referred to an order, then, that resists philosophy's founding opposition between the sensible and the intelligible. The order that resists this opposition, that resists it because it sustains it, is designated in a movement of differance (with an *a*) between two differences or between two letters. This differance belongs neither to the voice nor to writing in the ordinary sense, and it takes place, like the strange space that will assemble us here for the course of an hour, *between* speech and writing and beyond the tranquil familiarity that binds us to one and to the other, reassuring us sometimes in the illusion that they are two separate things.

Now, how am I to speak of the *a* of differance? It is clear that it cannot be *exposed.* We can expose only what, at a certain moment, can become *present,* manifest; what can be shown, presented as a present, a being-present in its truth, the truth of a present or the presence of a present. However, if differance ⌐is⌐ (I also cross out the "is") what makes the presentation of being-present possible, it never presents itself as such. It is never given in the present or to anyone. Holding back and not exposing itself, it goes beyond the order of truth on this specific point and in this determined way, yet is not itself concealed, as if it were something, a mysterious being, in the occult zone of the nonknowing. Any exposition would expose it to disappearing as a disappearance. It would risk appearing, thus disappearing.

Thus, the detours, phrases, and syntax that I shall often have to resort to will resemble—will sometimes be practically indiscernible from—those of negative theology. Already we had to note *that* differance *is not,* does not exist, and is not any sort of being-present (*on*). And we will have to point out everything *that* it *is not,* and, consequently, that it has neither existence nor essence. It belongs to no category of being, present or absent. And yet what is thus denoted as differance is not theological, not even in the most negative order of negative theology. The latter, as we know, is always occupied with letting a supraessential reality go beyond the finite categories of essence and existence, that is, of presence, and always hastens to remind us that, if we deny the predicate of existence to God, it is in order to recognize him as a superior, inconceivable, and ineffable mode of being. Here there is no question of such a move, as will be confirmed as we go along. Not only is differance irreducible to every ontological or theological—onto-theological—reappropriation, but it opens up the very space in which onto-theology—philosophy—produces its system and its history. It thus encompasses and irrevocably surpasses onto-theology or philosophy.

For the same reason, I do not know where to *begin* to mark out this assemblage, this graph, of differance. Precisely what is in question here is the requirement that there be a *de jure* commencement, an absolute point of departure, a responsibility arising from a principle. The problem of writing opens by questioning the *archē.* Thus what I put forth here will not be developed simply as a philosophical discourse that operates on the basis of a principle, of postulates, axioms, and definitions and that moves according to the discursive line of a rational order. In marking out differance, everything is a matter of strategy and risk. It is a question of strategy because no transcendent truth present outside the sphere of writing can theologically command the totality of this field. It is hazardous because this strategy is not simply one in the sense that we say that strategy orients the tactics according to a final aim, a *telos* or the theme of a domination, a mastery or an ultimate reappropriation of movement and field. In the end, it is a strategy without finality. We might call it blind tactics or empirical errance, if the value of empiricism did not itself derive all its meaning from its opposition to philosophical responsibility. If there is a certain errance in the tracing-out of differance, it no longer follows the line of logico-philosophical speech or that of its integral and symmetrical opposite, logico-empirical speech. The concept of *play* [*jeu*] remains beyond this opposition; on the eve and aftermath of philosophy, it designates the unity of chance and necessity in an endless calculus.

By decision and, as it were, by the rules of the game, then, turning this thought around, let us introduce ourselves to the thought of differance by way of the theme of strategy or stratagem. By this merely strategic justification, I want to emphasize that the efficacy of this thematics of differance very well may, and even one day must, be sublated, i.e., lend itself, if not to its own replacement, at least to its involvement in a series of events which in fact it never commanded. This also means that it is not a theological thematics.

I will say, first of all, that differance, which is neither a word nor a concept, seemed to me to be strategically the theme most proper to think out, if not master (thought being here, perhaps, held in a certain necessary relation with the structional limits of mastery), in what is most characteristic of our "epoch." I start off, then, strategically, from the place and time in which "we" are, even though my opening is not justifiable in the final account, and though it is always on the basis of differance and its "history" that we can claim to know who and where "we" are and what the limits of an "epoch" can be.

Although "differance" is neither a word nor a concept, let us nonetheless attempt a simple and approximative semantic analysis which will bring us in view of what is at stake [en vue de l'enjeu].

We do know that the verb "to differ" [différer] (the Latin verb differre) has two seemingly quite distinct meanings; in the Littré dictionary, for example, they are the subject of two separate articles. In this sense, the Latin differre is not the simple translation of the Greek diapherein; this fact will not be without consequence for us in tying our discussion to a particular language, one that passes for being less philosophical, less primordially philosophical, than the other. For the distribution of sense in the Greek diapherein does not carry one of the two themes of the Latin differre, namely, the action of postponing until later, of taking into account, the taking-account of time and forces in an operation that implies an economic reckoning, a detour, a respite, a delay, a reserve, a representation—all the concepts that I will sum up here in a word I have never used but which could be added to this series: temporalizing. "To differ" in this sense is to temporalize, to resort, consciously or unconsciously, to the temporal and temporalizing mediation of a detour that suspends the accomplishment or fulfillment of "desire" or "will," or carries desire or will out in a way that annuls or tempers their effect. We shall see, later, in what respects this temporalizing is also a temporalization and spacing, is space's becoming-temporal and time's becoming-spatial, is "primordial constitution" of space and time, as metaphysics or transcendental phenomenology would call it in the language that is here criticized and displaced.

The other sense of "to differ" [différer] is the most common and most identifiable, the sense of not being identical, of being other, of being discernible, etc. And in "differents," whether referring to the alterity of dissimilarity or the alterity of allergy or of polemics, it is necessary that interval, distance, spacing occur among the different elements and occur actively, dynamically, and with a certain perseverence in repetition.

But the word "difference" (with an e) could never refer to differing as temporalizing or to difference as polemos. It is this loss of sense that the word differance (with an a) will have to schematically compensate for. Differance can refer to the whole complex of its meanings at once, for it is immediately and irreducibly multivalent, something which will be important for the discourse I am trying to develop. It refers to this whole complex of meanings not only when it is supported by a language or interpretive context (like any signification), but it already does so somehow of itself. Or at least it does so more easily by itself than does any other word: here the *a* comes more immediately from the present particle [*différant*] and brings us closer to the action of "differing" that is in progress, even before it has produced the effect that is constituted as different or resulted in difference (with an *e*). Within a conceptual system and in terms of classical requirements, differance could be said to designate the productive and primordial constituting causality, the process of scission and division whose differings and differences would be the constituted products or effects. But while bringing us closer to the infinitive and active core of differing, "differance" with an *a* neutralizes what the infinitive denotes as simply active, in the same way that "parlance" does not signify the simple fact of speaking, of speaking to or being spoken to. Nor is resonance the act of resonating. Here in the usage of our language we must consider that the ending *-ance* is undecided between active and passive. And we shall see why what is designated by "differance" is neither simply active nor simply passive, that it announces or rather recalls something like the middle voice, that it speaks of an operation which is not an operation, which cannot be thought of either as a passion or as an action of a subject upon an object, as starting from an agent or from a patient, or on the basis of, or in view of, any of these *terms*. But philosophy has perhaps commenced by distributing the middle voice, expressing a certain intransitiveness, into the active and the passive voice, and has itself been constituted in this repression.

How are differance as temporalizing and differance as spacing conjoined?

Let us begin with the problem of signs and writing—since we are already in the midst of it. We ordinarily say that a sign is put in place of the thing itself, the present thing—"thing" holding here for the sense as well as the referent. Signs represent the present in its absence; they take the place of the present. When we cannot take hold of or show the thing, let us say the present, the being-present, when the present does not present itself, then we signify, we go through the detour of signs. We take up or give signs; we make signs. The sign would thus be a deferred presence. Whether it is a question of verbal or written signs, monetary signs, electoral delegates, or political representatives, the movement of signs defers the moment of encountering the thing itself, the moment at which we could lay hold of it, consume or expend it, touch it, see it, have a present intuition of it. What I am describing here is the structure of signs as classically determined, in order to define—a commonplace characterization of its traits—signification as the differance of temporalizing. Now this classical determination presupposes that the sign (which defers presence) is conceivable only *on the basis of* the presence that it defers and *in view of* the deferred presence one intends to reappropriate. Following this classical semiology, the substitution of the sign for the thing itself is both *secondary* and *provisional:* it is second in order after an original and lost presence, a presence from which the sign would be derived. It is provisional with respect to this final and missing presence, in view of which the sign would serve as a movement of mediation.

In attempting to examine these secondary and provisional aspects of the substitute, we shall no doubt catch sight of something like a primordial differance. Yet we could no longer even call it primordial or final, inasmuch as the characteristics of origin, beginning, *telos, eschaton,* etc., have always denoted presence—*ousia, parousia,* etc. To question the secondary and provisional character of the sign, to oppose it to a "primordial" differance, would thus have the following consequences:

1. Differance can no longer be understood according to the concept of "sign," which has always been taken to mean the representation of a presence and has been constituted in a system (of thought or language) determined on the basis of and in view of presence.

2. In this way we question the authority of presence or its simple symmetrical contrary, absence or lack. We thus interrogate the limit that has always constrained us, that always constrains us—we who inhabit a language and a system of thought—to form the sense of being in general as presence or absence, in the categories of being or beingness (*ousia*). It already appears that the kind of questioning we are thus led back to is, let us say, the Heideggerian kind, and that differance *seems* to lead us back to the ontic-ontological difference. But permit me to postpone this reference. I shall only note that between differance as temporalizing-temporalization (which we can no longer conceive within the horizon of the present) and what Heidegger says about temporalization in *Sein und Zeit* (namely, that as the transcendental horizon of the question of being it must be freed from the traditional and metaphysical domination by the present or the now)—between these two there is a close, if not exhaustive and irreducibly necessary, interconnection.

But first of all, let us remain with the semiological aspects of the problem to see how differance as temporalizing is conjoined with differance as spacing. Most of the semiological or linguistic research currently dominating the field of thought (whether due to the results of its own investigations or due to its role as a generally recognized regulative model) traces its genealogy, rightly or wrongly, to Saussure as its common founder. It was Saussure who first of all set forth the *arbitrariness of signs* and the *differential character of signs* as principles of general semiology and particularly of linguistics. And, as we know, these two themes—the arbitrary and the differential—are in his view inseparable. Arbitrariness can occur only because the system of signs is constituted by the differences between the terms, and not by their fullness. The elements of signification function not by virtue of the compact force of their cores but by the network of oppositions that distinguish them and relate them to one another. "Arbitrary and differential" says Saussure "are two correlative qualities."

As the condition for signification, this principle of difference affects the *whole sign,* that is, both the signified and the signifying aspects. The signified aspect is the concept, the ideal sense. The signifying aspect is what Saussure calls the material or physical (e.g., acoustical) "image." We do not here have to enter into all the problems these definitions pose. Let us only cite Saussure where it interests us:

> The conceptual side of value is made up solely of relations and differences with respect to the other terms of language, and the same can be said of its material side.... Everything that has been said up to this point boils down to this: in language there are only differences. Even more important: a difference generally implies positive terms between which the difference is set up; but in language there are only differences *without positive terms.* Whether we take the signified or the signifier, language has neither ideas nor sounds that existed before the linguistic system, but only conceptual and phonic differences that have issued from the system. The idea of phonic substance that a sign contains is of less importance than the other signs that surround it.[4]

The first consequence to be drawn from this is that the signified concept is never present in itself, in an adequate presence that would refer only to itself. Every concept is necessarily and essentially inscribed in a chain or a system, within which it refers to another and to other concepts, by the systematic play of differences. Such a play, then—differance—is no longer simply a concept, but the possibility of conceptuality, of the conceptual system and process in general. For the same reason, differance, which is not a concept, is not a mere word; that is, it is not what we represent to ourselves as the calm and present self-referential unity of a concept and sound [*phonie*]. We shall later discuss the consequences of this for the notion of a word.

The difference that Saussure speaks about, therefore, is neither itself a concept nor one word among others. We can say this *a fortiori* for differance. Thus we are brought to make the relation between the one and the other explicit.

Within a language, within the *system* of language, there are only differences. A taxonomic operation can accordingly undertake its systematic, statistical, and classificatory inventory. But, on the one hand, these differences *play a role* in language, in speech as well, and in the exchange between language and speech. On the other hand, these differences are themselves *effects.* They have not fallen from the sky ready made; they are no more inscribed in a *topos noētos* than they are prescribed in the wax of the brain. If the word "history" did not carry with it the theme of a final repression of differance, we could say that differences alone could be "historical" through and through and from the start.

What we note as *differance* will thus be the movement of play that "produces" (and not by something that is simply an activity) these differences, these effects of difference. This does not mean that the differance which produces differences is before them in a simple and in itself unmodified and indifferent present. Differance is the nonfull, nonsimple "origin"; it is the structured and differing origin of differences.

Since language (which Saussure says is a classification) has not fallen from the sky, it is clear that the differences have been produced; they are the effects produced, but effects that do not have as their cause a subject or substance, a thing in general, or a being that is somewhere present and itself escapes the play of difference. If such a presence were implied (quite classically) in the general concept of cause, we would therefore have to talk about an effect without a cause, something that would very quickly lead to no longer talking about effects. I have tried to indicate a way out of the closure imposed by this system, namely, by means of the "trace." No more an effect than a cause, the "trace" cannot of itself, taken outside its context, suffice to bring about the required transgression.

As there is no presence before the semiological difference or outside it, we can extend what Saussure writes about language in signs in general: "Language is necessary in order for speech to be intelligible and to produce all of its effects; but the latter is necessary in order for language to be established; historically, the fact of speech always comes first."[5]

Retaining at least the schema, if not the content, of the demand formulated by Saussure, we shall designate by the term *differance* the movement by which language, or any code, any system of reference in general, becomes "historically" constituted as a fabric of differences. Here, the terms "constituted," "produced," "created," "movement," "historically," etc., with all they imply, are not to be understood only in terms of the language of metaphysics, from which they are taken. It would have to be shown why the concepts of production, like those of constitution and history, remain accessories in this respect to what is here being questioned; this, however, would draw us too far away today, toward the theory of the representation of the "circle" in which we seem to be enclosed. I only use these terms here, like many other concepts, out of strategic convenience and in order to prepare the deconstruction of the system they form at the point which is now most decisive. In any event, we will have understood, by virtue of the very circle we appear to be caught up in, that differance, as it is written here, is no more static than genetic, no more structural than historical. Nor is it any less so. And it is completely to miss the point of this orthographical impropriety to want to object to it on the basis of the oldest of metaphysical oppositions—for example, by opposing some generative point of view to a structuralist-taxonomic point of view, or conversely. These oppositions do not pertain in the least to difference; and this, no doubt, is what makes thinking about it difficult and uncomfortable.

If we now consider the chain to which "differance" gets subjected, according to the context, to a certain number of nonsynonymic substitutions, one will ask why we resorted to such concepts as "reserve," "protowriting," "proto-trace," "spacing," indeed to "supplement" or "*pharmakon,*" and, before long, to "hymen," etc.[6]

Let us begin again. Differance is what makes the movement of signification possible only if each element that is said to be "present," appearing on the stage of presence, is related to something other than itself but retains the mark of a past element and already lets itself be hollowed out by the mark of its relation to a future element. This trace relates no less to what is called the future than to what is called the past, and it constitutes what is called the present by this very relation to what it is not, to what it absolutely is not; that is, not even to a past or future considered as a modified present. In order for it to be, an interval must separate it from what it is not; but the interval that constitutes it in the present must also, and by the same token, divide the present in itself, thus dividing, along with the present, everything that can be conceived on its basis, that is, every being—in particular, for our metaphysical language, the substance or sub-ject. Constituting itself, dynamically dividing itself, this interval is what could be called *spacing*; time's becoming-spatial or space's becoming-temporal (*temporalizing*). And it is this constitution of the present as a "primordial" and irre-ducibly nonsimple, and, therefore, in the strict sense nonprimordial, synthesis of traces, retentions, and protentions (to reproduce here, analogically and pro-visionally, a phenomenological and transcendental language that will presently be revealed as inadequate) that I propose to call protowriting, prototrace, or differance. The letter (is) (both) spacing (and) temporalizing.[7]

Given this (active) movement of the (production of) differance without ori-gin, could we not, quite simply and without any neographism, call it *differenti-ation?* Among other confusions, such a word would suggest some organic unity, some primordial and homogeneous unity, that would eventually come to be di-vided up and take on difference as an event. Above all, formed on the verb "to differentiate," this word would annul the economic signification of detour, tem-poralizing delay, "deferring." I owe a remark in passing to a recent reading of one of Koyré's texts entitled "Hegel at Jena."[8] In that text, Koyré cites long pas-sages from the Jena *Logic* in German and gives his own translation. On two oc-casions in Hegel's text he encounters the expression *"differente Beziehung."* This word (*different*), whose root is Latin, is extremely rare in German and also, I believe, in Hegel, who instead uses *verschieden* or *ungleich,* calling differ-ence *Unterschied* and qualitative variety *Verschiedenheit.* In the Jena *Logic,* he uses the word *different* precisely at the point where he deals with time and the present. Before coming to Koyré's valuable remark, here are some passages from Hegel, as rendered by Koyré:

The infinite, in this simplicity is—as a moment opposed to the self-identical—the negative. In its moments, while the infinite presents the totality to (itself) and in itself, (it is) excluding in general, the point or limit; but in this, its own (action of) negating, it relates itself immediately to the other and negates itself. The limit or moment of the present (*der Gegen-wart*), the absolute "this" of time or the now, is an absolutely negative simplicity, absolutely excluding all multiplicity from itself, and by this very fact is absolutely determined; it is not an extended whole or *quantum* within itself (and) which would in itself also have an undetermined aspect or qualitative variety, which of itself would be related, indifferently (*gleichgültig*) or externally to another, but on the contrary, this is an absolutely different relation of the simple.[9]

And Koyré specifies in a striking note: "Different relation: *differente Beziehung*. We could say: differentiating relation." And on the following page, from another text of Hegel, we can read: "*Diese Beziehung ist Gegenwart, als eine differente Beziehung*" (This relation is [the] present, as a different relation). There is another note by Koyré: "The term '*different*' is taken here in an active sense."

Writing "differing" or "differance" (with an *a*) would have had the utility of making it possible to translate Hegel on precisely this point with no further qualifications—and it is a quite decisive point in his text. The translation would be, as it always should be, the transformation of one language by another. Naturally, I maintain that the word "differance" can be used in other ways, too; first of all, because it denotes not only the activity of primordial difference but also the temporalizing detour of deferring. It has, however, an even more important usage. Despite the very profound affinities that differance thus written has with Hegelian speech (as it should be read), it can, at a certain point, not exactly break with it, but rather work a sort of displacement with regard to it. A definite rupture with Hegelian language would make no sense, nor would it be at all likely; but this displacement is both infinitesimal and radical. I have tried to indicate the extent of this displacement elsewhere; it would be difficult to talk about it with any brevity at this point.

Differences are thus "produced"—differed—by differance. But *what* differs, or *who* differs? In other words, *what* is differance? With this question we attain another stage and another source of the problem.

What differs? Who differs? What is differance?

If we answered these questions even before examining them as questions, even before going back over them and questioning their form (even what seems to be most natural and necessary about them), we would fall below the level we have now reached. For if we accepted the form of the question in its own sense and syntax ("What?," "What is?," "Who is?"), we would have to admit that differance is derived, supervenient, controlled, and ordered from the starting point of a being-present, one capable of being something, a force, a state, or power in the world, to which we could give all kinds of names: a *what,* or being-present as a *subject,* a *who.* In the latter case, notably, we would implicitly admit that the being-present (for example, as a self-present being or consciousness) would eventually result in differing: in delaying or in diverting the fulfillment of a "need" or "desire," or in differing from itself. But in none of these cases would such a being-present be "constituted" by this differance.

Now if we once again refer to the semiological difference, what was it that Saussure in particular reminded us of? That "language [which consists only of differences] is not a function of the speaking subject." This implies that the subject (self-identical or even conscious of self-identity, self-conscious) is inscribed in the language, that he is a "function" of the language. He becomes a *speaking* subject only by conforming his speech—even in the aforesaid "creation," even in the aforesaid "transgression"—to the system of linguistic prescriptions taken as the system of differences, or at least to the general law of differance, by conforming to that law of language which Saussure calls "language without speech." "Language is necessary for the spoken word to be intelligible and so that it can produce all of its effects."[10]

If, by hypothesis, we maintain the strict opposition between speech and language, then differance will be not only the play of differences within the language but the relation of speech to language, the detour by which I must also pass in order to speak, the silent token I must give, which holds just as well for linguistics in the strict sense as it does for general semiology; it dictates all the relations between usage and the formal schema, between the message and the particular code, etc. Elsewhere I have tried to suggest that this differance within language, and in the relation between speech and language, forbids the essential dissociation between speech and writing that Saussure, in keeping with tradition, wanted to draw at another level of his presentation. The use of language or the employment of any code which implies a play of forms—with no determined or invariable substratum—also presupposes a retention and protention of differences, a spacing and temporalizing, a play of traces. This play must be a sort of inscription prior to writing, a protowriting without a present origin, without an *archē*. From this comes the systematic crossing-out of the *archē* and the transformation of general semiology into a grammatology, the latter performing a critical work upon everything within semiology—right down to its matrical concept of signs—that retains any metaphysical presuppositions incompatible with the theme of differance.

We might be tempted by an objection: to be sure, the subject becomes a *speaking* subject only by dealing with the system of linguistic differences; or again, he becomes a *signifying* subject (generally by speech or other signs) only by entering into the system of differences. In this sense, certainly, the speaking or signifying subject would not be self-present, insofar as he speaks or signifies, except for the play of linguistic or semiological differance. But can we not conceive of a presence and self-presence of the subject before speech or its signs, a subject's self-presence in a silent and intuitive consciousness?

Such a question therefore supposes that prior to signs and outside them, and excluding every trace and differance, something such as consciousness is possible. It supposes, moreover, that, even before the distribution of its signs in space and in the world, consciousness can gather itself up in its own presence. What then is consciousness? What does "consciousness" mean? Most often in the very form of "meaning" ["*vouloir-dire*"], consciousness in all its modifications is conceivable only as self-presence, a self-perception of presence. And what holds for consciousness also holds here for what is called subjective existence in general. Just as the category of subject is not and never has been conceivable without reference to presence as *hypokeimenon* or *ousia,* etc., so the subject as consciousness has never been able to be evinced otherwise than as self-presence. The privilege accorded to consciousness thus means a privilege accorded to the present; and even if the transcendental temporality of consciousness is described in depth, as Husserl described it, the power of synthesis and of the incessant gathering-up of traces is always accorded to the "living present."

This privilege is the ether of metaphysics, the very element of our thought insofar as it is caught up in the language of metaphysics. We can only de-limit such a closure today by evoking this import of presence, which Heidegger has shown to be the onto-theological determination of being. Therefore, in evoking this import of presence, by an examination which would have to be of a quite peculiar nature, we question the absolute privilege of this form or epoch of presence in general, that is, consciousness as meaning [*vouloir-dire*] in self-presence.

We thus come to posit presence—and, in particular, consciousness, the being-next-to-itself of consciousness—no longer as the absolutely matrical form of being but as a "determination" and an "effect." Presence is a determination and effect within a system which is no longer that of presence but that of differance; it no more allows the opposition between activity and passivity than that between cause and effect or in-determination and determination, etc. This system is of such a kind that even to designate consciousness as an effect or determination—for strategic reasons, reasons that can be more or less clearly considered and systematically ascertained—is to continue to operate according to the vocabulary of that very thing to be de-limited.

Before being so radically and expressly Heideggerian, this was also Nietzsche's and Freud's move, both of whom, as we know, and often in a very similar way, questioned the self-assured certitude of consciousness. And is it not remarkable that both of them did this by starting out with the theme of differance?

This theme appears almost literally in their work, at the most crucial places. I shall not expand on this here; I shall only recall that for Nietzsche "the important main activity is unconscious" and that consciousness is the effect of forces whose essence, ways, and modalities are not peculiar to it. Now force itself is never present; it is only a play of differences and quantities. There would be no force in general without the difference between forces; and here the difference in quantity counts more than the content of quantity, more than the absolute magnitude itself.

Quantity itself therefore is not separable from the difference in quantity. The difference in quantity is the essence of force, the relation of force with force. To fancy two equal forces, even if we grant them opposing directions, is an approximate and crude illusion, a statistical dream in which life is immersed, but which chemistry dispels.[11]

Is not the whole thought of Nietzsche a critique of philosophy as active indifference to difference, as a system of reduction or adiaphoristic repression? Following the same logic—logic itself—this does not exclude the fact that philosophy lives *in* and *from* differance, that it thereby blinds itself to the *same*, which is not the identical. The same is precisely differance (with an *a*), as the diverted and equivocal passage from one difference to another, from one term of the opposition to the other. We could thus take up all the coupled oppositions on which philosophy is constructed, and from which our language lives, not in order to see opposition vanish but to see the emergence of a necessity such that one of the terms appears as the differance of the other, the other as "differed" within the systematic ordering of the same (e.g., the intelligible as differing from the sensible, as sensible differed; the concept as differed-differing intuition, life as differing-differed matter; mind as differed-differing life; culture as differed-differing nature; and all the terms designating what is other than *physis*— *technē, nomos,* society, freedom, history, spirit, etc.—as *physis* differed or *physis* differing: *physis in differance*). It is out of the unfolding of this "same" as differance that the sameness of difference and of repetition is presented in the eternal return.

In Nietzsche, these are so many themes that can be related with the kind of symptomatology that always serves to diagnose the evasions and ruses of anything disguised in its differance. Or again, these terms can be related with the entire thematics of active interpretation, which substitutes an incessant deciphering for the disclosure of truth as a presentation of the thing itself in its presence, etc. What results is a cipher without truth, or at least a system of ciphers that is not dominated by truth value, which only then becomes a function that is understood, inscribed, and circumscribed.

We shall therefore call differance this "active" (in movement) discord of the different forces and of the differences between forces which Nietzsche opposes to the entire system of metaphysical grammar, wherever that system controls culture, philosophy, and science.

It is historically significant that this diaphoristics, understood as an energetics or an economy of forces, set up to question the primacy of presence qua consciousness, is also the major theme of Freud's thought; in his work we find another diaphoristics, both in the form of a theory of ciphers or traces and an energetics. The questioning of the authority of consciousness is first and always differential.

The two apparently different meanings of differance are tied together in Freudian theory: differing [*le différer*] as discernibility, distinction, deviation, diastem, *spacing;* and deferring [*le différer*] as detour, delay, relay, reserve, *temporalizing.* I shall recall only that:

1. The concept of trace (*Spur*), of facilitation (*Bahnung*), of forces of facilitation are, as early as the composition of the *Entwurf,* inseparable from the concept of difference. The origin of memory and of the psyche as a memory in general (conscious or unconscious) can only be described by taking into account the difference between the facilitation thresholds, as Freud says explicitly. There is no facilitation [*Bahnung*] without difference and no difference without a trace.

2. All the differences involved in the production of unconscious traces and in the process of inscription (*Niederschrift*) can also be interpreted as moments of differance, in the sense of "placing on reserve." Following a schema that continually guides Freud's thinking, the movement of the trace is described as an effort of life to protect itself *by deferring* the dangerous investment, by constituting a reserve (*Vorrat*). And all the conceptual oppositions that furrow Freudian thought relate each concept to the other like movements of a detour, within the economy of differance. The one is only the other deferred, the one differing from the other. The one is the other in differance, the one is the differance from the other. Every apparently rigorous and irreducible opposition (for example, that between the secondary and primary) is thus said to be, at one time or another, a "theoretical fiction." In this way again, for example (but such an example covers everything or communicates with everything), the difference between the pleasure principle and the reality principle is only differance as detour (*Aufschieben, Aufschub*). In *Beyond the Pleasure Principle,* Freud writes:

> Under the influence of the ego's instincts of self-preservation, the pleasure principle is replaced by the reality principle. This latter principle does not abandon the intention of ultimately obtaining pleasure, but it nevertheless demands and carries into effect the postponement of satisfaction, the abandonment of a number of possibilities of gaining satisfaction and the temporary toleration of unpleasure as a step on the long indirect road (*Aufschub*) to pleasure.[12]

Here we touch on the point of greatest obscurity, on the very enigma of differance, on how the concept we have of it is divided by a strange separation. We must not hasten to make a decision too quickly. How can we conceive of differance as a systematic detour which, within the element of the same, always aims at either finding again the pleasure or the presence that had been deferred by (conscious or unconscious) calculation, and, *at the same time,* how can we, on the other hand, conceive of differance as the relation to an impossible presence, as an expenditure without reserve, as an irreparable loss of presence, an irreversible wearing-down of energy, or indeed as a death instinct and a relation to the absolutely other that apparently breaks up any economy? It is evident—it is evidence itself—that system and nonsystem, the same and the absolutely other, etc., cannot be conceived *together.*

If differance is this inconceivable factor, must we not perhaps hasten to make it evident, to bring it into the philosophical element of evidence, and thus quickly dissipate its mirage character and illogicality, dissipate it with the infallibility of the calculus we know well—since we have recognized its place, necessity, and function within the structure of differance? What would be accounted for philosophically here has already been taken into account in the system of differance as it is here being calculated. I have tried elsewhere, in a reading of Bataille,[13] to indicate what might be the establishment of a rigorous, and in a new sense "scientific," *relating* of a "restricted economy"—one having nothing to do with an unreserved expenditure, with death, with being exposed to nonsense, etc.—to a "general economy" or system that, so to speak, *takes account of* what is unreserved. It is a relation between a differance that is accounted for and a differance that fails to be accounted for, where the establishment of a pure presence, without loss, is one with the occurrence of absolute loss, with death. By establishing this relation between a restricted and a general system, we shift and recommence the very project of philosophy under the privileged heading of Hegelianism.

The economic character of differance in no way implies that the deferred presence can always be recovered, that it simply amounts to an investment that only temporarily and without loss delays the presentation of presence, that is, the perception of gain or the gain of perception. Contrary to the metaphysical, dialectical, and "Hegelian" interpretation of the economic movement of differance, we must admit a game where whoever loses wins and where one wins and loses each time. If the diverted presentation continues to be somehow definitively and irreducibly withheld, this is not because a particular present remains hidden or absent, but because differance holds us in a relation with what exceeds (though we necessarily fail to recognize this) the alternative of presence or absence. A certain alterity—Freud gives it a metaphysical name, the unconscious—is definitively taken away from every process of presentation in which we would demand for it to be shown forth in person. In this context and under this heading, the unconscious is not, as we know, a hidden, virtual, and potential self-presence. It is differed—which no doubt means that it is woven out of differences, but also that it sends out, that it delegates, representatives or proxies; but there is no chance that the mandating subject "exists" somewhere, that it is present or is "itself," and still less chance that it will become conscious. In this sense, contrary to the terms of an old debate, strongly symptomatic of the metaphysical investments it has always assumed, the "unconscious" can no more be classed as a "thing" than as anything else; it is no more of a thing than an implicit or masked consciousness. This radical alterity, removed from every possible mode of presence, is characterized by irreducible aftereffects, by delayed effects. In order to describe them, in order to read the traces of the "unconscious" traces (there are no "conscious" traces), the language of presence or absence, the metaphysical speech of phenomenology, is in principle inadequate.

The structure of delay (*retardement: Nachträglichkeit*) that Freud talks about indeed prohibits our taking temporalization (temporalizing) to be a simple dialectical complication of the present; rather, this is the style of transcendental phenomenology. It describes the living present as a primordial and incessant synthesis that is constantly led back upon itself, back upon its assembled and assembling self, by retentional traces and protentional openings. With the alterity of the "unconscious" we have to deal not with the horizons of modified presents—past or future—but with a "past" that has never been nor will ever be present, whose "future" will never be produced or reproduced in the form of presence. The concept of trace is therefore incommensurate with that of retention, that of the becoming-past of what had been present. The trace cannot be conceived—nor, therefore, can differance—on the basis of either the present or the presence of the present.

A past that has never been present: with this formula Emmanuel Levinas designates (in ways that are, to be sure, not those of psychoanalysis) the trace and the enigma of absolute alterity, that is, the Other [*autrui*]. At least within these limits, and from this point of view, the thought of differance implies the whole critique of classical ontology undertaken by Levinas. And the concept of trace, like that of differance, forms—across these different traces and through these differences between traces, as understood by Nietzsche, Freud, and Levinas (these "authors' names" serve only as indications)—the network that sums up and permeates our "epoch" as the de-limitation of ontology (of presence).

The ontology of presence is the ontology of beings and beingness. Everywhere, the dominance of beings is solicited by differance—in the sense that *sollicitare* means, in old Latin, to shake all over, to make the whole tremble. What is questioned by the thought of differance, therefore, is the determination of being in presence, or in beingness. Such a question could not arise and be understood without the difference between Being and beings opening up somewhere. The first consequence of this is that differance is not. It is not a being-present, however excellent, unique, principal, or transcendent one makes it. It commands nothing, rules over nothing, and nowhere does it exercise any authority. It is not marked by a capital letter. Not only is there no realm of differance, but differance is even the subversion of every realm. This is obviously what makes it threatening and necessarily dreaded by everything in us that desires a realm, the past or future presence of a realm. And it is always in the name of a realm that, believing one sees it ascend to the capital letter, one can reproach it for wanting to rule.

Does this mean, then, that differance finds its place within the spread of the ontic-ontological difference, as it is conceived, as the "epoch" conceives itself within it, and particularly "across" the Heideggerian meditation, which cannot be gotten around?

There is no simple answer to such a question.

In one particular respect, differance is, to be sure, but the historical and epochal *deployment* of Being or of the ontological difference. The *a* of differance marks the *movement* of this deployment.

And yet, is not the thought that conceives the *sense* or *truth* of Being, the determination of differance, as ontic-ontological difference—difference conceived within the horizon of the question of *Being*—still an intrametaphysical effect of differance? Perhaps the deployment of differance is not only the truth or the epochality of Being. Perhaps we must try to think this *unheard-of* thought, this silent tracing, namely, that the history of Being (the thought of which is committed to the Greco-Western logos), as it is itself produced across the ontological difference, is only one epoch of the *diapherein*. Then we could no longer even call it an "epoch," for the concept of epochality belongs within history understood as the history of Being. Being has always made "sense," has always been conceived or spoken of as such, only by dissimulating itself in beings; thus, in a particular and very strange way, differance (is) "older" than the ontological difference or the truth of Being. In this age it can be called the play of traces. It is a trace that no longer belongs to the horizon of Being but one whose sense of Being is borne and bound by this play; it is a play of traces or differance that has no sense and is not, a play that does not belong. There is no support to be found and no depth to be had for this bottomless chessboard where being is set in play.

It is perhaps in this way that the Heraclitean play of the *hen diapheron heautōi*, of the one differing from itself, of what is in difference with itself, already becomes lost as a trace in determining the *diapherein* as ontological difference.

To think through the ontological difference doubtless remains a difficult task, a task whose statement has remained nearly inaudible. And to prepare ourselves for venturing beyond our own logos, that is, for a differance so violent that it refuses to be stopped and examined as the epochality of Being and ontological difference, is neither to give up this passage through the truth of Being, nor is it in any way to "criticize," "contest," or fail to recognize the incessant necessity for it. On the contrary, we must stay within the difficulty of this passage; we must repeat this passage in a rigorous reading of metaphysics, wherever metaphysics serves as the norm of Western speech, and not only in the texts of "the history of philosophy." Here we must allow the trace of whatever goes beyond the truth of Being to appear/disappear in its fully rigorous way. It is a trace of something that can never present itself; it is itself a trace that can never be presented, that is, can never appear and manifest itself as such in its phenomenon. It is a trace that lies beyond what profoundly ties fundamental ontology to phenomenology. Like differance, the trace is never presented as such. In presenting itself it becomes effaced; in being sounded it dies away, like the writing of the *a*, inscribing its pyramid in differance.

We can always reveal the precursive and secretive traces of this movement in metaphysical speech, especially in the contemporary talk about the closure of ontology, i.e., through the various attempts we have looked at (Nietzsche, Freud, Levinas)—and particularly in Heidegger's work.

The latter provokes us to question the essence of the present, the presence of the present.

What is the present? What is it to conceive the present in its presence?

Let us consider, for example, the 1946 text entitled "Der Spurch des Anaximander." Heidegger there recalls that the forgetting of Being forgets about the difference between Being and beings:

> But the point of Being (*die Sache des Seins*) is to be the Being *of* beings. The linguistic form of this enigmatic and multivalent genitive designates a genesis (*Genesis*), a provenance (*Herkunft*) of the present from presence (*des Anwesenden aus dem Anwesen*). But with the unfolding of these two, the essence (*Wesen*) of this provenance remains hidden (*verborgen*). Not only is the essence of this provenance not thought out, but neither is the simple relation between presence and present (*Anwesen und Anwesenden*). Since the dawn, it seems that presence and being-present are each separately something. Imperceptibly, presence becomes itself a present. . . . The essence of presence (*Das Wesen des Anwesens*), and thus the difference between presence and present, is forgotten. *The forgetting of Being is the forgetting of the difference between Being and beings.*[14]

In recalling the difference between Being and beings (the ontological difference) as the difference between presence and present, Heidegger puts forward a proposition, indeed, a group of propositions; it is not our intention here to idly or hastily "criticize" them but rather to convey them with all their provocative force.

Let us then proceed slowly. What Heidegger wants to point out is that the difference between Being and beings, forgotten by metaphysics, has disappeared without leaving a trace. The very trace of difference has sunk from sight. If we admit that difference (is) (itself) something other than presence and absence, if it *traces,* then we are dealing with the forgetting of the difference (between Being and beings), and we now have to talk about a disappearance of the trace's trace. This is certainly what this passage from "Der Spruch des Anaximander" seems to imply:

> The forgetting of Being is a part of the very essence of Being, and is concealed by it. The forgetting belongs so essentially to the destination of Being that the dawn of this destination begins precisely as an unconcealment of the present in its presence. This means: the history of Being begins by the forgetting of Being, in that Being retains its essence, its difference from beings. Difference is wanting; it remains forgotten. Only what is differentiated—the present and presence (*das Anwesende und das Anwesen*)—becomes uncovered, but not *insofar* as it is differentiated. On the contrary, the matinal trace (*die frühe Spur*) of difference effaces itself from the moment that presence appears as a being-present (*das Anwesen wie ein Anwesendes erscheint*) and finds its provenance in a supreme (being)-present (*in einem höchsten Anwesen-den*).[15]

The trace is not a presence but is rather the simulacrum of a presence that dislocates, displaces, and refers beyond itself. The trace has, properly speaking, no place, for effacement belongs to the very structure of the trace. Effacement must always be able to overtake the trace; otherwise it would not be a trace but an indestructible and monumental substance. In addition, and from the start, effacement constitutes it as a trace—effacement establishes the trace in a change of place and makes it disappear in its appearing, makes it issue forth from itself in its very position. The effacing of this early trace (*die frühe Spur*) of difference is therefore "the same" as its tracing within the text of metaphysics. This metaphysical text must have retained a mark of what it lost or put in reserve, set aside. In the language of metaphysics the paradox of such a structure is the inversion of the metaphysical concept which produces the following effect: the present becomes the sign of signs, the trace of traces. It is no longer what every reference refers to in the last instance; it becomes a function in a generalized referential structure. It is a trace, and a trace of the effacement of a trace.

In this way the metaphysical text is *understood;* it is still readable, and remains to be read. It proposes *both* the monument and the mirage of the trace, the trace as simultaneously traced and effaced, simultaneously alive and dead, alive as always to simulate even life in its preserved inscription; it is a pyramid.

Thus we think through, without contradiction, or at least without granting any pertinence to such contradiction, what is perceptible and imperceptible about the trace. The "matinal trace" of difference is lost in an irretrievable invisibility, and yet even its loss is covered, preserved, regarded, and retarded. This happens in a text, in the form of presence.

Having spoken about the effacement of the matinal trace, Heidegger can thus, in this contradiction without contradiction, consign or countersign the sealing of the trace. We read on a little further:

> The difference between Being and beings, however, can in turn be experienced as something forgotten only if it is already discovered with the presence of the present (*mit dem Anwesen des Anwesenden*) and if it is thus sealed in a trace (*so eine Spur geprägt hat*) that remains preserved (*gewahrt bleibt*) in the language which Being appropriates.[16]

Further on still, while meditating upon Anaximander's τὸ χρεών, translated as *Brauch* (sustaining use), Heidegger writes the following:

> Dispensing accord and deference (*Fug und Ruch verfügend*), our sustaining use frees the present (*das Anwesende*) in its sojourn and sets it free every time for its sojourn. But by the same token the present is equally seen to be exposed to the constant danger of hardening in the insistence (*in das blosse Beharren verhärtet*) out of its sojourning duration. In this way sustaining use (*Brauch*) remains itself and at the same time an abandonment (*Aushändigung:* handing-over) of presence (*des Anwesens*) *in den Un-fug,* to discord (disjointedness). Sustaining use joins together the dis- (*Der Brauch fügt das Un-*).[17]

And it is at the point where Heidegger determines *sustaining use* as *trace* that the question must be asked: can we, and how far can we, think of this trace and the *dis-* of difference as *Wesen des Seins*? Doesn't the *dis* of difference refer us beyond the history of Being, beyond our language as well, and beyond everything that can be named by it? Doesn't it call for—in the language of being—the necessarily violent transformation of this language by an entirely different language?

Let us be more precise here. In order to dislodge the "trace" from its cover (and whoever believes that one tracks down some *thing?*—one tracks down tracks), let us continue reading this passage:

> The translation of τὸ χρεών by "sustaining use" (*Brauch*) does not derive from cogitations of an etymologico-lexical nature. The choice of the word "sustaining use" derives from an antecedent *translation* (*Übersetzen*) of the thought that attempts to conceive difference in the deployment of Being (*im Wesen des Seins*) toward the historical beginning of the forgetting of Being. The word "sustaining use" is dictated to thought in the apprehension (*Erfahrung*) of the forgetting of Being. Tò χρεών properly names a trace (*Spur*) of what remains to be conceived in the word "sustaining use," a trace that quickly disappears (*alsbald verschwindet*) into the history of Being, in its world-historical unfolding as Western metaphysics.[18]

How do we conceive of the outside of a text? How, for example, do we conceive of what stands opposed to the text of Western metaphysics? To be sure, the "trace that quickly disappears into the history of Being, . . . as Western metaphysics," escapes all the determinations, all the names it might receive in the metaphysical text. The trace is sheltered and thus dissimulated in these names; it does not appear in the text as the trace "itself." But this is because the trace itself could never itself appear as such. Heidegger also says that difference can never appear *as such:* "Lichtung des Unterschiedes kann deshalb auch nicht bedeuten, dass der Unterschied als der Unterschied erscheint." There is no essence of difference; not only can it not allow itself to be taken up into the *as such* of its name or its appearing, but it threatens the authority of the *as such* in general, the thing's presence in its essence. That there is no essence of difference at this point also implies that there is neither Being nor truth to the play of writing, *insofar* as it involves difference.

For us, difference remains a metaphysical name; and all the names that it receives from our language are still, so far as they are names, metaphysical. This is particularly so when they speak of determining difference as the difference between presence and present. (*Anwesen/Anwesend*), but already and especially so when, in the most general way, they speak of determining difference as the difference between Being and beings.

"Older" than Being itself, our language has no name for such a differance. But we "already know" that if it is unnamable, this is not simply provisional; it is not because our language has still not found or received this *name,* or because we would have to look for it in another language, outside the finite system of our language. It is because there is no *name* for this, not even essence or Being—not even the name "differance," which is not a name, which is not a pure nominal unity, and continually breaks up in a chain of different substitutions.

"There is no name for this": we read this as a truism. What is unnamable here is not some ineffable being that cannot be approached by a name; like God, for example. What is unnamable is the play that brings about the nominal effects, the relatively unitary or atomic structures we call names, or chains of substitutions for names. In these, for example, the nominal effect of "differance" is itself involved, carried off, and reinscribed, just as the false beginning or end of a game is still part of the game, a function of the system.

What we do know, what we could know if it were simply a question of knowing, is that there never has been and never will be a unique word, a master name. This is why thinking about the letter *a* of differance is not the primary prescription, nor is it the prophetic announcement of some imminent and still unheard-of designation. There is nothing kerygmatic about this "word" so long as we can perceive its reduction to a lower-case letter.

There will be no unique name, not even the name of Being. It must be conceived without *nostalgia*; that is, it must be conceived outside the myth of the purely maternal or paternal language belonging to the lost fatherland of thought. On the contrary, we must *affirm* it—in the sense that Nietzsche brings affirmation into play—with a certain laughter and with a certain dance.

After this laughter and dance, after this affirmation that is foreign to any dialectic, the question arises as to the other side of nostalgia, which I call Heideggerian *hope*. I am not unaware that this term may be somewhat shocking. I venture it all the same, without excluding any of its implications, and shall relate it to what seems to me to be retained of metaphysics in "Der Spruch des Anaximander," namely, the quest for the proper word and the unique name. In talking about the "first word of Being" (*das frühe Wort des Seins: τὸ χρεών*), Heidegger writes,

> The relation to the pre*sent*, unfolding its order in the very essence of pre*sence*, is unique (*ist eine einzige*). It is pre-eminently incomparable to any other relation; it belongs to the uniqueness of Being itself (*Sie gehört zur Einzigkeit des Seins selbst*). Thus, in order to name what is deployed in Being (*das Wesende des Seins*), language will have to find a single word, the unique word (*ein einziges, das einzige Wort*). There we see how hazardous is every word of thought (every thoughtful word: *denkende Wort*) that addresses itself to Being (*das dem Sein zugesprochen wird*). What is hazarded here, however, is not something impossible, because Being speaks through every language; everywhere and always.[19]

Such is the question: the marriage between speech and Being in the unique word, in the finally proper name. Such is the question that enters into the affirmation put into play by differance. The question bears (upon) each of the words in this sentence: "Being / speaks / through every language; / everywhere and always /."

NOTES

1. [The reader should bear in mind that "differance," or difference with an *a*, incorporates two significations: "to differ" and "to defer."—Translator.]
2. [For the term "facilitation" (*frayage*) in Freud, cf. "Project for a Scientific Psychology I" in *The Complete Psychological Works of Sigmund Freud*, 24 vols. (New York and London: Macmillan, 1964), I, 300, note 4 by the translator, James Strachey: "The word 'facilitation' as a rendering of the German '*Bahnung*' seems to have been introduced by Sherrington a few years after the *Project* was written. The German word, however, was already in use." The sense that Derrida draws upon here is stronger in the French or German; that is, the opening-up or clearing-out of a pathway. In the context of the "Project for a Scientific Psychology I," facilitation denotes the conduction capability that results from a difference in resistance levels in the memory and perception circuits of the nervous system. Thus, lowering the resistance threshold of a contact barrier serves to "open up" a nerve pathway and "facilitates" the excitatory process for the circuit. Cf. also J. Derrida, *L'Ecriture et la différence*, Chap. VII, "Freud et la scène de l'écriture" (Paris: Seuil, 1967), esp. pp. 297–305.—Translator.]
3. [On "pyramid" and "tomb" see J. Derrida, "Le Puits et la pyramide" in *Hegel et la pensée moderne* (Paris: Presses Universitaires de France, 1970), esp. pp. 44–45.—Translator.]
4. Ferdinand de Saussure, *Cours de linguistique générale*, ed. C. Bally and A. Sechehaye (Paris: Payot, 1916); English translation by Wade Baskin, *Course in General Linguistics* (New York: Philosophical Library, 1959), pp. 117–18, 120.
5. *Course in General Linguistics*, p. 18.
6. [On "supplement" see above, *Speech and Phenomena*, Chap. 7, pp. 88–104. Cf. also Derrida, *De la grammatologie* (Paris: Editions de Minuit, 1967). On "*pharmakon*" see Derrida, "La Pharmacie de Platon," *Tel Quel*, No. 32 (Winter, 1967), pp. 17–59; No. 33 (Spring, 1968), pp. 4–48. On "hymen" see Derrida, "La Double séance," *Tel Quel*, No. 41 (Spring, 1970), pp. 3–43; No. 42 (Summer, 1970), pp. 3–45. "La Pharmacie de Platon" and "La Double séance" have been reprinted in a recent text of Derrida, *La Dissémination* (Paris: Editions du Seuil, 1972).—Translator.]
7. [Derrida often brackets or "crosses out" certain key terms taken from metaphysics and logic, and in doing this, he follows Heidegger's usage in *Zur Seinsfrage*. The terms in question no longer have their full meaning, they no longer have the status of a purely signified content of expression—no longer, that is, after the deconstruction of metaphysics. Generated out of the play of differance, they still retain a vestigial trace of sense, however, a trace that cannot simply be gotten around (*incontournable*). An extensive discussion of all this is to be found in *De la grammatologie*, pp. 31–40.—Translator.]
8. Alexandre Koyré, "Hegel à Iéna," *Revue d'histoire et de philosophie religieuse*, XIV (1934), 420–58; reprinted in Koyré, *Etudes d'histoire de la pensée philosophique* (Paris: Armand Colin, 1961), pp. 135–73.

9. Koyré, *Etudes d'histoire*, pp. 153–54. [The quotation from Hegel (my translation) comes from "Jenenser Logik, Metaphysik, und Naturphilosophie," *Sämtliche Werke* (Leipzig: F. Meiner, 1925), XVIII, 202. Koyré reproduces the original German text on pp. 153–54, note 2.—Translator.]

10. De Saussure, *Course in General Linguistics*, p. 37.

11. G. Deleuze, *Nietzsche et la philosophie* (Paris: Presses Universitaires de France, 1970), p. 49.

12. Freud, *Complete Psychological Works*, XVIII, 10.

13. Derrida, *L'Ecriture et la différence*, pp. 369–407.

14. Martin Heidegger, *Holzwege* (Frankfurt: V. Klostermann, 1957), pp. 335–36. [All translations of quotations from *Holzwege* are mine.—Translator.]

15. *Ibid.*, p. 336.

16. *Ibid.*

17. *Ibid.*, pp. 339–40.

18. *Ibid.*, p. 340.

19. *Ibid.*, pp. 337–38.

JÜRGEN HABERMAS

"MORALITY AND ETHICAL LIFE: DOES HEGEL'S CRITIQUE OF KANT APPLY TO DISCOURSE ETHICS?"

In recent years Karl-Otto Apel and I have begun to reformulate Kant's ethics by grounding moral norms in communication, a venture to which I refer as "discourse ethics."[1] In this paper I hope to accomplish two things: first, to sketch the basic idea of discourse ethics and then to examine Hegel's critique of Kantian moral philosophy. In part I, I will deal with two questions: What is discourse ethics? and What moral intuitions does discourse ethics conceptualize? I will address the complicated matter of how to justify discourse ethics only in passing.

In part II, I will turn to the question of whether Hegel's critique of Kantian ethics applies to discourse ethics as well. The criticisms Hegel leveled against Kant as a moral philosopher are many. From among them I will single out four which strike me as the most trenchant. These are as follows:

- Hegel's objection to the *formalism* of Kantian ethics. Since the moral principle of the categorical imperative requires that the moral agent abstract from the concrete content of duties and maxims, its application necessarily leads to tautological judgments.[2]

Reprinted with permission from Jürgen Habermas, *Moral Consciousness and Communicative Action*, tr. Christian Lenhardt and Shierry Weber Nicholsen, Cambridge, MA: MIT Press, pp. 195–211.

- Hegel's objection to the *abstract universalism* of Kantian ethics. Since the categorical imperative enjoins separating the universal from the particular, a judgment considered valid in terms of that principle necessarily remains external to individual cases and insensitive to the particular context of a problem in need of solution.[3]
- Hegel's attack on the *impotence of the mere ought*. Since the categorical imperative enjoins a strict separation of "is" from "ought," it necessarily fails to answer the question of how moral insight can be realized in practice.[4]
- Hegel's objection to the terrorism of *pure conviction* (*Gesinnung*). Since the categorical imperative severs the pure postulates of practical reason from the formative process of spirit and its concrete historical manifestations, it necessarily recommends to the advocates of the moral worldview a policy that aims at the actualization of reason and sanctions even immoral deeds if they serve higher ends.[5]

I

1. What Is Discourse Ethics?

First I want to comment briefly on the general nature of Kantian moral philosophy. It has all of the following attributes: it is deontological, cognitivist, formalist, and universalist. Wanting to limit himself strictly to the class of justifiable normative judgments, Kant was forced to choose a narrow concept of morality. Classical moral philosophies had dealt with *all* the issues of the "good life." Kant's deals only with problems of right or just action. To him, moral judgments serve to explain how conflicts of action can be settled on the basis of rationally motivated agreement. Broadly, they serve to justify actions in terms of valid norms and to justify the validity of norms in terms of principles worthy of recognition. In short, the basic phenomenon that moral philosophy must explain is the normative validity (*Sollgeltung*) of commands and norms of action. This is what is meant by saying that a moral philosophy is *deontological*. A deontological ethics conceives the rightness of norms and commands on analogy with the truth of an assertoric statement. It would be erroneous, though, to equate the moral "truth" of normative statements with the assertoric validity of propositional statements, a mistake made by intuitionism and value ethics. Kant does not make this mistake. He does not confuse theoretical with practical reason. As for myself, I hold the view that normative rightness must be regarded as a claim to validity that is analogous to a truth claim. This notion is captured by the term "*cognitivist* ethics." A cognitivist ethics must answer the question of how to justify normative statements. Although Kant opts for the grammatical form of an imperative ("Act only according to that maxim by which you can at the same time will that it should become a universal law"), his categorical imperative in fact plays the part of a principle of justification that discriminates between valid and invalid norms in terms of their universalizability: what every rational being must be able to will is justified in a moral sense. This is what one means when one speaks of an ethics as being *formalist*. Discourse ethics replaces the Kantian categorical imperative by a procedure of moral argumentation. Its principle postulates,

> Only those norms may claim to be valid that could meet with the consent of all affected in their role as participants in a practical discourse.[6]

While retaining the categorical imperative after a fashion, discourse ethics scales it down to a principle of universalization (U). In practical discourses (U) plays the part of a rule of argumentation:

> (U) For a norm to be valid, the consequences and side effects of its general observance for the satisfaction of each person's particular interests must be acceptable to all.

Finally, an ethics is termed *universalist* when it alleges that this (or a similar) moral principle, far from reflecting the intuitions of a particular culture or epoch, is valid universally. As long as the moral principle is not justified—and justifying it involves more than simply pointing to Kant's "fact of pure reason"—the ethnocentric fallacy looms large. I must prove that my moral principle is not just a reflection of the prejudices of adult, white, well-educated, Western males of today. This is the most difficult part of ethics, a part that I cannot expound in this paper. Briefly, the thesis that discourse ethics puts forth on this subject is that anyone who seriously undertakes to participate in argumentation implicitly accepts by that very undertaking general pragmatic presuppositions that have a normative content. The moral principle can then be derived from the content of these presuppositions of argumentation if one knows at least what it means to justify a norm of action.[7] These, then, are the deontological, cognitivist, formalist and universalist assumptions that all moral philosophies of the Kantian type have in common. Let me make one more remark concerning the procedure I call practical discourse.

The viewpoint from which moral questions can be judged *impartially* is called the moral point of view. Formalist ethical theories furnish a rule explaining how something is looked at from the moral point of view. John Rawls, for example, recommends an original position, where those concerned meet as rational and equal partners who decide upon a contract, not knowing their own or each other's actual social positions.[8] G.H. Mead for his part recommends a procedure that he calls ideal role taking. It requires that any morally judging subject put itself in the position of all who would be affected if a problematic plan of action were carried out or if a controversial norm were to take effect.[9] As a procedure, practical discourse is different from these two constructs, the Rawlsian and the Meadian. Argumentation insures that all concerned in principle take part, freely and equally, in a cooperative search for truth, where nothing coerces anyone except the force of the better argument. Practical discourse is an exacting form of argumentative decision making. Like Rawls's original position, it is a warrant of the rightness (or fairness) of any conceivable normative agreement that is reached under these conditions. Discourse can play this role because its idealized, partly counterfactual presuppositions are precisely those that participants in argumentation do in fact make. That is why I think it unnecessary to resort to Rawls's fictitious original position with its "veil of ignorance." Practical discourse can also be viewed as a communicative process *simultaneously* exhorting *all* participants to ideal role taking. Thus practical discourse transforms what Mead viewed as *individual, privately enacted* role taking into a *public* affair, practiced intersubjectively by all involved.[10]

2. What Moral Intuitions Does Discourse Ethics Conceptualize?

How can it be argued that the *procedural* explanation discourse ethics gives of the moral point of view—in other words, of the impartiality of moral judgment—constitutes an adequate account of moral intuitions, which are after all *substantive* in kind? This is an open question that needs to be addressed.

Moral intuitions are intuitions that instruct us on how best to behave in situations where it is in our power to counteract the extreme vulnerability of others by being thoughtful and considerate. In anthropological terms, morality is a safety device compensating for a vulnerability built into the sociocultural form of life. The basic facts are the following: Creatures that are individuated only through socialization are vulnerable and morally in need of considerateness. Linguistically and behaviorally competent subjects are constituted as individuals by growing into an intersubjectively shared lifeworld, and the lifeworld of a language community is reproduced in turn through the communicative actions of its members. This explains why the identity of the individual and that of the collective are interdependent; they form and maintain themselves together. Built into the consensus-oriented language use of social interaction is an inconspicuous necessity for participants to become more and more individuated. Conversely, everyday language is also the medium by which the intersubjectivity of a shared world is maintained.[11] Thus, the more differentiated the structures of the lifeworld become, the easier it is to discern the simultaneous growth of the autonomous individual subject and his dependence on interpersonal relationships and social ties. The more the subject becomes individuated, the more he becomes entangled in a densely woven fabric of mutual recognition, that is, of reciprocal exposedness and vulnerability. Unless the subject externalizes himself by participating in interpersonal relations through language, he is unable to form that inner center that is his personal identity. This explains the almost constitutional insecurity and chronic fragility of personal identity—an insecurity that is antecedent to cruder threats to the integrity of life and limb.

Moral philosophies of sympathy and compassion (Schopenhauer) have discovered that this profound vulnerability calls for some guarantee of mutual consideration.[12] This considerateness has the twofold objective of defending the integrity of the individual and of preserving the vital fabric of ties of mutual recognition through which individuals *reciprocally* stabilize their fragile identities. No one can maintain his identity by himself. Consider suicide, for example. Notwithstanding the Stoic view that held that this final, desperate act reflects the imperious self-determination of the lone individual, the responsibility for suicide can never be attributed to the individual alone. This seemingly loneliest of deeds actually enacts a fate for which others collectively must take some of the blame, the fate of ostracism from an intersubjectively shared lifeworld.

Since moralities are tailored to suit the fragility of human beings individuated through socialization, they must always solve *two* tasks at *once*. They must emphasize the inviolability of the individual by postulating equal respect for the dignity of each individual. But they must also protect the web of intersubjective relations of mutual recognition by which these individuals survive as members of a community. To these two complementary aspects correspond the principles of justice and solidarity respectively. The first postulates equal respect and equal rights for the individual, whereas the second postulates empathy and concern for the well-being of one's neighbor. Justice in the modern sense of the term refers to the subjective freedom of inalienable individuality. Solidarity refers to the well-being of associated members of a community who intersubjectively share the same lifeworld. Frankena distinguishes a principle of justice or equal treatment from a principle of beneficence, which commands us to advance the common weal, to avert harm and to do good.[13] In my view, it is important to see that both principles have one and the same root: the specific vulnerability of the human species, which individuates itself through sociation. Morality thus cannot protect the one without the other. It cannot protect the rights of the individual without also protecting the well-being of the community to which he belongs.

The fundamental motif of an ethics of compassion can be pushed to the point where the link between the two moral principles becomes clear. In the past these principles have served as core elements of two contrary traditions in moral philosophy. Theories of duty have always centered on the principle of justice, whereas theories of the good have always emphasized the common weal. Hegel was the first to argue that we misperceive the basic moral phenomenon if we isolate the two aspects, assigning opposite principles to each. His concept of ethical life (*Sittlichkeit*) is an implicit criticism of two kinds of one-sidedness, one the mirror image of the other. Hegel opposes the abstract universality of justice manifesting itself in the individualist approaches of the modern age, in rational natural right theory and in Kantian moral philosophy. No less vigorous in his opposition to the concrete particularism of the common good that pervades Aristotle and Thomas Aquinas. The ethics of discourse picks up this basic Hegelian aspiration to redeem it with Kantian means.

This idea is not so remarkable if one keeps in mind that discourses, treating as they do problematic validity claims as hypotheses, represent a reflective form of communicative action. To put it another way, the normative content of the pragmatic presuppositions of argumentation is borrowed from that of communicative action, onto which discourses are superimposed. This is why all moralities coincide in one respect: the same medium, linguistically mediated interaction, is both the reason for the vulnerability of socialized individuals and the key resource they possess to compensate for that vulnerability. Every morality revolves around equality of respect, solidarity, and the common good. Fundamental ideas like these can be reduced to the relations of symmetry and reciprocity presupposed in communicative action. In other words, the common core of all kinds of morality can be traced back to the reciprocal imputations and shared presuppositions actors make when they seek understanding in everyday situations.[14] Admittedly, their range in everyday practice is limited. While equal respect and solidarity are present in the mutual recognition of subjects who orient their actions to validity claims, normative obligations usually do not transcend the boundaries of a concrete lifeworld, be it that of a family, a neighborhood, a city, or a state. There is only one reason why discourse ethics, which presumes to derive the substance of a universalistic morality from the general presuppositions of argumentation, is a promising strategy: discourse or argumentation is a more exacting type of communication, going beyond any particular form of life. Discourse generalizes, abstracts, and stretches the presuppositions of context-bound communicative actions by extending their range to include competent subjects beyond the provincial limits of their own particular form of life.

These considerations address the issues of whether and why discourse ethics, though organized around a concept of procedure, can be expected to say something relevant about substance as well and, more important perhaps, about the hidden link between justice and the common good, which have traditionally been divorced, giving rise to separate ethics of duty and the good. On the strength of its improbable pragmatic features, practical discourse, or moral argumentation, serves as a warrant of insightful will formation, insuring that the interests of individuals are given their due without cutting the social bonds that intersubjectively unite them.[15]

In his capacity as a participant in argumentation, everyone is on his own and yet embedded in a communication context. This is what Apel means by an "ideal community of communication." In discourse the social bond of belonging is left intact despite the fact that the consensus required of all concerned transcends the limits of any actual community. The agreement made possible by discourse depends on two things: the individual's inalienable right to say yes or no and his overcoming of his egocentric viewpoint. Without the individual's uninfringeable freedom to respond with a "yes" or "no" to criticizable validity claims, consent is merely factual rather than truly universal. Conversely, without empathetic sensitivity by each person to everyone else, no solution deserving universal consent will result from the deliberation. These two aspects—the autonomy of inalienable individuals and their embeddedness in an intersubjectively shared web of relations—are internally connected, and it is this link that the procedure of discursive decision making takes into account. The equal rights of individuals and the equal respect for the personal dignity of each depend upon a network of interpersonal relations and a system of mutual recognition. On the other hand, while the degree of solidarity and the growth of welfare are indicators of the quality of communal life, they are not the only ones. Just as important is that *equal* consideration be given to the interests of every individual in defining the general interest. Going beyond Kant, discourse ethics extends the deontological concept of justice by including in it those structural aspects of the good life that can be distinguished from the concrete totality of specific forms of life.

II

For all its affinities with Kant's moral theory, discourse ethics is rather different. Before going on to consider Hegel's objections to Kant's ethics, I want to focus briefly on three differences that strike me as important. First, discourse ethics gives up Kant's dichotomy between an *intelligible* realm comprising duty and free will and a *phenomenal* realm comprising inclinations, subjective motives, political and social institutions, etc.[16] The quasi-transcendental necessity with which subjects involved in communicative interaction orient themselves to validity claims is reflected only in their being *constrained* to speak and act under idealized conditions. The unbridgeable gap Kant saw between the intelligible and the empirical becomes, in discourse ethics, a mere tension manifesting itself in *everyday communication* as the factual force of counterfactual presuppositions. Second, discourse ethics rejects the monological approach of Kant, who assumed that the individual tests his maxims of action *foro interno* or, as Husserl put it, in the loneliness of his soul. The singularity of Kant's transcendental consciousness simply takes for granted a prior understanding among a plurality of empirical egos; their harmony is preestablished. In discourse ethics it is not. Discourse ethics prefers to view shared understanding about the generalizability of interests as the *result* of an intersubjectively mounted *public discourse*. There are no shared structures preceding the individual except the universals of language use. Third, discourse ethics improves upon Kant's unsatisfactory handling of a specific problem of justification when he evasively points to the alleged "fact of pure reason" and argues that the effectiveness of the "ought" is simply a matter of experience. Discourse ethics solves this problem by deriving (U) from the universal presuppositions of argumentation.

1. On the Formalism of the Moral Principle

Neither Kantian ethics nor discourse ethics lays itself open to the charge that since it defines the moral principle in formal or procedural terms, it can make only tautological statements about morality. Hegel was wrong to imply that these principles postulate logical and semantic consistency and nothing else. In fact, they postulate the employment of a substantive moral point of view. The issue is not whether normative statements must have the grammatical form of universal sentences. The issue is whether we can *all* will that a contested norm gain binding force under given conditions.[17] The content that is tested by a moral principle is generated not by the philosopher but by real life. The conflicts of action that come to be morally judged and consensually resolved grow out of everyday life. Reason as a tester of maxims (Kant) or actors as participants in argumentation (discourse ethics) *find* these conflicts. They do not create them.[18]

There is a somewhat different sense in which Hegel's charge of formalism does ring true. Any procedural ethics must distinguish between the structure and the content of moral judgment. Its deontological abstraction segregates from among the general mass of practical issues precisely those that lend themselves to rational debate. They alone are subjected to a justificatory test. In short, this procedure differentiates *normative* statements about the hypothetical justice of actions and norms from *evaluative* statements about subjective preferences that we articulate in reference to what our notion of the good life happens to be, which in turn is a function of our cultural heritage. Hegel believed it was this tendency to abstract from the good life that made it impossible for morality to claim jurisdiction over the substantive problems of daily life. He has a point, but his criticism overshoots its aim. To cite an example, human rights obviously embody generalizable interests. As such they can be morally grounded in terms of what all could will. And yet nobody would argue that these rights, which represent the moral substance of our legal system, are irrelevant for the ethics (*Sittlichkeit*) of modern life.

In the back of Hegel's mind was a theoretical question that is rather more difficult to answer: Can one formulate concepts like universal justice, normative rightness, the moral point of view, and the like independently of any vision of the good life, i.e., independently of an intuitive project of some privileged but concrete form of life? Noncontextual definitions of a moral principle, I admit, have not been satisfactory up to now. Negative versions of the moral principle seem to be a step in the right direction. They heed the prohibition of graven images, refrain from positive depiction, and as in the case of discourse ethics, refer negatively to the damaged life instead of pointing affirmatively to the good life.[19]

2. On the Abstract Universalism of Morally Justified Judgment

Neither Kantian ethics nor discourse ethics lays itself open to the objection that a moral point of view based on the generalizability of norms necessarily leads to the neglect, if not the repression, of existing conditions and interests in a pluralist society. As interests and value orientations become more differentiated in modern societies, the morally justified norms that control the individual's scope of action in the interest of the whole become ever more general and abstract. Modern societies are also characterized by the need for regulations that impinge *only* on particular interests. While these matters do require regulation, a discursive consensus is not needed; compromise is quite sufficient in this area. Let us keep in mind, though, that fair compromise calls for morally justified procedures of compromising.

Hegel's objection sometimes takes the form of an attack on rigorism. A rigid procedural ethics, especially one that is monologically practiced, fails to take account, so the argument goes, of the consequences and side effects that may flow from the generalized observance of a justified norm. Max Weber was prompted by this objection to counterpose an ethics of responsibility to what he termed Kant's ethics of conviction. The charge of rigorism applies to Kant. It does not apply to discourse ethics, since the latter breaks with Kant's idealism and monologism. Discourse ethics has a built-in procedure that insures awareness of consequences. This comes out clearly in the formulation of the principle of universalization (U), which requires sensitivity to the results and consequences of the general observance of a norm for every individual.

Hegel is right in another respect too. Moral theories of the Kantian type are specialized. They focus on questions of *justification,* leaving questions of *application* unanswered. An additional effort is needed to *undo* the abstraction (from particular situations and individual cases) that is, initially at least, an inevitable part of justification. No norm contains within itself the rules for its application. Yet moral justifications are pointless unless the decontextualization of the general norms used in justification is compensated for in the process of application. Like any moral theory, discourse ethics cannot evade the difficult problem of whether the application of rules to particular cases necessitates a separate and distinct faculty of *prudence* or judgment that would tend to undercut the universalistic claim of justificatory reason because it is tied to the parochial context of some hermeneutic starting point? The neo-Aristotelian way out of this dilemma is to argue that practical reason should forswear its universalistic intent in favor of a more contextual faculty of judgment.[20] Since judgment always moves within the ambit of a more or less accepted form of life, it finds support in an evaluative context that engenders *continuity* among questions of motivation, empirical issues, evaluative issues, and normative issues.

In contrast to the neo-Aristotelian position, discourse ethics is emphatically opposed to going back to a stage of philosophical thought prior to Kant. Kant's achievement was precisely to dissociate the problem of justification from the application and implementation of moral insights. I argue that even in the prudent application of norms, principles of practical reason take effect. Suggestive evidence is provided by classical *topoi,* for instance, the principles that all relevant aspects of a case must be considered and that means should be proportionate to ends. Such principles as these promote the idea of *impartial* application, which is not a prudent but a moral point of view.

3. On the Impotence of the "Ought"

Kant is vulnerable to the objection that his ethics lacks practical impact because it dichotomizes duty and inclination, reason and sense experience. The same cannot be said of discourse ethics, for it discards the Kantian theory of the two realms. The concept of practical discourse postulates the inclusion of all interests that may be affected; it even covers the critical testing of interpretations through which we come to recognize certain needs as in our own interests. Discourse ethics also reformulates the concept of autonomy. In Kant, autonomy was conceived as freedom under self-given laws, which involves an element of coercive subordination of subjective nature. In discourse ethics the idea of autonomy is intersubjective. It takes into account that the free actualization of the personality of one individual depends on the actualization of freedom for all.

In another respect Hegel is right. Practical discourse does disengage problematic actions and norms from the substantive ethics (*Sittlichkeit*) of their lived contexts, subjecting them to hypothetical reasoning without regard to existing motives and institutions. This causes norms to become removed from the world (*entweltlicht*)—an unavoidable step in the process of justification but also one for which discourse ethics might consider making amends. For unless discourse ethics is undergirded by the thrust of motives and by socially accepted institutions, the moral insights it offers remain ineffective in practice. Insights, Hegel rightly demands, should be transformable into the concrete duties of everyday life. This much is true: any universalistic morality is dependent upon a form of life that *meets it halfway.* There has to be a modicum of congruence between morality and the practices of socialization and education. The latter must promote the requisite internalization of superego controls and the abstractness of ego identities. In addition, there must be a modicum of fit between morality and sociopolitical institutions. Not just any institutions will do. Morality thrives only in an environment in which postconventional ideas about law and morality have already been institutionalized to a certain extent.

Moral universalism is a *historical result.* It arose, with Rousseau and Kant, in the midst of a specific society that possessed corresponding features. The last two or three centuries have witnessed the emergence, after a long seesawing struggle, of a *directed* trend toward the realization of basic rights. This process has led to, shall we cautiously say, a less and less selective reading and utilization of the universalistic meaning that fundamental-rights norms have; it testifies to the "existence of reason," if only in bits and pieces. Without these fragmentary realizations, the moral intuitions that discourse ethics conceptualizes would never have proliferated the way they did. To be sure, the gradual embodiment of moral principles in concrete forms of life is not something that can safely be left to Hegel's absolute spirit. Rather, it is chiefly a function of collective efforts and sacrifices made by sociopolitical movements. Philosophy would do well to avoid haughtily dismissing these movements and the larger historical dimension from which they spring.

4. On the Subject of "Virtue and the Way of the World"

Neither Kantian ethics nor discourse ethics exposes itself to the charge of abetting, let alone justifying, totalitarian ways of doing things. This charge has recently been taken up by neoconservatives. The maxim that the end justifies the means is utterly incompatible with both the letter and the spirit of moral universalism, even when it is a question of politically implementing universalistic legal and constitutional principles. A problematic role is played in this connection by certain notions held by philosophers of history, Marxists, and others. Realizing that the political practice of their chosen macrosubject of society is sputtering, if not paralyzed, they delegate revolutionary action to an avant-garde with proxy functions. The error of this view is to conceive of society as a subject writ large and then to pretend that the actions of the avant-garde need not be held any more accountable than those of the higher-level subject of history. In contrast to any philosophy of history, the intersubjectivist approach of discourse ethics breaks with the premises of the philosophy of consciousness. The only higher-level intersubjectivity it acknowledges is that of public spheres.

Hegel rightly sets off action *under* moral laws from political practice that aims to bring about, or at least to promote, the institutional prerequisites for general participation in moral reasoning of a posttraditional type. Can the realization of reason in history be a meaningful objective of intentional action? As I argued earlier, the discursive justification of norms is no guarantee of the actualization of moral insight. This problem, the disjunction between judgment and action on the output side, to use computer jargon, has its counterpart on the input side: discourse cannot by itself insure that the conditions necessary for the actual participation of all concerned are met. Often lacking are crucial institutions that would facilitate discursive decision making. Often lacking are crucial socialization processes, so that the dispositions and abilities necessary for taking part in moral argumentation cannot be learned. Even more frequent is the case where material living conditions and social structures are such that moral-practical implications spring immediately to the eye and moral questions are answered, without further reflection, by the bare facts of poverty, abuse, and degradation. Wherever this is the case, wherever existing conditions make a mockery of the demands of universalist morality, moral issues turn into issues of political ethics. How can a political practice designed to realize the conditions necessary for a dignified human existence be morally justified?[21] The kind of politics at issue is one that aims at changing a form of life from moral points of view, through it is not reformist and therefore cannot operate in accordance with existing laws and institutions. The issue of revolutionary morality (which incidentally has never been satisfactorily discussed by Marxists, Eastern or Western) is fortunately not an urgent one in our type of society. Not so moot are cognate issues like civil disobedience, which I have discussed elsewhere.[22]

III

In sum, I argue that Hegel's objections apply less to the reformulation of Kantian ethics itself than to a number of resulting problems that discourse ethics cannot be expected to resolve with a single stroke. Any ethics that is at once deontological, cognitivist, formalist, and universalist ends up with a relatively narrow conception of morality that is uncompromisingly abstract. This raises the problem of whether issues of justice can be isolated from particular contexts of the good life. This problem, I believe, can be solved. But a second difficulty makes its appearance, namely whether practical reason may be forced to abdicate in favor of a faculty of judgment when it comes to applying justified norms to specific cases. Discourse ethics, I think, can handle this difficulty too. A third problem is whether it is reasonable to hope that the insights of a universalist morality are susceptible to translation into practice. Surely the incidence of such a morality is contingent upon a complementary form of life. This by no means exhausts the list of consequent problems. I mention only one more: How can political action be morally justified when the social conditions in which practical discourses can be carried on and moral insight can be generated and transformed do not exist but have to be created? I have so far not addressed two other problems that flow from the self-limitation of every nonmetaphysical point of view.

Discourse ethics does not see fit to resort to an objective teleology, least of all to a countervailing force that tries to negate dialectically the irreversible succession of historical events—as was the case, for instance, with the redeeming judgment of the Christian God on the last day. But how can we live up to the principle of discourse ethics, which postulates the consent of *all,* if we cannot make restitution for the injustice and pain suffered by previous generations or if we cannot at least promise an equivalent to the day of judgment and its power of redemption? Is it not obscene for present-day beneficiaries of past injustices to expect the posthumous consent of slain and degraded victims to norms that appear justified to us in light of our own expectations regarding the future?[23] It is just as difficult to answer the basic objection of ecological ethics: How does discourse ethics, which is limited to subjects capable of speech and action, respond to the fact that mute creatures are also vulnerable? Compassion for tortured animals and the pain caused by the destruction of biotopes are surely manifestations of moral intuitions that cannot be fully satisfied by the collective narcissism of what in the final analysis is an anthropocentric way of looking at things.

At this point I want to draw only one conclusion from these skeptical considerations. Since the concept of morality is limited, the self-perception of moral theory should be correspondingly modest. It is incumbent on moral theory to explain and ground the moral point of view. What moral *theory* can do and should be trusted to do is to clarify the universal core of our moral intuitions and thereby to refute value skepticism. What it cannot do is make any kind of substantive contribution. By singling out a procedure of decision making, it seeks to make room for those involved, who must then find answers on their own to the moral-practical issues that come at them, or are imposed upon them, with objective historical force. Moral philosophy does not have privileged access to particular moral truths. In view of the four big moral-political liabilities of our time—hunger and poverty in the third world, torture and continuous violations of human dignity in autocratic regimes, increasing unemployment and disparities of social wealth in Western industrial nations, and finally the self-destructive risks of the nuclear arms race—my modest opinion about what philosophy can and cannot accomplish may come as a disappointment. Be that as it may, philosophy cannot absolve anyone of moral responsibility. And that includes philosophers, for like everyone else, they face moral-practical issues of great complexity, and the first thing they might profitably do is to get a clearer view of the situation they find themselves in. The historical and social sciences can be of greater help in this endeavor than philosophy. On this note I want to end with a quote from Max Horkheimer from the year 1933: "What is needed to get beyond the utopian character of Kant's idea of a perfect constitution of humankind, is a materialist theory of society."[24]

NOTES

1. See the essays by K.-O. Apel in K.-O. Apel, D. Böhler, and G. Kadelbach, eds., *Praktische Philosophie/Ethik* (Frankfurt, 1984), and J. Habermas, "Discourse Ethics," in this volume.

2. "But the content of the maxim remains what it is, a specification or singularity, and the universality conferred on it by its reception into the form is thus a merely analytic unity. And when the unity conferred on it is expressed in a sentence purely as it is, that sentence is analytic and tautological." G.W.F. Hegel, *Natural Law*, trans. T.M. Knox (Philadelphia: University of Pennsylvania Press, 1975), p. 76. The same formalism manifests itself in the fact that any maxim at all can take the form of a universal law. "There is nothing whatever which cannot in this way be made into a moral law." Hegel, *Natural Law*, p. 77.

3. "The moral consciousness as the simple knowing and willing of pure duty is ... brought into relation with the object which stands in contrast to its simplicity, into

relation with the actuality of the complex case, and thereby has a complex moral relationship with it. . . . As regards the many duties, the moral consciousness heeds only the pure duty in them; the many duties qua manifold are specific and therefore as such have nothing sacred about them for the moral consciousness." G.W.F. Hegel, *Phenomenology of Spirit*, trans. A.V. Miller (Oxford: Oxford University Press, 1977), pp. 369–370. The counterpart to abstracting from the particular is hypostatizing the particular, for it becomes unrecognizable in the form of the universal: "By confusing absolute form with conditioned matter, the absoluteness of the form is imperceptibly smuggled into the unreal and conditioned character of the content; and in this perversion and trickery lies the nerve of pure reason's practical legislation." *Natural Law*, p. 79.

4. "The moral consciousness . . . learns from experience that Nature is not concerned with giving it a sense of the unity of its reality with that of Nature. . . . The nonmoral consciousness . . . finds, perhaps by chance, its realization where the moral consciousness sees only an occasion for acting, but does not see itself obtaining, through its action, the happiness of performance and the enjoyment of achievement. Therefore it finds rather cause for complaint about such a state of incompatibility between itself and existence, and about the injustice which restricts it to having its object merely as pure duty, but refuses to let it see the object and itself realized." *Phenomenology*, p. 366.

5. In the *Phenomenology of Spirit* Hegel devotes a famous section entitled "Virtue and the Way of the World" to a discussion of Jacobin moral zeal (*Gesinnungsterror*). In it he shows how morality can be turned into a means to bring "the good into actual existence by the sacrifice of individuality." P. 233.

6. K.H. Ilting seems to have missed the fact that the notion of what can be consented to merely operationalizes what he himself calls the "imposability" of norms. Only those norms are imposable for which a discursive agreement among those concerned can be reached. See K.H. Ilting, "Der Geltungsgrund moralischer Normen," in W. Kuhlmann and D. Böhler, eds., *Kommunikation und Reflexion* (Frankfurt, 1982), pp. 629ff.

7. The concept of the justification of norms must not be too strong, otherwise the conclusion that justified norms must have the assent of all affected will already be contained in the premise. I committed such a *petitio principii* in the essay on "Discourse Ethics" cited in note 1 above. [Habermas is referring here to the first edition of *Moralbewusstsein und kommunikatives Handeln*. In the second edition, on which this translation was based, the appropriate changes were made. . . .–Trans.]

8. "The idea of the original position is to set up a fair procedure so that any principles agreed to will be just." J. Rawls, *A Theory of Justice* (Cambridge, Mass., 1971), p. 136.

9. G.H. Mead, *Mind, Self and Society* (Chicago: Chicago University Press, 1934), "Fragments on Ethics," pp. 379–389. The concept of ideal role taking also underlies Kohlberg's theory of moral development. Also see H. Joas, *G.H. Mead: A Contemporary Re-examination of His Thought* (Cambridge, Mass., 1985), chapter 6, pp. 121ff.

10. Practical discourse can fulfill functions other than critical ones only when the subject matter to be regulated touches on generalizable interests. Whenever exclusively particular interests are at stake, practical decision making necessarily takes the form of compromise. See J. Habermas, *Legitimation Problems in Late Capitalism* (Boston, 1975), pp. 111ff.

11. J. Habermas, *The Theory of Communicative Action*, vol. 2, *Lifeworld and System* (Boston, 1987), pp. 58ff.

12. Compare my critique of Arnold Gehlen: "The profound vulnerability that makes necessary an ethical regulation of behavior as its counterpoise is rooted, not in the biological weaknesses of humans, not in the newborn infant's lack of organic faculties and not in the risks of a disproportionately long rearing period, but in the cultural systems that are constructed as compensation. The fundamental problem of ethics is guaranteeing mutual consideration and respect in a way that is effective in actual conduct. That is the core of truth in any ethics of compassion." J. Habermas, "Imitation Substantiality," in J. Habermas, *Philosophical-Political Profiles* (Cambridge, Mass., 1983), p. 120.

13. W. Frankena, *Ethics* (Englewood Cliffs, N. J., 1973), pp. 45ff.

14. This is an old topic of action theory. See A. Gouldner, "The Norm of Reciprocity," *American Sociological Review* 25 (1960): 161–178.

15. Michael Sandel has justly criticized Rawls for saddling his construct of an original position with the atomistic legacy of contract theory. Rawls envisions isolated, independent individuals who, prior to any association, possess the ability to pursue their interests rationally and to posit their objectives monologically. Accordingly, Rawls views the basic covenant not so much in terms of an agreement based on argumentation as in terms of an act of free will. His vision of a just society boils down to a solution of the Kantian problem of how the individual will can be free in the presence of other individual wills. Sandel's own anti-individualist conception is not without problems either, in that it further deepens the separation between an ethics of duty and an ethics of the good. Over against Rawls's presocial individual, he posits an individual who is the product of his community; over against the rational covenant of autonomous individuals, he posits a reflective awareness of prior social bonds; over against Rawls's idea of equal rights, he posits the ideal of mutual solidarity; over against equal respect for the dignity of the individual, he posits the advancement of the common good. With these traditional juxtapositions Sandel blocks the way to an intersubjectivist extension of Rawls's ethics of justice. He roundly rejects the deontological approach and instead returns to a teleological conception that presupposes an objective notion of community. "For a society to be a community in the strong sense, community must be constitutive of the shared self-understandings of the participants and embodied in their institutional arrangements, not simply an attribute of certain of the participants' plans of life," M.J. Sandel, *Liberalism and the Limits of Justice* (Cambridge, 1982), p. 173. Clearly, totalitarian (i.e., forcibly integrated) societies do not fit this description, which is why Sandel would have to explicate carefully the normative content of such key notions as community, embodied, and shared self-understanding. He does not do so. If he did, he would realize just how onerous the burden of proof is that neo-Aristotelian approaches must bear, as in the case of A. MacIntyre in *After Virtue*, (London, 1981). They must demonstrate how an objective moral order can be grounded without recourse to metaphysical premises.

16. K.-O. Apel, "Kant, Hegel und das aktuelle Problem der normativen Grundlagen von Moral und Recht," in D. Henrich, ed., *Kant oder Hegel* (Stuttgart, 1983), pp. 597ff.

17. G. Patzig, "Der Kategorische Imperativ in der Ethikdiskussion der Gegenwart," in G. Patzig, *Tatsachen, Normen, Sätze* (Stuttgart, 1980), pp. 155ff.

18. The controversial subjects Kant focused upon, the stratum-specific "maxims of action" in early bourgeois society, were not produced by law-giving reason but simply taken up by law-testing reason as empirical givens. Thus Hegel's attack on Kant's deposit example (*Critique of Practical Reason*, section 4, "Remark") becomes groundless.

19. Conversely, one might critically ask what evidence there is for the suspicion that universal and particular are always *inextricably* interlocked. We saw earlier that practical discourses are not only embedded in complexes of action but also represent, at a higher plane of reflection, continuations of action oriented toward reaching understanding. Both have the same structural properties. But in the case of communicative action there is no need to extend the presuppositions about symmetry and reciprocity to actors *not* belonging to the particular collectivity or lifeworld. By contrast, this extension into universality does become necessary, indeed forced, when argumentation is at issue. It is no wonder that ethical positions starting from the ethics (*Sittlichkeit*) of such concrete forms of life as the polis, the state, or a religious community have trouble generating a universal principle of justice. This problem is less troublesome for discourse ethics, for the latter presumes to justify the universal validity of its moral principle in terms of the normative content of communicative presuppositions of *argumentation* as such.

20. E. Vollrath, *Die Rekonstruktion der politischen Urteilskraft* (Stuttgart, 1977).

21. Compare J. Habermas, *Theory and Practice*, trans. J. Viertel (Boston, 1973), pp. 32ff.

22. J. Habermas, *Die neue Unübersichtlichkeit* (Frankfurt, 1985), and *The New Conservatism*, trans. Shierry Weber Nicholsen (Cambridge, Mass., 1989). The only comment I want to make on this subject here is that problems of this kind do not lie on the same plane of complexity as the objections discussed earlier. First, the relation of morality, law, and politics has to be clarified. While these universes of discourse may overlap, they are by no means identical. In terms of justification, posttraditional ideas about law and morality are structurally similar. At the heart of modern legal systems are basic moral norms which have attained the force of law. On the other hand, law differs from morality, *inter alia*, in that the target group of a law—those who are expected to comply with a legal norm—are relieved of the burdens of justifying, applying, and implementing it. These chores are left to public bodies. Politics too has an intimate relation to morality and law. Basic political issues are moral issues. And exercising political power is tantamount to making legally binding decisions. Also, the legal system is for its part tied up with politics via the legislative process. As far as the field of public will formation is concerned, the main thrust of politics is to pursue collective ends in an agreed-upon framework of rules rather than to redefine this framework of law and morality.

23. See H. Peukert, *Science, Action, and Fundamental Theology* (Cambridge, Mass., 1984), and C. Lenhardt, "Anamnestic Solidarity," *Telos*, no. 25, 1975.

24. M. Horkheimer, "Materialismus und Moral," *Zeitschrift für Sozialforschung* 2 (1933): 175. English translation, "Materialism and Morality," *Telos*, no. 69 (1986): 85–118.

SUGGESTIONS FOR FURTHER READING

THEODOR ADORNO

Negative Dialectics, tr. E.B. Ashton. New York: Seabury Press, 1973.

JACQUES DERRIDA

Speech and Phenomena, tr. David B. Allison. Evanston, IL: Northwestern University Press, 1973.

Of Grammatology, tr. Gayatri Chakravorty Spivak. Baltimore, MD: Johns Hopkins University Press, 1974.

FERDINAND DE SAUSSURE

Course in General Linguistics, tr. Wade Baskin. New York: McGraw-Hill, 1959.

MICHEL FOUCAULT

Discipline and Punish: The Birth of the Prison, tr. Alan Sheridan. New York: Random House, 1977.

The History of Sexuality, Vol. 1: An Introduction, tr. Robert Hurley. New York: Random House, 1978.

HANS-GEORG GADAMER

Truth and Method. New York: Crossroad, 1975.

JÜRGEN HABERMAS

Knowledge and Human Interests, tr. Jeremy J. Shapiro: Boston: Beacon Press, 1972.

The Theory of Communicative Action, Vols. 1, and 2, tr. Thomas McCarthy. Boston: Beacon Press, 1984 and 1987.

MARTIN HEIDEGGER

Being and Time, tr. John Macquarrie and Edward Robinson. New York: Harper & Row, 1962.

On the Way to Language, tr. Peter D. Hertz. New York: Harper & Row, 1971.

Max Horkheimer
 Eclipse of Reason. New York: Continuum, 1974.

Max Horkheimer and Theodor Adorno
 Dialectic of Enlightenment, tr. John Cumming. New York: Continuum, 1972.

Edmund Husserl
 Cartesian Meditations: An Introduction to Phenomenology, tr. Dorion Cairns. The Hague: Nijhoff, 1977.
 The Crisis of European Sciences and Transcendental Phenomenology, tr. David Carr. Evanston, IL: Northwestern University Press, 1970.

Luce Irigaray
 This Sex Which Is Not One, tr. Catherine Porter with Carolyn Burke. Ithaca, NY: Cornell University Press, 1985.
 Speculum of the Other Woman, tr. Gillian C. Gill. Ithaca, NY: Cornell University Press, 1985.

Julia Kristeva
 Desire in Language: A Semiotic Approach to Literature and Art, tr. Thomas Gora, Alice Jardine, and Leon S. Roudiez. New York: Columbia University Press, 1980.
 Powers of Horror: An Essay in Abjection, tr. Leon S. Roudiez. New York: Columbia University Press, 1982.

Jacques Lacan
 Écrits, tr. Alan Sheridan. New York: Norton, 1977.

Claude Lévi-Strauss
 The Elementary Structures of Kinship, tr. James Harle Bell, John Richard von Sturmer, and Rodney Needham. Boston: Beacon Press, 1969.
 Tristes Tropiques, tr. John Russell. New York: Atheneum, 1965.

Jean-François Lyotard
 The Postmodern Condition: A Report on Knowledge, tr. Geoff Bennington and Brian Massumi. Minneapolis: University of Minnesota Press, 1984.
 The Differend: Phrases in Dispute, tr. Georges Van Den Abbeele. Minneapolis: University of Minnesota Press, 1988.

Maurice Merleau-Ponty
 Phenomenology of Perception, tr. Colin Smith. London: Routledge and Kegan Paul, 1962.
 The Visible and the Invisible, tr. Alphonso Lingis. Evanston, IL: Northwestern University Press, 1968.

Paul Ricoeur
 The Conflict of Interpretations: Essays in Hermeneutics, tr. Don Ihde. Evanston, IL: Northwestern University Press, 1974.
 Interpretation Theory: Discourse and the Surplus of Meaning. Fort Worth, TX: Texas Christian University Press, 1976.